Natural Deduction Rules for Sentence Logic (cont.)

GROUP B

RULE 9.   Double Negation (DN): A is interchangeable with $\sim\sim A$

RULE 10.   Transposition (Trans.): $A \to B$ is interchangeable with $\sim B \to \sim A$

RULE 11.   Commutation (Com.):

$A \lor B$ is interchangeable with $B \lor A$
$A \mathbin{\&} B$ is interchangeable with $B \mathbin{\&} A$

RULE 12.   Association (Assoc.):

$A \lor (B \lor C)$ is interchangeable with $(A \lor B) \lor C$
$A \mathbin{\&} (B \mathbin{\&} C)$ is interchangeable with $(A \mathbin{\&} B) \mathbin{\&} C$

RULE 13.   Distribution (Dist.):

$A \mathbin{\&} (B \lor C)$ is interchangeable with $(A \mathbin{\&} B) \lor (A \mathbin{\&} C)$
$A \lor (B \mathbin{\&} C)$ is interchangeable with $(A \lor B) \mathbin{\&} (A \lor C)$

RULE 14.   De Morgan's Laws (DeM):

$\sim(A \mathbin{\&} B)$ is interchangeable with $\sim A \lor \sim B$
$\sim(A \lor B)$ is interchangeable with $\sim A \mathbin{\&} \sim B$

RULE 15.   The Conditional (Con.): $A \to B$ is interchangeable with $\sim A \lor B$

RULE 16.   The Biconditional (Bicon.): $A \leftrightarrow B$ is interchangeable with $(A \to B) \mathbin{\&} (B \to A)$

RULE 17.   Exportation (Exp.): $(A \mathbin{\&} B) \to C$ is interchangeable with $A \to (B \to C)$

RULE 18.   Absorption (Abs.): $A \to B$ is interchangeable with $A \to (A \mathbin{\&} B)$

RULE 19.   Tautology (Taut.):

A is interchangeable with $A \lor A$
A is interchangeable with $A \mathbin{\&} A$

LOGIC

Consulting Editor:

V. C. CHAPPELL,
UNIVERSITY OF MASSACHUSETTS

The painting reproduced on the cover is *Composition No. 7,* by Piet Mondrian. In this style of painting the artist is, in Mondrian's words, "concerned exclusively with relations."

LOGIC

A FIRST COURSE

Albert E. Blumberg

LIVINGSTON COLLEGE
RUTGERS UNIVERSITY

Alfred A. Knopf   *New York*

THIS IS A BORZOI BOOK
PUBLISHED BY ALFRED A. KNOPF, INC.

First Edition

987654321

Copyright © 1976 by Alfred A. Knopf, Inc.

All rights reserved under International and Pan-American Copyright Conventions. No part of this book may be reproduced in any form or by any means, electronic or mechanical, including photocopying, without permission in writing from the publisher. All inquiries should be addressed to Alfred A. Knopf, Inc., 201 East 50th Street, New York, N.Y. 10022. Published in the United States by Alfred A. Knopf, Inc., New York, and simultaneously in Canada by Random House of Canada Limited, Toronto. Distributed by Random House, Inc., New York.

Library of Congress Cataloging in Publication Data

Blumberg, Albert Emanuel.
    Logic : a first course.

    Bibliography: p.
    Includes indexes.
    1. Logic. I. Title.
BC108.B545   1976   160   75-38679
ISBN 0-394-31442-5

For granting of permission to reproduce materials, grateful acknowledgment is made as follows:

The painting on the front cover: Piet Mondrian, COMPOSITION NO. 7, courtesy Munson-Williams Proctor Institute, Utica, New York.

Excerpts from *The New York Times* issues of September 24, 1968; July 13, August 1, August 25, and October 2, 1969; June 8, and November 8, 1970; February 18, July 5, and July 7, 1974: © 1968, 1969, 1970, and 1974 by The New York Times Company. Reprinted by permission.

A portion of a Webster's Dictionary definition: By permission. From *Webster's New College Dictionary;* © 1975 by G. & C. Merriam Co., Publishers of the Merriam-Webster's Dictionaries.

Excerpts from an article and an editorial from the *New York Post:* Reprinted by permission of *New York Post.* © 1969 and 1971, New York Post Corporation.

Excerpts from *The Way of Life:* From *The Way of Life* by Lao Tzu, as translated by Raymond B. Blakney. Copyright © 1955 by Raymond B. Blakney. By arrangement with The New American Library, Inc., New York, N.Y.

Manufactured in the United States of America

To my parents,
to my wife,
to all my philosophy teachers and students,
in gratitude for what they taught me

Preface

Why study logic?

The logician Hao Wang remarks that logic is of value not so much for its explicit use, but "more as a way of acquiring the habit of precise thinking."[1] This answer nicely captures the element of truth in the familiar but simplistic view that logic teaches us "how to think."

Properly encouraged, precise thinking can be habit forming. We learn to recognize and avoid certain typical errors in reasoning. We learn to exercise care in defining and using terms. We learn how to test certain kinds of arguments to see if their conclusions do indeed follow, in the sense claimed, from their premises.

At the same time, we come to understand that logical error does not always announce itself boldly and clearly, that misplaced precision easily degenerates into semantic game playing, and that mastery of a few logical techniques does not immediately enable us to sort out all arguments into two neat piles, the good and the bad.

The problems that trouble our times cannot be solved by logic alone. But modern logic does offer modern society a precision instrument of great power. It is an essential tool in all the sciences and professions. It is equally needed in the making of social policy and in the life of the individual in society.

There are many ways to go about the study of logic, and *Logic: A First Course* is intended to be helpful over a fairly broad spectrum of choices. One approach would put the main emphasis on informal and applied logic. For a course of this type, one might begin with Chapters 1 (*argument, deductive and nondeductive arguments, valid and sound arguments*), 2 (especially

---

[1] Hao Wang, *From Mathematics to Philosophy* (London: Routledge and Kegan Paul, 1974), p. ix.

§11 on *fallacies*), and 3 (especially §15 on *definitions*). Then, after a brief look at §16 of Chapter 4 on the *uses of deductive arguments*, one would proceed to the Appendix on the traditional logic of the *Aristotelian syllogism* and to Chapters 5 and 6 on the modern *logic of sentences* (truth tables, truth trees), concluding with Chapters 13 and 14 on *nondeductive arguments*.

A second approach would distribute the weight more evenly between the formal and the informal, the pure and the applied. Here a likely sequence might be Chapter 1; §11 of Chapter 2, §15 of Chapter 3, and §16 of Chapter 4; the Appendix; §17 on the *criterion of deductive validity*, in Chapter 4; Chapters 5 and 6 on *sentence logic with truth trees*; and Chapters 9 and 10 on *first-order predicate logic with truth trees*. A variant of this approach omits the Appendix.

A third approach would stress the formal side. Material for such a course would include Chapter 1; §§17 and 18 of Chapter 4; and Chapters 5, 6, perhaps 7 on sentence logic using *natural deduction*, and 8 on *sentence logic and ordinary language*. It would cover Chapters 9, 10, perhaps 11 on first-order logic using *natural deduction*, and surely 12 on *first-order predicate logic and ordinary language*.

There are several matters of pedagogy to be briefly noted. First, placing Aristotle in an appendix is a concession to the view that a person setting out to study logic need not be compelled to recover so much of the history of the subject. It is not, however, an endorsement of that view. The syllogistic, aside from its historical and cultural value, has often served as a simple, intuitive example with which to begin the study of systems of logic.

Second, the discussion of "translating" ordinary English sentences into the symbolism of modern logic has been divided: some of it comes before the symbolism is used by the student to test validity, but much of it comes afterward. In the case of sentence logic, the topic is touched on in Chapter 5, §22, and returned to in Chapter 8, §34. For first-order logic, the preliminary discussion appears in Chapter 9, §38, and a more extended treatment in Chapter 12, §50. This division has been questioned. In its defense it may be argued that while early practice in "translating" does help motivate the effort required to master the symbolism, too much "translation" too soon may discourage and actually impede that effort.

Finally, a considerable store of exercises has been provided. It should be supplemented generously from that richest of all sources—daily life in contemporary society. For

I hear and I forget, I see and I remember, I do and I understand

is a bit of ancient wisdom still worth repeating.

There is sometimes a tendency to assign only exercises directed toward mastering some technique for testing validity. But there are other purposes that exercises should serve. One is to help develop clarity in the definition and use of such pivotal concepts as *validity*, *truth-functional compound, tautology,* and *quantification.* Another, certainly, is to foster an appreciation and understanding of the fundamental notion of *proof.* It is hoped that the varied exercises included in this book (with solutions provided for about three-quarters of them) will serve all these purposes.

Acknowledgments are due first to all the instructors and students who taught me what logic I know. Footnotes record my specific indebtedness to the logic texts of Professors W. V. Quine, Richard C. Jeffrey, Irving Copi, Patrick Suppes, Benson Mates, and Brian Skyrms.

In preparing the manuscript, I was helped especially by two close friends and former students. Douglas Wagner examined all the earlier versions of Parts I and II, contributed a stream of substantive suggestions, and guided my efforts to correct the many errors and inadequacies that he uncovered. His untimely death in the fall of 1974 brought to a tragic end what would have been a brilliant career in logic and philosophy.

Richard Nagel, now teaching at North Carolina State University at Raleigh, reviewed the manuscript and exercises in detail, made a number of extremely useful comments, and—perhaps more than he realized—provided throughout a much needed source of encouragement.

Among the busy friends and colleagues who took time out to read one or more chapters and to aid me with their advice were Professors David Rosenthal, Chauncey Downes, Robert Martin, and Vere Chappell. I am very much indebted to the anonymous readers, supplied by the publisher, who unsparingly dissected the first drafts of Parts I and II and considerably influenced their final shape. Many of the exercises, particularly for Part II, were supplied by Thomas J. McKay, who also offered several important criticisms. Christopher Ake was very helpful with the proofs.

My special thanks go to Jane Cullen, project editor for Random House. She suggested innumerable improvements in content and form, painstakingly supervised the final editing of the manuscript, and firmly and often gently held me to schedule.

Lastly, my wife, Dorothy Rose, took untold hours from her own writing to scrutinize every draft. A firm believer in the principle that if something can be said at all it can be said clearly, she set a standard of intelligibility that, if not always reached, was more closely approximated because of her insistence. A respecter of words, ever on the search for the *mot juste,* she did a great deal to lighten the burden of composition. She alone knows how much I have depended on her assistance, understanding, and boundless good spirits.

For the typing of the manuscript, I have no one to thank but myself.

As always, the author is solely responsible for the slips, errors, blunders, and idiosyncratic extravagances that remain. My gratitude will go out to anyone kind enough to call them to my attention.

September 24, 1975   A.E.B.

Contents

I Language and Argument

II   The Logic of Deductive Arguments

III Nondeductive Arguments

LOGIC

First, bear with me while we define what "logic" is. "Logic" (in its broadest sense) is "the science of verbal expression and argumentative reasoning." Sometimes "logic" is used with more restricted extension, and limited to the rules of reasoning. Whether logic teaches only the ways of reasoning, or embraces all rules relative to words, surely those who claim that it is useless are deluded. For either of these services may be proved by incontrovertible arguments to be very necessary.

John of Salisbury (1115/20–1180), *The Metalogicon* I, 10

1

Introduction

Our subject is "logic." The quotation marks serve as an early warning that the noun they enclose and the adjective derived from it have a variety of uses. Some of these are shown in the following sentences:

> The logic of Perkins's argument is unassailable.
>
> The logical thing for Perkins to do is drop the course.
>
> Perkins is a very logical man.
>
> Perkins understands the logic of events.

Thus in ordinary conversation the words 'logic' and 'logical' are applied to events, actions, persons, arguments, and much else. In our discussion, however, these words will be applied exclusively to arguments.

§1 What Is Logic?

We shall use the term 'logic' as a name for the general study of *arguments* and of the principles and procedures that enable us to distinguish good arguments from bad ones.

Accordingly, logic does not merely *describe* arguments; rather it also seeks to *evaluate* them. Its commitment is to search for rules, norms, or criteria—some precise, some not so precise—that will allow us to appraise arguments and determine on which of them we may rely.

---

§2   *What Is an Argument?   An Inference?*

Technically, an argument is a sequence of statements together with a claim. The sequence is made up of two or more statements; the claim is that one of these statements, called the "conclusion," *follows in some sense* from the others, called the "premisses."

An argument, then, is not the same thing as a dispute, altercation, rhubarb, or hassle, although any of these may have an argument in the strict sense as a constituent.   The following are examples of arguments:

(1)   All men are mortal.

Socrates is a man.

Therefore Socrates is mortal.

(2)   Heisenberg is a philosopher or Heidegger is a physicist.

Heisenberg is not a philosopher.

Hence Heidegger is a physicist.

(3)   Professor Able's logic text is easy.

Professor Baker's logic text is easy.

Professor Charles's logic text is easy.

Therefore all logic texts are easy.

It is worth taking a moment to unpack the definition of argument, especially with reference to the notions of sequence, claim, and statement.

SEQUENCE

Consider the following passage:

(4)   When Shem was a hundred years old, he became the father of Arpach'shad two years after the flood; and Shem lived after the

birth of Arpach'shad five hundred years, and had other sons and daughters.   When Arpach'shad had lived thirty-five years, he became the father of Shelah; and Arpach'shad lived after the birth of Shelah four hundred and three years, and had other sons and daughters.   When Shelah had lived thirty years, he became the father of Eber; and Shelah lived after the birth of Eber four hundred and three years, and had other sons and daughters.

[*Genesis* 11: 10–14]

This is certainly a sequence of statements.   However, it is not an argument; it is a chronicle.   It tells us that certain events followed other events, but there is no claim that any statements follow from any other statements. Thus while every argument includes a sequence of statements, not every sequence of statements is an element in an argument.

Two further comments need to be made about the number and order of statements in an argument.   Both are illustrated in

(5)   Socrates, being a man, is mortal, since all men are.

First, although this is a single sentence grammatically, it does convey an argument—in fact, the very argument made by the three-sentence sequence in (1).   The point is that it is possible for us to use a single sentence to make several statements at once.   Subject to this qualification, we reaffirm that all arguments must contain at least two statements: one or more premises and a conclusion.

Second, the three statements made by using sentence (5) are, in the order of their appearance,

> Socrates is a man.
>
> Socrates is mortal.
>
> All men are mortal.

Notice that the conclusion of argument (1) appears in the middle of (5) instead of at the end.   The French film director Henri-Georges Clouzot once asked his Italian colleague Michelangelo Antonioni, "Don't you think in every film there has to be a beginning, a middle, and an end?" Antonioni replied, "Yes, Georges, but not necessarily in that order."[1] The situation is similar with regard to arguments.

CLAIM

The second essential element in an argument is the claim that the conclusion follows in some sense from the premises.   This claim is the particular concern of the logician, who distinguishes it from another claim

---

[1]   Jerry Tallmer, *New York Post*, September 28, 1968.

normally made with respect to an argument—namely, that the premisses from which the conclusion is said to follow are themselves true, well-confirmed, or otherwise worthy of acceptance. These two kinds of claims are referred to when, in our ordinary talk about arguments, we make a distinction between one's "logic" and one's "facts." By "logic" we mean here the justification offered for drawing a conclusion from premisses, and by "facts" we mean the premisses held to be true.

Now not only are the claims different, they are quite independent of each other. Either may be accepted or rejected without prejudice to the other. This independence is also recognized in our everyday discourse. Thus we often say that someone's "logic is all right but his facts are wrong," as in the case of a person who advances the following argument:

(6)   All college students stand in awe of the faculty.

Perkins is a college student.

Therefore Perkins stands in awe of the faculty.

Again, we speak of "granting the premisses for the sake of the argument," so as then to show that the supposed conclusion does not follow, as in

(7)   Everyone loves somebody.

Hence somebody loves everyone.

To repeat, when we advance arguments we generally make "factual" claims as well as "logical" ones. Logicians, however, are occupied professionally only with "logical" claims. They do not assume the responsibility (except in a few quite special cases) of certifying the truth of the premisses. This task they are happy to leave to common sense and to those extensions and refinements of common sense we call science.

SENTENCE AND STATEMENT

It is useful to distinguish between the terms 'sentence' and 'statement'. In general, *sentences* are expressions used to perform linguistic jobs of various sorts. One sort of job is to *make statements* to the effect that something is or is not the case (the statement being true if what it says is the case, and false if it is not). Of the making of statements—as of books—there is no end. But sentences are also used for many other purposes: to ask questions, to issue instructions, to perform ceremonies, to utter prayers, to cite examples, and the like. Consider the following sentences:

(8)   What is an algorithm?

Bring in two examples of arguments.

I now pronounce you husband and wife.

The first is used customarily to ask a question, the second to issue an instruction, the third to perform a ceremony.   (In the present instance, of course, these sentences are being cited as *examples*, rather than being used in the ordinary way.)

With this distinction in mind, we now widen our definition of argument to read "sequence of sentences" instead of "sequence of statements." For there are many arguments that involve sentences other than those used to make statements.   Consider, for example, the sequence

(9)   Buy me a racquet at the biggest sports shop in town.

Ellsworth Kramer's is the biggest sports shop in town.

Hence buy me a racquet at Ellsworth Kramer's.[2]

Although the first and last of these sentences are used to make requests, not statements, there seems to be no reason why we should not regard this sequence and similar ones as expressing arguments.   Indeed, especially within the last few years, a large body of literature has grown up devoted to just such arguments, and writers now refer to "logics" of commands, questions, and so forth.   This discussion, however, must be confined to the "logic" of what for brevity shall be called "statement-making sentences," or even just plain "sentences."

While we shall speak of statement-making sentences, we of course recognize that it is not the sentences that make statements but we who use sentences for that purpose among others.   Likewise, while we shall say that arguments "make" claims, obviously it is not the arguments that make claims, but we who do so when we advance various arguments to various ends.

Arguments composed only of statement-making sentences are also of many kinds.   The most important distinction between kinds of arguments will be described after we dispose of one last matter of terminology.

INFERENCE

In our everyday talk we sometimes use the word 'inference' to stand for an argument, sometimes for the conclusion of an argument, and sometimes for the drawing of the conclusion of an argument—an ambiguity that should not be passed over in silence.   For an argument is a *sequence of sentences together with a claim*, a conclusion is a *sentence*, and the drawing of a conclusion is an *act*.   These are three different types of things, and what can be said rightly or wrongly about one may not be applicable at all to the other two.   In order to avoid confusion, we shall confine the word

---

[2]   The example is adapted from R. M. Hare, *The Language of Morals* (New York: Oxford University Press, 1952, 1961).

'inference' to just one of its three uses: by an inference we shall always mean the *act of drawing a conclusion* and never the conclusion itself or the argument.

EXERCISES

2.1. Which of the following examples contain arguments?

> a. If Shem had no sons or daughters, he had no descendants. But he had descendants, so he must have had sons or daughters.
>
> b. After two terms as a popular governor and ten years as a distinguished senator, it followed naturally that he should try to get his party's nomination for the Presidency.
>
> c. All dogs are fish.   All fish bark.   Hence all dogs bark.
>
> d. Since he will arrive late, and no party ever begins without him, the party will begin late.   But be prepared for his arrival.
>
> e. All dogs are mammals.   All trout are fish.   All oaks are trees.   And each other living thing also falls within some biological category.
>
> f. Despite what you say, I believe I have the correct view.   Furthermore, I do not think you really believe what you are saying. In any case I refuse to be swayed.

2.2. Now see if you can tell which of the following quoted passages contain arguments and which are merely narratives.   For each argument, try to pick out the premiss(es) and conclusion.

> a. Shortly after establishing their political dominance in Central Mexico in the 16th century, the Spanish moved to many new regions, among them the west coast of Mexico . . .   In a series of brutal military campaigns, the Spanish soon subjugated and largely eliminated the native civilizations of the west coast, leaving this area to be recorded in history as merely a marginal province of Mesoamerica.   [C. W. Meighan, " Prehistory of West Mexico," *Science*, June 21, 1974]
>
> b. "If we can go fusion for Lindsay," the Liberal Party source said, "then there's a contest.   If we can't go fusion for Lindsay, it becomes a one-way affair.   So if we go independent or take a Democrat, the election is over right now."   [*New York Post*, April 14, 1969]

c.   When the Epidamnians found that no help could be expected from Corcyra, they were in a strait what to do next.   So they sent to Delphi and inquired of the god . . .   The answer he gave them was to deliver their city, and place themselves under the protection of the Corinthians.   So the Epidamnians went to Corinth and delivered over the colony in obedience to the commands of the oracle.   [Thucydides, *The Peloponnesian War*, Chapter 2]

d.   In a typical laboratory or wildlife situation, an animal generally can engage in any of several alternative activities.   Since at any one moment one alternative occurs to the exclusion of others, behavior generally implies choice.   [W. M. Baum, "Choice in Free-ranging Pigeons," *Science*, July 5, 1974]

e.   [T]he committee's Annual Report on the Economic Status of the Profession notes that faculty members have actually lost ground economically.   The average college and university professor had $271 less buying power this year than last because of spiraling inflation, even though the average professor received salary and fringe benefit increases amounting to $979 during the 1973–74 academic year.   ["Hard Times: Academic Salaries Lag," *Academe*, American Association of University Professors, June 1974]

f.   The Exploratorium in San Francisco . . . is the creation of one man—Frank Oppenheimer, scientist, physicist, humanist . . .   To supplement the experiential aspects of the Exploratorium, Oppenheimer uses high school students to talk to the public about the exhibits . . .   They are especially helpful as an alternative to using tape recordings, says Oppenheimer.   "If you are going to appeal to a wide audience, you can't use tapes, because tapes say the same thing to everybody."   ["Profile of a Man and His Museum," *Bulletin*, American Association for the Advancement of Science, June 1974]

---

§3   *What Is a Deductive Argument?*
A Nondeductive Argument?

An essential element in any argument is the claim that the conclusion follows—in some sense of 'follow'—from the premisses.   We now distinguish two senses of 'follow' and on this basis divide all arguments into two classes: deductive and nondeductive (sometimes called 'inductive').

A *deductive* argument includes the claim that the conclusion follows from the premises in the sense that it is *impossible* for the conclusion to be false if the premises are all true. The deductive claim may also be expressed by saying that the premises, if accepted, furnish conclusive grounds for accepting the conclusion; that the premises *entail* or *logically imply* the conclusion; that the conclusion is a *logical consequence of* or is *deducible from* the premises. The essential idea of a deductive argument was first formulated by Aristotle (384–322 B.C.), the father of logic.

Samples of deductive arguments are (1) and (2) in §2. Another is

(1)   A man dies because he is guilty.

A man is guilty because he is one of Caligula's subjects.

Now all men are Caligula's subjects.

Ergo, all men are guilty and shall die.

It is only a matter of time and patience.[3]

Any argument that is not deductive we shall call nondeductive. The characteristic feature of a *nondeductive* argument is the claim that the conclusion follows from the premises in the sense that it is *improbable* that the conclusion is false, given that the premises are all true.[4] The nondeductive claim accordingly admits the possibility, which deductive claims exclude, of the conclusion's being false even if all the premises are true.

An instance of a nondeductive argument is (3) in §2. Another is

(2)   Freshmen generally have trouble with calculus.

Perkins is a freshman.

Therefore Perkins is having trouble with calculus.

In this case the claim is only that given the truth of the premises, it is improbable that the conclusion is false. Clearly, there is no claim that the premises, if true, make it impossible for the conclusion to be false.

Thus the difference between these two classes of arguments is simply the difference between two sorts of claims that may be made in arguments concerning the relationship between the truth of the premises and the truth of the conclusion. Whether the claim made in a particular argu-

---

[3]   Albert Camus, *Caligula and Three Other Plays*, trans. Stuart Gilbert (New York: Random House, 1958), p. 29. The next line reads: "Caligula (laughing): 'There's logic for you, don't you agree?'"

[4]   This way of describing nondeductive arguments derives in part from Brian Skyrms, *Choice and Chance* (Belmont, Calif.: Dickenson Pub. Co., 1966), Chapter 1. We shall return to it in Part III.

ment is deductive or nondeductive can usually be learned from the wording of the argument or from the context in which it is offered.

Warning: Don't assume that a nondeductive argument is necessarily a *bad* argument—specifically a bad deductive argument—just because its conclusion *may* be false even when its premises are all true. The difference between a deductive and a nondeductive argument is not that between a good argument and a bad one, but between the two sorts of claims that an argument, good or bad, may make about the sense in which its conclusion *follows from* its premises.

---

§4   *What Is a Good Argument?*

We turn now from description to appraisal. How can we tell if an argument is good or bad?

In everyday life we use a rich variety of adjectives in evaluating arguments. We commend them for being fresh, elegant, ingenious, persuasive, incisive, clear, valid, sound, and so on. And we criticize them if we find that they lack these or like traits. Hence there are as many possible senses of 'good' in the phrase 'good argument' as there are possible combinations of one or more good-making qualities.

Which of these qualities should be regarded as essential? Which will best serve as necessary conditions for a good argument?

Here we may allow ourselves to be guided, up to a point, by common sense—which in this context is merely another name for our pretheoretical intuitions or feelings about arguments. We begin by testing our intuitions on a series of deductive arguments, reserving for later in this section a brief comment on nondeductive arguments.

APPRAISING DEDUCTIVE ARGUMENTS

One example of a deductive argument is

(1)   If Perkins is a registered Democrat, he can vote in November.

Perkins can vote in November.

Therefore Perkins is a registered Democrat.

Common sense tells us at once that this argument is faulty. The deductive claim is that the conclusion must be true if the premises are all true. Here this claim is not sustained. Obviously, Perkins can qualify as a voter in November without registering as a Democrat; he may register in some other party or without designating a party.

It is therefore quite natural to lay down as the *first* essential condition for a good deductive argument that its claim be justified: that its conclusion follow from its premises in the sense that it is indeed *impossible* for the conclusion to be false if the premises are all true. Deductive arguments that fulfill this condition we shall call *valid*.

There is a second quality that common sense generally demands of a good argument. Consider the following example:

(2)   If Perkins is seventeen, he can vote in November.

Perkins is seventeen.

Therefore Perkins can vote in November.

A moment's thought will confirm that this argument is perfectly valid; *if* its premises were all true, its conclusion would have to be true. Nevertheless, it is a bad argument, because its conclusion is false. The trouble in this instance is not with the "logic" but with the "facts": the first premiss is false.

Accordingly, common sense adds a *second* condition for a good deductive argument—namely, that its premises *all* be true. Arguments that are valid and also have all true premisses we shall call *sound*. An example of a sound argument is

(3)   If Perkins is a registered Democrat, he can vote in November.

Perkins is a registered Democrat.

Therefore Perkins can vote in November.

Here both conditions for a good deductive argument are met. These are
1. If the premisses are all true, the conclusion cannot possibly be false.
2. The premisses must all be true.
To repeat, deductive arguments that satisfy condition 1 are called valid. Those that satisfy conditions 1 *and* 2 are called sound.

NONDEDUCTIVE ARGUMENTS

Condition 2 above also applies to nondeductive arguments, although with some qualifications to be noted later. Condition 1, however, is concerned not with the *truth* of premises but solely with the *relationship* between the truth of the premises and the truth of the conclusion, and it is on precisely this point that deductive and nondeductive claims differ.

The deductive claim is that it is *impossible* for the conclusion to be false while the premises are all true, and impossibility does not admit of degrees. Either the truth of the premises guarantees the truth of the conclusion, the claim is sustained, and the argument is valid; or it does not, the claim is not sustained, and the argument is invalid.

On the other hand, the nondeductive claim is that it is *improbable* that the conclusion is false given that all the premises are true. Now improbability is indeed a matter of degree; hence the evidential claim in this case is by its very nature of the more-or-less variety.

Accordingly, when appraising a nondeductive argument, we ask *how much* support is claimed for the conclusion on the basis of the premises, and whether *this* claim is justified.   Notice that such an appraisal seems to presuppose that we have some way of *measuring* the degrees of evidential support that various premises give to various conclusions.   This presupposition is one of the many problems that attend the analysis of nondeductive arguments and that had best await a later discussion.

Again we emphasize that whether an argument is deductive or nondeductive, the competence and concern of the logician extend only to the relationship between the truth of the premises and the truth of the conclusion—not to the truth or falsity of the premises themselves.   The sole appointed task of the logician is to determine whether the conclusion actually does follow from the premises in the sense claimed.

INTUITION AND THEORY

Our intuitions about arguments have led us to a more or less serviceable notion of goodness in arguments.   Can we conclude, as many do, that unaided intuition can guide us all the way; that "logic" itself is nothing but ordinary common sense, and that common sense need not be refined and extended by any special study of logical theory and technique?

We very soon find that our unschooled intuitions—especially about validity—have distinct limitations.   Suppose we are asked to decide whether the following argument is valid:

(4)   All the world loves a lover.

Bob does not love Jane.

Therefore Jane does not love herself.

why does he think ≠ INVALID?

If all we have to go on are our ordinary intuitions about what follows from what, we are likely either to confess defeat, or to answer incorrectly that the argument is invalid.

That our intuitions can benefit from schooling appears, indeed, to be a general phenomenon.   The businessman's "sense" of the market gives way to market research; flying by instrument takes over from flying by the seat of your pants.   To be sure, the process of disciplining intuition is not without its dangers.   For instance, we may come to distrust our old, unschooled intuitions before we have mastered the theory and the technique with which to educate them.   But this is a risk to which anyone is exposed who engages in serious study.

EXERCISES

4.1.   Which of the following are valid *deductive* arguments?   (Use the commonsense test for deductive validity: a deductive argument is valid if it is *impossible* for the conclusion to be false *if* the premises are all true.

Later, in Chapter 4, we begin the process of replacing this rough criterion with a more precise one.)

a. If Quincy has quit school, then Perkins will need a new tennis partner. Quincy has quit school. So Perkins will need a new tennis partner.

b. If Quincy has quit school, then Perkins will need a new tennis partner. Perkins will need a new tennis partner. Hence Quincy has quit school.

c. Usually if Perkins plays too much tennis, he gets a headache. If Perkins plays more than three sets, he plays too much tennis. So if Perkins plays more than three sets, he gets a headache.

d. If I go to the movies, I will stay up late and wake up tired. If I wake up tired, I will not be able to go to work the next day. Therefore if I go to the movies, I will not be able to go to work the next day.

e. If she goes to New York City she will confer with the mayor. If she goes to Albany she will talk to the governor. Hence she will either confer with the mayor or talk to the governor.

f. All examined rubies have been red and all examined emeralds have been green. So if the queen's jeweler finds blue stones for her tiara, they will not be emeralds or rubies.

g. All rubies are red and all emeralds are green. Hence the blue jewel on the queen's pendant is not an emerald or a ruby.

h. There are 500,000 lottery tickets and only one will win. Almost everyone with a ticket will lose. I have a ticket. I will lose.

i. If someone says something significant, the commencement will be a success. Everyone will say what he or she is supposed to say, and the commencement will be a success. Hence someone will say something significant.

j. If John brings root beer, the picnic will be a great success. If John remembers to bring root beer, he will bring it. John will remember to bring root beer if Paul reminds him. So if Paul reminds John to bring root beer, then the picnic will be a great success.

4.2. Which of the following deductive arguments are *valid*? Which are *sound*? (Use the commonsense test again for deductive validity, and let "common knowledge" be your guide in determining whether premises are true.)

a. All station wagons are cars. Some Fords are station wagons. Therefore some Fords are cars.

b. If Freud was a physicist, then he was a scientist. Freud was a scientist. Therefore Freud was a physicist.

c. Hyenas are felines. Felines do not roar. Hence hyenas do not roar.

d. All violinists are classicists. All musicians are classicists. Therefore all violinists are musicians.

e. The person who gets the most electoral votes will win the Presidency. A person gets some electoral votes for each state he or she carries. Hence the person who carries the most states will win the Presidency.

f. An even integer is divisible by 2. A positive integer is prime if it is greater than 1 and its only positive divisors are itself and 1. It follows that the only even prime is 2.

g. No third-party candidate has been elected President of the United States in this century. Stevenson was elected President in 1956. Hence Stevenson was not a third-party candidate.

h. Punishment is a crime. Incarceration is punishment. Therefore incarceration is a crime.

4.3. Which of the following statements about *deductive* arguments are true?

a. An argument may be valid and yet have a false conclusion.

b. An argument may have a true conclusion and yet be invalid.

c. An argument may have false premisses and a true conclusion and yet be sound.

d. An argument may have true premisses and a false conclusion and yet be valid.

True → e. An argument may have true premisses and a true conclusion and yet be unsound.

4.4. Find or construct your own examples of the following:

a. A nondeductive argument.

b. A sound deductive argument.

c. A deductive argument that is valid but unsound.

d. A valid deductive argument with a false conclusion.

e. An invalid deductive argument with a true conclusion.

4.5. Turn back to Exercise 2.2. Is the argument contained in *b* deductive or nondeductive, and if deductive, is it valid?

4.6. From the definitions given in the text, *prove* that

> a. A sound deductive argument cannot have a false conclusion.
>
> b. If a valid deductive argument has a false conclusion, it must have at least one false premiss.

Note: These proof problems are intended as simple beginning exercises, on a par, say, with the following proof that 2 is the only even prime:

> We are given the following definitions:
>
> I. An integer is even if it is divisible by 2.
>
> II. A (positive) integer is prime if it is greater than 1 and its only positive divisors are itself and 1.
>
> The proof that 2 is the only even prime is then
>
> 1. 2 is even by definition I.
> 2. 2 is prime by definition II.
> 3. Any positive even integer other than 2 will have as divisors at least itself, 1, and 2, and hence will not be prime. Thus 2 is the only even prime.

---

§5   *More on the True, the Valid, and the Sound*

Whenever the medieval student thought a lecturer or disputant had failed to draw some pertinent distinction, he was wont to rise from his bench and cry, " *Distinguo!* " If the " point of distinction " proved well-taken, he earned great credit in the eyes of his master. The period in general was one of extremism in the hunt for distinctions, and it is still recalled in such pejorative phrases as " hair-splitting," " nit-picking," and " logic-chopping " and in the image of the scholar as a person intent on making two distinctions grow where but one grew before.

Moderation would appear to be the sensible course; distinctions, like William of Ockham's entities, ought not be multiplied without necessity. With this thought in mind, we want to say a few words more about two quite necessary distinctions.

TRUE SENTENCES; VALID ARGUMENTS AND INFERENCES

In ordinary discourse we do not draw a clear line between how we use ' true ' or 'false' and how we use 'valid' or 'invalid'.   We speak as freely of false arguments and invalid conclusions as we do of invalid arguments and false conclusions.   But in technical discussion it is helpful to distinguish sharply between what may be asserted rightly or wrongly about sentences and what may be asserted rightly or wrongly about arguments.   Roughly speaking, a statement-making sentence is false if what it says is not the case.   But when is an argument false?   When the premisses are false?   The conclusion false?   The evidential claim not sustained?   Some measure of confusion can be avoided if we agree to say that sentences (but not arguments) are true or false and that arguments (but not sentences) are valid or invalid.

Furthermore, where an argument is valid, we shall say that its conclusion has been validly drawn or *inferred* from the premisses and, thus, that the *inference* made in the argument is *valid*.   Accordingly, we shall also talk of invalid or valid inferences, but never of false or true inferences.

VALID DEDUCTIVE ARGUMENTS; SOUND DEDUCTIVE ARGUMENTS

Many students find the valid-sound distinction especially troublesome, perhaps because they tend to dismiss it as "merely a matter of terminology."   No doubt the choice of the particular words 'valid' and ' sound' to stand for particular properties of deductive arguments is in a sense arbitrary, but the difference on which the distinction rests is quite real.

The essential point is that there are two things we want to know about a deductive argument:

> 1.   If the premisses are true, does the conclusion necessarily follow?
>
> 2.   Are the premisses in fact true?

The answer to question 1 turns only on the relationship between the truth of the premisses and the truth of the conclusion; the answer to question 2 turns on the truth or falsity of the premisses themselves.   Hence the two questions are distinct.   If the answer to question 1 is yes, the argument is valid; and if the answers to questions 1 and 2 are both yes, the argument is sound.   *A sound argument is thus a valid argument whose premisses are true.*

Questions 1 and 2 are not only distinct; they are—as Aristotle long ago recognized—entirely independent of each other. Take, for example, these two arguments:

(1)   Sophocles is a philosopher or Socrates is a dramatist.
       Sophocles is not a philosopher.
       Therefore Socrates is a dramatist.

(2)   Sophocles is a philosopher or Socrates is a philosopher.
       Sophocles is not a philosopher.
       Therefore Socrates is a philosopher.

In both cases common sense tells us that if the premisses are true the conclusion follows necessarily, and hence that the argument is valid. But in the first case the first premiss is false, as is the conclusion; and in the second case it is true, and so is the conclusion.   Thus the question of validity, question 1, is quite independent of the question as to whether the premisses are all true, question 2.

The valid-sound distinction may also be described in these terms: If an argument is *invalid*, we learn nothing from it about the actual truth or falsity of its conclusion.   If an argument is valid, we know that the conclusion cannot be false *if* the premisses are all true; but we do not know *whether* the premisses are true.   If an argument is *sound*, we know that the conclusion must be true because the argument is valid and the premisses are all true.

EXERCISES

5.1. This is a drill on terminology.   Consider the argument

> All freshmen take calculus.
> Perkins is a freshman.
> Therefore Perkins takes calculus.

Suppose the facts are these: it is *not* the case that all freshmen take calculus; Perkins is a freshman; Perkins is taking calculus.

Now the statements below purport to describe this argument.   In which of them are the terms 'valid', 'invalid', 'sound', 'unsound', 'true', and 'false' used *correctly*, as defined in the text.   In which *incorrectly*?   Correct the statements in which any of these terms is used incorrectly.

a.   The argument is *false* because its first premiss is *invalid*.

b.   Since the first premiss is *unsound*, the argument, though *valid*, is *false*.

c.   The argument is *sound* because if the premisses were all true, the conclusion would have to be *true*.

d.   The argument is *valid*; but since the first premiss is *false*, the argument is *unsound*.

e.   The conclusion is *valid*; but since the first premiss is *false*, the argument is *unsound*.

---

§6   *Recognizing Arguments*

Thus far the discussion of arguments has been tied to a group of very simple examples.   The choice was deliberate.   "Pure" cases were used to begin with because basic notions, such as that of *argument*, are best grasped if they are first examined in very simple settings.

The cases we encounter in real life, however, are almost always "impure."   Arguments rarely make their appearance with premisses and conclusions all present and neatly labeled.   Quite the contrary.   They come embedded in lectures, debates, research papers, monographs, committee reports, and party platforms and clothed in all manner of linguistic raiment.   Frequently, they are linked together to form complex, extended chains of reasoning.   More often than not, the conclusion is stated first or tucked in between premisses; and one or more of the premisses or even the conclusion may be omitted altogether as being "obvious from the context."   Hence the problem is to be able to recognize arguments in their natural habitat, to be able to tell whether some *actual* bit of discourse represents an argument or whether it is merely a recital or some other kind of communication.

An actual piece of discourse represents an argument if 1) it contains a sequence of at least two sentences and 2) this sequence is associated with a claim that one of its members follows in some sense from the other or others.

There are, of course, exceptions to requirement 1: some arguments may take the grammatical form of a single sentence (see §2).   This is most likely to occur where arguments are being *reported* rather than *offered*, as in the following sentence from a *New York Times* editorial:

(1)   The chief argument now being advanced for going ahead with the Safeguard antiballistic missile system (ABM) is the alleged need to avoid a defeat for the President that would undermine his prestige just as he enters strategic arms limitation talks with the Soviet Union.   [July 13, 1969]

Generally, however, the presence of the necessary *sequence* is fairly obvious.

The problem then reduces to one of verifying the presence of the second element of an argument: the *claim* that one sentence in the sequence follows in a certain sense from the others.   Here two kinds of situations must be considered.

First, the sentences in the sequence may contain specific words commonly used to signal the fact that an appropriate claim is being made. Words such as 'hence', 'therefore', or 'so' perform that function by announcing the conclusion, while words like 'since' or 'for' do so by pointing out a premiss.   Such words may furnish all the evidence we need to decide whether what we have is an argument.   If at the same time we supply any understood but unstated premiss or conclusion, we can determine just what the argument is.   A case in point is the following:

(2)   But if we're doomed to have black schools—and whites are determined that we are—then blacks ought to control them. [Dr. Troy Duster, quoted in *The New York Times*, September 24, 1968]

What has been omitted here as obvious is the conclusion that follows from the two premisses: "Therefore blacks ought to control black schools."

Second, in a great many situations the appropriate claim is present only implicitly, if at all.   When the argument is oral, we can perhaps ask the person who advances it to " be more explicit ": Does he intend to claim that such and such a sentence follows in such and such a sense from such and such other sentences?   He may tell us and, in this instance, solve for us the problem of argument recognition.   But more often the argument will appear in printed material, and the author will not be at hand to be questioned.   Then we must rely on common sense and on miscellaneous clues provided by the context if we are to be able to determine whether an appropriate claim is being made and, if so, just what it is. Consider this passage from a statement on the draft issued April 18, 1969, by 253 student-body presidents and college newspaper editors:

(3)   Most of us have worked in electoral politics and through other channels to change the course of America's foreign policy.   We will continue, but the possible results of these efforts will come too late for those whose deferments soon expire.   We must make an agonizing choice: to accept induction, which we feel would be irresponsible to ourselves, our country and our fellow man; or to refuse induction, which is contrary to our respect for law and involves injury to our personal lives and careers.

Left without a third alternative, we will act according to our conscience.   Along with thousands of our fellow students, we campus leaders cannot participate in a war which we believe to be immoral and unjust.   We publicly and collectively express our intention to refuse induction and to aid and support those who decide to refuse. We will not serve in the military as long as the war in Viet Nam continues.

Do these paragraphs offer or report one or more arguments, or are they merely a recital? If the former, how would you state the arguments?

Questions such as these do have answers, but not always uniquely "correct" ones. Ordinary language is far too complex for us to be able to write a *general* argument-recognition program. There is no algorithm, or set of precise instructions, by which a person or a machine, presented with an arbitrary body of actual discourse, can mechanically pick out in a finite number of steps just those sequences of sentences that are associated with appropriate claims and thus constitute arguments. Human beings have the ingenuity and understanding to cope with the task of recognizing an ordinary language argument, but they must work at it and think about it. A machine cannot do the job.

EXERCISES

6.1. Each of the following passages may be viewed as containing, implicitly if not explicitly, one or more arguments. See if you can unearth the premises and the conclusions, noting those that are *implicit* and thus have to be supplied. You may rephrase sentences (while preserving their intended meanings) if this will help bring out the argument more clearly.

For example, a recent full-page advertisement for a prominent conglomerate included a passage that ran something like this:

> The characteristic feature of monopoly is the absence of or decline in competition. The *X* Corporation knows only too well that competition abounds in each industry in which it is represented.

The argument contained here may be formulated as follows:

> *First premiss:* If monopoly is present, competition declines or is absent.
>
> *Second premiss:* Competition abounds in each industry in which the *X* Corporation is represented.
>
> *Conclusion* (supplied): Hence there is no monopoly in any industry in which the *X* Corporation is represented.

> a. Either Thieu implements the Paris agreements and loses, or he refuses to implement them and he loses. [A North Vietnamese, quoted in *The New York Times*, February 18, 1974]

b.   When inflation spreads and expectations of hyperinflation appear, Governmental countermeasures are unlikely to be even-handed or well-planned.   The public anxiety becomes too great and the pressure to do something impetuously is given added impetus not only from the sharply rising prices, but also from strikes, shortages of goods and services, and the increasing skepticism of the people in the Governmental process.   Consequently the country becomes ripe for a sharp shift to the left or to the right. [Economist Henry Kaufman, in *The New York Times*, Section 3, July 7, 1974]

c.   That *God is to be worshipped* is, without doubt, as great a truth as any that can enter into the mind of man . . .   But it can by no means be thought innate, unless the ideas of *God* and *worship* are innate.   That the idea the term 'worship' stands for is not in the understanding of children, and a character stamped on the mind in its first original, I think will be granted by anyone that considers how few there be amongst grown men who have a clear and distinct notion of it . . .   [John Locke, *An Essay Concerning Human Understanding*, Book I, Chapter 3]

d.   On this occasion, I realize that the position I am in is a unique one—one that will never come again—because since I am the first American President ever to pay a state visit to Indonesia, the next American president who comes here will not be in the position I presently find myself in.   [Richard Nixon, quoted in *The New York Times*, August 1, 1969]

e.   If the moon is devoid of seismic activity from internal sources, this leads to the conclusion that there are no significant internal energy sources and that the moon could not have a partially molten mantle or a molten core.   As discussed above, the absence of a hot interior, in turn, indicates either (i) that excess heat has been removed in the past by extensive volcanism; or (ii) that the proportion of radioactive materials in the moon is much lower than that for the earth or for meteoroids; or (iii) that the moon was formed much later than the earth and radiogenic heating has not had time to produce important effects.   Thus the complete absence of internal seismic activity in the moon will be of considerable significance relative to the thermal history of the moon.   [G. Latham et al., "The Apollo Passive Seismic Experiment," *Science*, July 18, 1969]

f.   We have maintained that the problems and techniques of the school are not the problems and techniques of practical life or the traditional home.   The school's knowledge base, value system and dominant learning situations and the functional learning systems to which they give rise are all in conflict with those of the student's traditional culture. If we take this opposition seriously, certain implications follow for educational policy. For one thing, it is not necessary to look further for explanations of the difficulties formal education may present to people who rely heavily on informal education in their basic method. The problem does not lie " in them." Searches for specific " incapacities" and " deficiencies" are socially mischievous detours. [Sylvia Scribner and Michael Cole, " Cognitive Consequences of Formal and Informal Education," *Science*, November 9, 1973]

g. The failure of the Nixon-Brezhnev summit to make a breakthrough toward a second strategic arms limitation treaty (SALT II) covering offensive nuclear weapons testifies to the continued fragility of " détente." [An editorial in *The New York Times*, July 5, 1974]

h. Now while I'm all for conserving energy and eliminating waste, I'm also aware of what has been accomplished . . . during this generation. World resources and reserves of petroleum have been greatly extended by off-shore oil-drilling techniques . . . Nuclear power technology has been brought to maturity. And the groundwork has been laid for future advances in breeder reactors, fusion and hydrogen technology. My point is that this generation need not be apologetic about its use of energy because it will leave behind it, through its technological advances, more new resources and reserves than it has used up. [Dr. Thomas O. Paine, senior vice president of General Electric, in *General Electric Investor*, Summer 1974]

i. In as many ways as equivalent syllogisms may be varied, in so many may the technical forms be varied likewise. As, for instance: "If you had borrowed and not paid, you owe me money; but you have not borrowed and not paid; therefore you do not owe me money." To perform these processes skillfully, is held to be the peculiar mark of a philosopher. [*The Discourses of Epictetus*, Chapter 8, " That Logical Subtleties Are Not Safe to the Uninstructed."]

j. Now the President may be right in how he reads the Constitution. But he may also be wrong. And if he is wrong, who is there to tell him so? And if there is no one, then the President, of course, is free to pursue his course of erroneous interpretations. What then becomes of our constitutional form of government? [Leon Jaworski, oral argument before the Supreme Court, *The New York Times*, July 9, 1974]

6.2. For each argument you identify under 6.1, state whether you think it is deductive, nondeductive, or interpretable either way. If you decide that it is being offered as a deductive argument, then using the common-sense criterion, give your best judgment as to its validity.

For example, the argument contained in the *X* Corporation advertisement, formulated as above, is surely valid. (We leave it to the economists to determine whether it is also sound.)

---

§7   *On the Three Divisions of Our Subject*

Our subject, we have said, is logic, or the general study of arguments and of the principles and procedures used in evaluating them. We have defined the term 'argument', have distinguished in a preliminary way between deductive and nondeductive arguments, and have identified the principal qualities that constitute goodness in a deductive argument. The logician's task now is to examine just one of those qualities, *validity*, and to determine the criteria by which one may verify its presence or absence in arguments.

We shall follow custom and divide our discussion into three parts. The first, "Language and Argument," may be described as an informal linguistic preface to logic, in which the connecting thread is the role played by language in argument. So we first comment briefly on *human language*, the *uses* of ordinary language, and *fallacies in argument*, including in particular those due to language. We then review some theories of *linguistic meaning* and conclude with a discussion of *definitions*. The reader will find that a great many of the questions touched on in Part I do not yet have widely accepted answers. Some of the questions are not even clearly formulated; others are still quite "open." But work proceeds, and some of this we shall try to report.

The other two divisions of our subject comprise logic in a stricter sense. Part II, "The Logic of Deductive Arguments," is given over to appraising the validity of deductive arguments. A deductive argument is valid if it is impossible for the conclusion to be false when the premises are all true. But what is meant by 'impossible'? What is the logical "bond" that joins premises and conclusion in a valid deductive argument? By what criterion do we establish deductive validity? Here, in contrast to Part I, precise answers will be forthcoming for a number of questions. Elementary modern logic furnishes a generally recognized set of principles and procedures that enables us to distinguish between the valid and the invalid *for certain classes of deductive arguments*. The fragment of modern logic known as *sentence logic* does this for a small class of arguments. *First-order predicate logic*, which includes sentence logic, does the same thing for a much wider class of arguments (among them the traditional Aristotelian syllogisms). We shall consider each of the two logics in turn.

Finally, in Part III—"Nondeductive Arguments"—we shall once more find ourselves moving, for much of the way, over still uncertain ground. The widespread agreement on elementary matters that prevails among deductive logicians is absent in the nondeductive field.   Here authorities differ even in their notions of what a nondeductive argument is and, therefore, on how to conceive of a *logic* of nondeductive arguments, or an "inductive" logic.   We shall be content to review some elementary material on nondeductive arguments and to consider certain uses of such arguments in science and daily life.

1

Language
and Argument

SOCRATES: . . . *If I had not been poor, I might have heard the fifty-drachma course of the great Prodicus, which is a complete education in grammar and language—these are his own words—and then I should have been at once able to answer your question about the correctness of names. But, indeed, I have only heard the single-drachma course, and therefore I do not know the truth about such matters. I will, however, gladly assist you and Cratylus in the investigation of them.*

Plato, *Cratylus*, 384

2

Language

Logic is the study of arguments. These, as we have seen, are made up of sentences, which in turn are basic structures of language. Thus logic and language are closely related, and it is tempting to begin a course in logic with an extended discussion of language.

Some writers reject this temptation altogether. They move at once into logic proper, often on the ground that the really interesting problems of language are so resistant that whatever can be said about them in brief is bound to be either false or trivial. Others succumb fully, exploring the "foothills" of language so thoroughly that exhaustion sets in long before they can begin to scale the "peaks" of logic. In this situation, moderation would seem to be the wisest course.

There are at least two reasons why it seems wrong to skip matters of language entirely. First, in studying arguments we often learn more from faulty ones than from good ones—as in physiology, where a pathological specimen may be more instructive than a healthy one—and a great many *fallacies*, or typical faults in argument, turn on misuses of language. Second, arguments are often difficult to appraise because they contain terms that are not reasonably clear in meaning. It may therefore be helpful to give some thought to what is meant by the meaning of a linguistic expression and in particular to how we fix such meanings in *definitions*.   These reasons motivate the present chapter and the one that follows it.

We begin with brief comments on the nature and importance of language and on some of the puzzles it presents to scholar and student. Thereafter natural (or ordinary) languages are distinguished from artificial (in particular, formal) languages.   Some of the varied uses of natural languages are suggested.   And we consider less hurriedly those errors in argument that are traditionally called "informal fallacies."

---

§8   *The Nature of Human Language*

Language is an essential and pervasive feature of human society.   We *listen to* lectures, *ask* and *answer* questions, *read* books, *write* papers.   We may not be born talking, but we very soon acquire the habit.   And if circumstances are favorable, reading and writing follow in due course.

ON THE IMPORTANCE OF LANGUAGE

Before we enter into the actual discussion of language, we note two common errors that interfere with a proper appreciation of its role.   First, the importance of language is often underestimated.   Since linguistic phenomena are so much a part of our daily lives, we are likely to take them for granted and hence fail to make them an object of study and reflection.   But unless we give careful thought to language and how we use it, we cannot hope to improve the quality of our own linguistic communication, upon which so much depends, in school and out.

Second, its importance is at times overestimated.   Thus it is often said of nations, races, or generations that "they do not speak the same language"—as if language alone is responsible for the great "communication gaps" of our age.   But if this were the case, there would be no difficulty in bridging the "gaps."   All that would be needed (assuming grammar is not at issue) would be an appropriate dictionary—a lexicon for two generations, for example, with suitable definitions of such expressions as 'cop-out', 'hangup', 'uptight', 'loose', and the like.   Of course, the whole notion is absurd.   What causes the major breakdowns in communication is not vocabulary as such, but a whole range of differing moral, social, and political ideas.   The point is not that one side does not understand what the other is saying but, rather, that it does not agree with what is being said—or even that it does not believe the other side actually means what it is saying.   Since such gaps are not due primarily to language, language alone cannot provide the chief means of overcoming them; and to expect it to do so only diverts attention from the real problems.

SOME DEFINITIONS OF LANGUAGE

Experts differ on what language is and even on what questions about language a theory of language should ask and try to answer. There is, however, a measure of agreement on certain fundamentals, and this is enough to get us started.

Thus Professor Chao has said that language is

> a conventional system of habitual vocal behavior by which members of a community communicate with one another.[1]

From a layman's standpoint this definition is very close to that given by Professor Hughes, for whom 'language' means

> a system of arbitrary vocal symbols by which thought is conveyed from one human being to another.[2]

The two have the following points in common:

1. *Language is a system.* The units that make up a language—words, syllables, or whatever—are systematically interconnected; they are not a mere collection of items.

2. *Language is a system of conventional, or arbitrary, signs.* The meaningful units of language—words, certain sequences of sounds—receive their meanings solely from the practices of a particular language community, not from any other source.

3. *Language is a system of conventional vocal signs.* Experts agree that *speech* is primary and that written or other representations of language are derivative from speech.

4. *Language is a system of conventional vocal signs used for communication among human beings.*

These points all fit in fairly well with our commonsense or intuitive notion of language, and we shall let them serve as the initial basis for our discussion.

Note, though, that the two definitions are not in perfect accord: Professor Chao speaks of communicative *behavior*, while Professor Hughes speaks of arbitrary symbols conveying *thought*. Some of the differences will be reviewed in Chapter 3 under the topic of *meaning*. Note, too, that if these definitions are accepted, it follows that all linguistic communication is human (although animals communicate, they do not do so by "language"); but it does not follow that human communication is solely linguistic (we also communicate by means of shrugs, winks, yawns, scowls, and so on).

---

[1] Yuen Ren Chao, *Language and Symbolic Systems* (New York: Cambridge University Press, 1968), p. 1.

[2] John P. Hughes, *The Science of Language* (New York: Random House, 1962), p. 6.

Finally, implicit in the definitions is a crucial feature of language, the significance of which is likely to escape our attention.   Consider the following sentence:

Shakespeare was fond of rock music.

The chances are that the reader has never seen it before, yet he or she can understand it without difficulty.   Thus a fifth point can be added:

5.   *Language is a system of communication with the property that anyone who is acquainted with the signs (vocabulary) and the rules for their use (grammar) can understand and produce combinations of signs (sentences) that he or she has never previously encountered.*

THE STUDY OF LANGUAGE

The scientific study of language is known today as linguistics, and those who pursue it are called, if somewhat unhappily, linguists (' linguisticians ' might be a better term).   Their ample writings contain what to the layman seems a heady array of challenging facts, ingenious analyses, unsolved puzzles, and unresolved controversies.   We sample the array briefly before continuing with our main discussion.

Among the facts about language that linguists and laymen find particularly striking are the following:[3]

1.   Language is ubiquitous.   All known human societies, without exception, use language—that is, their members perform individual speech acts, or utterances, in accordance with one or another conventional system of communication.

2.   While languages are quite numerous (some 2,800 are said still to be in use today) and differ widely in sound, vocabulary, and grammar, there is a remarkable unity in the midst of this diversity: *all* languages have in common certain features in addition to those they possess by definition.   These shared features the linguist calls "language universals." They vary from the obvious—that every language has vowels—to the not so obvious or indeed not certain—that every language has a distinction between one-place and two-place "predicates" (between 'Perkins *is learned*' and 'Perkins *admires* Quincy ').   A modest stock of "universals" has been assembled, and work continues apace to locate others.[4]

3.   There are no "undeveloped" languages.   All known human societies—no matter how "unsophisticated" their tools, economies, or

---

[3]   These and a great many other matters about language are discussed with clarity and authority by Max Black in *The Labyrinth of Language* (New York: New American Library, 1969).

[4]   See *Universals of Language*, 2d ed., ed. Joseph H. Greenberg (Cambridge, Mass.: MIT Press, 1966). The second example of "universals" is taken from Charles F. Hockett's essay in this volume, "The Problem of Universals in Language," p. 23.

other culture traits may be—possess fully developed languages with extensive vocabularies and complex grammars.

These and other facts raise many questions. What exactly are the basic units of language and how do they combine to form the system—or group of interconnected systems—of sounds and lexical items and grammar we call a language? What is the origin of language? How does a child first acquire a language? Is it proper to identify language as exclusive to human beings if some other animal can be taught to use some form of "human language"? Can an adequate theory of language be given solely in terms of observed behavioral regularities? Just what is a theory of language a theory *of*?

Of these questions—and they are only a few—there seems to have been marked progress on the first, especially in regard to the phonology or sound system of language. The second—the origin of language—has for the time being been ruled out of court by the linguists themselves on the ground of insufficient evidence. The remaining topics—particularly language acquisition and the fundamental nature of a theory of language—are today the subject of intensive study and pungent debate.

---

§9   *Ordinary (Natural) and Formal (Artificial) Languages*

The languages we have been talking about are called *natural* languages. We now distinguish between these and various systems of human communication known as *artificial* languages.

As the name suggests, natural languages are ordinary languages—English, Spanish, Swahili, Italian, Chinese, Hindustani, Russian, and the like. Especially relevant to the natural-artificial distinction are such characteristics of natural languages as the following:

> 1. They have developed *historically* (they were not devised at a particular time for a particular purpose).
>
> 2. They are *socially* learned (we acquire our first language not as isolated individuals but in the context of the family or some other social group).
>
> 3. They are *orally* transmitted (we learn to speak our native language before we learn to read it).[5]

---

[5] See Morton W. Bloomfield and Leonard Newmark, *A Linguistic Introduction to the History of English* (New York: Alfred A. Knopf, 1963), pp. 9ff.

In particular, the grammars of natural languages are set down only *after* the languages are in use: use determines rules of use.

Not so the artificial languages. These are *constructed* systems of conventional signs, deliberately put together for a specific purpose. Hence their grammars must be formulated *before* the languages can be used: "rules of use" determine use.

Artificial languages are called "languages" by analogy with the natural variety. But this terminology is often objected to on the ground that there is an unbridgeable, qualitative difference in expressive power between natural languages and even the most elaborate of constructed languages. In the absence of a theory of natural language that is universally considered to be adequate, however, this issue may be regarded as still open. Meanwhile, the use of the word 'language' seems justified if for no other reason than that artificial languages share with natural ones the highly significant property mentioned above in §8: if we know the signs and the rules of a language, we can understand and produce combinations of signs (sentences, formulas) we have not previously encountered.

Before considering artificial languages, we should remove a minor source of confusion by illustrating the distinction between a language and a code. For example, Morse code is not an artificial language but a way of representing a natural language; and American deaf-mutes who communicate by finger-spelling English words are simply encoding spoken English. But if instead of employing a manual alphabet, they communicate by means of the American Sign Language, they are then using a constructed language with its own gestural signs and rules of use.

There are various types of artificial languages. The diversity of these languages reflects the diversity of the needs they are designed to fill. Such needs include international communication, communication between people and computers, and the formal treatment of logic and mathematics.

International communication. During the late nineteenth and early twentieth centuries several attempts were made to further international understanding by constructing a simple new language for general international use. The purpose, apparently, was to create a *full-fledged substitute* for natural languages, a project which in effect assumed that it was possible to *construct* a "natural" language. But the end results— chiefly Esperanto and its variants—were in reality nothing other than simplified natural languages (specifically, Romance languages), and they never gained wide acceptance.

Communication between people and computers. Computers at present are not equipped to "take directions" expressed in ordinary words and sentences; they do not "understand" natural language. Hence it is necessary to construct artificial (computer) languages if digital computers are to be instructed about various problems and the procedures for solv-

ing them.   Such "programming languages" will vary with the nature
and range of the tasks we wish to assign.   But in each case they will
contain 1) a complete list of admissible symbols and 2) a complete list of
rules for combining admissible symbols into admissible sequences, or
strings, of admissible symbols.   Some well-known computer languages
are FORTRAN (Formula Translator), ALGOL (Algorithm-Oriented
Language), and of a different species, SNOBOL (String-Oriented Symbolic
Language).

The formal treatment of logic and mathematics.   As we all know, mathematics makes extensive use of nonverbal symbols (that is, symbols other
than words).   There are at least two reasons for this.

First, nonverbal symbols often speak more clearly than words.   In
many situations they are more *perspicuous*: their import can more easily
be taken in at a glance.   Compare the formula

$$x^n + y^n = z^n$$

with its equivalent written out in words

> If you take a quantity and multiply it by itself a certain num-
> ber of times and add to it a second quantity that has been
> multiplied by itself the same number of times, the sum will be
> equal to a third quantity that has been multiplied by itself that
> same number of times.

Second, nonverbal symbols can be assigned single, precise meanings,
whereas ordinary words generally carry vague or multiple meanings (and
even when they are assigned precise meanings their other uses often get
in the way).   Take, for instance, the sentences

> Socrates is a man.
>
> The tiger is a predator.

The word 'is' in the first sentence is used in the sense of 'is a member of '
("Socrates is a member of the set of men"); in the second, it is used in the
sense of 'is a subset of' ("The set of tigers is a subset of the set of preda-
tors").   The mathematical theory of sets guards against confusion by
employing two different symbols for these two meanings— '∈' (epsilon)
to mean the same as 'is a member of' and '⊂' (the symbol for *set-
inclusion*) to mean the same as 'is a subset of '.

It seems plausible, then, that when fully rigorous and explicit proofs
of theorems are desired, nonverbal symbols should take over altogether.
This is why constructed symbolic languages are used in formal mathematics and logic.

Formal languages, as these symbol systems are often called, also vary widely depending on the nature of the logical and mathematical theories we wish to express in them. All such languages, however, contain 1) a complete list of symbols called the symbols of that particular formal language; 2) a list of rules for combining these symbols into one or more kinds of admissible or *well-formed* expressions of the language; and if the formal language is given an *interpretation*, 3) rules that assign "meanings" to the symbols and well-formed expressions of the language. The reader who is especially interested in formal languages may want to try his or her hand at constructing one—that is, a list of symbols and rules of grammar—say, for elementary algebra.

§10   *Some Uses of Ordinary Language*

Traditional grammar divides the sentences of ordinary language into four classes—declarative, interrogative, imperative, exclamatory—each with its appointed use. These uses are, respectively, to convey information, to ask questions, to issue instructions, and to exclaim. All of them are quite important.

This listing, however, does not do justice to the richly varied uses of ordinary language. What is needed is a closer view of the kinds of tasks performed with language and of the kinds of sentences used in performing these tasks. In the beginning, though, was the utterance, not the sentence. Therefore we start by discussing utterances, go on to sentences, and proceed thence to our goal: a more comprehensive account of the uses of language.

UTTERANCES AND SENTENCES[6]

Utterances are instances of actual speech having brief careers through time. They are always produced by someone at some place and generally to some end. This is how one linguist describes them:

> An UTTERANCE is any stretch of talk, by one person, before and after which there is silence on the part of the person.[7]

Sentences, in contrast, are more abstract. Should a person on some occasion say 'Logic is useful' and on a later occasion say 'Logic is

---

[6]   On utterances and sentences, see John Lyons, *Introduction to Theoretical Linguistics* (New York: Cambridge University Press, 1968), pp. 51ff., 170ff.

[7]   Zellig S. Harris, *Structural Linguistics* (Chicago: University of Chicago Press, 1951, 1951, 1961), p. 14.

useful ', he or she has produced two quite distinct utterances.   Nonetheless these utterances have something in common.   Thus sentences might be thought of as what all utterances having the same (relevant) sound pattern have in common.

Linguists draw a fundamental distinction between utterances as units of speech and sentences as units of grammatical description.   Utterances are the data with which the linguist begins the study of a language; sentences are part of the apparatus in terms of which the linguist develops a science of language.[8]

Definitions of 'Sentence'

What remains is to mark off sentences from other grammatical units. This is not as simple as it once seemed.   Tradition defined 'sentence ' as 'a linguistic unit that expresses a complete thought '.   But this definition would not be satisfactory today—for after all, *what* is a complete thought?   Yet it does contain the essential ingredients—namely, the elements of completeness and independence.   We see these in some recent definitions:

(1)   [E]ach sentence is an independent linguistic form, not included by virtue of any construction in any larger linguistic form.

(2)   [T]he sentence is the largest unit of grammatical description.

(3)   [A] sentence is the smallest linguistic unit that can be used to perform a complete action that is distinctively linguistic.[9]

Taken together, these would appear to say that a sentence is the largest grammatically *independent* linguistic unit (as contrasted with syllables, words, phrases) and the smallest linguistically *complete* one (as contrasted, say, with paragraphs).   Accordingly, sentences are the basic units of linguistic study.   Indeed, a language is sometimes regarded as just the set of its "grammatical" sentences.

One final observation.   We shall allow ourselves to talk of uttering *sentences*.   But we shall mean by this the producing of *utterances* that the linguist characterizes by means of the grammatical units known as sentences.

---

[8]   See John Lyons, op. cit., pp. 51, 52.

[9]   Definition (1) is from Leonard Bloomfield's *Language* (New York: Holt, Rinehart, Winston, 1933, 1966), p. 170; (2) is John Lyons's interpretation (op. cit., p. 172) of the point of (1); (3) is from William P. Alston, a philosopher of language, and appears in his *Philosophy of Language* (Englewood Cliffs, N.J.: Prentice-Hall, 1964), p. 33.   Since there are one-word sentences (exclamations and replies to questions), Alston in a footnote qualifies his definition thus: "To perform a complete linguistic action we must utter a sentence or some expression which in that context is elliptical for a sentence."

SENTENCES AND THE USES OF LANGUAGE

An account of the uses of ordinary language is in essence an account of the purposes served by the sentences we utter. We shall first summarize the standard version and then move a step or two beyond it.[10]

The Standard Account

It has been the custom to group the uses or functions of language under three loosely defined headings: *informative*, *expressive*, and *directive*.

The first of these functions centers on the communication of information. Although "information" is a complex notion, we are all acquainted from everyday life and from science with sentences that impart information. Examples of sentences that either inform or purport to inform are

(4)   Congress adopted the resolution of independence on July 2, 1776.

Dry breakfast cereals are uniformly high in nutrient value.

The second function—the expressive—is to evoke or to give vent to emotions. Although "emotion" too is a complex notion, examples of sentences that serve this purpose can readily be cited. A favorite source is poetry. But there is also political oratory, and there are the exclamations and imprecations of ordinary life. Thus we have

(5)   The Moving Finger writes, and having writ / Moves on.

All theory, dear friend, is gray,
But green the golden Tree of Life

A spirit of national masochism prevails, encouraged by an effete corps of impudent snobs who characterize themselves as intellectuals.

Zounds!

The third function—the directive—is to bring about or to prevent certain actions. This is carried out in diverse ways by the use of commands, instructions, requests (including questions—that is, requests for information), exhortations, and so on. There is no dearth of familiar examples. Here are a few:

(6)   Right turn!

You are to find the defendant not guilty unless you are persuaded beyond reasonable doubt that he is guilty.

---

[10]   See M. Black, op. cit., Chapter 5, "The Many Uses of Language," pp. 115–142, for a full analysis of the older and newer views.

Please pass the catsup.

When do classes begin?

Vote for the only man who offers you a choice, not an echo!

Each of the four traditional forms of sentences has a characteristic function: the declarative, to inform; the imperative—and the interrogative —to announce instructions or make various kinds of requests; the exclamatory to vent emotions.   But as the standard account itself emphasizes, there is no one-to-one correspondence between form and function.[11]

The four sentence forms cannot be neatly paired with certain functions because, for one thing, there are numerous exceptions to the characteristic uses.   Thus declarative sentences often serve a directive function, as in

(7)   I should like a copy of Frege's *Foundations of Arithmetic.*

Or they may serve an essentially expressive function, as in the second sentence under (5).

Another obstacle to the pairing of form and function is that many sentences serve more than one function in a given context.   The following are illustrations:

(8)   The only way to learn mathematics is to do mathematics. (informative-directive)

Why not victory? (directive-expressive)

War is bad for children and other living things. (expressive-directive-informative)

Finally, sentences serve different functions in *different* contexts.   For instance, the interrogative sentence

(9)   So what else is new?

can be used to ask a simple question—What else *is* new?—but in certain situations may also be used to vent an emotional attitude of disinterest or even disgust.

Thus it is not "grammatical" form alone that determines the purposes served by sentences, but other factors too—especially context.   While context dependency is particularly evident in the expressive use of language (this is discussed further in §13, where the "emotive meaning" of linguistic expressions is considered), it pervades language use as a whole.   Indeed,

---

[11]   These matters are discussed in Irving M. Copi's widely used text *Introduction to Logic*, 3rd ed. (New York: Macmillan, 1968), pp. 34–43.

it is by stressing context and situation that we gain a larger appreciation of the manifold uses of language.

Wittgenstein's Insight

The influential Austrian philosopher Ludwig Wittgenstein (1889–1951), in a by now classic passage of his *Philosophical Investigations*, asked: "But how many kinds of sentences are there?" He went on:

> Say assertion, question, and command?—There are *countless* kinds: countless different kinds of use of what we call "symbols," "words," "sentences." And this multiplicity is not something fixed, given once for all; but new types of language, new language-games, as we may say, come into existence, and others become obsolete and get forgotten. . . .

> Here the term "language-*game*" is meant to bring into prominence the fact that the *speaking* of language is part of an activity, or of a form of life.

> Review the multiplicity of language-games in the following examples and others:

> Giving orders, and obeying them—
> Describing the appearance of an object, or giving its measurements—
> Constructing an object from a description (a drawing)—
> Reporting an event—
> Speculating about an event—
> Forming and testing an hypothesis—
> Presenting the results of an experiment in tables and diagrams—
> Making up a story; and reading it—
> Play-acting—
> Singing catches—
> Guessing riddles—
> Making a joke; telling it—
> Solving a problem in practical arithmetic—
> Translating from one language to another—
> Asking, thanking, cursing, greeting, praying.[12]

Wittgenstein's emphasis here on the limitless and changing panorama of language uses seems entirely just. The wonder is that no one had quite made the point earlier, and that it remained for him—and indepen-

---

[12]   Ludwig Wittgenstein, *Philosophical Investigations*, 3rd ed., trans. G. E. M. Anscombe (New York: Macmillan, 1967), pp. 11 and 12.

dently the English philosopher John L. Austin (1911–1960)—to "break the news." Perhaps the chief reason for the delay was that for a very long time those who looked into these matters—philosophers, scientists, teachers—had their attention fixed exclusively on the use of sentences to make statements—that is, to say something either true or false.[13]   This concentration, natural as it was, in effect shut out serious study of other uses of sentences.

Clearly, not every sentence we utter is used to make a statement—to say something we would ordinarily call true or false.   In fact, if we were to keep a log of the sentences we utter in the course of a day, we should probably find that only a minority of them are statement-making sentences. Most of our sentences serve other purposes, where the question of truth or falsity does not even arise.   For example, the promise we make is neither true nor false, it is kept or broken; a prayer may be answered or not; a greeting acknowledged or ignored; an apology accepted or re-jected.   While this may seem obvious, the tendency to view all sentences in terms of the statement-making model has hampered the philosophical analysis of other kinds of sentences.

Language Uses and Logic

In §2 it was noted that arguments may contain sentences other than those used to make statements.   The fact that "logics" are only now being developed to deal with these other kinds of sentences—a logic of com-mands, of questions, and the like—is itself a reflection of the past one-sided preoccupation with statement-making sentences.   These "logics" have not yet reached the stage where they can be included in an intro-ductory discussion.   Thus in using the term 'logic' we shall continue to mean the basic logic of statement-making sentences.

Sentences and Statements: A Further Remark

Sentences have been described as the fundamental units of grammatical description and the making of *statements* as one of the principal uses to which sentences are put.   To make a statement is to utter or write a sen-tence for the purpose of saying how things are.[14]

We note now that different sentences may be used to make the same statement ("*Llueve*" and "*Es regnet*," for example, or in English, "It is raining").   And the "same" sentence may be used to make different statements ("I am tired," say, uttered by two different people).

---

[13]   See Max Black, op. cit., pp. 117–118.

[14]   The reader will find that other logic texts use the term 'proposition' and not ' statement-making sentence '.   Without entering into any of the issues involved, we suggest that no harm will result if the reader puts the expression 'statement-making sentence' in place of 'proposition expressed by a sentence'.

TYPES AND TOKENS

There is a useful distinction, going back to the American philosopher Charles Sanders Peirce (1839–1914), between sentences and words as *types*, and sentences and words as *tokens*. An example will make this clear. Suppose we write

(10)   To err is human, to forgive divine.

How many *words* are there in this sentence? Obviously, either seven or six depending on whether we count the repetition of 'to' as two words or as two *occurrences* of one word. Now suppose we again write

(11)   To err is human, to forgive divine.

Are (10) and (11) two sentences or two occurrences of the same sentence? Again the answer depends on how we are to understand our terms.

Here the type-token distinction comes into play. The answer to the first question is that the sentence contains seven word *tokens*, representing six word *types*. The answer to the second is that (10) and (11) are two sentence *tokens* of the same sentence *type*.

---

§11   *Some Misuses of Ordinary Language in Argument: Informal Fallacies*

No less varied than the uses of ordinary language are its misuses. Many of these enter into the stream of argument, producing disturbances of diverse sorts. The resulting typical faults in argument (along with certain others) are known as *fallacies*. A number of them will be reviewed in detail.

WHAT IS A FALLACY?

All fallacies are errors, but only typical errors are called fallacies. Thus it is an error but not a fallacy if Perkins, when asked to identify Sophocles, replies that he was an ancient Greek philosopher who was condemned to death for "not believing in the gods the state believes in, and also for corrupting the young." Again, while all fallacies are typical errors, not all typical errors are termed fallacies. For instance, a typical error in calculating is to reverse a pair of numbers—to read 31, say, for 13—but this is not called a fallacy.

As commonly used, the word 'fallacy' is reserved for typical errors in belief and in argument.   Its use in connection with beliefs is illustrated in the following two passages:

(1)   The greatest fallacy of politics and political opinion in 1968 is that police action can prevent or control disorder in cities. [Mayor Richard Hatcher of Gary, Indiana, speaking at De Pauw University, October 11, 1968 (*I. F. Stone's Weekly*, October 21, 1968)]

(2)   The nonbiologist frequently and mistakenly thinks of genes as being directly responsible for one property or another; this leads him to the fallacy of dichotomizing everything as being dependent on either genes or environment.   [Professor Eric H. Lenneberg, "On Explaining Language," *Science* 164 (May 9, 1969), 638]

In logic, however, the term 'fallacy' is restricted to typical or recurrent errors in *argument*, and here it shall be used only in that sense.

FALLACIES IN ARGUMENT

Fallacious arguments have been a topic of study ever since Aristotle considered them in his *De Sophisticis Elenchis* (*On Sophistical Refutations*). "That some reasonings are genuine," he wrote, "while others seem to be so but are not, is evident.   This happens with arguments, as also elsewhere, through a certain likeness between the genuine and the sham."

With Aristotle's words in mind, let us say that a deductive argument is fallacious if it 1) fails, in some typical way, to be sound (" genuine "), and yet 2) seems to be sound.   Thus no sound argument can be fallacious; and no "sham" argument can be fallacious either unless it bears a "certain likeness " to a sound one.[15]

Now a deductive argument is sound if it fulfills the two conditions described in §4.   These are 1) that the inference or inferences contained in the argument be valid, and 2) that its premises be true.   Clearly, arguments may, in typical ways, fail to meet either or both of these conditions and, hence, be fallacious.

All this appears simple enough; but there are several complicating factors.   One is the set of problems raised by the question, What makes an argument *seem* to be sound when it isn't?   Is it vague and ambiguous language?   Individual prejudice?   Pressure to conform?   The list of possible answers is long.

Another complicating factor is the strong tradition that divides all fallacies into two groups: *formal* and *informal*.   There are several difficulties with this classification.   One is that the division is made uncertain

---

[15]   The application of the notion of fallacy to nondeductive arguments is left for Part III.

because 'formal' has two senses, in one of which many so-called informal fallacies may be said also to be formal.   A second difficulty is that the standard repertory of "informal" fallacies includes items that are *not* fallacious arguments because they are not arguments at all, but substitutes for argument.   A third is that the classification leaves unplaced at least one type of error that really merits the name 'fallacy', as well as some other errors that are of special interest even though they may not merit the name.

FORMAL FALLACIES ILLUSTRATED

To say that an inference or argument is *formal* is to say that its validity depends not on the particular subject matter or content of the sentences making up the argument, but solely on their *form*.   What this signifies we shall discuss in detail in Part II; an illustration will suffice for now.

Take the argument

(3)   No men are angels.

Therefore no angels are men.

Obviously the inference contained in (3) is *valid* (it is impossible for the conclusion to be false if the premiss is true).   So is the one contained in

(4)   No astrologers are scientists.

Therefore no scientists are astrologers.

In fact, (3) and (4) are easily seen to be instances of the same "form" or pattern of argument, which can be represented as

(5)   No *A* are *B*

Therefore no *B* are *A* ,

where the letters '*A*' and '*B*' serve as stand-ins or place-holders for the names of classes.   We therefore say that (5) is a *valid form* of inference.

On the other hand, the argument

(6)   All mathematicians are scholars

Therefore all scholars are mathematicians

contains an inference that is clearly *invalid* (since it is indeed possible for the premiss to be true and the conclusion false), as is the inference contained in

(7)   All fascists are reactionaries.

Therefore all reactionaries are fascists.

Arguments (6) and (7) are instances of the "form"

(8)   All A are B

   Therefore all B are A,

which is thus seen to be an *invalid form* of inference or argument.

   Now one of the errors often made is to accept (8) as a valid form of argument and to accept instances of (8), such as (6) and (7), as valid arguments.   This is a formal error—that is, one with respect to the *form* of an argument.   Thus we commit a formal fallacy—in the strict sense—if in some typical fashion and due to a "certain likeness" between them, we mistake an invalid form of inference for a valid one.

   There is also a looser sense of 'formal fallacy', according to which *any* instance of an invalid form of argument is an instance of a formal fallacy.   Consider the "argument"

(9)   All sophomores are perspicacious.

   Therefore all fallacies are trivial.

It is obviously invalid (the conclusion may well be false even if the premiss is true), and its form

(9')   All A are B

   Therefore all C are D

is an invalid form.   Therefore, in the looser sense, (9) is an instance of a formal fallacy.

   But is it strictly an instance of a formal fallacy?   Is the error in connection with (9) that an invalid form of inference is mistaken for a valid one?   Obviously not; no one is likely to mistake (9') for a valid form.

   Thus the error in (9) turns *not* on the *form* of the argument but on something else: the premiss is irrelevant to the conclusion.   Hence the notion of a formal fallacy in the looser sense is misleading.   If there is a fallacy in (9), it is better to term it *informal* or *nonformal*.

INFORMAL FALLACIES

Informal fallacies have generally been arranged in several families. The members of these families include many prominent enough to have received special names—for example, the fallacy of *petitio principii* ("begging the question").   The listing presented here will not stray far from the usual one.   It is offered with the warning that not every fallacious argument fits neatly under just one particular informal fallacy (an argument may be an instance of more than one fallacy) and that the roll call of informal fallacies will of necessity be incomplete.

We shall review informal fallacies under two headings: *fallacies of irrelevance*—those that involve the lack of an appropriate (or of any) connection between the premisses and the conclusion of an argument— and *fallacies of ambiguity*—those that arise because certain terms in an argument are not reasonably clear in meaning.

Fallacies of Irrelevance

An argument whose premisses are not properly related to its conclusion is said to be an instance of a fallacy of irrelevance if the fault is a typical one.

Arguments are advanced to establish or defend a conclusion, to draw consequences from a set of premisses, and so on—purposes that certainly cannot be served by arguments whose premisses "have nothing to do with the case." Yet such arguments are offered all the time. We shall consider a number of varieties of irrelevant argument, touching on the first half dozen only briefly and allotting more space to several others that are more interesting.

Argument ad baculum (*"appeal to the stick"*). This fallacy is usually defined as the appeal to force or to the threat of force to obtain acceptance of a conclusion. It evokes the image of the policeman's club, the general's weaponry, and the diplomat's "big stick," as well as the many less obvious ways in which power and authority are employed to *compel* assent. While all these may be referred to loosely as instances of the *ad baculum* fallacy, it would seem more accurate to describe them not as *errors* in argument, but as the *abandonment* of argument.

In the strict sense, one can speak of an *ad baculum* fallacy only if the threat is embodied in a premiss and the premiss is irrelevant to the conclusion. An example might be the argument contained in this dialogue:

> The club members want to run Mort for coroner.
>
> I don't want Mort for coroner.
>
> You'd better want Mort for coroner, or the members will make life miserable for you.
>
> All right. I want Mort for coroner.

But in such situations does it really make much difference whether what one faces is a threat or a premiss?

Argument ad hominem (*"to the man"*). This fallacy consists in offering statements about a person's character or circumstances as premisses to oppose his conclusion. It is a fallacy of irrelevance since in general such matters have nothing to do with the truth or falsity of a person's views. (An attack on the credibility of a witness is clearly an exception to this.)

There are two main forms of the *ad hominem* fallacy.   The first, called the "abusive," makes the character of a person the issue ("Perkins's room-mate is wrong about the war in Indochina; look how angry he gets when anyone disagrees with him").   The other, the "circumstantial," makes the circumstances of a person the issue ("Linda is wrong when she says that women are discriminated against in hiring; how about her important job at CBS").

The familiar *tu quoque* ("you're another") fallacy—replying in kind to an opponent's abuse—may also be counted as a form of this fallacy.

Argument **ad ignorantiam** (*"from ignorance"*).   To commit this fallacy is to argue that a conclusion should be accepted because it has not been disproved or that it should be rejected because it has not been proved. Examples are

> Extrasensory perception exists because no one has been able to prove that it does not.
>
> Extraterrestrial life does not exist because no one has been able to prove that it does.

The *ad ignorantiam* fallacy is one of irrelevance because the fact that we lack premises from which to infer a conclusion is *in general* not itself a relevant premise with respect to that conclusion.

Argument **ad misericordiam** (*"appeal to pity"*).   Here the fallacy consists in presenting an appeal to pity as if it were a proper premiss from which to infer a conclusion.   The stock example is the defense attorney in a felony trial who asks acquittal on the ground that her client was reared in unhappy circumstances.   Technically, no doubt, this is a fallacy.   Yet most defendants in such trials *were* so reared, and this fact seems somehow relevant as well as troubling.   It is a matter of law, however, and not of logic.   (Perhaps the law is wrong in excluding certain kinds of premises —psychological and social—as irrelevant, thus often leaving the defense with no alternative but to make logically questionable and otherwise uncer-tain appeals to pity.)

Argument **ad populum** (*"to the people"*).   An argument is said to be an instance of the *ad populum* fallacy if it relies on an appeal to the "emotions of the crowd" to gain assent to its conclusion.   Those who exploit this fallacy are called demagogues.

Usually *ad populum* is illustrated from political oratory and lawyers' speeches to juries.   Those who offer these illustrations presumably have in mind situations in which the person offering the argument 1) lacks (or chooses not to use) premises sufficient to establish the desired con-clusion and 2) strives to win assent to it by playing on the sentiments and prejudices of a mass audience.   And there can be no doubt that audiences often do accept conclusions on emotional grounds (as much in the privacy of their TV rooms as in public assemblages).

But there are certain objections to the "fallacy" as traditionally conceived.   First, those taken in by an *ad populum* appeal are perhaps better described not as victims of a *fallacy in* argument but (as in the case of *ad baculum*) as victims of a *substitute for* argument.

Second, what is labeled an *ad populum* argument intended to obtain assent to a certain conclusion often turns out, on closer view, to be something quite different: an exhortation to act in behalf of a conclusion to which the audience has already given assent.   (An example, perhaps, is the William Jennings Bryan "Cross of Gold" speech to the Democratic National Convention in 1896.)

Finally, the traditional *ad populum* fallacy conjures up a picture of mobs of ignorant, easily misled people.   This is a very negative view of the populace.   Before we rush to accept it, let us be careful lest in characterizing a fallacy in argument we commit a fallacy in belief.

Argument ad **verecundiam** (*"appeal to authority"*).   This is the fallacy of appealing to an authority in an area that lies outside of his or her competence.   Thus if Rod Laver were to endorse a tennis racquet, there would be no *ad verecundiam* fallacy; but if he were to endorse a breakfast cereal there might be, unless he has a competence in nutritional science.

Most of the conclusions we accept in ordinary life are taken on someone's, often unsupported, word.   Awareness of the *ad verecundiam* fallacy is helpful if it disposes us 1) to check the credentials of the alleged authority and 2) to get some idea of the kinds of premisses from which the authority derives the conclusion in question.

We should also take note of a related error.   Frequently, we are asked to approve an important public policy solely on the ground that the person asking us to do so "knows best."   But isn't this an appeal to authority in an area in which in a sense there is no "authority," in which each of us is or properly should be his or her own authority?

Accident.   The fallacy of *accident* is committed when we argue from some general principle to some particular case whose "accidental" features make it an exception to the principle.   An example is

> The failure to prove something true doesn't prove it false.
>
> Therefore the failure to prove a person guilty doesn't prove him or her innocent.

Here the general principle is correct (see the discussion of *ad ignorantiam*). But it is wrongly applied to a case whose special circumstance—the legal presumption that a person is innocent unless proven guilty—makes the principle irrelevant.

Converse accident, or *hasty generalization*, which is the converse of the fallacy of accident, is sometimes included with it as a fallacy of irrelevance.   An example would be

> Perkins never opens a book and makes all A's.
>
> Therefore anyone who never opens a book will make all A's.

The "fallacy" consists in unwisely taking an exceptional case—Perkins is phenomenally brilliant—as the basis for a generalization.   This error, however, relates not to deductive arguments but to nondeductive ones, and it is best dealt with in that context.

For the seven informal fallacies examined thus far, the error lies in using *premises that are irrelevant to the question at issue.*   In the three fallacies now to be considered, the problem of irrelevance centers on difficulties concerning the *question itself.*

Many questions, or complex question.   This is the familiar "have you stopped beating your wife" fallacy.   It arises when two or more questions are asked as one, with the insistence that they be given a single yes-or-no answer.

More generally, this fallacy arises whenever a question is asked that carries a presupposition such that any responsive answer to the question appears to concede the truth of the presupposition.   Some examples of such questions are

(10)   How long will you continue to abuse our patience, O Catiline?

(11)   When will students begin acting responsibly?

(12)   Why are college courses so irrelevant?

The fallacy is actually committed when an answer to the question—for example, "It's hard to say" as a reply to (11)—is used as a premiss from which to infer that the person being interrogated concedes the truth of the presupposition.   ("Ah! So you admit that students have been behaving irresponsibly!")

Obviously, the way to handle such a situation is to insist that the many questions be separated.   The complex question should be divided, and each part should be considered in the light of the premises relevant to it.

Petitio principii ("*begging the question*").   An argument that has its conclusion as one of its premises is said to commit the fallacy of *petitio principii.*   It begs the question by assuming what is to be proved.   But the notion of fallacy involved here requires some qualification.   Consider the following argument:

(13) $2 + 2 = 4$
         Therefore $2 + 2 = 4$.

The argument is valid (if the premiss is true, then obviously the conclusion cannot be false); moreover, it is sound (since the lone premiss is true). Yet by our definition of *petitio principii*, (13) commits that fallacy.   How can a sound argument, however trivial, be fallacious?

The apparent contradiction is resolved if we recall the purposes of argument.   One of these is to provide support or defense for particular conclusions.   But an argument in which the conclusion appears as a premiss brings the conclusion no *new* support and in that respect is pointless.   It is in this extended sense that (13) is "fallacious."

The interesting forms of *petitio* are of course those in which it is not so easy to recognize that the question has been begged.   One is the so-called *circular argument*.   This is a chain argument in which a conclusion turns out to be a premiss from which a premiss was inferred, from which another premiss was inferred, from which the conclusion itself was inferred.   Where the chain has many links, "arguing in a circle" can often go undetected.   A simple example of a circular argument is found in the following:

> Philosophers love learning because they are scholars; intellectuals because they are philosophers; and scholars because they are intellectuals.

When all premisses and conclusions in the chain are made explicit, we have

(14)   *All scholars love learning.
        All philosophers are scholars.
        Therefore all philosophers love learning.

        All philosophers love learning.
        All intellectuals are philosophers.
        Therefore all intellectuals love learning.

        All intellectuals love learning.
        All scholars are intellectuals.
        *Therefore all scholars love learning.

(where the asterisks point out the closing of the circle).

A *petitio* may also occur in connection with the fallacy of many questions.   For instance, an inquiry to determine a person's past or present membership in some organization begs the question if the inquisitor begins by asking, "When did you leave the *X* organization?"

Finally, some of the most subtle instances of *petitio* are found where unclear and ambiguous language conceals the fact that a particular conclusion has been "built into" the premisses.   Take, for example, certain "intelligence test" results that purport to show regional or racial inferiority with respect to a "capacity to learn." If the tests have been so constructed as to put at a disadvantage those who come from certain environments, then at most what has been demonstrated is an "inferior" *performance* in certain areas. And this finding itself has been predetermined by the choice of test material. Much of the talk about differences in "intelligence" and "capacity to learn" suffers from just such a *petitio.*

Ignoratio elenchi ("*arguing beside the point*"). In the most general sense, any argument that commits a fallacy of irrelevance is guilty of arguing beside the point, and thus all fallacies of irrelevance are cases of *ignoratio.* In a more specific sense, the fallacy is committed when premisses are addressed to the *wrong conclusion.* This is the supreme fallacy of irrelevance, and it occurs continually. How often do we find ourselves saying, "But that's not the point," or, "Let's get back to the point," or, "What you are saying is beside the point."

An illustration of *ignoratio* may be cited in the deliberations of a jury in a recent criminal case. A preliminary vote had shown seven to five for acquittal. One of the five then said, "I wish I could be sure that the defendant is innocent." Now this remark revealed a line of reasoning that was "beside the point." For the jury had been asked to determine whether it had been given premisses (testimony, judge's instructions, and so forth) sufficient to sustain the conclusion: the defendant is guilty beyond a reasonable doubt. But this juror was evidently weighing the premisses in relation to a different conclusion: the defendant is innocent beyond a reasonable doubt.

Of course, the definition of *ignoratio* presupposes that the context will allow us to determine what the point really is, or to what conclusion the premisses should rightfully be addressed. And while this is sometimes difficult to do, it is almost always possible.

Fallacies of Ambiguity

The family of fallacies known as fallacies of ambiguity are most directly connected to the misuses of ordinary language. An argument is an instance of a fallacy of ambiguity if, though unsound, it is made to appear sound as a result of the multiple and shifting uses of some of its terms, phrases, or sentences. Such fallacies are customarily arranged under three or four headings, depending on the source and nature of the ambiguity.

In discussing fallacies of ambiguity, we need first to differentiate vagueness from ambiguity. A word is *vague* if its use is imprecise. In ordinary language, all words are more or less vague; and generally, this does not create a problem. One soon learns to apply the appropriate degree of precision to the given occasion. We might say of a neighbor's child, "My, how big you've grown!" In this situation, we would feel no need to express the increase in centimeters or millimeters. On the other hand, one would not report a laboratory experiment by stating: "I applied some heat to a piece of metal and it got bigger."

Ambiguity is a different matter.   A word or expression is ambiguous in a particular context if 1) it has more than one meaning, 2) the meanings are easily confused, and 3) it is not clear in that context which of the meanings is intended.   Notice that words are not ambiguous in themselves, but only relative to a particular context.   Words encountered in this book that are ambiguous in this technical sense include 'logic ', 'argument ', ' inference ', 'valid ', 'meaning', and 'ambiguous '.   An example of an ambiguous sentence is "You can fool all of the people some of the time."

Although ambiguous expressions can be harmless (when they are meant as puns, for example), they generate all kinds of trouble when they appear in arguments.

Equivocation.   A fallacy of equivocation is committed when an ambiguous term is used to shift senses in the same argument.   What has been established with respect to one sense of the term is then wrongly regarded as having been proved with respect to another.   We say that such an argument commits an equivocation *on* that term.

The offending term may occur in two different senses in the premisses. One example is

(15)   Happiness is the end (= goal) of life.

The end (= termination) of life is death.

Therefore happiness is death.

Another is this favorite of freshman logic classes:

(16)   Salt dissolves in water.

Joe is an old salt.

Therefore Joe dissolves in water.

Again, a term may be used in one sense in the premisses and in a different sense in the conclusion.   Thus in the specific "intelligence test" situation mentioned above, the premisses report findings with respect to intelligence = "ability to perform certain tasks," but the conclusions are drawn with respect to intelligence = "capacity to learn."

Composition and division.   Composition and division are paired fallacies and represent special cases of equivocation.   Here the equivocation is on general terms, expressions that denote wholes or classes.   Some of these expressions are used only *collectively*: they are properly applied only to wholes or classes and not to each part or member individually. An example is the expression 'the average American family' in the sentence 'The average American family has two and a half children'. But others have a *distributive* use as well: they may be applied either to each part or member or to the whole or class, depending on the context. An example is the expression 'class', as in

(17)   The class met irregularly.   (collective use)

(18)   The class passed the course.   (distributive use)

Here is a fertile source of ambiguity.

The fallacy of *division* is committed when a person argues that what is true collectively of a whole or a class *must* be true of each part or member. The fallacy of *composition* is the same kind of error in reverse.   Often these fallacies occur because we unwittingly slip from a collective use of a term into a distributive use, or vice versa.

Two arguments that are instances of the fallacy of division are

(19)   The faculty at State is brilliant.

The Philosophy Department is part of the faculty at State.

Therefore the Philosophy Department at State is brilliant.

(20)   The signs of the Zodiac are twelve in number.

Aquarius is a sign of the Zodiac.

Therefore Aquarius is twelve in number.

An example of the fallacy of composition would be to argue that since an orchestra (distributively) consists of first-rate musicians, the orchestra (collectively) is therefore first-rate.

Amphiboly.   This is a fallacy in which the ambiguity attaches not to a word but to an entire sentence.   Such a sentence is said to be amphibolous; amphiboly, like ambiguity, is relative to context.   Some examples of amphibolous sentences are:

(21)   PAINT MARS ENVOY'S HOME.   [from a newspaper headline]

(22)   Can you spell backwards?

These, of course, can easily be disambiguated.   If (21) is taken out of capitals (of course, Mars is not yet represented in Washington) and single quotation marks are used in (22) to indicate that a word is being referred to rather than being used, the sentences then read:

Paint mars envoy's home.

Can you spell 'backwards'?

A well-used example of an amphibolous conclusion is taken from the story in Herodotus (*Histories*, Book I) about Croesus and the Oracle at

Delphi.   The wealthy ruler wished to know what would happen if he made war against Cyrus the Great of Persia, and he accompanied his query with a large gift of not very pure gold.   The Oracle sent back word that if Croesus went to war, "he would destroy a great empire."   Thus encouraged, Croesus did go to war; but the empire he destroyed was his own.

Accent.   Some sentences vary in meaning depending on which of their words are stressed.   Compare Leibniz's "This is the best of all *possible* worlds" with Dr. Pangloss's "This is the *best* of all possible worlds." If the source of the ambiguity lies in stress, then the fallacy of amphiboly is sometimes called a fallacy of accent.

THE FALLACY OF INCONSISTENT PREMISSES

A typical error that is not considered either a formal or an informal fallacy is the fallacy of inconsistent premisses.   Condition 2 for a sound argument requires that all the premisses be true.   In general, the truth of premisses is not for logic to determine, but for the sciences and common sense.   There is one exception, however.   This is the case when not only are the premisses not all true, but when in addition they *cannot possibly* all be true—in short, when the premisses are inconsistent or mutually contradictory.   Obviously, it is impossible for such a set of premisses to meet condition 2.   Yet sets of inconsistent premisses are offered in argument frequently enough for the error to count as a fallacy.

An instance of the fallacy of inconsistent premisses is the following argument:

(23)   If Perkins is admitted to Princeton, he will go to summer school.

If he goes to summer school, he cannot take a job this summer.

Perkins will take a job this summer.

Perkins has been admitted to Princeton.

Therefore?

There are no possible circumstances under which *all* of these premisses would be true; hence the set is inconsistent.

Another instance is the "proof" that $2 = 1$, here in a form used for illustrative purposes by the English logician Augustus De Morgan (1806–1871):[16]

---

[16]   W. V. Quine (*The Ways of Paradox*, New York: Random House, 1966, p. 5) cites this as an example of what he calls a "falsidical paradox."

(24) 1. $x = 1$ By hypothesis
     2. $x^2 = x$ From step 1 by multiplying both sides by x
     3. $x^2 - 1 = x - 1$ From step 2 by subtracting 1 from both sides
     4. $x + 1 = 1$ From step 3 by dividing both sides by $x - 1$
     5. $1 + 1 = 1$ From step 4 by substituting 1 for x, since $x = 1$
                                              by hypothesis

     6. $2 = 1$

The error is that since $x = 1$, to divide by $x - 1$ is to divide by zero. This of course is not permitted by the laws of arithmetic, which here are assumed as part of the premisses of the argument. Hence step 4 of the "proof" rests on contradictory premisses: the justification given for step 4 assumes that division is defined for zero as a divisor, whereas the laws of arithmetic state that division is *not* defined for division by zero. And this is the fallacy.

TACIT USE OF AN UNSTATED PREMISS

Often an argument or a proof uses as a premiss a statement not specifically listed in the set of its premisses. The premiss may go unlisted simply because it is "obvious from the context." But at times premisses are omitted because of a failure to recognize that they are required in order to obtain the desired conclusion. The result is a gap in the proof, a defective argument.

Errors of this sort may go unnoticed for a very long time. A classic illustration concerns the proof that $2 + 2 = 4$, offered by the German philosopher, mathematician, statesman, and historian Gottfried Wilhelm Leibniz (1646–1716). The flaw in his proof was pointed out in 1884 by the German logician and mathematician Gottlob Frege (1848–1925).[17]

The stated premisses (offered as complete) are three definitions and one axiom:

DEFINITIONS

      1.   2 is $1 + 1$
      2.   3 is $2 + 1$
      3.   4 is $3 + 1$

AXIOM   When equals are substituted for equals the results are equal.

The proof then proceeds as follows:

      1. $2 + 2 = 2 + 1 + 1$ By definition 1
      2. $= 3 + 1$ By definition 2
      3. $= 4$ By definition 3

---

[17]   See G. Frege, *The Foundations of Arithmetic* (German original, 1884; English trans. J. L. Austin, New York: Philosophical Library, 1953), p. 7.

Frege observed that although the proof seemed free of errors, there was actually a gap in it. The gap had gone unnoticed because parentheses had been omitted. Strictly, the steps in the proof should be written:

$$
\begin{array}{lll}
1. & 2+2 = 2+(1+1) & \text{By definition 1} \\
1'. & \quad\ = (2+1)+1 & \\
2. & \quad\ = 3+1 & \text{By definition 2} \\
3. & \quad\ = 4 & \text{By definition 3}
\end{array}
$$

When this is done, we see that the proof can proceed from step 1 to step 1' only if

$$2 + (1 + 1) = (2 + 1) + 1.$$

But this equality can be asserted only if we have as one of our premisses the axiom of which it is a special case—namely, the Law of Association for Addition:

$$a + (b + c) = (a + b) + c$$

It is this law that is the tacitly used, unstated premiss in Leibniz's proof, and therein lies the error in the argument. The defect is cured when the law is listed as a premiss.

EXERCISES

11.1. Which of the following illustrate fallacies in argument? For those that do, indicate what fallacies are committed.

  a. If the mayor is reelected, this town will be in trouble. He will be reelected if we do not work for our candidate. So we must work for our candidate if we are to prevent trouble.

  b. Perkins's dog Fido is very friendly. To be friendly is to be able to carry on a good conversation. Hence Fido must be able to carry on a good conversation.

  c. The members of the class of '76 had higher average SAT scores than the members of the class of '75. Perkins is a member of the class of '76. So Perkins had a higher SAT score than the average member of the class of '75.

  d. Mr. Adams is against capital punishment. He says it is morally wrong to take human life. But since he's a minister, you could hardly expect him to say anything else.

  e. The commission on governmental corruption argued that since the Senator had always done important work for his state and country and since he had sponsored legislation that everyone agreed was in the public interest, he must not be guilty of the bribery charges that have been brought against him.

f.   Logic is an indispensable aid to careful thought.   For anyone who wishes to think carefully must think logically.

g.   Why has the policy of open admissions been a failure?

h.   Three and two are odd and even.   Three and two are five. Hence five is odd and even.

i.   If x is kin to y and y is kin to z, then x is kin to z. x is kin to x.   If x is kin to y, then y is kin to x.   John and Mary are kin to Bill and Bill is kin to Jim and Jane, but John is not kin to Jane. Hence Mary must be kin to Jim.

j.   The Senator has supported the President's view that no nation without a strong military establishment can survive, and no one has demonstrated that a nation without such an institution can survive.   We must conclude that any nation that can survive has a strong military establishment.

k.   Truths are as plentiful as falsehoods, since each falsehood admits of a negation which is true.   [Willard Van Orman Quine, *Methods of Logic* (New York: Henry Holt, 1959), p. xi]

l.   When not enough money circulates, there's a scarcity of money.   When there's a scarcity of money, interest rates rise. Hence when not enough money circulates, interest rates rise. [Adapted from J. S. Mill, *A System of Logic*, 8th ed. (London: Longmans, 1872), p. 531]

m.   Let me get this straight.   In order to be grounded I have to be crazy.   And I must be crazy to keep flying.   But if I ask to be grounded—that means I'm not crazy and I have to keep flying. [Yossarian, in the Joseph Heller book and movie *Catch 22*, quoted from *The New York Times Magazine*, March 16, 1969]

11.2.   More fallacy hunting: The following quotations may each be viewed as containing or reporting one or more fallacies.   Which, in your opinion, are fallacies in belief only?   Which are fallacies in argument? For the latter identify the type(s) of fallacy committed.

a.   You argue that a man cannot inquire either about that which he knows, or about that which he does not know; for if he knows, he has no need to inquire; and if not, he cannot; for he does not know the very subject about which he is to inquire.   [Socrates, in Plato's dialogue *Meno* (New York: Random House, 1937), 80*d*]

b. *Mihi à docto doctore* I, a learned scholar,
    Domandatur causam et Am asked the cause and
    rationem quare reason why
    Opium facit dormire Opium puts one to sleep.
    A quoi respondeo To which I reply:
    Quia est in eo Because it possesses
    Virtus dormitiva A dormitive power
    Cuius est natura Whose nature it is
    Sensus assoupire To make the senses drowsy.
    [Molière, *Le Malade imaginaire*, cited in J. S. Mill, *A System of Logic*, 8th ed., p. 539]

c. The King to Oxford sent a troop of horse,
    For Tories own no argument but force:
    With equal skill to Cambridge books he sent,
    For Whigs admit no force but argument.
    [Sir William Browne (1692–1774), in *The Oxford Dictionary of Quotations*]

d. All criminal actions ought to be punishable by law. Prosecutions for theft are criminal actions. Therefore prosecutions for theft ought to be punishable by law. [Example cited by A. De Morgan, *Formal Logic* (London: Open Court, 1847, 1926), p. 281]

e. All the angles of a triangle are equal to two right angles. ABC is an angle of a triangle. Therefore ABC is equal to two right angles. [Example cited by Archbishop Richard Whately, *Elements of Logic*, rev. ed. (Boston and Cambridge: James Munroe, 1859), p. 213]

f. [W]e argue from principles that hold good normally, without even settling what conditions constitute the normal, or satisfying ourselves that they are present in the case about which we are arguing. Freedom is good, and therefore it is supposed that every community should have free institutions, though perhaps there are some races only fit for a very moderate degree of "freedom." [Example cited by H. W. B. Joseph, *An Introduction to Logic*, 2d ed. (Oxford: Oxford University Press, 1916), p. 589]

g. [W]e have a tendency to project and to treat as objective, as belonging to some external state of affairs, the feeling that the state of affairs arouses in us (the *pathetic fallacy*) . . . [J. L. Mackie, "Fallacies," *The Encyclopedia of Philosophy*, 1967]

h.   [*N*]*o complete and consistent account has ever been given of the manner in which the Christian Religion, supposing it a human contrivance, could have arisen and prevailed* as it did.   And yet this may obviously be demanded with the utmost of fairness of those who deny its divine origin.   The Religion exists: that is the phenomenon; those who will not allow it to have come from God are bound to solve the phenomenon on some other hypothesis less open to objections. . . . That infidels have never done this, though they have had 1800 years to try, amounts to a confession that no such hypothesis can be devised, which will not be open to greater objections than lie against Christianity. [An *argument used* by Archbishop Richard Whately, *Elements of Logic*, rev. ed., 1859, p. 242]

11.3.   Find or construct examples of fallacies (in argument) of the following types:

a.   Equivocation.

b.   *Petitio principii.*

c.   *Ignoratio elenchi.*

d.   Division.

e.   Accident.

f.   Inconsistent premisses.

3

Meaning and Ordinary Language

Red means danger. Dark clouds mean rain. 'Perspicuous' means the same as 'clear'. '*Il pleut*' means the same in French as 'It is raining' means in English. But what does 'mean' mean?

Meaning is a difficult notion, the most difficult we shall encounter. It is also a very controversial one. Linguists have sometimes sought to work without the notion of meaning, and philosophers have often worked with it; but neither group has as yet achieved results that command universal acceptance.

Our own interest in meaning is linked to our concern for argument and to the demand that terms in an argument be reasonably clear in meaning. Of many possible questions about meaning, two will be considered in this chapter. First, what is meant by 'the meaning of an expression', or more exactly, what is it for a linguistic expression to have a certain meaning? Second, how are the meanings of expressions explained or established?

In the nature of the case, we cannot expect this chapter to provide "definitive" answers to these questions. It will be enough if we are able to clarify the questions and report some of the attempts to answer them.

The first step will be to narrow down the target area by distinguishing and setting aside a number of nonlinguistic uses of 'mean' and 'meaning'. We then ask what a *theory of meaning* is and review some of the past and current efforts to formulate such a theory. Following this, we examine some proposals on how to draw a line between *meaningful* and *meaningless* expressions and we conclude with a discussion of procedures used in *defining,* or explaining the meaning of, terms.

§12   *Meaning: Linguistic and Nonlinguistic*

There are many uses of 'mean' and 'meaning'. The following sentences—and many more could be added—illustrate some of the *nonlinguistic* uses of these terms:[1]

(1)   Perkins is not a mean man.

(2)   Perkins's academic record is no mean achievement.

(3)   Perkins means to succeed.

(4)   Academic success means everything to Perkins.

(5)   Perkins maintains a mean position between liberalism and conservatism.

(6)   Abolition of the draft means that Perkins will go to graduate school.

(7)   Perkins finds Sartre's philosophy full of meaning.

(8)   Perkins wonders what is the meaning of his rejection by Harvard.

Each of these sentences uses 'mean' or 'meaning' in a different way: (1) for 'ungenerous'; (2) for 'insignificant'; (3) for 'intend', (4) for 'all-important'; (5) for 'middling'; (6) for 'will result in'; (7) for 'significance'; (8) for 'explanation'. All of these uses are nonlinguistic in the sense that the sentences (1) through (8) refer not to linguistic expressions but to persons, actions, attitudes, events, and circumstances.

One way to test whether a particular use of 'mean' is linguistic or nonlinguistic is to see whether 'means the same as' can be substituted for 'means' without appreciably altering the sense of the sentence in

---

[1]   This list is freely adapted from Chapter 1 of William P. Alston's *Philosophy of Language* (Englewood Cliffs, N.J.: Prentice-Hall, 1964). His book and his article "Language" in *The Encyclopedia of Philosophy*, ed. Paul Edwards (New York: Macmillan, 1967), have influenced the present chapter at many points.

which that use occurs.   Now in none of the sentences (1) through (8) can this be done.   For example, under this substitution (3) and (4) become

(3′)   Perkins *means the same as* to succeed.

(4′)   Academic success *means the same as* everything to Perkins.

But the substitution goes through without difficulty in the two sentences

(9)   ' Perspicuous' means *clear*

(10)   ' *Il pleut*' means *it is raining* in French,

provided that when the substitution is made, the expressions 'clear' and 'It is raining' are enclosed in single quotation marks (and of course the italics are removed).   Thus (1) through (8) contain nonlinguistic uses, (9) and (10) linguistic ones.

---

§13   *Some Theories of Linguistic Meaning*

There are some questions for which we cannot even try to find answers unless we first determine more clearly what it is we are asking.   One of these is: What is linguistic meaning?   How this question is answered— the theory of meaning arrived at—depends very much on how it is asked.

For instance, if we put the question in the form

(1)   What kind of things are meanings?

we assume in advance that meanings are a kind of *thing*; and this assumption will shape the sort of theory we propose.   If, on the other hand, we construe our question in some such form as

(2)   What are we saying about a linguistic expression when we specify its meaning?   [William P. Alston],

the range of inquiry broadens.

In fact these are two of the main forms in which students of language have asked the question about meaning.   The kinds of answers they have proposed will be dealt with in this section.   First, however, we consider an important but often mishandled distinction between two aspects of linguistic meaning and explain why we limit our further inquiry to just one of them.

LITERAL AND NONLITERAL MEANING

According to the standard account (§10), two of the major uses of language are to convey information and to vent or evoke emotions. In discussing these uses, some writers on language distinguish two corresponding kinds of meaning: *literal*, or cognitive, and *emotive*. The former they associate with the informative use of language, as in scientific discourse; the latter with the expressive use of language, as in poetry and politics. Stock examples of expressions that have the same literal meaning but differ in their emotive meaning are

(3)   government bureaucrat, government official, public servant,

or the adjectives that occur in Russell's famous conjugation of the verb ' to be ':

(4)   I am firm; you are obstinate; he is a pig-headed fool.

The literal-emotive distinction, however, is an oversimplification. Expressions that have the same literal meaning may exhibit differences in many aspects of meaning that cannot properly be classified as emotive. Such aspects include political implications, social and ethnic overtones, aesthetic values, and so on. This observation the reader may easily test for herself or himself. One need only reflect on the role played in recent American diplomatic and social history by the following pairs of words that have the same literal meaning, at least in some uses, but that differ in other respects:

(5)   incursion   invasion
         disadvantaged   poor
         respond   retaliate

Thus the basic distinction with regard to the meaning of an expression is not between its literal meaning and its emotive meaning, but between its literal meaning and a whole complex of factors (including emotive) associated with the use of the expression. The German logician and mathematician Gottlob Frege (1848–1925) had a name for the nonliteral aspect of meaning. He called it the "coloring" of an expression, as distinguished from its "sense."[2]

---

[2] The emotive-literal distinction is scrutinized by M. Black in *The Labyrinth of Language* (New York: New American Library, 1969), pp. 129–138. For a summary of Frege's views on language, see "Frege" by M. F. Dummett in *The Encyclopedia of Philosophy*.

For expressions that occur in statement-making sentences, the literal-nonliteral distinction can be made fairly precise.   Consider the sentences

(6)   Some man is looking for Perkins.

Some guy is looking for Perkins.

Some chap is looking for Perkins.

Clearly all three make the same statement.   They are all true or false under exactly the same circumstances.   And this is a consequence of the fact that the words 'man', 'guy', and 'chap' have the same *literal* meaning and differ only in matters of idiom, style, and the like.   It therefore seems plausible to define the literal meaning of an expression (Frege's "sense") as *the part of its meaning that helps to determine the truth conditions* of the statement made by the sentence in which the expression occurs.   (By 'the truth conditions of a statement' we mean simply the conditions under which the sentence would be true and those under which it would be false.)

Now elementary logic, as noted in §10, is confined to sentences used to make statements, to say something true or false about how things are. Since only literal meaning, not "coloring," contributes directly to determining the circumstances under which statements are true or false, we may in general set nonliteral meaning aside.

The reader should be warned, however, that some of the theories of meaning we are about to review do not accept the literal-nonliteral distinction as we have drawn it.   But, then, some of them do not even accept the way of separating linguistic from nonlinguistic uses of 'mean' illustrated in §12.   Indeed, theories of meaning vary so widely that any brief and schematic review such as this one is bound to omit a great deal and oversimplify what is left.   At best it serves as a plea for further study.

MEANINGS AS THINGS, OR ENTITIES

Of the theories that assume meanings to be *things*, or entities, there are two main varieties.   The distinction between the two varieties depends on what kinds of entities meanings are taken to be.

Meanings as Ideas

One variety of entity theory of meaning—sometimes called the "ideational" or "image" theory—identifies the meaning of a word or phrase with the *ideas* or images associated with it.   Often cited as an example is the view of the British philosopher John Locke (1632–1704) that "words signify ideas." Thus in his *An Essay Concerning Human Understanding* (Book III, Chapter 2, §§1, 2), he writes:

> The comfort and advantage of society not being to be had without communication of thoughts, it was necessary that man should find some external sensible signs, whereof those invisible ideas, which his thoughts are made up of, might be made known to others. . . . Thus we may conceive how *words*, which were by nature so well adapted to that purpose, came to be made use of by men as the signs of their ideas; . . . The use, then, of words, is to be sensible marks of ideas; and the ideas they stand for are their proper and immediate signification.
>
> The use men have of these marks being either to record their own thoughts, for the assistance of their own memory; or, as it were, to bring out their ideas, and lay them before the view of others: words, in their primary or immediate signification, stand for nothing but *the ideas in the mind of him that uses them*, how imperfectly soever or carelessly those ideas are collected from the things they are supposed to represent.

Here Locke seems to be endorsing the ideational theory of meaning: the meanings of words ("their proper and immediate signification") are ideas; they are "in" the mind. Stripped to essentials, the reasoning appears to be that meanings are what human beings communicate when they use language; to communicate is to give verbal expression to thoughts or ideas; hence meanings are ideas.

This interpretation of Locke's position, however, has recently been placed in doubt, at least in part.[3] Accordingly, the usual objections, which are summarized below, are to be thought of as addressed not so much to Locke but to anyone who might still accept the ideational theory in its full-blown form.

The objections are abundant. If the ideational theory is taken literally so that meanings are identified with ideas in the sense of somebody's *mental events*, then those who support it must cope with unhappy consequences such as these: 1) No word can have the same meaning for two persons, since presumably no two persons can have the very same experience. 2) No words can mean (refer to, denote, stand for) nonmental objects, such as sticks and stones. 3) Words like 'or', 'and', 'not', and so on, with which we associate no particular ideas, must be declared meaningless.

If the theory is construed more liberally so that meanings are ideas in

---

[3] See Norman Kretzmann, "The Main Thesis of Locke's Semantic Theory," *The Philosophical Review* 77 (1968), pp. 175–196.

the sense of notions or concepts, then we begin to move in a circle.   For what are concepts or notions if not the "meanings" of terms?

It would seem that it is precisely this cluster of ambiguities surrounding the word 'idea' that long shielded the ideational theory from effective criticism.   Frege gave a new turn to the discussion of meaning when he warned against confusing purely psychological matters with concepts and meanings.

Meanings as Entities Referred To

The second variety of entity theory of meaning—known as the "referential" theory—identifies the meaning of an expression with the entity or entities to which it refers.

The error in this theory is its assumption that all meaning is referring. In its simplest form, the theory takes as the model or paradigm for meaning situations the relation between a name and what it names, between the *word* 'Fido', say, and the *dog* Fido.   This assimilation of meaning to naming—or the 'Fido'-Fido principle, as he called it—has been challenged in particular by the English philosopher Gilbert Ryle.

It is not difficult to find fatal objections to the referential theory. Here are two:

1. Not all meaningful expressions *refer*.   Such words as 'or', 'and', 'not', and the like cannot be said to refer to any object, yet they are meaningful; it is thus clear that referring is only one of the functions performed by words.

2. Of the expressions that do refer, some have the same reference yet differ in meaning; others have the same meaning yet differ in reference.

Frege supplied the classic example for the first part of objection 2. The expressions 'the Morning Star' and 'the Evening Star' both refer to the same object, the planet Venus.   Hence by the referential theory they must have the same meaning.   We should then expect to be able to put one for the other in any sentence in which either occurs without altering the meaning of that sentence.   Consider now the sentences

(7)   The Morning Star is the Morning Star.

(8)   The Morning Star is the Evening Star.

Since (8) is obtained from (7) by putting 'the Evening Star' in place of the second occurrence of 'the Morning Star' in (7), then (8) should have the same meaning as (7).   But this is not so: (7) is a simple statement of identity, whose truth is evident on the face of it, whereas (8) makes a statement whose truth can be asserted only if certain astronomical facts are known.   It follows that (7) and (8) do not have the same meaning, since in Frege's terminology, the statements they make do not have the same truth conditions.   Thus two expressions with the same reference need not have the same meaning, and meaning therefore cannot be identified with reference. (Of course, Frege's argument holds for any two proper names or definite descriptions that name or describe the same object; for example, we could just as well have used 'the Democratic Presidential nominee of 1964' and 'the husband of Lady Bird Johnson'.)

As for the second part of objection 2, a favorite example used by critics to counter the referential theory is the word 'I'. Clearly, its reference varies with the person speaking, but not so its meaning.

We conclude that the entity theories of meaning are unsatisfactory. Among other weaknesses, they tend to look at the meanings of words standing alone. Frege counseled that we should never ask for the meaning of a word in isolation but always in the context of a sentence. We shall see that his advice is followed in some of the theories to be discussed in the remainder of this section.

This rather summary rejection of entity theories should not, however, be taken to mean that they display no positive features. Ideational theories emphasize, if one-sidedly, the psychological element in meaning situations; referential theories stress, although exaggeratedly, the importance of the referring function. Both bring to the fore aspects of linguistic communication for which any adequate theory of meaning must make suitable provision.

MEANING AS BEHAVIOR

The term 'behavioral' (sometimes 'causal') is used for theories that identify the meaning of an expression with the stimuli that prompt its utterance and the response or range of responses that the utterance produces.

As a brief and schematic example, take this "behavioral" version of the meaning of 'It is raining'. The *stimulus* for the utterance would include such events as the speaker's looking out the window and noticing precipitation; the *response* to the utterance would include such actions on the part of the hearer as also looking out the window and putting on a raincoat. The regular association of stimuli and responses such as these in this sort of situation is said to constitute the meaning of 'It is raining'.

(Notice the analogy between the behavioral approach to linguistic meaning and the sense we attribute to 'Dark clouds mean rain'. In both cases, meaning is thought of as a regular association, in a certain kind of situation, between utterances or signs, and responses or consequences.)

Those who favor behavioral theories are moved in part by their view of science. In their opinion, sound scientific practice demands that we reject the ideational theory of meanings as *private mental entities* and attempt to account for meaning solely in terms of *publicly observable aspects* of our communication by language. They believe that a proper stimulus-response theory of meaning will be flexible enough to avoid the kinds of errors that reduce meaning to naming and make meanings into things.

Behavioral theories vary with the particular notion of "behavior" on which they are founded. There are said to be two main varieties: the "crude" and the "refined."

"Crude" Behavioral Theories

The crude variety of behavioral theory bases the meaning of an expression on behavior in the sense of actual *overt responses*—that is, on what speakers and especially hearers actually *do*.

But there are innumerable kinds of things that hearers may do on the varied occasions when such a sentence as 'It is raining' is uttered. Which of them are to enter into its meaning? Obviously, not all of the things will be done on each such occasion, nor is it at all likely that any one thing will be done on every such occasion. Hence if meaning is identified with overt responses, the meaning of 'It is raining' will vary widely from occasion to occasion; yet in ordinary life its meaning is relatively constant. And what of the meaning of sentences to which there may be no overt responses at all?

"Refined" Behavioral Theories

The second variety identifies the meaning of an expression with the situation of its utterance and with certain *dispositions* on the part of the hearers to respond in certain ways. The refinement thus lies in replacing *overt response* with *disposition to respond*.

What is to be understood by the phrase 'a disposition to respond'? The notion is not an easy one to pin down, but it can be explained roughly as follows. When we describe people and how they behave, we do so in either or both of two ways. Sometimes we simply report what they *do*. More often, though, we talk of their likes and dislikes, sentiments and attitudes, qualities of character and intellect, fears and hopes, competences and failings. Now none of these can be specified merely by listing a person's overt acts. We can describe them adequately only by stating something to the effect that under such and such conditions this person is disposed to do such and such things, and under such and such other conditions he or she is disposed to do such and such other things. Consider, for example, these two sentences:

(9)   Perkins bought a copy of Frege's *Foundations of Arithmetic*.

(10)   Perkins likes the philosophy of mathematics.

The first sentence describes a particular act performed by Perkins. But what does (10) describe? Not one or more acts, but rather a disposition, under certain conditions, to perform certain acts—to obtain and read a book if it is about the foundations of mathematics, to discuss with anyone who has a similar interest such topics as the nature of mathematical proof and truth, to do research on the relationship between mathematics and the empirical sciences.

To construe meaning as disposition to respond rather than as overt response does bring some advantage. It is no longer necessary to seek the meaning of 'It is raining' in the endless, unmanageable range of responses that its utterance may in fact evoke (the hearer frowns, turns over, and goes back to sleep; looks at the clock, says "Thank God"; and so forth). Instead, it may be sought in the much more limited repertoire made up of such of the hearer's dispositions to respond as are regularly associated with the utterance of the sentence (to put on a raincoat if about to go out, to close the windows if they are open, to seek shelter if outside, and so on).

This shift, however, does not really solve the problem. For when the behavioral theorists are required to specify exactly which dispositions enter into the determination of the meaning of a particular expression, they are apt to do what we have just done with the dispositions associated with 'It is raining': list two or three as illustrations, and then wave off the others with an "and so on." And what is true of a sentence about something concrete, such as the weather, is surely all the more true when the subject matter is abstract, as in the case of the sentences "Einstein's general theory of relativity is now undergoing reexamination" and "Perkins likes the philosophy of mathematics." Thus the defect noted in the crude behavioral theory seems to persist, if on a lesser scale, in the more refined theory.

There is another difficulty. Even sophisticated stimulus-response theories tend to focus their attention on response and to reduce stimulus to mere utterance of sounds. But this leaves aside the crucial element of meaning that is generally called the *intention* of the speaker—what the speaker aims to accomplish with the utterance, or the *point* of uttering it. The question is still open as to whether *any* behavioral theory of meaning can deal in a satisfactory manner with this element, short of substantially enlarging and altering the usual notion of *behavior*. In any event the basic behavioral insight—that linguistic expressions have meaning only by reason of the roles they play in human activity—is almost certain to be regarded as an essential component in any adequate theory of meaning.

MEANING AS USE

This survey concludes with a comment on an approach to meaning associated primarily with the name of Ludwig Wittgenstein. It is an approach that is easily sloganized—"Don't look for the meaning, look for the use"—and hence easily distorted. Properly understood, however, it may indeed, as William P. Alston has suggested, lead to an analysis of meaning that avoids the defects of all the other theories.

Wittgenstein's ideas on language and meaning are set forth in a kind of running attack on the naming theory of meaning and, more generally, on the tendency to view all uses of language in the light of its use to convey information. The following passages from his *Philosophical Investigations* give some indication of what he is getting at:

> §40. . . . It is important to note that the word "meaning" is being used illicitly if it is used to signify the thing that 'corresponds' to the word. That is to confound the meaning of a name with the *bearer* of the name. When Mr. N. N. dies one says that the bearer of the name dies, not that the meaning dies. . . .

> §43. For a *large* class of cases—though not for all—in which we employ the word "meaning" it can be defined thus: the meaning of a word is its use in the language.

> And the *meaning* of a name is sometimes explained by pointing to its *bearer*.

> §421. . . . Look at the sentence as an instrument, and its sense as its employment.[4]

Here and elsewhere in his writings the principal features that characterize Wittgenstein's approach to meaning are:

1. Meaning is sought neither in the mind nor in some world of abstract entities, but in the role language plays in human behavior.

2. The meaning of an expression is identified not with an *entity* or thing, but with the *use* of that expression in the language.

3. The uses of language are not simply to inform and to refer, but are unlimited in their diversity.

4. The focus is not merely on the utterance of an expression and the hearer's responses or dispositions to respond, but is also on the speaker and what he or she is using the expression to accomplish.

Wittgenstein's basic doctrine is often misunderstood. He *is* saying that the meaning of a word is to be explained in terms of its *use* in the language (rather than the other way around). But he is *not* saying that an adequate explanation of the meaning of a word is given merely by describing its *usage*—that is, simply by stating the circumstances in which we make use of the word and those in which we do not. We must still explain the *point* of using the word, what we use it *for*. And if we miss

---

[4] Ludwig Wittgenstein, *Philosophical Investigations*, 3rd ed., trans. G. E. M. Anscombe (New York: Macmillan, 1967), pp. 20–21, 126.

out on this aspect, then, as Michael F. Dummett has observed, we do not understand the "point" of Wittgenstein's doctrine.[5]

AUSTIN'S THEORY OF ILLOCUTIONARY FORCES

The interest in meaning as use, aroused by Wittgenstein's ideas, has been further heightened by the writings of the English philosopher John L. Austin (1911–1960).   The latter's chief concern was the detailed analysis of ordinary language, as a means of solving fundamental problems in philosophy.[6]

Austin was early struck by the fact that many of the declarative sentences we utter do not make statements and hence cannot be characterized as being true or false.   This holds, for instance, in the cases of these utterances:

(11)   I name this ship The Athos.

(12)   I promise to return your copy of *Seize the Time* this evening.

For (11) is not a *report* of the christening of a vessel, but *part* of the christening; and (12) *makes a promise*, it is not a statement about the making of a promise.   Such utterances Austin called "performative," and he distinguished them from "constative" utterances, those we properly call true or false.

In pursuing his studies further, Austin found that the distinction tended to break down, so he replaced it with his theory of *illocutionary forces*. This rests on an elaborate analysis of the various kinds of acts performed when something is said.   There is always a *phonetic* act of uttering certain noises, as well as a *phatic* (saying) act of uttering certain vocables, or words, in conformity with a certain grammar.   But beyond these, Austin distinguished three other kinds of acts, which he called 1) locutionary, 2) illocutionary, and 3) perlocutionary.

To illustrate briefly: A *locutionary* act is what Perkins performs when he uses an utterance with a more or less definite meaning and reference— when in speaking to his roommate, for example, he utters "Your watch is slow" as a sentence in English referring to a particular person and that person's watch.   *In* performing this locutionary act, Perkins may at the same time be performing any of a number of *illocutionary* acts, such as the act of stating something or of hinting (at the danger of coming late to a concert, for instance).   Finally, *by* performing his illocutionary act

---

[5]   M. F. Dummett, "Truth," *Proceedings of the Aristotelian Society* 59 (1958–59), pp. 141–162.   Reprinted in *Philosophical Logic*, ed. P. F. Strawson (London: Oxford University Press, 1967); see especially pp. 51 and 68 in the latter.

[6]   A brief and very clear account of Austin's work is given by J. O. Urmson in his article "Austin" in *The Encyclopedia of Philosophy*.

(of stating or of hinting), he may succeed in performing a *perlocutionary* act, such as the act of getting his roommate to reset his watch or of inducing him to hurry.

This line of inquiry into meaning and use—which Wittgenstein and Austin began independently of each other—was promptly taken up by many students of the philosophy of language and of philosophy generally. The resulting movement soon came to be known as "ordinary language" or "linguistic" philosophy, and as such tended to dominate the Anglo-American philosophical scene during the 1950s and 1960s.

---

§14   *The Meaningful and the Meaningless*

Thus far we have discussed one question about meaning, namely,

(1)   What are we saying about a linguistic expression when we specify its meaning?

But there are actually two questions that philosophers have asked. The second is

(2)   What condition(s) must a linguistic expression satisfy if it is to be called meaningful?

An answer to (1) is a *theory* of meaning, an account of the *nature* of meaning; an answer to (2) is a *criterion* or test of meaningfulness, an account of what is required to indicate the *presence* of meaning.

The motive in seeking a serviceable criterion of meaningfulness is quite clear. If one was available, the *meaningful*—or as they are also called, the *significant*—expressions could be separated from the meaningless ones. The saving in philosophical energy would be considerable.

The distinction between an account of the nature of something and a criterion of its presence has general application. Take, for instance, the notion *good student*. Here the questions would be phrased

(1′)   What are we saying when we say someone is a good student?

(2′)   What condition(s) must someone satisfy to be called a good student?

Now there was a time when it was considered a *criterion* of someone's being a good student that he or she passed all courses with a grade of B or better. But it was never considered—or certainly ought never to have been considered—that this accomplishment made up the *whole nature* of being a good student.

We often find ourselves saying, "But that's no criterion." What is meant is that a condition proposed by someone as a criterion fails of the purpose—as when a person tells us that long hair in the male is an infallible sign of political radicalism or a hard hat an infallible sign of political conservatism. A criterion serves as a sifter. If the meshes are too coarse (as in the case of long hair and hard hats), items are let through that should be excluded; if too fine, items are excluded that should be let through. Formulating an effective criterion can indeed be difficult, especially—and this applies above all to meaning—if there is no general agreement as to the nature of the something the presence of which is to be tested for.

THEORIES OF MEANING AND CRITERIA OF SIGNIFICANCE

Preoccupation with the two questions about meaning was a distinctive feature of a new movement in philosophy that came into being in Vienna during the twenties and early thirties of this century. This movement— led by two German philosophers, Moritz Schlick (1882–1936) and Rudolf Carnap (1891–1970)—was first given the name "logical positivism" and later became known as "logical empiricism." Its aim was reform in philosophy. Its members had observed that whereas scientists were making brilliant progress in solving their problems, philosophers— and particularly metaphysicians—seemed forever bogged down in questions that defied solution. Perhaps the reason was that many of these questions, although undoubtedly possessed of great *emotive* import, lacked cognitive, or literal meaning. This was the context in which a search was mounted for the sort of criterion of (cognitive) *meaningfulness*, or *significance*, that would enable philosophers to identify and eliminate meaningless questions.

The Vienna School was thus primarily concerned with a criterion of significance rather than a theory of meaning. There is, of course, a relationship between the two. A theory of meaning may determine a corresponding criterion of significance. For instance, some logical positivists at one time held a theory of meaning according to which the meaning of a statement-making sentence is identified with the "method of its verification." If this account of meaning is accepted, then a particular criterion of significance is also established: a sentence is (cognitively) meaningful only if it is in some sense *verifiable*. For if meaning lies in the method of verification, then a sentence that lacks any method of verification must also lack any meaning.

A criterion of significance, however, does not necessarily determine a particular theory of meaning. We may accept a verifiability criterion of significance without thereby committing ourselves to the theory that the method of verification *is* the meaning of the sentence. Thus we may want to say that a sentence is significant only if there is some possible empirical evidence somewhere that somehow counts for or against it.

But this is not to say that the meaning of the sentence is merely that piece of evidence.

THE PROBLEM OF AN EMPIRICIST CRITERION OF SIGNIFICANCE

The logical positivists' search for a viable criterion of significance was in a sense a failure. It did not produce a criterion that philosophers in general might accept. Yet both friends and critics of the Vienna School agree that the effort sensitized a whole generation of philosophers to the question of the meaningful and the meaningless.

Only a few of the problems the logical positivists encountered along the way will be mentioned here. And to simplify matters, our discussion of successive versions of the empiricist criterion will omit the part that covers the sentences of logic and mathematics and sentences expressing contradictions. A full analytical account will be found in the works of a leading member of the search party, the Berlin-born logical empiricist Carl Hempel, for many years a professor of philosophy at Princeton.[7]

The desired criterion of significance was first advanced in the form of the *verifiability requirement*. According to it,

> A sentence is significant if and only if it is capable, at least in principle, of being completely verified (or falsified) by the evidence of observation.

Notice that the criterion was expressed in terms of verif*ability*, not of verif*ication*; it was never contemplated that a sentence would be significant if and only if its truth or falsity had already been established.

Under the pressure of criticism, the range of admissible observational evidence was broadened, and the verifiability criterion underwent several changes. But it remained subject to the fatal defect of being overly restrictive: it excluded as meaningless certain sentences that obviously are meaningful. In particular, the criterion ruled out as meaningless all sentences that state scientific laws. Since such laws are open-ended generalizations—they are asserted to hold for *all* instances, future as well as past, of the phenomena in question—they are not *conclusively* verifiable.

Once it had been shown to be too strong a requirement, verifiability was replaced by *confirmability*. The criterion then read:

> A sentence is significant if and only if it is possible, at least in principle, to specify observations that, if carried out, would in some degree serve to confirm or disconfirm it.

---

[7]   See Carl Hempel, "Empirical Criteria of Cognitive Significance," in his *Aspects of Scientific Explanation and Other Essays in the Philosophy of Science* (New York: Free Press, 1965), pp. 101–122; also see William P. Alston, op. cit., Chapter 4.

But this more liberal criterion also ran into difficulties—difficulties centering around the notion of confirmation, with which we shall be concerned in Part III.

The development today continues in the direction of declining expectations, of more limited goals.   In Hempel's recent writings, it is no longer assumed that a hard and fast line can be drawn between the meaningful and the meaningless.   And even a rough criterion is applicable at best only to sentences in the context of theories and systems, and not to sentences in isolation.   *Testability in principle* survives as a sort of rule of thumb to help us separate the theories and systems that seem worth bothering about from all the rest.

TYPES OF MEANINGLESSNESS OR NONSENSE

Lacking a firm criterion to mark off the meaningful from the meaningless, we must fall back on a rule of thumb aided by our intuitions.   The task is lightened, however, if we first differentiate among the various kinds of expressions usually lumped together under the catch-all heading of "nonsense."   We shall touch briefly on seven types, some trivial, some important.   The first two are obvious forms of intentional nonsense; the last two are a bit odd but not really nonsense at all.

Double-Talk

Webster's Eighth New Collegiate Dictionary defines 'double-talk' in part to mean the same as 'language that appears to be earnest and meaningful but in fact is a mixture of sense and nonsense'.   Although Lewis Carroll had already dabbled in double-talk,[8] it was Al Kelly (Abraham Kalish, 1896–1966) who made a profession of it.   As perfected by him, double-talk is discourse equipped with all the gestures and intonation of ordinary speech, but with meaningless wordlike sounds—especially in noun, verb, and adjective positions—strategically interspersed among real words. For instance, Kelly claimed he once attended a medical meeting where, posing as a doctor, he reported that he had been able to

> rehabilitate patients by daily injections of triprobe into the right differnarium which translucentizes the stoline producing a black greel which enables you to stame the klob.   [*The New York Times*, September 7, 1966]

Thus double-talk is meant to be nonsense; its point is to amuse.

---

[8]   "'Twas brillig, and the slithy toves / Did gyre and gimble in the wabe; / All mimsy were the borogoves, / And the mome raths outgrabe."   From the poem "Jabberwocky," in *Through the Looking Glass*, by Lewis Carroll (Charles Lutwidge Dodgson, 1832–1898).

Nonsense Syllables

The inventor of nonsense syllables was the German psychologist Hermann Ebbinghaus (1850–1909).   An early student of memory, he found that he needed uniformly *un*associated material for his research.   Since words would not do (associations among them would already have been built up), Ebbinghaus hit upon the idea of assembling random pairs of consonants separated by a vowel.   He thus obtained a pool of some 2,300 "nonsense" syllables, such as *zat, bok*, and *sid*, to use in his experiments in memorizing.   Although these syllables, like double-talk, are deliberate nonsense, their purpose is to provide material for scientific studies.

Various kinds of nonintentional nonsense result when a string, or sequence, of words, or of what purport to be words, *seems* to be a sentence, but fails to be a "good" sentence.   The string may fail for any of several reasons.

Bad Grammar

One type of nonsense occurs when the language's rules of grammar are violated, as in

(3)   Perkins is between the devil and.

(4) $5 > 4 = 7$.

The string (3) violates the grammar of 'is between '; for 'is between ' is a three-place predicate, yet here only two places are filled, by 'Perkins ' and 'the devil '.   As to (4), the grammar of a constructed language suitable for algebra would require that ' $=$ ', the sign for equality, be flanked on both sides by *terms*; but in (4), ' $=$ ' stands between a *sentence* of arithmetic ('$5 > 4$') and a *term* (the numeral '7').   The grammars of the respective languages rule out (3) and (4) as nonsense.

Pseudo-Words

A string may also fail to be a "good" sentence if it contains something that purports to be a word but is not in the vocabulary of our particular language, and so may be called a "pseudo-word."   An example is the string

(5)   Bekos is the staff of life.

Here the trouble is not with the rules of grammar, but with the vocabulary: 'bekos' is not in our dictionary (that is, in any dictionary that correctly reports what the vocabulary of English is).

Grammatical but Nonsensical " Sentences"

Consider now the string

(6)   Colorless green ideas sleep furiously.

In this case there is no problem with either the grammar or the vocabulary. Yet (6) is nonsensical. It was in fact devised some years ago by the distinguished American linguist Noam Chomsky precisely in order to show that not every grammatically well-formed sentence is (intuitively) significant or meaningful.[9]   Here, then, is another kind of nonsense.

There is a species of nonsensical "sentence" that is often regarded as coming under this category but that has attracted considerable interest in its own right.   For example, take the two sentences

(7)   Harold Wilson is a prime minister.

(8)   Harold Wilson is a prime number.

Both are grammatically correct.   Moreover, (7) is certainly meaningful and, as of July 1975, true.   But what of (8)?   Is it nonsense or just false? And how are we to decide?   We might want to say that (8) is meaningless because a person is not the sort of entity of which it can be meaningfully said either that it is or that it is not a prime number.   The problem then would be to build into the structure of our language some appropriate rules about the "sorts" or "categories" of expressions that may be applied significantly to various kinds of objects.   Differences in *category* would be part of the semantic or meaning aspect of our language.   Then (8) could be called nonsensical on the ground that it contains a *category-mistake*.[10]

The two final kinds of "nonsense" are sentences, as was noted above, that may seem to be, and are often called, "nonsensical" but in fact are not.

Self-Contradictions

Is the sentence

(9)   Perkins is six feet tall and Perkins is not six feet tall

nonsensical?   Not really.   It would certainly be *odd* to use it in a piece of everyday discourse.   But it contains no errors of grammar, no pseudo-

---

[9]   Noam Chomsky, *Syntactic Structures* ('s-Gravenhage: Mouton, 1957), p. 15.
[10]   The discussion of *categories* goes back to Aristotle's short treatise of the same name.   In recent times the importance of category-mistakes has been stressed by Gilbert Ryle in *The Concept of Mind* (London: Hutchinson, 1949).

words, no category-mistakes; thus it is not *on those accounts* devoid of sense.   As a matter of fact, we know that in general if we have two sentences each of which makes sense, the result of writing 'and' between them will be a sentence that also makes sense.   And (9) is just such a sentence.   But its oddity can be explained if we note that the sentence that follows 'and' countersays what the sentence preceding the ' and ' says.   Consequently, (9) makes a statement that is always false; it is self-contradictory.   Thus it is better to describe (9) not as an example of nonsense, but rather as an example of "countersense."[11]

In connection with arguments, self-contradictions play the important role of distress signals.   As has been seen, if an argument is valid, it is impossible for its premises all to be true and its conclusion false.   Hence if a self-contradiction can be validly inferred from a set of premises or assumptions, then—since a self-contradiction is always false—it follows that at least one member of the set must be false.

Paradoxes and Antinomies

Willard Van Orman Quine, the Harvard logician and philosopher of language, has defined 'paradox' as 'any conclusion that at first sight seems absurd but that has an argument to sustain it' and ' antinomy ' as a *paradox* that 'produces a self-contradiction by established ways of reasoning '—that is, reasoning free of visible error or fallacy.[12]

An example of a paradox that is *not* an antinomy is found in the story of the village barber who shaves all and only those male villagers who do not shave themselves.   Does the barber shave himself?   The answer is given by the following argument:

> *Premiss:*   There is a village in which the barber shaves any male villager if and only if that villager does not shave himself.
>
> *Conclusion:*   Therefore, the barber shaves himself if and only if he does not shave himself.

The conclusion is self-contradictory.   Hence the premiss from which it is validly inferred—that there is a barber with the indicated property— must be false.   Thus what the paradox shows is simply that there is no such village barber.

An example of a paradox that *is* an antinomy is the one discovered by

---

[11] The distinction between 'nonsense' (German ' *Unsinn* ') and 'countersense' (German ' *Widersinn* ') is due to the German philosopher Edmund Husserl (1859–1938); see "Husserl's Conception of a Purely Logical Grammar," in *Philosophy and Phenomenological Research* 17 (1956–57), pp. 363–369, by Yehoshua Bar-Hillel, the Hebrew University linguist.

[12]   See the illuminating title essay in W. V. Quine, *Ways of Paradox and Other Essays* (New York: Random House, 1966), pp. 3–20.

Kurt Grelling in 1908: Call an adjective autological if it is true of itself (for instance, the adjective 'short' is short) and heterological if it is not true of itself (for instance, the adjective 'monosyllabic' is not monosyllabic). Is the adjective 'heterological' *itself* heterological or autological?

Antinomies are sometimes divided into two groups: those that turn on questions of language (such as Grelling's) and those that turn on questions of logic. The most celebrated "logical" antinomy is the one discovered in 1901 by Bertrand Russell (1872–1970), which he always referred to as "The Contradiction." We give it in detail for purposes of illustration.

At the time of Russell's discovery, the assumption was that for any condition that can be formulated—for instance, the condition of being an object in a classroom—there exists a set or class whose members are the objects satisfying this condition. It was also understood that we can form sets whose members are sets, sets whose members are sets of sets, and so forth.

Consider the condition that a set not be a member of itself. This condition is satisfied by most sets—the set of all books is not a book, a class of students is not another student. Now form the set of objects that meet this condition—that is, the set whose members are all and only the sets that are not members of themselves. Call this set R, the Russell set. Then ask if R is a member of itself, or (using '$\in$' as the symbol for set membership) $R \in R$?

Let us assume that the answer is yes, that $R \in R$. Then R must satisfy the defining condition that it cannot be a member of itself. Thus

(10)   If $R \in R$, then $R \notin R$

(where '$\notin$' stands for 'is not a member of'). Notice that (10) is not an antinomy. It simply proves that $R \in R$ is false—that is, that $R \notin R$. (Any sentence that implies its own negation is false.) Now we have $R \notin R$. But if $R \notin R$, then R meets the condition of not being a member of itself, and so $R \in R$. Hence

(11)   If $R \notin R$, then $R \in R$.

Now (11) proves that $R \notin R$ is false, that is, that $R \in R$ is true. Therefore (10) and (11) taken together prove that

(12) $R \notin R$ and $R \in R$,

which is a self-contradiction. In short, the "established ways of reasoning"—in particular, the assumption that for *any* condition we can state, there exists a corresponding set—have produced a self-contradiction. (No assumption of this sort is present in the case of the village barber.)

The discovery of this antinomy by the young Russell had a profound effect on the development of set theory and on the foundations of mathematics.

---

§15   *Meaning and Definition*

Despite the problems that beset meaning, we usually manage to communicate with one another quite well.   Just as we can operate power tools without knowing exactly what electricity is, so we can use words correctly without knowing what "meaning" is.   In fact, we use them correctly although we may not even be able to *define* them, to express their meaning in words.   In most cases it is enough if we know generally when to apply a particular word and when not.

Yet many times we find it necessary to follow Voltaire's admonition: "Define your terms . . . or we shall never understand one another."   The occasion may be a discussion, a debate, a dispute; it may be a class report, a term paper, a research project.   Or it may happen that events themselves place a strain on certain words, forcing us to reflect more carefully on their meanings.   For example, an economic decline focuses attention more sharply on the meanings of such terms as 'recession' and 'unemployment', while heart transplant experiments cause the reexamination of what is meant by 'death'.   Thus we are constantly involved in a process of definition and redefinition.

The last part of the discussion of meaning will therefore be devoted to some questions about definitions: what they are, how they differ in purpose and status, what the traits of a good definition are, what theoretical problems are raised by definitions, and when a dispute about words is merely a verbal dispute.

WHAT IS A DEFINITION?

In its most general sense, a "definition" is *any* explanation of the meaning or use of a word or phrase.   Thus it is a definition if, when someone asks "What is a hippie?", we point to one.   Definition by pointing is known as *ostensive* definition.

In the more restricted sense, which is adopted here, 'definition' is defined as a 'sentence that is used to fix, determine, or explain the meaning or use of a word or phrase' —in short, a verbal definition.   It is of the form

'———— ' means the same, or is to mean the same, as '**** ',

where in the space ——— the word or phrase to be defined (the *definiendum*) is mentioned, and in the space ∗∗∗∗, the word or phrase in terms of which it is being defined (the *definiens*).   An example of a definition is

'Perspicuous' means the same as 'clear '.

DEFINITIONS CLASSIFIED BY PURPOSE

Definitions differ widely in kind.   A convenient way to classify them initially is by the purposes they serve.

Stipulative Definitions

Definitions may be employed to fix the meaning of a new word or to assign a new use to an old one.   Definitions that serve this purpose are called *stipulative definitions.*

The current impatience with jargon should not blind us to the many real needs that stipulative definitions and the coining of new words (neologisms) may satisfy.   These include the following:

> *Naming a new kind of object or phenomenon.*   Recent examples are the introduction of the term 'pulsar' to mean (at present) the same as 'neutron star of enormous density and incredibly high rate of spin '; and 'conglomerate' to mean the same as 'company that grows not so much by increasing its own output as by absorbing other, usually unrelated, companies '.

> *Replacing an old word that is ambiguous or intolerably vague.* Thus ' germ' in one of its uses has been supplanted by 'microorganism '; and the many maladies once grouped together by Victorians as "the vapors" are now denoted severally by a whole battery of medical and psychological terms.

> *Abbreviating technical discourse.*   It is obviously simpler and clearer to say that a relation—call it *R*—is *transitive* than to say that *R* is a relation such that, for all objects *a, b, c*, if *R* holds between *a* and *b* and between *b* and *c*, then it also holds between *a* and *c*.

> *Supplying a brief term for a longer or more roundabout expression in everyday conversation.*   For instance, despite the arbiters of style, the neologism that consists in assigning to 'hopefully ' the same meaning as 'I am hoping that' continues to gain adherents.

Stipulative definitions, then, are sentences of the form

(1)   I (we) propose that '———' mean the same as '∗∗∗∗ ',

where in ——— we mention the newly introduced word or phrase, the *definiendum*, and in **** the familiar words or phrases making up the *definiens*.

Notice that stipulative definitions have the status not of statement-making sentences but of sentences that are used to make proposals. Hence such definitions are not true or false and are to be judged solely on the merits of the proposals they make.

Lexical Definitions

Definitions may be employed to report the accepted or standard usage(s) of a word or phrase. Definitions that fulfill this function are called *lexical definitions*; most dictionary definitions are of this type. They are used chiefly to increase one's vocabulary and to settle doubts or disputes about correct usage.

The notion of "accepted or standard usage" is connected with two familiar facts. One is that words are defined not in isolation but as symbols belonging to a language spoken by a particular community; the other is that language communities, by a rather complex process, permit small groups of their members (the lexicographers) to rule on which usages of words are to count as *correct* ones.

Lexical definitions may thus be regarded as sentences of the form

(2)   In language community *X*, when '———' is used correctly, it means the same as '**** '.

An example of such a sentence is

> In the English-speaking community, when 'tomentose' is used correctly, it means the same as 'covered with densely matted hairs '.

Lexical definitions, unlike stipulative definitions, do make statements. They report facts about correct usage, and these reports will be true or false depending on the facts.

Here we should be careful not to confuse two kinds of questions about usage: "What is the correct usage of a word *W*?" and "On what basis is this or that usage of *W* held to be correct?" Lexical definitions answer only the first kind of question. The second is left to critics of the dictionary makers.

Explicative Definitions

Definitions may be designed to clarify or explicate for one or another purpose the use(s) of familiar but imprecise words or phrases. Definitions intended to serve this end are called *explicative*. They are found wherever there is some need to refine the meaning(s) of a commonly used term beyond the level of ordinary correct usage. While they are especially plentiful in law, they also perform important functions in mathematics, the sciences, and philosophy.

For example, the lexical definition of 'basement', as given in *The Random House Dictionary of the English Language*, is 'a story of a building, partly or wholly underground'. But the New York State Multiple Dwelling Act explicates 'basement' as 'story partly below street level but having at least one half of its height above'.

Thus explicative definitions involve three elements rather than two:

1. The term that is being considered.

2. The imprecise common or intuitive use of the term.

3. The proposed more precise amended use of the term.

Such definitions are therefore sentences of the form

(3)   I (we) propose (or declare) that '———', which in language community X means the same as '****', be redefined to mean the same as '////'.

Notice that the new use (the legal 'basement') must be *similar* to the old one (the dictionary 'basement') in the sense that it must be applicable in most situations in which the old one was applicable. The process of explication does not create a wholly new use; it *transforms* an old imprecise use into a more exact, more clearly delineated one.[13]

A second example may be cited, this time from mathematics. The Soviet mathematician A. A. Markov, in his *Theory of Algorithms* (1954), offers an explication of the term 'algorithm'. Mathematicians, he notes, commonly understand that term to denote an exact set of rules determining a process of computation that leads from various initial data to a desired result. But this use is not precise enough for a mathematical theory of algorithms. Markov therefore proposes to replace the old use with an amended one, where in effect the expressions 'set of rules' and 'process of computation' are spelled out with maximum precision in terms of alphabets of symbols and specified lists of substitution formulas.

Finally, it is clear from (3) that explicative definitions have a mixed status. Inasmuch as they contain a clause stating the correct usage, they resemble lexical definitions. Yet they also resemble stipulative definitions in that they propose or institute an amended use. The part that states the correct usage is to be judged on its truth or falsity, the definition as a whole on its merits as a proposal.

---

[13] See Rudolf Carnap, *Logical Foundations of Probability* (Chicago: University of Chicago Press, 1950), Chapter 1.

Theoretical and Persuasive "Definitions"

There are two additional categories of sentences that are often called definitions but that cannot be looked upon simply as statements or proposals as to the uses of words or phrases.

The first are the so-called *theoretical* definitions. These are attempts to answer such questions as "What is electricity?" "What is life?" "What is meaning?" and the like. But questions of this sort are about the *nature* of phenomena or things, and cannot in general be answered merely by defining words. What is required, and what those who ask these questions really seek, are *theories*—sets of sentences (including appropriate kinds of definitions) that explain or describe the nature of phenomena or things.

Theoretical definitions, then, generally turn out to be theories or parts of theories rather than definitions in the proper sense. Definitions, especially explicative definitions, do play a major role in theory construction, but they should not be mistaken for the theories themselves.

Second, certain so-called definitions are not really intended to introduce, state, or clarify the use of a term but to influence people's attitudes. Such sentences are called *persuasive* definitions, following Charles L. Stevenson, who first described them.[14] They pervade politics, but also appear frequently in other arenas of controversy.

A persuasive definition operates very simply. Consider any familiar term with strong emotional associations— 'fascist ', for instance. Under the pretext of giving the "real" or "more precise" meaning of the term, the persuader undertakes to alter its literal meaning. For example, he may argue that the word 'fascist ', rather than meaning someone who advocates replacing parliamentary democracy with a military-industrial dictatorship, really means someone who participates in street demonstrations. Meanwhile, the emotive component of the meaning is left unchanged. The effect is to transfer the emotional associations of the familiar literal meaning to the newly proposed one.

In short, persuasive definitions are essentially appeals to emotions under the guise of explication. The unmasking takes place when we consider just what change in use is being proposed, to what end and with what consequences.

QUALITIES OF A GOOD DEFINITION

We have seen that definitions, classified by purpose, form three main groups. Each has its characteristic criteria of goodness.

Stipulative definitions, it will be recalled, are not true or false, but useful or useless. They are useful (and good) if they name a new object,

---

[14]   See Charles L. Stevenson, *Ethics and Language* (New Haven: Yale University Press, 1944, 1960), Chapter 9.

eliminate an ambiguity, or abbreviate discourse. They are useless (hence bad) if the new object can be named just as conveniently by some existing word or phrase, if the elimination of the ambiguity introduces a new one of greater consequence, or if the economy in discourse is more than offset by the effort required to learn the new word.

Lexical definitions, as defined above, are not intended to create or justify correct usage, but only to report it. Hence they are good if the statements they make are true, bad if they are false or inaccurate. The more interesting questions about *how* and *why* a language community selects certain usages as correct lie beyond the realm of purely lexical definitions.

Explicative definitions serve not simply to report correct usage but to propose changes in it. They are therefore subject to rather complicated criteria. It is easy enough to assess their lexical components in terms of truth or falsity. The problem is: How can proposals to amend existing usage be evaluated?

Take, for example, Professor Markov's explicative definition of 'algorithm'. Here the criteria that suggest themselves include: Is the new use sufficiently similar to the old so that the sort of things called algorithms in the past (for instance, Euclid's algorithm for finding the Greatest Common Divisor of two integers) will for the most part be covered by the new use? Is the new use fruitful in the sense that it enables us to construct a mathematical theory of intrinsic interest and possible theoretical application? Criteria such as these also seem appropriate in the sciences and philosophy. Others would, of course, be suitable in law.

In addition to the separate criteria for each type of definition, there are some rather obvious requirements that apply to all definitions. For one thing, definitions should not be expressed in obscure, high-flown language. Little is gained if 'beauty' is taken to mean the same as 'wondrous property that defies description'. For another, definitions should not be circular—that is, the *definiendum* should not appear in the *definiens*. Circularity is not always easy to detect. Thus until the French mathematician H. C. R. Méray pointed out the error in 1869, mathematicians had for some decades been defining the limit of a sequence as a real number and at the same time defining a real number as a limit of a sequence (of rational numbers).[15]

MORE ABOUT DEFINITIONS

Thus far we have taken definitions to be sentences that make statements or proposals about the *uses of words*. And we have classified these definitions solely on the basis of their purposes. There are, however, other ways of looking at definitions, as well as other points that can be made about them.

---

[15] See Carl B. Boyer, *A History of Mathematics* (New York: John Wiley, 1968), pp. 606 ff.

Nominal definitions and real definitions. Richard Robinson has suggested that views about definitions may be divided into three classes depending on how they answer the question: What do we define—*things* or *concepts* or *words*?[16] In our own discussion the assumption has been that we define *words* with the aid of other words. But a tradition going back to Plato and Aristotle holds that we define *things*. Indeed, Aristotle defined ' definition' as "a phrase signifying the essence of a thing." Aristotelian definitions are known as *real* definitions (from the Latin *res*, meaning things), as distinguished from *nominal* definitions (from *nomina*, meaning words). For Aristotle, a true real definition represented the most important kind of knowledge, since it stated the essence of a thing. Today, however, the notion *essence* is regarded by many as too imprecise to be very useful, unless, of course, it is identified simply with *nature*. But in that event we would look to theories rather than to definitions alone to inform us about the "essence" of things.

The view that what we define are *concepts* seems to suffer from similar disabilities. We therefore continue to assume that what we define are words.

Explicit definitions and contextual definitions. Certain definitions simply specify an expression for which the *definiendum* may always be directly substituted. Examples are

(4)   ' Pusillanimous' means the same as ' faint-hearted '.

' 4 ' means the same as ' 3 + 1 ' .

They are known as *explicit definitions.*

Other definitions accomplish their task by specifying how *contexts* in which the *definiendum* occurs can be rephrased as contexts in which it does not occur. These are called contextual definitions, or definitions in use. An example is Russell's definition of ' the ', as illustrated in

' The author of *Waverley* is Scotch' means the same as 'At least one person wrote *Waverley*, and at most one person wrote *Waverley*, and whoever wrote *Waverley* was Scotch '.[17]

Here one can see how a context in which the word ' the ' appears can be rephrased so that ' the ' disappears.

Explicit definitions merely put synonyms for synonyms and can be used only where these are available. Contextual definitions, on the other hand, play a much wider role. They bring to mind Frege's dictum that

---

[16]   Richard Robinson, *Definition* (Oxford: Oxford University Press, 1954), pp. 7 ff.

[17]   Bertrand Russell, *Introduction to Mathematical Philosophy* (London: George Allen and Unwin, 1919), p. 177.

the meaning of a word (hence its definition) is to be sought not in isolation, but in the context of *sentences.*

Definitions using necessary and sufficient conditions; descriptions in terms of "*family resemblances.*" It has long been assumed that for a large class of cases a proper definition must obey a certain structural requirement: the *definiens* must indicate *all* and *only* the characteristics an entity has to possess if the *definiendum* is to be correctly applicable to it. An example is

(5)   ' *x* is a prime number' means the same as ' *x* is an integer, and the only divisors of *x* are *x* and 1 ' ,

which says that an object may be called a 'prime number' if and only if 1) it is an integer and 2) its only divisors are itself and 1. The structure of (5) is

> ' *X* is a *Y*' means the same as ' *X* has characteristics $c_1, c_2, \ldots . c_n$ '.

The possession of *each* of these characteristics is necessary and the possession of *all* of them is sufficient for anything to be called a *Y*. Definitions that meet this structural requirement may be termed *definitions by necessary and sufficient conditions.* They are general in mathematics, and have been taken as models for all areas.

Recently, however, a number of philosophers, following Wittgenstein, have sharply questioned the universal applicability of the necessary-and-sufficient-condition model. They point out that many terms are so used that the objects or phenomena to which they are correctly applied may not have any *common* characteristics at all. The classic passage in Wittgenstein (*Philosophical Investigations*, §§65–67) speaks for itself:

> §65. . . . Instead of producing something common to all that we call language, I am saying that these phenomena have no one thing in common which makes us use the same word for all,— but that they are *related* to one another in many different ways. And it is because of this relationship, or these relationships, that we call them all "language." I will try to explain this.
>
> §66. Consider for example the proceedings that we call "games." I mean board-games, card-games, ball-games, Olympic games, and so on. What is common to them all?—Don't say: "There *must* be something common, or they would not be called 'games'"—but *look and see* whether there is anything common to all.—For if you look at them you will not see something that is common to *all*, but similarities, relationships, and a whole series of them at that. . . .

> And the result of this examination is: we see a complicated net-
> work of similarities overlapping and criss-crossing: sometimes
> overall similarities, sometimes similarities of detail.

> §67. I can think of no better expression to characterize these
> similarities than "family resemblances"; for the various resem-
> blances between members of a family—build, features, colour of
> eyes, gait, temperament, etc. etc.—overlap and criss-cross in the
> same way.—And I shall say 'games' form a family.[18]

What Wittgenstein has said here about defining the words 'language '
and 'game' obviously holds for a great many words of ordinary language.
For that matter, even a comparatively technical term like 'recession '
seems to have such fuzzy boundaries that a description in terms of "family
resemblances" may prove more useful than a definition by necessary and
sufficient conditions.

DISPUTES ABOUT WORDS

It is often said that a particular dispute or disagreement is *verbal*, not *real*.
What is meant is best made clear if we sort out several kinds of disagreements.

We first distinguish, with Charles L. Stevenson, between disagreements
in *belief* and disagreements in *attitude*.[19] Suppose someone maintains
approvingly that Britain in the 1930s pursued a policy of appeasing Hitler.
The person is doing two things: expressing a belief and evincing an
attitude. And we may find ourselves in disagreement with the belief,
with the attitude, or with both. Here we leave aside matters of attitude
and confine ourselves to matters of belief.

A disagreement in *belief* may relate 1) to facts other than those about
how words are used, 2) to facts about how words are used, or 3) to both.
If the first, the disagreement is likely to be called "factual" or "real"; if
the second, "verbal"; if the third, "mixed." For example, suppose
there is a disagreement in belief concerning the statement made by the
sentence

(6)   Britain in the 1930s pursued a policy of appeasement toward
        Hitler.

Here there are three possible grounds for disagreement. The parties to the
dispute may agree on the definition of 'appeasement' ; in that event their
dispute is only about the *facts* of British foreign policy. Or they may
agree about these facts but use different definitions of 'appeasement' —

---

[18]   Wittgenstein, op. cit., pp. 31–32.
[19]   Op. cit., Chapter 1.

one of them perhaps taking it to mean the same as 'making concessions in a context of encouraging aggression' and the other taking it to mean the same as 'making concessions in a context of stemming aggression'. In that event the disagreement is about how the two parties use certain words. Lastly, they may disagree about facts *and* words.

It is not always clear which of the three kinds of disagreement in belief is present. In many cases a disagreement that seems to be about non-linguistic facts turns out in reality to be about how words are used. Then we are apt to say that the disagreement is "verbal, not real"—that it is "just a matter of semantics." (Likewise, what appears to be an agreement on nonlinguistic facts may, if conflicting definitions are employed, turn out actually to be an agreement in *words* but a disagreement as to *facts*.) Many disagreements in philosophy as well as in politics are of the "verbal, not real" character. And that is one of the reasons why in these fields the cry must so often be raised: "Define your terms!"

One final caution. When we say that disagreements in belief about the uses of words are "verbal," we do not necessarily mean that they are "unreal." On the contrary, many disputes about words are quite real. For example, we can be in genuine disagreement about the utility of a particular stipulative definition, the accuracy of a lexical definition, or the fruitfulness of an explicative definition.

EXERCISES

15.1. Which of the following would you regard as definitions? For each definition, indicate the expression defined (the *definiendum*) and the expression(s) in terms of which it is defined (the *definiens*).

    a. A sound deductive argument is a valid deductive argument with all true premisses.

    b. A definition is any explanation of the meaning or use of a word or phrase.

    c. If there are ever perfect days, they come in June.

    d. The repetition by an infant of syllables resembling those used in adult speech is called babbling.

    e. A perfect number is a number that is the sum of its divisors (excluding itself and including 1).

    f. Life is short and art is long; the crisis is fleeting, experiment risky, decision difficult.

    g. Ontology is the study of what there is.

    h. ' Force' is a vague term in ordinary discourse. By 'the force of x' we shall mean the same as 'the mass of x times the acceleration of x'.

i.   A multinational enterprise is a large enterprise that has extensive interests in subsidiaries and branches outside its home country.

j.   It is one of the maxims of the civil law that definitions are hazardous.   [Dr. Samuel Johnson (1709–1784), in *Bartlett's Familiar Quotations*]

k.   I had rather feel compunction, than understand the definition thereof.   [Thomas à Kempis (1380–1471), in *The Oxford Book of Quotations*]

15.2.   Consider now those examples in 15.1 that contain definitions. See if you can classify each one according to the purpose(s) it serves: stipulative, lexical, explicative, theoretical, "persuasive." Remember that a definition may serve more than one purpose, there may be borderline cases, and the example itself may not supply enough context for you to decide.

15.3.   Now see if you can do the same thing for the following passages, each of which contains a definition:

a.   EVOKE, *v.t.*, to call up or produce . . .   [*The Random House Dictionary of the English Language*, 1966]

b.   The first truly international standard of length was a bar of platinum-irridium alloy called the *standard meter*, kept at the International Bureau of Weights and Measures near Paris, France.   The distance between two fine lines engraved on gold plugs near the ends of the bar was defined to be *one meter*.   [D. Halliday and D. Resnick, *Fundamentals of Physics* (New York: John Wiley, 1970), p. 3]

c.   The wavelength of the orange-red light of krypton-86 has replaced the platinum-irridium bar as the world standard of length. Formerly the wavelength of this light was defined as a function of the length of the meter bar.   Now the meter is defined as a multiple (1,650,763.73) of the wavelength of the light.   [Ibid., p. 720, quoted from *Scientific American*, December 1960, p. 75]

d.   The *weight* of a body is the gravitational force exerted on it by the earth.   [Ibid., p. 70]

e.   By Manners, I mean not here, Decency of behavior; as how one man should salute another, or how a man should wash his mouth, or pick his teeth before company, and such other points of the *Small Morals*; But those qualities of man-kind that concern their living together in Peace and Unity.   [Thomas Hobbes, *Leviathan*, 1651]

f.   A miracle may be accurately defined, *a transgression of a law of nature by a particular volition of the Deity, or by the interposition of some invisible agent.* [David Hume, "Of Miracles," in *An Inquiry Concerning Human Understanding*, 1758]

g.   I am bound by my own definition of criticism: a disinterested endeavor to learn and propagate the best that is known and thought in the world. [Matthew Arnold, *Essays in Criticism, First Series*, 1865]

h.   What is poetry? The suggestion, by the imagination, of noble grounds for the noble emotion. [John Ruskin, *Modern Painters*, 1888, vol. 3]

i.   The word *antibiosis* was first used by Vuillemin in 1889, to describe the phenomenon where one organism is in opposition to the life of another. [Paul R. Burkholder, "Antibiotics," *Science*, May 29, 1959]

j.   Twice I have been startled to find my use of 'intuitive' misconstrued, as alluding to some special and mysterious avenue of knowledge. By an intuitive account I mean one in which terms are used in habitual ways, without reflecting on how they might be defined or what presuppositions they might conceal. [Willard Van Orman Quine, *Word and Object* (Cambridge, Mass., and New York: Technology Press of M.I.T. and John Wiley, 1960), p. 36*n.*]

k.   An important aim of theoretical biology is an abstract definition of life . . .   For a working principle, we might again rely upon the evolutionary concept: a living system has those properties (of self-replication and metabolism) from which we may with more or less confidence deduce an evolutionary scheme that would encompass self-evidently living organisms. [Joshua Lederberg, "Exobiology: Approaches to Life Beyond the Earth," *Science*, August 12, 1960]

l.   AA, *n.*, basaltic lava having a rough surface. [*The Random House Dictionary of the English Language*, 1966]

m.   An increased scale of human activity has brought with it pollution, defined as "an undesirable change in the physical, chemical, or biological characteristics of our air, land, and water that may or will harmfully affect human life or that of any other desirable species, or industrial processes, living conditions, or cultural assets; or that may or will waste or deteriorate our raw material resources." [S. Fred Singer, *Science*, December 13, 1968, quoting from "Waste Management and Control," Committee on Pollution, National Academy of Sciences–National Research Council, 1966]

n. "It's a story told with music and words," he said, laying down a minimal definition of opera. "It uses the methods and means of opera. It's opera in a new language." [assistant manager of the Metropolitan Opera, speaking of *Tommy*, a rock opera created by The Who; *The New York Times*, June 8, 1970]

o. In recognition of this progress toward economic stability, I think we should define a recession as a sustained decline in the rate of growth relative to the long-term trend; or, alternatively, as a decline in the proportion of available labor and capital resources employed in production. [Solomon Fabricant, *The New York Times*, November 8, 1970]

p. Zoonoses may be defined as "those diseases and infections which are naturally transmitted between vertebrate animals and man." [Dr. Illar Muul, *Science*, December 18, 1970, quoting from World Health Organization Report Series No. 169, 1958]

q. QUESTION: Must we accept a permanent higher rate of unemployment, defining "full employment" as a jobless rate of 5 per cent rather than 4 per cent?
SAMUELSON: That's the figure Mr. Nixon's economists are using. If you can't deliver the pie in the sky, you'd better redefine pie!
[Paul Samuelson, interviewed in *Newsweek*, January 31, 1972]

15.4.   As far as you can judge, are the definitions in 15.2 good ones? That is, do they avoid circularity and high-flown or vague language? Do they fulfill the purpose(s) you think they are intended to serve?

15.5.   Find examples of your own to illustrate the following sorts of definitions: 1) stipulative, 2) explicative, 3) contextual, 4) explicit.

15.6.   A miscellany.

a. How would you classify the following definition as between contextual and explicit?

We eliminate ' $=$ ' by paraphrasing all expressions of the same form as '$a = b$' by sentences of the same form as the following: 'Any property that a has is also had by b, and any property that b has is also had by a'.

b. Compare these two definitions of 'melting point of a solid '. Which is better and why?

1. The melting point of a solid is the temperature at which it melts.

2.   According to the theory of solids, the addition of thermal energy increases the amplitude of vibration of the lattice particles about their equilibrium positions until, finally, some of the amplitudes become so large that the lattice is ruptured. The temperature at which this first occurs is rather sharply defined for crystalline solids and is known as the *melting point* of the material.   [W. Wallace McCormick, *Fundamentals of College Physics* (New York: Macmillan, 1965), p. 49]

c.   The following definition of 'ethnography' may be regarded as a *definition by necessary and sufficient conditions*.   It uses the term 'culture'.   Is it possible to find—say, in some anthropology text—the same kind of definition of 'culture'?   Or does this term perhaps admit only of a *description in terms of "family resemblances"*?

Cultural anthropology has as its central interest the description and analysis of a certain kind of regularities in human social behavior.   The regularities in question are the customs —or, to use the technical term, the culture—of the group. The work of describing such regularities within the boundaries of a particular society during a brief cross section of time is called ethnography.   [Anthony C. F. Wallace, "Culture and Cognition," *Science*, February 2, 1962]

d.   George Levine gives this account of his definition of 'the novel' :

[M]y definition is in large part stipulative, but unless I specifically say otherwise, I have particularly in mind certain qualities which, though perhaps never uniformly present in any single novel, may reasonably be taken as qualities of Victorian fiction in general. I am quite deliberately not thinking of the minimal definition of the novel as an extended fictional narrative in prose ...   [T]he idea of "the novel" in this book is largely the idea of the realistic novel of mid-nineteenth-century England . . . [T]raditionally, when we speak of the novel as a form, we refer, as Northrop Frye defines it, to a work governed by the demands of plot or character development, which constructs a realistic atmosphere, which presents character within the context of a society, and which is concerned with social modes or manners. In particular, I mean to emphasize the portrayal of character and the related conventions of realism.   [*The Boundaries of Fiction* (Princeton, N.J.: Princeton University Press, 1968), p. 7]

Now list all the definitions of 'the novel' contained in this passage. Professor Levine describes his own definition as "in large part stipulative." Is this correct? If not, how would you describe his definition?

II

The Logic of Deductive Arguments

Now reasoning is an argument in which, certain things being laid down, something other than these necessarily comes about through them.

Aristotle, *Topics*

4

Deductive Arguments

We begin our account of logic proper with some introductory remarks on *deductive logic*—the study of the principles and procedures that may be used to determine which deductive arguments are valid.

The fundamental question for deductive logic is, *How can we tell whether a deductive argument is valid?* This is really two questions in one. First, what are the *criteria* for deductive validity? Second, what are the *procedures* for determining which deductive arguments meet these criteria? Deductive logic is in essence the search for just such criteria and procedures.

The present chapter initiates this search. The point of departure is the commonsense criterion: a deductive argument is valid if and only if it is impossible for the premisses all to be true and the conclusion false. This criterion is refined and reformulated, with the aid of the notions of *logical form* and *logical truth*, into a *general* criterion of deductive validity. Succeeding chapters then set up *specific* criteria for specific areas of logic, as well as procedures for applying these criteria.

A few words on the nature and uses of deductive arguments set the stage for the discussion of criteria. A remark on the aims and scope of deductive logic brings it to a close.

§16   *Deductive Arguments and Their Uses*

Let us first review briefly what is meant by a deductive argument, and note some of the purposes it serves.

THE NOTION OF A DEDUCTIVE ARGUMENT

We start our consideration of deductive arguments by defining in summary form three technical terms: 'argument', 'deductive', and 'valid'. By an *argument* we understand a sequence of two or more sentences together with the claim that one of these sentences (called the 'conclusion') follows in some sense from the others (called the 'premisses'). An argument is *deductive* if the claim made is that the conclusion follows from the premisses in the precise sense that it is impossible for the conclusion to be false if the premisses are all true.   Finally, a deductive argument is *valid* if the deductive claim is correct—that is, if it is indeed impossible for the conclusion to be false if the premisses are all true. Consider the following:

(1)   All emeralds previously examined have been green.

Therefore the next emerald examined will be green.

(2)   If Edward Kennedy is a registered Democrat, he can vote in the general elections.

Edward Kennedy can vote in the general elections.

Therefore Edward Kennedy is a registered Democrat.

(3)   If Edward Kennedy is a registered Democrat, he can vote in the general elections.

Edward Kennedy cannot vote in the general elections.

Hence Edward Kennedy is not a registered Democrat.

(4)   If Edward Kennedy is a registered Democrat, he can vote in the general elections.

Edward Kennedy is a registered Democrat.

Hence Edward Kennedy can vote in the general elections.

These are all arguments.   But as can be easily verified from the definitions, only (2), (3), and (4) are deductive arguments, and only (3) and (4) are valid deductive arguments.

Notice that (1) is not classified as a deductive argument.   On the contrary, it is a nondeductive argument.   Clearly, the claim made in (1) is not that it is *impossible* for the conclusion to be false if the premiss is true, but only that it is *improbable* that the conclusion will be false, granted that the premiss is true.   Thus the distinction between deductive and nondeductive arguments turns on the kind of claim made.   Which kind is intended is generally, though not always, obvious from the context.

Two further details of terminology should be added.   First, the word ' inference' is used to refer only to the act of drawing a conclusion from premisses, and not to the conclusion or to the argument as a whole.   And we say that an inference is deductive if the argument in which it occurs is deductive, valid if that argument is valid.   Second, the term 'sound' is reserved for deductive arguments that 1) are valid *and* 2) have all true premisses, as in (4) above.   Note that conditions 1) and 2) are quite independent of each other: a deductive argument may be invalid even if all of its premisses (and for that matter its conclusion) are true—see (2) above; it may be valid even if one or more of its premisses (and its conclusion) are false—see (3) above.   But a deductive argument cannot be valid if its premisses are all true and its conclusion is false.

Whether a premiss is true is in general a matter of *fact*, not of *logic*, and must be judged by those familiar with the facts.   Hence deductive logic appraises only the validity of arguments, not their soundness.   It may thus be defined in brief as the *study of valid deductive inference.*

THE USES OF DEDUCTIVE ARGUMENTS

No one today supposes—perhaps no one ever really did—that people can live and learn by deductive inference alone.   (Indeed, the present tendency is, if anything, to downgrade its role.)   Yet a quick review of some of the uses of deductive arguments will show that both in life and in learning they play an indispensable part.   Such a review will also provide some additional experience in *recognizing* and *following* arguments; this will be of help when we come later to *evaluate* them and, most important, to *construct* valid ones of our own.

We are often able to recognize a piece of discourse as making or reporting an argument by the fact that it contains such "signal" words as ' therefore', 'hence', 'so', 'since', 'whereas', and the like.   Similarly, there are rough language cues that indicate the kind of argument it is. Thus when the tie between conclusion and premisses is expressed in such phrases as 'follows necessarily (or logically) from', 'is (logically) implied by', 'is entailed by', 'is a logical consequence of', or 'is deducible from', it can normally be concluded that the argument is *deductive.*   On the other hand, when such expressions as 'is supported by', 'follows probably from', or 'is confirmed by' are used to characterize the tie, the argument is generally intended as a *nondeductive* one. With these guides in mind, we turn to the uses of deductive arguments in three main areas.

Mathematics

The most familiar example of a deductive argument is a proof in high school geometry. The premises in this case are Euclid's axioms and postulates; the conclusion is the theorem to be demonstrated—say, the Pythagorean theorem. If these axioms and postulates are designated by the letters $A_1, A_2, \ldots, A_n$ and the theorem by the letter B, then the argument may be represented schematically as

> A_1
> A_2
> $\vdots$
> A_n
> Therefore B.

Such an argument or chain of arguments (since each step in the proof may itself be viewed as the last step of an argument) is clearly deductive. The claim is not that the theorem "is made probable by" or "is confirmed by" the axioms and postulates, but that it follows necessarily from them, that it is impossible for the theorem to be "false" if all of these axioms and postulates are "true."

What holds for geometry holds for mathematics generally. (Even high school algebra is finally coming to include as a topic the development of algebraic theorems from postulates.) Deductive logic is used throughout in proving theorems, in organizing and reorganizing existing mathematical knowledge, and in creating new branches such as recursive function theory, information theory, and the like.

The Sciences

Mathematics is preeminently a deductive discipline. The sciences, however, employ a procedure that in its overall aspect is *nondeductive*. In mathematics one *proves* theorems; in the sciences one *confirms* laws and theories. The Pythagorean theorem follows necessarily from its premises, but Newton's law of universal gravitation is accepted only until an alternative with a wider basis of confirmation takes its place. In short, to discover a scientific law or theory is often to hit upon the conclusion of a nondeductive argument whose premises, among other things, state the evidence on which some degree of confirmation is claimed for that law or theory.

Nonetheless, deduction plays a crucial role within this framework. First, physics and many other sciences rely heavily on the procedures of mathematics, where *deductive inference* is an essential element. Thus deductive arguments enter wherever mathematics is applied. Second, all sciences seek to test hypotheses, and this can be done only if consequences are derived or *deduced* from them. Thus deductive arguments are often used in testing hypotheses. Finally, the sciences look on their hypotheses and laws not as discrete particles of knowledge but as candidates for incorporation into theories or systems of laws. The aim is to show that large numbers of laws (for example, Kepler's laws of planetary motion and Galileo's free fall law) are *deducible from*, or are logical consequences of, a small number of more general laws (Newton's laws of motion and law of universal gravitation). Thus deductive arguments are present wherever scientific knowledge is organized into systems or theories.

Daily Life

Deduction dominates mathematics and pervades the sciences, but it is little evident in our daily affairs. Perhaps this is because life is so much a matter of making decisions (which vocation to follow, whom to marry, what to believe), and decisions seem best described as conclusions of *nondeductive*, rather than of deductive, arguments. These nondeductive arguments are distinguished by the fact that some of their premisses assign positive or negative values (in accordance with various value systems) to the consequences of alternative courses of action. But even here deduction plays a significant, if indirect, role. All our decisions involve cause-effect hypotheses, and in confirming hypotheses we rely in part on deduction.

In addition to its role in decision making, deduction is present implicitly in many of the simple modes of everyday intuitive reasoning. For example, we "argue" that Perkins must be very bright, since he holds a Phi Beta Kappa key. If the missing premiss is supplied, the argument reads:

(5)   All holders of Phi Beta Kappa keys are very bright.

Perkins is the holder of a Phi Beta Kappa key.

Therefore Perkins is very bright.

This is an instance of a familiar form of argument in traditional deductive logic. We shall encounter other argument forms that are familiar from daily life when we come to examine deductive inference in detail.

---

§17   *Deductive Validity and Logical Form*

Deductive logic seeks to determine what follows necessarily from what. Its basic findings are cast in the form of 1) criteria or standards of validity and 2) procedures, devices, or routines by which to decide which deductive arguments meet these criteria. The particular criteria proposed for *specific classes* of deductive arguments we shall take up in later chapters. Here we wish to say something about criteria of deductive validity *in general.*

To be useful, criteria of validity should be precise—that is, they should take some such form as "An argument belonging to such and such a class of arguments is valid if and only if it has this or that *clearly defined* property." Now precision of this sort is not come by easily. On the contrary, several formulations must be gone through before a more or less serviceable model for validity criteria is reached. A natural starting point is the criterion, borrowed from common sense, that was introduced in §16.

A PRELIMINARY CRITERION OF DEDUCTIVE VALIDITY

Thus far, in discussing deductive arguments, we have used the following criterion:

> *An argument is valid if and only if it is* impossible *for the conclusion to be false when the premisses are all true, i.e., if and only if it is* impossible *to find a set of circumstances that would make the premisses all true and the conclusion false.*

But this criterion is not sufficiently precise. The critical term 'impossible' has many senses. If it is to be used in formulating a criterion of validity, we must sort out some of these senses and determine which one we want.

Take the following (intuitively) valid argument:

(1)   Hipparchus is a philosopher or Hypatia is a philosopher.

Hipparchus is not a philosopher.

Therefore Hypatia is a philosopher.

Now in what sense is it "impossible" to find a set of circumstances such that 1) Hipparchus *or* Hypatia is a philosopher and 2) Hipparchus is *not* a philosopher, and yet 3) Hypatia *also* is *not* a philosopher? Is it merely impossible *practically*, as it once was impossible practically to go to the moon? Obviously a different and stronger sense of 'impossible' is desired. Is it impossible *physically*? Would the existence of such a state of affairs merely contravene some present law of science? Might such a state of affairs conceivably exist in a universe different from ours (or even in our own universe, if the "law" turned out to require modification)? Again, no. What is needed is a third sense—namely, impossible *logically*. The existence of the set of circumstances in question would somehow violate what will later be called the "principles" or "truths" of logic. Accordingly, we revise our preliminary criterion to read:

> *An argument is valid if and only if it is* logically *impossible for the conclusion to be false when the premisses are all true.*

Logical Impossibility and Logical Necessity

It is also said that a deductive argument is valid if and only if the truth of its conclusion "follows necessarily from" the truth of its premisses. Actually, this is just a restatement of the revised criterion. For if it is *logically impossible* that the conclusion be false when the premisses are all true, then it is *logically necessary* that the conclusion be true when the premisses are all true (and vice versa). In more general terms, logical necessity and logical impossibility are interdefinable with the aid of negation. If something is logically impossible, then its negation is logically necessary; if something is logically necessary, then its negation is logically impossible.

This revised criterion, then, rests on the notion of logical impossibility. What can be done to make this notion and that of logical necessity more precise? Any effort in this direction seems inevitably to involve two other notions that are difficult and still quite controversial: logical form and logical truth.

LOGICAL FORM AND THE FORMAL CHARACTER OF VALIDITY

According to deductive logic, both traditional and modern, the *validity* of a deductive argument is independent of the truth or falsity of its premisses and conclusion. It is also independent of the particular *content* or *subject matter* of the sentences that compose the argument. What determines validity is solely the logical *form*, or *structure*, of these sentences. In short, *validity* is *formal*. And deductive logic, as the theory of valid deductive inference, need therefore attend only to the form of the argument, not to its content. For this reason it is often referred to simply as "formal" logic.

Now what is to be understood by logical form? And how does one determine that the validity of an argument depends solely on the logical form of its premisses and conclusion and not on their content?

Although there is no generally accepted account of logical form, we can get at least a rough idea by examining and comparing various arguments. Consider, for example, the following:

(2)   Heidegger is a physicist or Heisenberg is a physicist.

Heidegger is not a physicist.

Therefore Heisenberg is a physicist.

If we compare (2) with (1), we find that although the casts of characters and what is said about them are quite different, the two arguments do have something in common that may be regarded as their logical form. It can be exhibited quite simply. Let the letters 'P' and 'Q' be place-holders for noncompound (simple) sentences—that is, let them stand in place of *any* such sentences—and let the word 'not' have the force of ' It is not the case that '. Substituting in (2), we obtain

(2') P or Q
Not-P
Therefore Q ,

which we take to represent the logical form of (2). Under the same substitutions, (1) becomes

(1') P or Q
Not-P
Therefore Q ,

which is the same as (2'). Thus (2) and (1) have their logical form in common, or (2) and (1) are both instances of the same *argument form.*

The notion of logical form can also be illustrated by traditional syllogistic arguments, such as

(3)   All mathematicians are scholars

All algebraists are mathematicians

Therefore all algebraists are scholars

and

(4)   All registered voters are eligible to vote in the general elections.

All registered Democrats are registered voters.

Therefore all registered Democrats are eligible to vote in the general elections.

Here let the letters 'S', 'M', and 'P' be place-holders for words that stand for classes. Then (3) becomes

(3')   All *M* are *P*
          All *S* are *M*
          Therefore all *S* are *P*,

and so does (4).   Hence (3) and (4) have the same logical form, or are
instances of the same argument form.

Thus we may think of the *logical form* of a sentence as being constituted
by the *kinds* of terms or parts it contains, together with *the way these are
combined* in the sentence.   Roughly, the form is what remains of the
sentence after place-holders are substituted for specific terms (' mathematicians ') or parts (' Heisenberg is a physicist ').   The logical form of
the argument, or the *argument form*, is then given by the logical forms of
the sentences that make up the argument.

So much for logical form.

Next, how do we determine that the validity of an argument depends
solely on its form?   We do so by showing that given a valid argument—
say, (1) above—any other arbitrarily chosen argument of the same form
will also be valid.   Let

(5)   Perkins publishes or Perkins perishes

          Perkins does not publish

          Therefore Perkins perishes

be such an argument.   As the reader will verify, it is of the same form
as (1).   Moreover, it too is valid, for it is *logically* impossible to find a
set of circumstances such that 1) Perkins publishes *or* perishes and 2)
Perkins does *not* publish and yet 3) Perkins also does not perish.

Again, the choice of (5) as a second argument of the same form was
quite arbitrary.   Must we then test a third, a fourth, . . . , an *n*th argument of the same form in order to make sure that *all* arguments of that
form are valid?   Or can we generalize on the basis of an arbitrarily
selected instance?[1]

The Problem of " Nonformal " Validity

Are all valid deductive arguments valid by reason of their logical form
alone?   Take the following example:

(6)   Today is Monday.

          So tomorrow is Tuesday.

---

[1]   While it can be shown that any instance of a valid argument form is valid, the
companion statement—that any instance of an invalid argument form is invalid—
requires qualification.   On this, see §25.

This is surely a valid deductive argument: no set of circumstances—barring willful changes in the uses of words—could possibly make its premiss true and its conclusion false.   But is it valid in virtue of its logical form?   Indeed, what is its logical form?   As the argument stands, *what* place-holders could we put *where* in order to obtain anything we might call the logical form?

Views here differ.   Most writers hold that deductive validity is *always* formal and that apparent exceptions can be taken care of by supplying "missing" premisses.   In the case of (6), the supplied premiss might read: "If any day is Monday, then the following day is Tuesday."   Others object that any "premisses" that have to be supplied in such situations are the kind of premisses that are true *solely* by virtue of how we use words and thus add no nonlinguistic information to what has been provided by the other premisses.   These writers hold that an argument like (6) is valid as it stands.   They therefore reject the assertion that all valid deductive arguments are valid only by reason of being instances of valid argument forms.[2]

There might perhaps be a third view, which concurs with the second in rejecting the first.   In this view, deductive logic is seen as an ongoing enterprise that has already succeeded in working out formal criteria of validity for certain classes of sentences (for example, those dealt with by sentence logic and first-order predicate logic) and that is prepared to examine *additional* classes of sentences.   To the extent that the examination is successful, *new* logical forms and *new* formal criteria of validity will be obtained.   And the set of arguments valid by reason of form will be correspondingly enlarged.

As far as our present purposes are concerned, however, this whole question can very well be put aside.   Since deductive logic now considers only arguments for which validity is known to be formal, these alone shall be attended to in what follows.

THE SIGNIFICANCE OF THE FORMAL CHARACTER OF VALIDITY

What is so special about the fact that deductive validity depends solely on form?

In the first place, if validity is formal, then deductive logic does not have to assume the impossible burden of making a separate finding of validity for each individual argument.   All that is required is to determine which *forms* of argument are valid; for if a form is valid, then each instance of that form will also be valid.   Thus it is the formal character of validity that gives logic its generality, its power.

---

[2]   See Max Black, *The Labyrinth of Language* (New York: New American Library, 1969), pp. 103–105.

In the second place, if *validity* is formal, then any *criterion* of validity must likewise be formal. If the validity of an argument depends solely on its form, then the "clearly defined property" that an argument must possess if it is to be valid can only be a *formal property*.

The questions then are, What formal property of arguments could serve as a criterion of validity? And what relation would this property bear to the notion of logical impossibility and to our preliminary criterion?

EXERCISES

17.1. Later certain *formal* criteria by which to determine whether various *argument forms* are valid will be considered. Meanwhile, it may be useful to test your own commonsense intuitions on the following argument forms. Which seem valid? Which invalid? For each one that you think *in*valid, verify this by constructing an *argument* of that form that is *in*valid (i.e., that has all true premisses but a false conclusion). For example,

> All *M* are *P*
>
> No *S* are *M*
>
> Therefore no *S* are *P*

is an argument form. Now replace the letter '*M*' with 'sound arguments', '*P*' with 'valid arguments', and '*S*' with 'arguments with false premisses'. You will then obtain the following argument:

> All sound arguments are valid.
>
> No arguments with false premisses are sound.
>
> Therefore no arguments with false premisses are valid.

The premisses of this argument are all true, but the conclusion is false. Hence the argument is invalid, as is the form of the argument.

> a. If *P*, then *Q*
>   *Q*
>   Therefore *P*
>
> b. If *P*, then *Q*
>   Not-*Q*
>   Therefore not-*P*
>
> c. *Q* or not-*P*
>   *P*
>   Therefore *Q*
>
> d. If *P*, then *Q*
>   Therefore if not-*Q*, then not-*P*

e.   No M are P
     No S are M
     Therefore no S are P

f.   No M are P
     All S are M
     Therefore no S are P

---

§18   *Deductive Validity and Logical Truth*

In this section, we shall try to formulate a *general* criterion of deductive validity in terms of a *formal property* of deductive arguments.   We shall try at the same time to show that this property helps clarify the notion of logical impossibility on which our preliminary criterion of validity relies. The central role in this undertaking will be played by a notion of *logical truth*.   But first an auxiliary concept must be introduced and carefully defined.

CORRESPONDING CONDITIONAL
Consider a two-premiss argument represented schematically by

(1) A_1

         A_2

         Therefore B.

Connect the two premisses by 'and'.   We then have the conjunction

         A_1 and A_2.

Next, form a *conditional*, or an "if-then," sentence from this argument. Do so by making 'A_1 and A_2' the *antecedent*, or "if-part," and the conclusion B the *consequent*, or "then-part":

(2)   If (A_1 and A_2), then B.

Thus (2) will represent the conditional sentence corresponding to the argument represented by (1) and known as the *corresponding conditional* of that argument.   For instance, the argument

(3)   Sophocles is a philosopher or Socrates is a philosopher

         Sophocles is not a philosopher

         Therefore Socrates is a philosopher

will have as its corresponding conditional

(4)   If [(Sophocles is a philosopher or Socrates is a philosopher) and
         Sophocles is not a philosopher], then Socrates is a philosopher.

Corresponding conditionals can in like manner be constructed for arguments with any number of premisses.

   To each argument there corresponds just one conditional sentence.
Similarly, to each argument form there corresponds just one conditional
"sentence form."   For example, the argument (3) is an instance of the
form

(3′)   *P* or *Q*
         Not-*P*
         Therefore *Q*,

and the corresponding conditional sentence form for (3′) will be

(5)   If [(*P* or *Q*) and not-*P*], then *Q*.

LOGICAL TRUTH AND A FORMAL CRITERION OF VALIDITY

Writers on logic generally agree on which sentences are to be counted as
logically true, however much they may disagree on what it is for a sentence to be logically true.   An example of a logical truth is

(6)   It is raining or it is not raining.

This sentence is true if it rains and also true if it does not rain.   What
distinguishes it is that, while its component sentences may be either true
or false in the ordinary sense (depending on whether what they say is the
case), the compound sentence is so formed that it cannot be false.   For
the time being, we shall mean by a logical truth a sentence of this sort.

   Using the notion of a corresponding conditional, we may now formulate the following general criterion of deductive validity:

> *An argument is valid if and only if its corresponding
> conditional is a logical truth.*[3]

Thus the property that characterizes a valid deductive argument is that
of *having a corresponding conditional that is logically true.*

---

[3]   The Stoic logicians of antiquity were the first to state a general criterion, or rule, of
deductive validity in terms of logical truth.   See Benson Mates, *Stoic Logic* (Berkeley
and Los Angeles: University of California Press, 1953, 1961), p. 4.

We can illustrate the use of this criterion if we return for a moment to the argument (3). According to the criterion, (3) is valid if and only if its corresponding conditional (4) is a logical truth. It is not difficult to see that (4), like (6), cannot be false. Hence (4) is a logical truth, and (3) is valid.

Extension of the New Criterion to Argument Forms

Suitably modified, the new criterion of deductive validity may be extended from arguments to argument forms in the following way:

> *An* argument form *is valid if and only if all of its instances have corresponding conditionals that are logical truths.*

For example, the argument form

(3′)   *P* or *Q*
         Not-*P*
         Therefore *Q*

meets this criterion and is a valid argument form. For not only does its instance (3) have a corresponding conditional (4) that is logically true, but so will any arbitrarily chosen instance of (3′), such as

(7)   We hang together or we hang separately.

        We do not hang together.

        Therefore we hang separately.

The Formal Character of Logical Truth

Two things should be said about the new criterion at this point. First, the property of being a logical truth is a formal property; hence the new criterion is a formal one. Second, if logical impossibility is defined in terms of logical truth, the revised preliminary criterion of deductive validity reduces to the new one.

In general, whether a sentence is true or false cannot be determined simply from its form, or structure. But there are exceptions—namely, logically true sentences (and also logically false ones, or self-contradictions). Logically true sentences such as (6) and (4) are "true" no matter what the case may be. They are true, as has been seen, by virtue of how they are formed from sentences that are capable of being true or false in the ordinary sense. Thus being a logical truth—whatever else we may eventually wish to say about it—is a formal, or structural, property of sentences. It follows that the property of having a corresponding conditional that is logically true is a formal property of deductive arguments and that this new criterion of validity is indeed a formal one.

Logical Impossibility and Logical Truth

It has been shown (in §17) that logical possibility may be defined in terms of logical necessity and negation:

> A sentence is logically impossible if and only if its negation is logically necessary.

If we now identify logically necessary sentences (sentences that *cannot* be false) with logical truths, then our preliminary criterion of deductive validity readily reduces to our new one in the following manner:

> *An argument is valid if and only if it is* logically impossible *for the conclusion to be false when the premisses are all true.*
>
> *An argument is valid if and only if it is* logically necessary *that if the premisses are all true the conclusion also is true.*
>
> *An argument is valid if and only if its corresponding conditional—the sentence whose antecedent is the conjunction of the premisses and whose consequent is the conclusion—is itself a logical truth.*

Logical Truth, Logical Implication, Logical Consequence

The notion of logical truth may also be used to provide compact, informal definitions for the notions of *logical implication* and *logical consequence*. These are stated briefly now, and treated in more detail in later chapters.

To say that a sentence A logically implies a sentence B or that B is a logical consequence of A is simply to say that the conditional

If A, then B

is a logical truth.   Inserting these definitions in the criterion for deductive validity, we have

> *An argument is valid if and only if the conjunction of its premisses* logically implies *its conclusion.*
>
> *An argument is valid if and only if its conclusion is a* logical consequence *of the conjunction of its premisses.*

Thus the burden is placed squarely on the notion of logical truth. Since there is considerable agreement as to which sentences are logically true, we can make practical use of the criterion without having to go beyond the still-vague characterization of logical truths as sentences that are "true" by virtue of how they are formed. But the underlying question—what, more precisely, is to be understood by logical truth?—remains unresolved and continues to be debated.

A CONCLUDING WORD ON LOGICAL TRUTH

Philosophers in the past have often described the truths, principles, or laws of deductive logic as "truths of reason." Today, however, scholars are more disposed to seek a characterization of logical truth at or near the interface of logic and language.

A widely discussed definition is one given by Willard Van Orman Quine. Logical truths, he says, are sentences that

> not only are true but stay true even when we make substitutions upon the component words and phrases as we please, provided merely that the so-called "logical" words . . . 'or', 'not', 'if-then', 'everything', 'something', etc., stay undisturbed.[4]

Let us apply Professor Quine's definition to the example of logical truth used above:

(6)   It is raining or it is not raining.

Now (6) is true. Furthermore, it stays true no matter what sentences are substituted for 'It is raining', provided only that the "logical" (or "form") words 'or' and 'not' are left undisturbed. To take an arbitrary instance, if 'Socrates is a philosopher' is substituted for each occurrence of 'It is raining' in (6), the result is

(8)   Socrates is a philosopher or Socrates is not a philosopher.

This is also true; thus (6) is a logical truth.

Incorporating Quine's definition into our criterion of deductive validity, we have

> *An argument is valid if and only if its corresponding conditional is true and stays true under any substitutions for its nonlogical words.*

---

[4] W. V. Quine, *Methods of Logic* (New York: Henry Holt, 1950, 1959), p. xv. For refinements of his own view and a discussion of alternative formulations, see his *Philosophy of Logic* (Englewood Cliffs, N. J.: Prentice-Hall, 1970), especially Chapters 4 and 7.

Let us apply this criterion to argument (3), with its corresponding conditional (4). Now (4) is true. Moreover, it stays true under any substitution of sentences for its sentence components, provided we leave the words 'if-then', 'or', 'and', and 'not' unchanged. If we put, say, 'Perkins publishes' for 'Sophocles is a philosopher' and 'Perkins perishes' in place of 'Socrates is a philosopher', then (4) becomes

(9)   If [(Perkins publishes or Perkins perishes) and Perkins does not publish], then Perkins perishes,

which is also true. Thus (3) is a valid argument.

Quine's way, it must be noted, has not been universally accepted. On the contrary, it has been under considerable attack and may well need significant revision. His definition raises a number of questions. Some of them are: How are we to draw the kind of boundary line between "logical" and "nonlogical" words that Quine seems to require? What determines which substitutions are appropriate or permissible for the nonlogical words and phrases? But whatever difficulties are attached to it, his view has profoundly influenced the whole discussion, and many of its chief features are likely to survive in any alternative that may prove more satisfactory.

In any event, our present purposes are served. For Quine's view helps motivate an account of valid inference and argument that will be sensitive only to specified structural features of sentences and thus will be *formal*.

EXERCISES

18.1. For each of the following arguments, 1) write the argument form, 2) write the corresponding conditional of the argument form, and 3) find another argument of the same form.

a. If Perkins has his Ph.D., he will be appointed assistant professor.
He will not be appointed assistant professor.
Hence he does not have his Ph.D.

b. Perkins is appointed assistant professor or he does not accept the job offer.
Perkins does accept the job offer.
Hence Perkins is appointed assistant professor.

c. If Perkins has his Ph.D., he will be appointed assistant professor.
Hence if he is not appointed assistant professor, he does not have his Ph.D.

d.   If Perkins publishes, he will be promoted.
If Perkins does not publish, he will not be reappointed.
Either Perkins publishes or Perkins does not publish.
Hence either Perkins will be promoted or he will not be reappointed.

e.   If Perkins publishes, he will be promoted.
If Perkins is promoted, he will be able to work on his book this summer.
Hence if Perkins publishes, he will be able to work on his book this summer.

18.2.   Which of the following sentences are logical truths? For *d* through *g*, write an argument whose corresponding conditional is of the same form as that sentence.

. a.   (Gonzales wins or Gonzales does not win) and (Laver wins or Laver does not win).

. b.   If [(Gonzales and Laver win the doubles) and (Gonzales and Laver win the doubles only if Smith and Ashe withdraw)], then Smith and Ashe withdraw.

c.   (Gonzales wins and Laver withdraws) or (Gonzales does not win and Laver does not withdraw).

·d.   If [(Gonzales wins or Laver wins) and (if Gonzales wins, the gallery will be pleased) and (if Laver wins, the gallery will be pleased)], then the gallery will be pleased.

e.   If [(if the competition is keen, Gonzales plays well) and (Gonzales plays well and Laver plays well)], then the competition is keen.

f.   If [(Gonzales plays well or Gonzales loses his concentration) and (if Gonzales plays well, he wins)], then (if Gonzales does not lose his concentration, he wins).

g.   If {[if (Gonzales plays and the competition is not keen) then he wins easily] and (the competition is not keen)}, then (if Gonzales plays, he wins easily).

---

§19   *The Tasks and Scope of Deductive Logic*

As a discipline, deductive logic has rather an odd history.   More than two millennia separate the careers of its two founding fathers: Aristotle (384–322 B.C.) and Gottlob Frege (1848–1925).   During this long interval there was an elaboration of what was at hand, but little or no substantive growth.

It was Aristotle who

Introduced the basic notion of a deductive argument.

First treated deductive validity in terms of logical form, using letters as place-holders for class terms so as to exhibit the form of certain types of sentences.

Created the first system of deductive logic, the famous categorical syllogistic. [5]

In the fourth and third centuries B.C. the Stoic logicians developed the essentials of what today is called sentence logic. But their writings survived only in fragments, and their work eventually had to be done anew. Medieval logicians of the twelfth to the fourteenth centuries seem to have contributed rather to the philosophy of logic than to its content. Gottfried Wilhelm Leibniz (1646–1716) caught glimpses of the future, as did the little-appreciated Bernard Bolzano (1781–1848). And the English mathematician George Boole (1815–1864) was the first to apply algebraic methods to what was still traditional logic.

But it was Frege who really initiated the modern development of deductive logic with the publication in 1879 of his small book, the *Begriffs-schrift* ("Concept Writing," or "Ideography"). To him we owe

The first actual system of sentence logic.

The first system of quantification theory, embodying first- and second-order predicate logic and replacing the traditional subject-predicate analysis of sentences with an argument-function model.

The fundamental notion of a formal system.

Modern logic was then speeded on its course by the appearance in 1910–1913 of the massive, three-volume *Principia Mathematica* of Alfred North Whitehead (1861–1947) and Bertrand Russell (1872–1970). In their preface they acknowledge that "in all questions of logical analysis our chief indebtedness is to Frege."

THE TASKS OF A DEDUCTIVE LOGIC

Modern deductive logic differs from ancient and traditional logic in the enormously greater range of forms it considers and in the extensive use it makes of symbolism and mathematical methods. But the basic aim of deductive logic has remained the same from Aristotle to Frege. From

---

[5]   For a brief summary of Aristotelian logic see the Appendix.

the standpoint of the use of logic in argument, it may be described as the creation of a theory—today logicians would say a series of theories—of formally valid deductive inference.

In the light of what has been said in this chapter, each such logical theory has three specific tasks:

1. to analyze the *forms* of the particular classes of sentences with which it proposes to deal.

2. to formulate a *criterion* of validity for arguments composed of sentences belonging to these classes.

3. to devise the most economical *procedures* for deciding which of these arguments meet the criterion and hence are valid.

THE SCOPE OF DEDUCTIVE LOGIC

The logic we are about to study is modern, standard, elementary deductive logic.   It is modern as distinguished from ancient or medieval.   It is standard (or as it is now called, "classical") as distinguished from *intuitionistic* and other logics which cannot be gone into here.   It is elementary in that it is limited to 1) *sentence logic* (hereafter abbreviated as SL), which is also known as propositional logic and as the theory of truth-functions; and 2) *first-order predicate logic* (hereafter abbreviated as PL-1), which absorbs the sentential fragment into a broader and much more powerful theory of deductive inference.   Thus elementary logic does not extend to such topics as the theory of sets, second-order predicate logic, formal arithmetic, and the like.   These belong to advanced logic.

5

Sentence Logic
Sentence Forms and
Their Truth Tables

This is an introduction to sentence logic, or SL for short. SL studies a certain class of arguments in order to obtain a *criterion* that will enable us to determine which arguments belonging to that class are *valid*.

More specifically, SL may be defined as the fragment of modern logic that 1) considers certain whole unanalyzed sentences together with certain compounds formed from these sentences, and 2) constructs a theory of inference for just those arguments whose validity depends solely on whole sentences and on how these are combined into compound sentences.

There are two fundamental notions in SL: that of *truth-functional connective* (hence the practice of calling SL the theory of truth-functions) and that of *tautology*, or tautological sentence form. To grasp these notions clearly is to understand the essentials of SL.

In conducting its study, SL makes extensive use of nonverbal symbols (thus the term 'symbolic logic'). It is not too different in this respect from elementary algebra, which employs such special symbols as ' x ', ' y ', ' $+$ ', ' $=$ ', and the like.

§20   *Sentences, Sentence Connectives, Truth-Functional Compounds*

SL, like any other logical theory, deals with a particular class of arguments or, rather, forms of arguments.   To make clear which class this is, we first review the kinds of sentences (or forms of sentences) that may serve as premisses or conclusions in such arguments (or argument forms).

SENTENCES

SL does not consider sentences normally used to ask questions, make assignments, utter prayers, cheer the home team, perform ceremonies, and the like.   Examples of such sentences are

> What is the difference between a statement and a sentence?
>
> Give an example of a sentence used to issue an instruction.
>
> Forgive us our trespasses as we forgive those who trespass against us.
>
> We want a touchdown!
>
> I now confer on you the degree of Bachelor of Arts.

SL is concerned exclusively with sentences used to make statements—to say something that ordinarily can be called true or false, depending on what is the case.   Examples of these are

> It is raining.
>
> Austin is the capital of Texas.
>
> They create a desolation and they call it peace.

In a word, SL confines itself to *statement-making* sentences.

Truth-Values

We shall call a *sentence* true if the statement it is normally used to make is true, false if the statement is false.   Truth and falsity are known as *truth-values,* and to say that a sentence has the truth-value *truth* is simply to say that the sentence is true.   Sentences considered by SL have one or the other (but not both) of *two* truth-values.   For this reason, SL is referred to as a two-valued logic, in contrast to other sentence logics in which sentences may take any of three or more truth-values.

Warning: To avoid confusion, we must distinguish clearly between saying that a sentence may have either of two truth-values and saying which of the two truth-values it in fact has.   It is one thing to know that a sentence is either true or false, quite another to know that it *is* true or to know that it *is* false.   In general, it is *not* the business of logic to tell us which sentences are true and which are false.   All that is required for logic is that a statement-making sentence be regarded as something *capable* of being either true or false.

It should also be noted that SL considers simple or noncompound statement-making sentences as *wholes*.   No attempt is made *in SL* to analyze their internal structure or form.   This task is left to first-order predicate logic.

Symbols for Sentences

Like mathematics, sentence logic relies heavily on nonverbal symbols of several sorts, among them symbols for whole sentences.   For these we shall use Latin capital letters, sometimes with numerical subscripts.   In particular, we shall select

(1) $P \quad Q \quad R \quad S \quad T \quad U$ or $P_1 \quad P_2 \quad P_3 \quad P_4 \quad P_5 \quad P_6$

to serve as *sentence letters*.   They will act as *place-holders* for whole sentences in somewhat the way that "reserved for faculty" signs on seats at a commencement hold places for faculty members.

In addition, we shall use at times miscellaneous Latin capitals as convenient *abbreviations* for specified whole sentences.   For example, we might use the letter '*B*' for the sentence

(2)   Bolzano died in 1848

or the letter '*F*' for the sentence

(3)   Frege was born in 1848.

But these letters are not to be confused with sentence letters, which are stand-ins for *any* whole sentence, not abbreviations for *particular* whole sentences.

SENTENCE CONNECTIVES AND TRUTH-FUNCTIONAL COMPOUNDS

Besides whole unanalyzed sentences, SL also considers certain *compounds* formed from these sentences.

In ordinary discourse, we form all manner of compound sentences, employing for that purpose such words as 'and', 'or', 'but', 'whereas', 'while', and the like.   The grammarian calls such compounding devices "conjunctions," and they are numbered in the hundreds.

SL, however, uses only a handful of compounding devices, the so-called *SL sentence connectives*, or operators on sentences. All (but one) of these derive from familiar "conjunctions"; but none of them is, or is intended to be, a perfect analogue to its counterpart in ordinary language. The most important SL sentence connectives are those patterned on ' and ' , ' or', 'if-then' , and 'if and only if' , and on the adverb 'not '.

Truth-Functional Connectives and Truth-Functional Compounds

The SL sentence connectives are characterized by a unique property: *truth-functionality*. The notion of truth-functionality is one of the two notions crucial to SL, and requires very careful definition and illustration.

To say that a sentence connective is a *truth-functional* connective is to say that the compound sentence it forms is a *truth-functional* compound. We then define a *truth-functional compound* as a *compound sentence whose own truth or falsity depends entirely on the truth or falsity of its component sentences*, and not on anything else. In particular, the truth value of a truth-functional compound does *not* depend on 1) the content of the sentences that make it up, 2) the specific context in which the compound happens to appear, or 3) any relation of dependency that might exist between the truth-value of one component sentence and that of some other.

In other words a sentence connective is a truth-functional connective if the compound sentence it generates is a *truth-function* of its component sentences—that is, if the truth-value of the compound sentence is a *function* of (depends on in the sense that it is uniquely determined by) the truth-values of these components.

The language here reflects that of mathematics. In expressions of the form $y = f(x)$, the *numerical* value of y is said to be a *function* of the numerical value of x. To find the value of y all we need know are 1) the numerical value of x and 2) the rule that assigns to each value of x a unique value of y. For example, let $y = x^2$. Then for $x = 1$, $y = 1$; for $x = 2$, $y = 4$; and so forth.

Similarly, to find the *truth-value* of a truth-functional compound, all we need know are 1) the truth-value of its component sentences and 2) the rule that specifies in what way the truth-value of the compound depends on the truth-values of its components. The specific rule is determined by the particular sentence connective that generates the compound.

Consider, for example, the compound sentence

(4)   Life is short and art is long.

We want to show that in this sentence 'and' acts as a truth-functional connective and thus that (4) is a truth-functional compound. Now there are just four possibilities with respect to the truth or falsity of the two component sentences of (4): they may both be true, one true and the other false, one false and the other true, or both false. Here 'and' is used in such a way that we call (4) true if and only if both component sentences are true; in the other three cases, we call (4) false. Putting all this in table form, we have

'Life is short'	'Art is long'	'Life is short and art is long'
true	true	true
true	false	false
false	true	false
false	false	false

Clearly, to find the truth-value of (4) all we need know are the truth-values of its component sentences and the rule for the use of 'and'. It is not necessary to ask about the content of these components (any other pair of true-false sentences would do just as well), or the context in which (4) appears, or any possible relationship between the truth-values of the components themselves. In sum, 'and' is used here as a truth-functional connective and (4) is a truth-functional compound.

Now consider this compound sentence:

(5)   Heidegger is a physicist *or* Heisenberg is a physicist.

We now show that (5) also is a truth-functional compound. First, however, it must be noted that 'or' has two distinct uses, both of which may play a truth-functional role. These correspond respectively to the uses of the Latin words '*vel*' and '*aut*' —that is, 'or' used as 'either or both' and 'or' used as 'either but not both'.

Assume that the 'or' in (5) is the former, the *nonexclusive* 'or'. Now this 'or' is used in such a way that we call (5) false if and only if both components are false (i.e., if and only if neither German scholar is in fact a physicist); otherwise we call (5) true. The table is

'Heidegger is a physicist'	'Heisenberg is a physicist'	The compound
true	true	true
true	false	true
false	true	true
false	false	false

Again we need know only the truth-values of the components and the rule for the use of 'or' in order to find the truth-value of (5). Accordingly, (5) is a truth-functional compound.

Not all compound sentences are truth-functional compounds. Take, for instance, belief-sentences, such as

(6)   Perkins believes there is life on Mars.

Technically, (6) may be regarded as a compound sentence, since it contains a part—'There is life on Mars'—that is a sentence. But it is not a truth-functional compound. For its truth-value is not determined by the truth-value of the sentence 'There is life on Mars'. Like the rest of us, Perkins may truly believe false sentences as well as true ones. Hence (6) is not a truth-functional compound.

There are many other departures from truth-functionality in the compounds that occur in ordinary discourse. Take, for example, the sentence

(7)   If the book is blue, the book is colored.

The truth-value of (7) does to an extent depend on the truth-values of its components. But isn't there also present a certain relationship between the truth-values of the separate components themselves? If 'The book is blue' is true, is it *possible* for the sentence 'The book is colored' to be false? We shall return to this point in §35.

By way of summary, it should be emphasized again that the only compound sentences SL deals with are those generated by truth-functional connectives. And the only element of internal sentence structure it considers is the truth-functional compounding of otherwise unanalyzed sentences.

Symbols for Truth-Functional Connectives

Earlier the letters 'P', 'Q', 'R', 'S', 'T', and 'U' were introduced as place-holders for sentences. We now add a second set of symbols, those for the truth-functional connectives. The symbols

$$\& \qquad \vee \qquad \rightarrow \qquad \leftrightarrow \qquad \sim$$

will be used to stand for, respectively, the SL connectives patterned on 'and', 'or', 'if-then', 'if and only if' (often abbreviated as 'iff'), and 'not'. These five are not the only truth-functional connectives, but they are the only ones that here warrant special symbols.

EXERCISES

20.1. Which of the following would you classify as sentences normally used to make statements?

a.   Goethe or Schiller wrote *Wilhelm Tell.*

b.   Is there an odd perfect number?

c.   Barnum and Bailey were partners.

d.   If today is Tuesday, tomorrow is Wednesday.

e.   Hegel was greatly influenced by Aristotle, Spinoza, and Kant.

f.   Perkins thinks that he understands Heidegger.

g.   See me after class and I shall try again to explain the notion of truth-functional compound.

h.   The ball is foul.   (Said by the umpire)

20.2.   Which of the statement-making sentences in Exercise 20.1 are compound sentences, and which of these would you list as truth-functional compounds?

---

§21   *Truth Tables for Truth-Functional Connective Symbols*

The clearest way to *define* SL connective symbols and to *represent* SL compounds is by means of a *truth table*.   This is simply a device for listing 1) all possible different ways of assigning the truth-values—truth and falsity—to a given number of distinct sentences and 2) the particular truth-value that *each* such assignment determines for a truth-functional compound formed from these sentences.   Actually of ancient vintage, truth tables were first used explicitly and systematically in 1921 by both Wittgenstein and Emil L. Post in two independent publications.

In writing truth tables for SL connective symbols, we shall employ sentence letters rather than sentences.   This can be done because only the truth-values of the component sentences, not their content, enter into the determination of the truth-values of truth-functional compounds.   Strictly speaking, of course, it is not the sentence letter that is true or false but the sentences for which it holds a place—or rather the statements these sentences are used to make.   But it will save time and do no great harm if we allow ourselves to speak of '*P*' and '*Q*' as taking truth-values. And it will save space if we abbreviate 'true' as 'T' and 'false' as 'F'.

CONJUNCTION, DISJUNCTION

The truth tables for '&', which symbolizes the connective used to form the *conjunction* of two sentences, and '∨', which symbolizes the connective used to form the *disjunction* of two sentences, are given in Table 5.1.

The connectives so symbolized are patterned on 'and' and the nonexclusive 'or' ('or' in the sense of 'either or both'.)   Their tables contain four rows, one for each possible different assignment of truth or falsity to two sentences.   The columns headed by the two compounds list for each assignment the truth-value of the compound and thus constitute definitions or rules for the use of the two connective symbols.   Here, as later, the name of the particular truth-functional compound ('conjunction', 'disjunction', and the like) is the same as the name of the connective that generates the compound.   Thus '*P* & *Q*' is referred to as "the conjunction '*P* & *Q*'" and '*P* ∨ *Q*' as "the disjunction '*P* ∨ *Q*'."

TABLE 5.1   RULES FOR THE USE OF '&' AND '∨'

P	*Q*		*P* & *Q*	*P* ∨ *Q*
T	T		T	T
T	F		F	T
F	T		F	T
F	F		F	F

(*Note:* In listing the possible assignments of truth-values to sentence letters, the custom is to alternate T's and F's by ones under the rightmost sentence letter—in Table 5.1, '*Q*'—and by twos under the sentence letter standing directly to the left—in Table 5.1, '*P*'.   If three distinct sentence letters are involved, simply alternate by fours under the third letter to the left; if four, by eights under the fourth letter, and so on. This procedure will automatically generate all possible different assignments of truth-values to any given number of sentence letters.)

NEGATION

The symbol '∼' is used in representing the *negation* of a sentence: the sentence that is false if the original sentence is true and true if it is false. The connective or operator symbolized by '∼' is patterned on 'not', or better, 'It is not the case that'.   As can be seen in Table 5.2, its truth table contains just two rows, since the truth-value of the "compound" it forms depends on the truth-value of a single sentence component.

TABLE 5.2   RULE FOR THE USE OF '∼'

P	∼*P*
T	F
F	T

CONDITIONAL, BICONDITIONAL

The last SL connectives to be discussed are those symbolized by ' → ' and ' ↔ ', which form respectively the *conditional* of two sentences and the *biconditional* of two sentences.   These are patterned (quite roughly) on 'if-then' and 'iff' ('if and only if'), respectively.   For a variety of reasons the conditional in particular offers special difficulties.   These will be approached with caution and by stages.   For the time being, we simply present the truth tables for ' → ' and ' ↔ ' (see Table 5.3); explanation and "defense" will come in a little while.

TABLE 5.3   RULES FOR THE USE OF
' → ' AND ' ↔ '

P	Q	P → Q	P ↔ Q
T	T	T	T
T	F	F	F
F	T	T	F
F	F	T	T

Some vital information about truth-functional connectives and compounds is summarized in Table 5.4, on page 126.   As a matter of interest, other systems of notation are listed in Table 5.5.

TABLE 5.5   ALTERNATE SYSTEMS OF NOTATION

	Whitehead-Russell	Hilbert	Polish	Other
negation	$\sim P$	$\bar{P}$	Np	$\neg, -$
conjunction	$P \cdot Q$	$P \mathbin{\&} Q$	Kpq	$\wedge$
disjunction	$P \vee Q$	$P \vee Q$	Apq	
conditional	$P \supset Q$	$P \rightarrow Q$	Cpq	
biconditional	$P \equiv Q$	$P \sim Q$	Epq	$\leftrightarrow$

Note that in tables 5.1 through 5.5, connective symbols were used with single sentence letters or pairs of sentence letters.   SL connective symbols, however, may be applied not only to sentence letters to form truth-functional compounds, but also to truth-functional compounds to form additional truth-functional compounds.   For example, we may apply '&' not only to 'P' and 'Q', say, to form 'P & Q', but also to

TABLE 5.4   TRUTH-FUNCTIONAL CONNECTIVES AND COMPOUNDS

Name of Connective (and of Compound)	Symbol for Connective	Name of Symbol	Connective Patterned on	Compound Generated	Rule for Use of Connective Symbol
negation	~	tilde	'not'	'~P'	Compound is T iff the component is F; it is F iff the component is T.
conjunction	&	ampersand	'and'	'P & Q'	Compound is T iff both components are T; otherwise it is F.
disjunction	∨	wedge	'or' (non-exclusive)	'$P \vee Q$'	Compound is F iff both components are F; otherwise it is T.
conditional	→	arrow	'if-then'	'$P \rightarrow Q$'	Compound is F iff the antecedent is T and the consequent is F; otherwise it is T.
biconditional	↔	double arrow	'if and only if' ('iff')	'$P \leftrightarrow Q$'	Compound is T iff the two components have the same truth-value; otherwise it is F.

'*P* & *Q*' and '*R*', say, to form '(*P* & *Q*) & *R*', or to '*P* → *Q*' and '*Q* → *P*' to form the expression '(*P* → *Q*) & (*Q* → *P*) '.

PUNCTUATION OF SL EXPRESSIONS

Certain SL expressions, unless punctuated, can be read in more than one way. An example is ' ~*P* ∨ *Q* ', which is open to two interpretations:

1.   The negation of '*P*' disjoined with '*Q*', or ' ~*P* ∨ *Q*'.

2.   The negation of the disjunction of '*P*' with '*Q*', or ' ~ *P* ∨ *Q*'.

There are a number of ways to ensure unambiguous readings.   One is to use the Polish or parenthesis-free notation, a set of symbols for which no punctuation at all is required.   For our symbols, however, the simplest procedure seems to be

1.   To employ parentheses, supplemented on occasion by brackets or braces, with the proviso that the parentheses that surround an entire expression will be omitted (as has been done thus far) if no confusion results.

2.   To agree that the negation sign ' ~ ' extends only to the next letter (or negation thereof, in the case of an expression such as ' ~ ~*P* ') unless parentheses indicate otherwise.

These punctuation conventions permit removal of the ambiguity from the example.   The first interpretation may then be written as ' ~*P* ∨ *Q*' and the second as ' ~(*P* ∨ *Q*) '.

EXERCISES

21.1.   Write truth tables for

a.   *P* ∨ ~*Q*

b.   *P* & ~*Q*

c.   *P* → ~*Q*

d.   *P* ↔ ~*Q*

For example, the truth table for '*P* ∨ ~*Q*' is obtained as follows:

P	*Q*	~*Q*	*P* ∨ *Q*	*P* ∨ ~*Q*
T	T	F	T	T
T	F	T	T	T
F	T	F	T	F
F	F	T	F	T

21.2.   Write truth tables for the *negations* of

    a. $P \vee Q$

    b. $P \mathbin{\&} Q$

    c. $P \rightarrow Q$

    d. $P \leftrightarrow Q$

21.3.   A drill on punctuation.   Using parentheses and the convention that ' $\sim$ ' extends only to the next sentence letter (or negation thereof) unless parentheses indicate otherwise, write three different versions of

    a. $P \vee \sim Q \rightarrow R$

    b. $\sim P \mathbin{\&} Q \leftrightarrow \sim R$

21.4.   Using punctuation signs as in Exercise 21.3, write the following in symbols:

    a.   The disjunction of '*P*' with the conditional whose antecedent is ' $\sim Q$' and whose consequent is ' *R* '.

    b.   The disjunction of '*P*' with the negation of the conditional whose antecedent is ' *Q* ' and whose consequent is ' *R* '.

    c.   The conditional whose antecedent is the disjunction of '*P*' with the negation of ' *Q* ' and whose consequent is ' *R* '.

21.5.   Write truth tables for

    a. $Q \vee P$

    b. $Q \mathbin{\&} P$

    c. $Q \rightarrow P$

Compare these with the tables for '$P \vee Q$ ', '$P \mathbin{\&} Q$ ', '$P \rightarrow Q$ '.   What does this show?

21.6.   Write the truth table for

    $\sim (P \mathbin{\&} \sim Q)$

and compare it with the table for '$P \rightarrow Q$ '.

§22   *Truth-Functional Connectives and Ordinary-Language Counterparts*

The SL connectives, as noted above, do not attempt to capture all the uses of the ordinary language "conjunctions" on which they are patterned. The closeness of the fit varies from connective to connective.   In illustrating this briefly, we at the same time begin to see some of the difficulties in moving back and forth between ordinary language and the symbolism used by SL.   We also take this occasion to discuss in detail the problem of ' → ' and its relation to 'if-then'.

CONJUNCTION

In the case of 'and' and '&', the fit seems rather close.   Yet there are important differences.   For one thing, 'and' is used to join not only sentences but words or phrases, as in

(1)   Heidegger and Heisenberg are Germans.

(2)   Franklin and Eleanor are cousins.

(3)   Perkins is between the devil and the deep blue sea.

The first of these can easily be rephrased as the compound sentence

(4)   Heidegger is a German and Heisenberg is a German.

But not so the other two.   They are in fact simple sentences, and the occurrences in them of 'and' are not occurrences of a grammatical conjunction.   Furthermore, '&' is commutative—that is, '*P* & *Q*' and '*Q* & *P*' *always* have the same truth conditions.   This is not the case with all occurrences of 'and'.   Take, for instance, the sentence

(5)   Jane and Bob got married *and* Jane and Bob had a baby.

Here the italicized 'and' does serve as a conjunction, but it also carries the sense of succession in time.   It is 'and' as 'and then'.   Hence when the two sentences that form (5) are interchanged, or commuted, the compound obtained does not have the same truth conditions as the original one.

DISJUNCTION

In general, 'or' and ' ∨ ' do not offer much difficulty, once the two uses of 'or' are distinguished and disjunction is identified with the nonexclusive 'or' ('either or both'). Unlike 'and', 'or' is always commutative and uniformly serves, or can be construed as serving, to connect sentences. Moreover, the second use of 'or' ('either but not both') also has a truth-functional analogue, *alternation* (abbreviated as 'alt'). The difference between the two is expressed in Table 5.6.

TABLE 5.6

P	Q		P ∨ Q	P alt Q
T	T		T	F
T	F		T	T
F	T		T	T
F	F		F	F

NEGATION

The chief use of 'not' is to negate a sentence—that is, to construct a sentence whose truth-value is the opposite of that of the original sentence. Hence 'not' generally fits quite well with ' ~ '. But several points should be noted. First, ordinary language has many other ways of negating a sentence or denying its truth, as illustrated by the expressions "Nonsense!" and "You gotta be kidding!". Second, even the truth-functional uses of 'not' sometimes raise questions of interpretation. For example, the negation of 'Some men are rational' is not 'Some men are not rational' but 'No men are rational'. Often such difficulties can be obviated if instead of inserting the word 'not', we form the negation by simply prefixing 'It is not the case that . . .'

It should be noted that some writers on logic distinguish between the *negation* of a sentence and the *denial* of a sentence. To negate a sentence is to form its negation; to deny a sentence is to assign it the truth-value false. Thus the negation of 'It is raining' is 'It is not raining'; the denial of 'It is raining' is the statement "The sentence 'It is raining' is false." Although important in some contexts, this distinction does not enter into an informal account of SL. For in a standard two-valued logic such as SL, there is no practical difference between saying that '*P*' is false and negating '*P*'.

THE CONDITIONAL

The greatest difficulties arise in the case of 'if-then' and ' → ', due in part to terminology. The fact that '*P* → *Q*' is called a *conditional*, with '*P*' as *antecedent* and '*Q*' as *consequent*, leads us to expect a close fit between ' → ' and the most common use of 'if-then'—namely, to form such everyday conditionals as

(6)   If it rains today, Perkins takes his umbrella.

But several factors intervene to prevent such a fit.   For one thing, we use 'if-then' not only to generate various kinds of conditional sentences but in other ways as well—for example, in the sense of 'since-therefore' to indicate an argument.   For another, '→' itself does not capture *completely* even the most common uses of 'if-then', such as the one in (6).   We shall postpone to §35 a discussion of the confusions caused by other uses of 'if-then'; here we confine ourselves to examining the divergence between the truth-functional '$P → Q$' and the *ordinary* conditional.

Let us introduce a purely hypothetical connective '∗' (read 'star') with the stipulation that it is to be a faithful analogue of the ordinary 'if-then'.   With (6) as a guide, we now proceed line by line to construct a truth table for '$P ∗ Q$'.

Line 1 is no problem.   If it rains today and Perkins takes his umbrella, we count the conditional (6) as true.   In terms of sentence letters this reads

P	Q		P ∗ Q
T	T		T

Line 2 is also easy to determine.   For if it rains today and Perkins does *not* take his umbrella, we count (6) as false, or

P	Q		P ∗ Q
T	F		F

Notice that up to this point '$P ∗ Q$' coincides with '$P → Q$', and both are faithful to the ordinary conditional.

P	Q	P → Q	P ∗ Q
T	T	T	T
T	F	F	F
F	T	T	
F	F	T	

But suppose the antecedent of the conditional (6) is false—that is, suppose it doesn't rain today.   How does this affect the truth-value of (6)?   What is entered on lines 3 and 4 of the table for '$P ∗ Q$'?

If the antecedent of (6) is false, there are three possible choices:

First, we may count (6) as false, and enter F's on the last two lines of the table for '$P ∗ Q$', which would then read: TFFF.   But this won't do.

For TFFF is the truth table for 'P & Q' (see Table 5.1 above). We would simply be identifying '∗' with '&', thus making (6) read

(6′)   It rains today and Perkins takes his umbrella,

which obviously is not faithful to the ordinary use of 'if-then'. Thus the first choice in effect abandons the search for a truth-functional conditional by *abandoning the search for a conditional.*

Second, we may regard (6) as having no truth-value at all, and leave lines 3 and 4 blank. We might argue, that is, along the following lines: When we use a conditional, like (6), the statement we seek to make is addressed only to the possibility that it rains today; if it doesn't rain today, the statement simply does not apply and the sentence used to make it is neither true nor false. But in that case, if '∗' is to be faithful to 'if-then', the table for 'P ∗ Q' will have gaps and '∗' will not serve as an SL connective symbol. For remember, in order for a symbol to be an SL connective symbol, it must determine exactly one truth-value, T or F, for *each* of the possible assignments of truth-values to the sentence letters. Thus the second choice abandons the search for a truth-functional conditional by *abandoning the search for truth-functionality.*

Lastly, we may count (6) as true and enter T's for 'P ∗ Q' on lines 3 and 4. Then we do obtain a truth-functional conditional, for 'P ∗ Q' is now identical with '$P \rightarrow Q$'. Note that construed in this fashion, (6) is false *only* if it rains today and Perkins fails to take his umbrella.[1]

We may therefore conclude that if there is to be a truth-functional conditional at all, it must be '$P \rightarrow Q$'. And it will coincide with the ordinary conditional at lines 1 and 2 (whence the term 'conditional') but will in general diverge at lines 3 and 4.

In Defense of the Truth-Functional Conditional

Now that the truth-functional conditional has been described, we add a few words in its defense.

The objection is sometimes made that if we admit truth-functional conditionals, bizarre consequences follow. For the truth-value of a truth-functional conditional depends solely on the truth-values of its sentence components, and these need not be at all related in content. Consequently, not only will the sentence

(7)   If Quincy is President of the United States, then $2 + 2 = 4$

be true, but so will the sentence

(8)   If Quincy is President of the United States, then $2 + 2 = 5$.

---

[1]   (To complete the account) if we enter T on line 3 and F on line 4, we have TFTF, which simply reproduces the table for 'Q'. If we enter F on line 3 and T on line 4, we have TFFT, which is the table for '$P \leftrightarrow Q$'.

But is this consequence bizarre? Only if we mistakenly demand of truth-functional conditionals what we generally expect of ordinary conditionals—namely, that their sentence components be closely related in content. It may help us understand the difference between the two kinds of conditionals if we bear in mind that '$P \rightarrow Q$' has the same truth table as, and is therefore equivalent to, '$\sim P \vee Q$'. (The reader may wish to verify this equivalence, as an exercise.) Accordingly, if we interpret (7) and (8) as truth-functional conditionals, we may write them as

(7')   Quincy is *not* President of the United States *or* $2 + 2 = 4$.

(8')   Quincy is *not* President of the United States *or* $2 + 2 = 5$.

Both, of course, are true. And there is nothing bizarre about this.

On the positive side, we may cite in behalf of the truth-functional conditional its indispensable role in mathematics and logic. It seems that all essential uses of 'if-then' in mathematics are truth-functional or rest on truth-functionality. Moreover, the standard account of deductive validity in terms of the logical truth of the corresponding conditional (see §18) views the conditional as truth-functional.

Finally, '$P \rightarrow Q$' coincides with the ordinary conditional at lines 1 and 2, and thus shares with it what may be called the essential minimum sense of conditionality. This makes it possible to apply '$\rightarrow$' not only to the relatively few cases in ordinary discourse where 'if-then' is used purely truth-functionally, but also to the many cases where, as in (6), no harm is done if the conditional is treated as truth-functional and the gaps at lines 3 and 4 are filled in with T's. On this basis, '$\rightarrow$' has a wider range of application than might at first be supposed.

BICONDITIONAL

Once the relation between '$\rightarrow$' and 'if-then' is understood, that between '$\leftrightarrow$' and 'iff' offers no difficulty. For the biconditional '$P \leftrightarrow Q$' is only the conjunction of the two truth-functional conditionals '$P \rightarrow Q$' and '$Q \rightarrow P$', as shown in the accompanying truth table.

P Q	$P \leftrightarrow Q$	$P \rightarrow Q$	$Q \rightarrow P$	$(P \rightarrow Q)$ & $(Q \rightarrow P)$
T T	T	T	T	T
T F	F	F	T	F
F T	F	T	F	F
F F	T	T	T	T

NECESSARY AND SUFFICIENT CONDITIONS

The expressions 'sufficient condition', 'necessary condition', and 'necessary and sufficient condition' are used regularly in mathematics, often in other sciences, and occasionally even in ordinary discourse. They can be distinguished and presented with the aid of ' → ' and ' ↔ ', as follows:

SL Compound	Ordinary Language Variant	Condition Expressed
' $Q \to P$ '	' P if Q '	' Q ' is a *sufficient* condition of ' P '; if ' $Q \to P$ ' is true, then the truth of ' Q ' is sufficient to ensure the truth of ' P '.
' $P \to Q$ '	' P only if Q '	' Q ' is a *necessary* condition of ' P '; if ' $P \to Q$ ' is true, then the truth of ' Q ' is necessary for ' P ' to be true, for if ' Q ' is false, ' P ' must also be false.
' $P \leftrightarrow Q$ '	' P if and only if Q '	' Q ' is a *necessary* and *sufficient* condition of ' P ' (and ' P ' of ' Q ').

EXERCISES

22.1.   Here are some ordinary language sentences with the words ' and ', ' or ', and ' not ' (or their variants—for example, ' neither-nor '). In which of the sentences do these words occur truth-functionally—that is, as counterparts to truth-functional connectives? For each such sentence, write the corresponding symbolic expression.

    a.   Marx admired Dante and Goethe.

    b.   Quincy leaned too far over and fell in.

    c.   Neither Novalis nor Hölderlin wrote *Wilhelm Tell*.

    d.   The sum of two and four is six.

    e.   Either I am Caesar or I am nothing.

22.2.   For each of the following sentences, write the corresponding symbolic expression, treating all occurrences of ' if-then ', ' and ', ' or ', and ' not ' as truth-functional. Put ' P ' for ' The Democrats adopt a good platform '; ' W ' for ' The Democrats will win '; ' C ' for ' The Democrats name Canavan '; ' R ' for ' The Republicans name Robinson '; ' J ' for ' The Democrats name Johnson '; ' F ' for ' The Republicans name Firth '; ' I ' for 'An independent candidate will enter the field '.

    a. If the Democrats do not adopt a good platform, they will not win.

b. If the Democrats adopt a good platform and name Canavan, they will win.

c. If the Republicans name Robinson, then, if the Democrats name Johnson, the Democrats will not win.

d. If the Republicans name Firth and the Democrats name Johnson, then an independent candidate will enter the field.

22.3. An exercise on *necessary and sufficient conditions.* Suppose that Rogers graduates if and only if he earns 120 credits and completes a major. Which of the following sentences then are true?

a. Earning 120 credits is a sufficient condition for Rogers to graduate.

b. Completing a major is a necessary condition for Rogers to graduate.

c. A necessary and sufficient condition for Rogers to graduate is that he earn 120 credits.

d. Completing a major and earning 120 credits are separately necessary and jointly sufficient (conditions) for Rogers to graduate.

22.4. A continuation of Exercise 22.3. Write out symbolic expressions for the following sentences. (Put '*G*' for 'Rogers graduates'; '*E*' for 'Rogers earns 120 credits'; '*C*' for 'Rogers completes a major'.)

a–d.
Sentences *a* through *d* of Exercise 22.3.

e. Earning 120 credits is a necessary condition for Rogers to graduate.

f. Rogers graduates only if he earns 120 credits.

g. Rogers does not graduate unless he earns 120 credits.

---

§23 *Definition of SL Sentence Form*

Since SL is a formal logic, its primary concern is with sentence forms, not sentences. The notion of an *SL sentence form*, which will now be defined, spells out for SL the general notion of the logical form of a sentence (see §17):

> *An SL sentence form is an expression that 1) consists exclusively of sentence letters, symbols for truth-functional connectives, and punctuation symbols and 2) becomes a true-false sentence when distinct sentence letters are uniformly replaced by distinct true-false sentences and the connective symbols are uniformly replaced by their ordinary language counterparts.*

Any expression that satisfies condition 1 may be called an *SL expression*; any expression that satisfies both conditions 1 and 2 is called an SL *sentence form*.   For example, the following expressions are *not* SL expressions:

$$(2 + 2 = 4) \ \& \ Q \qquad P \ \$ \ Q$$

The following SL expressions are *not* SL sentence forms:

$$P \vee \qquad Q \sim \to (P \vee R)$$

But the following SL expressions *are* SL sentence forms:

$$P \qquad P \vee Q \qquad P \ \& \ Q \qquad Q \to \ \sim(P \vee R)$$

SUBSTITUTION INSTANCES OF AN SL SENTENCE FORM

A true-false sentence obtained by making appropriate replacements in an SL sentence form is called a *substitution instance* of that sentence form. Thus

(1)   Heidegger is a physicist or Heisenberg is a physicist

is a substitution instance of the SL sentence form '$P \vee Q$'.   The latter may be said to express the *logical form, according to SL*, of (1).

Note that (1) is not a substitution instance of '$P \vee P$', since the replacement of sentence letters by sentences would not then be uniform.

SYMBOLS FOR SL EXPRESSIONS

It is useful to have some way of referring to *any* SL expression—that is, to any expression consisting exclusively of sentence letters, SL connective symbols, and punctuation symbols.   To that end we introduce, as variables ranging over SL expressions, the letters

$$A \qquad B \qquad C \qquad \ldots$$

The use of these variables will be illustrated below.   But first a remark.

The Distinction Between Variables and Place-Holders

Note that the letters '*A*', '*B*', '*C*', . . . are not simply place-holders, like '*P*' or '*Q*', but variables in the strict mathematical sense.

A *variable* is a symbol that denotes *any* of a set of objects. The *members* of that set are said to be the *values* of that symbol; the *names* of members of the set are called *substituends* for the symbol. Thus in algebra the symbols '*x*', '*y*' and '*z*' are variables; their values are numbers (3, 4, and the like) and their substituends are the numerals ('3', '4', and the like) that *name* the numbers. Another example of the use of variables will crop up in a later chapter.

There is a class of symbols—often confused with variables—that we here have called 'place-holders'. These symbols, like variables, have substituends; unlike variables, however, they are not required to *denote* any of a set of objects. Thus sentence letters such as '*P*' or '*Q*' are place-holders. They have as substituends statement-making sentences, but they are not used here to denote any of a set of objects.

The distinction is motivated in part by philosophic controversies (about the "reference" of linguistic expressions) that are beyond the scope of our discussion.

VARIABLES OVER SL EXPRESSIONS

The letters '*A*', '*B*', '*C*', . . . , then, are variables. Their values are the members of the set of all SL expressions; their substituends (i.e., the expressions that may be put in place of them) are the names of SL expressions. Names of SL expressions, like the names of any expressions, may be formed by enclosing the expression in single quotation marks, which we have already done whenever we have had occasion to *mention* an expression as distinguished from using it.

Here is a typical illustration of how variables ranging over SL expressions are employed. Suppose we want to make a general statement to the effect that the negation of any SL sentence form is itself an SL sentence form. We simply write:

If *A* is an SL sentence form, so is the negation of *A*.

To obtain an instance of this general statement, we put in place of the letter '*A*' the name of an SL expression—for example, '*P*'—and we have:

If '*P*' is an SL sentence form, so is '~*P*'.

For reference purposes, the several kinds of letter symbols introduced in this section will now be listed.

1.   *P*   *Q*   *R*   *S*   *T*   *U*

These are *sentence letters* and serve only as place-holders for true-false sentences.

2.   *A   B   C   . . .*

These are *variables* ranging over SL expressions and having as substituends names of SL expressions.

3.   Miscellaneous Latin capital letters.

EXERCISES

23.1.   Which of the following expressions are SL expressions?

    a. Q

    b. $(P \lor P) = (Q \lor Q)$

    c. $P \leftrightarrow \sim Q$

    d. $[(P \& Q) \lor R] \& A$

    e. $P \sim Q$

    f. $\sim R($

    g. $P . (P \lor S)$

    h. $\sim (P \leftrightarrow Q) \leftrightarrow (P < P)$

23.2.   Which of the following SL expressions are SL sentence forms?

    a. $\& Q$

    b. $P \rightarrow (Q \rightarrow R)$

    c. $\sim \sim P \rightarrow (R \& S)$

    d. $P \sim \leftrightarrow Q$

    e. $\sim (P \& \sim Q) \rightarrow (R \& \sim S)$

    f. $\sim P(Q \rightarrow R)$

    g. $(P \rightarrow \sim P) \rightarrow \sim P$

    h. $[(P \rightarrow Q) \rightarrow R] \rightarrow S$

23.3.   For each of the SL *sentence forms* in Exercise 23.2, write an ordinary language sentence that is a substitution instance of that sentence form.

23.4. For each of the following sentences, write its sentence form according to SL.

a. Either Perkins passes the comprehensive examinations and completes an acceptable dissertation, or he does not get his Ph.D.

main break

b. If Perkins does not receive his Ph.D., he will teach part-time or try to get a research grant.

c. Perkins will get a full-time or part-time teaching position if and only if he completes his graduate course work and passes the comprehensive examinations.

d. If Perkins is awarded his Ph.D., then if he gets a job offer and the job is in the West, he will accept the offer.

e. If Perkins gets his Ph.D. and does not find a teaching job, he will try for a postdoctoral fellowship, or if that fails, he will look for work as a computer programmer.

f. If Perkins's dissertation is not accepted, then he will not get his Ph.D., and if he does not get his Ph.D., he will teach part-time if he can find a job.

g. Perkins will get his Ph.D. only if his dissertation is approved.

h. For Perkins to get a teaching position, it is a necessary condition that he have his Ph.D. or have completed his course work and passed the comprehensive examinations.

---

§24 *Truth Tables for SL Sentence Forms in General*

By definition, SL sentence forms consist entirely of occurrences of a certain number, n, of distinct sentence letters and a finite number of occurrences of SL connective symbols. It is therefore possible to construct a truth table for *any* SL sentence form and exhibit its truth-value as a function of the truth-values of its component sentence letters. The number of rows in the truth table will be 2^n, where n is the number of *distinct* letters in the sentence form. (We allow ourselves to talk of sentence forms as being "true" or "false"—just as we talk of sentence letters as being true or false.)

There are various ways to construct such tables, two of which are illustrated below. The sample SL sentence form is '$[(P \rightarrow Q) \& \sim P] \rightarrow \sim Q$'.

FIRST METHOD

We begin by listing all possible assignments of truth-values to the two sentence letters '*P*' and '*Q*' that appear in the sentence form. Next to the two letters we write the sentence form itself. Then under each occurrence of a sentence letter in the sentence form we repeat the table of that letter:

STEP 1

P	Q		$[(P \to Q)$ & $\sim P] \to \sim Q$			
T	T		T	T	T	T
T	F		T	F	T	F
F	T		F	T	F	T
F	F		F	F	F	F

We then write under each negation (if any) of a *single* sentence letter the truth table for that negation:

STEP 2

P	Q		$[(P \to Q)$ & $\sim P] \to \sim Q$			
T	T		T	T	F T	F T
T	F		T	F	F T	T F
F	T		F	T	T F	F T
F	F		F	F	T F	T F

Next we proceed to the other connectives, writing under each connective symbol the truth-value of the compound it generates. We begin with the connective symbol that generates the *smallest* compound and end with the connective symbol—called the *major* connective—whose compound is the *entire* sentence form. In this example, the order is '$P \to Q$', '$(P \to Q)$ & $\sim P$', and finally '$[(P \to Q)$ & $\sim P] \to \sim Q$'—that is, the sentence form itself.

STEP 3

P	Q		$[(P \to Q)$ & $\sim P] \to \sim Q$			
T	T		T T T	F T	F T
T	F		T F F	F T	T F
F	T		F T T	T F	F T
F	F		F T F	T F	T F

Step 4

P	Q		$[(P \rightarrow Q) \ \& \sim P] \rightarrow \sim Q$	
T	T		T T T F F T	F T
T	F		T F F F F T	T F
F	T		F T T T T F	F T
F	F		F T F T T F	T F

Step 5

P	Q		$[(P \rightarrow Q) \ \& \ \sim P] \rightarrow \sim Q$
T	T		T T T F F T T F T
T	F		T F F F F T T T F
F	T		F T T T T F F F T
F	F		F T F T T F T T F

The truth table created by Step 5 is the desired one for the sentence form. Once we are sufficiently familiar with the rules for the use of the connective symbols, we can reduce the clutter somewhat by omitting step 1.

(*Note:* Do not confuse the negation of a single letter with the negation of a compound expression. For example, if the expression ' $\sim (P \lor Q)$ ' had occurred in the sample sentence form, we would have had to enter the table for '$P \lor Q$' *before* entering the table for the negation of '$P \lor Q$'.)

SECOND METHOD

The truth table for the same SL sentence form can also be constructed by *stages*, as follows:

Step 1

P	Q		$\sim P$
T	T		F
T	F		F
F	T		T
F	F		T

Step 2

P	Q		$P \rightarrow Q$
T	T		T
T	F		F
F	T		T
F	F		T

STEP 3

P	Q	$\sim P$	$P \rightarrow Q$	$(P \rightarrow Q)\ \&\ \sim P$
T	T	F	T	F
T	F	F	F	F
F	T	T	T	T
F	F	T	T	T

STEP 4

P	Q	$\sim P$	$P \rightarrow Q$	$(P \rightarrow Q)\ \&\ \sim P$	$[(P \rightarrow Q)\ \&\ \sim P] \rightarrow \sim Q$
T	T	F	T	F	T
T	F	F	F	F	T
F	T	T	T	T	F
F	F	T	T	T	T

The last column is the desired truth table for the sentence form.

Either method can be extended to the cases of $n = 3$ or more. For example, the truth table for '$P \rightarrow (Q \vee R)$', where '$\rightarrow$' is the major connective, is

P	Q	R	$Q \vee R$	$P \rightarrow (Q \vee R)$
T	T	T	T	T
T	T	F	T	T
T	F	T	T	T
T	F	F	F	F
F	T	T	T	T
F	T	F	T	T
F	F	T	T	T
F	F	F	F	T

EXERCISES

24.1.   Write truth tables for the following SL sentence forms, indicating in each case the major connective:

a. $Q \rightarrow (Q \rightarrow P)$

b. $(P \vee \sim Q)\ \&\ (\sim P \vee Q)$

c. $\sim P \leftrightarrow (Q \vee R)$

d. $[P \rightarrow (Q \rightarrow R)] \rightarrow (P \rightarrow R)$

e. $(P \leftrightarrow Q)\ \&\ (P\ \&\ \sim Q)$

f. $[P\ \&\ (P \rightarrow Q)] \rightarrow Q$

24.2. Let '*P*' and '*Q*' stand in place of true sentences and '*R*' and '*S*' in place of false sentences.   Which of the following are true?

    a. (*P* & *R*) ∨ (*Q* & *R*)

    b. ~(*P* & *R*) ∨ *S*

    c. (*P* ∨ ~*R*) & ~(*P* & *Q*)

    d. *P* → [*Q* & ~(*R* ∨ *S*)]

    e. *R* → (*P* & *Q*)

    f. ~*R* → (*P* & *Q*)

    g. (*R* ∨ *P*) ∨ ~(*P* & *S*) ∨ (*Q* & *S*)

    h. (~*R* & *P*) → [~*P* & (*Q* ∨ *S*)]

    i. (*P* & *Q*) ∨ (*R* & *S*)

    j. (*P* & *R*) ∨ (*Q* & *S*)

    k. ~[~(*P* & *R*) & ~(*Q* & *S*)]

    l. {(*P* & ~*R*) & ~ [*Q* & (*P* & *S*)]} & ~(*P* & *R*)

24.3. For each of the following SL sentence forms, list the assignments of truth-values to '*P*', '*Q*', '*R*', and '*S*' that make the compound true.   (That is, list the lines of the truth tables on which these SL sentence forms take the truth-value true.)

    a. *P* & (*Q* ∨ *R*)

    b. *P* & ~(*Q* & ~*R*)

    c. ~*P* ∨ ~(*P* → *Q*)

    d. ~(*P* & *Q*) & ~(*Q* & *R*)

    e. (*P* & ~*Q*) → [(*Q* & *R*) → *P*]

    f. ~{[*P* & ~(*P* & *Q*)] & (*Q* ∨ *R*)}

    g. [(*P* ∨ *Q*) ∨ *R*] ∨ ~(*P* & *Q*)

    h. (*P* & ~*Q*) ∨ (*R* & ~*S*)

24.4. Using only '~' and '∨', write SL sentence forms that will have the same truth tables, respectively, as

    a. *P* & *Q*

    b. *P* → *Q*

    c. *P* ↔ *Q*

6

Sentence Logic
Argument Forms
and Their Validity:
Truth Trees

We now know exactly what kinds of sentences (or sentence forms) may serve as premisses or conclusions in sentence logic arguments (or argument forms). The next step—and the business of the present chapter—is to set up a *theory of inference* for SL argument forms. Such a theory will consist essentially of 1) a specific criterion of validity for SL argument forms and 2) some simple procedures for finding out which SL argument forms satisfy this criterion.

---

§25 *Definition of SL Argument Form*

The notion of an SL argument form spells out for SL the general notion of the logical form of an argument. The definition is

> *An SL argument form is a sequence of SL sentence forms such that, when we uniformly replace distinct sentence letters with distinct true-false sentences and uniformly replace connective symbols with their ordinary language counterparts, the result is a valid or invalid deductive argument.*

Any argument obtained by making appropriate substitutions in a particular SL argument form is called a *substitution instance* of the SL argument form.

Thus

(1) $P \vee Q$
         $\sim P$
         Therefore Q

is an SL argument form. For when appropriate substitutions are made in the sentence forms of (1), the result is an argument, say,

(1′)   Heidegger is a physicist or Heisenberg is a physicist.

         Heidegger is not a physicist.

         Therefore Heisenberg is a physicist.

On the other hand,

(2) $P \rightarrow (2 + 2 = 4)$
         P
         Therefore $2 + 2 = 4$

and

(3) $P \vee Q$
         Q

are not SL argument forms, because (2) is not a sequence of SL sentence forms and (3) does not yield an argument when appropriate substitutions are made in it.

THE RELATIONSHIP BETWEEN ARGUMENT AND ARGUMENT FORM

Many arguments may have the same form. Can the same argument have many forms? Take (1′), for instance. We may, if we wish, write its form as

(1″) P
         Q
         Therefore R,

where 'P', 'Q', and 'R', which are place-holders for true-false sentences, represent respectively the "forms" of the three sentences that enter into the argument. Thus we see that (1′) and virtually all other arguments can

—in a sense—have more than one form.   However, suppose we stipulate that all SL sentence forms are to be written out in such a way as to exhibit *all* occurrences of ordinary-language counterparts of the SL connective symbols.   Then (1′) will have just one form—namely, (1)—and we may accordingly talk of *the* form of an SL argument.

One further note.   In obtaining substitution instances from SL sentence forms, we require (see §23) that *distinct* sentence letters be replaced uniformly by *distinct* true-false sentences.   Were it not for this requirement, it would be necessary to accept as a substitution instance of the invalid argument form

(4) $P \lor Q$
          Therefore P

such an obviously valid "argument" as

It is raining or it is raining.

Therefore it is raining.

In fact, this is a substitution instance not of (4) but of the obviously *valid* argument form

$P \lor P$
Therefore P.

EXERCISES

25.1.   Which of the following expressions are SL argument forms?

a. $P \to Q$
     Q
     Therefore P

b. $5 > 4 \to P$
     $5 > 4$
     Therefore P

c. $P \to (Q \to R)$
     $P \to Q$

d. $P \leftrightarrow (Q \ \& \ R)$
     Q
     Therefore P

e. $(P = Q) \leftrightarrow (R = S)$
     $R = S$
     Therefore $P = Q$

f. $P \rightarrow (Q \rightarrow R)$
$P \rightarrow Q$
Therefore $P \rightarrow R$

g. $P \sim \rightarrow Q$
$\sim Q$
Therefore $\sim P$

25.2. For each SL argument form in Exercise 25.1, write an argument that is a substitution instance of that SL argument form.

---

§26 *Tautology in SL*

Just as truth-functionality is the key to the analysis of SL sentence forms, so the notion of *tautology* in SL is the key to the SL theory of valid inference. The basic notion of tautology is due independently to Wittgenstein and Post, and the use of the word 'tautology' in this connection to Wittgenstein.

TAUTOLOGY IN SL DEFINED
Tautology in SL can be defined in two ways:

> *1. A tautology is an SL sentence form that receives the truth-value T for all possible assignments of truth-values to its sentence letters—that is, its truth table contains only T's in the column under the major connective.*
>
> *2. A tautology is an SL sentence form all the substitution instances of which are true sentences.*

Notice how the two definitions differ. In the first, the defining property is *having all truth-values T*; in the second, it is *having all substitution instances true*. The two definitions, however, are equivalent. Any SL sentence form that is a tautology according to definition 1 will also be a tautology according to definition 2, and vice versa. For the present, we shall confine ourselves to illustrating definition 1.

First example of tautology: '$P \vee \sim P$'

P	$\sim P$	$P \vee \sim P$
T	F	T
F	T	T

Second example of tautology: '$Q \rightarrow (P \vee Q)$'

P	Q	$P \vee Q$	$Q \rightarrow (P \vee Q)$
T	T	T	T
T	F	T	T
F	T	T	T
F	F	F	T

Third example of tautology: '$[P \rightarrow (Q \rightarrow R)] \rightarrow [(P \rightarrow Q) \rightarrow (P \rightarrow R)]$'

P Q R	$[P \rightarrow (Q \rightarrow R)]$	$\rightarrow$	$[(P \rightarrow Q)$	$\rightarrow$	$(P \rightarrow R)]$
T T T	T T T T T	T	T T T	T	T T T
T T F	T F T F F	T	T T T	F	T F F
T F T	T T F T T	T	T F F	T	T T T
T F F	T T F T F	T	T F F	T	T F F
F T T	F T T T T	T	F T T	T	F T T
F T F	F T T F F	T	F T T	T	F T F
F F T	F T F T T	T	F T F	T	F T T
F F F	F T F T F	T	F T F	T	F T F

CLASSIFICATION OF SL SENTENCE FORMS

With the aid of truth tables, SL sentence forms can now be grouped into three mutually exclusive and jointly exhaustive classes, as follows:

  1. An SL sentence form is *contingent* if its truth table contains at least one T and at least one F under the major connective.

  2. An SL sentence form is *self-contradictory* (or a contradiction) if its truth table contains only F's under the major connective.

  3. An SL sentence form is *tautological* (or a tautology) if its truth table contains only T's under the major connective.

SOME SIMPLE THEOREMS ABOUT TAUTOLOGIES

Certain theorems about tautologies follow readily from these definitions. These and their proofs follow. (Recall that 'A' and 'B' are variables ranging over SL expressions; they stand for any SL expression, such as '$P \rightarrow Q$'.)

THEOREM 1. If A is a tautology, then $\sim A$ is a contradiction.[1]

---

[1] Technically, instead of writing '$\sim A$' we should either write 'the result of applying negation to A' or else use some special quotation device; the same holds for '$A \vee B$' and '$A \rightarrow B$'.

Proof. If A is a tautology, then by definition its truth table contains only T's. Now negation reverses all truth-values. Hence the negation of a tautology has a truth table containing only F's and is therefore by definition a contradiction.

THEOREM 2. If A is a tautology, then so is $A \vee B$.

Proof. If A is a tautology, then by definition its truth table contains only T's. A disjunction takes the value T if at least one disjunct is T. But A always takes T. Hence $A \vee B$ always takes T, and is thus a tautology.

THEOREM 3. If A and $A \rightarrow B$ are tautologies, so is B.

Proof. If A and $A \rightarrow B$ are tautologies, then by definition their truth tables contain only T's. Now if B were not a tautology, its table would contain at least one F. Hence there would be a line on which A takes T and B takes F. But then $A \rightarrow B$, by the definition of '$\rightarrow$', would take F on that line. This would contradict what we are given, namely, that $A \rightarrow B$ is a tautology. Hence if A and $A \rightarrow B$ are tautologies, then B too must be a tautology.

EXERCISES

26.1. Determine by truth tables whether the following are tautologies, contradictions, or contingent SL sentence forms.

    a. $(P \& Q) \rightarrow (P \vee Q)$

    b. $(\sim P \rightarrow P) \& (P \rightarrow \sim P)$

    c. $(P \vee Q) \rightarrow (P \& Q)$

    d. $\sim (P \& Q) \& (P \vee Q)$

    e. $P \rightarrow (Q \rightarrow P)$

    f. $\sim [P \& \sim (P \vee Q)] \rightarrow [Q \& \sim (Q \vee P)]$

    g. $(Q \& R) \rightarrow [(Q \vee P) \& (R \vee \sim P)]$

    h. $\sim (\{[(\sim P \vee R) \vee \sim R] \& [(\sim Q \vee \sim R) \vee R]\} \& \sim R)$

26.2. Prove the following theorems:

    a. If A and $A \leftrightarrow B$ are tautologies, so is B.

    b. If $A \& B$ is a tautology, so are A and B.

    c. If $A \vee B$ is a contradiction, so are A and B.

    d. If $\sim B$ and $A \vee B$ are tautologies, so is A.

§27   Tautology and Validity: Truth-Table Test

The definitions of tautology bring us to the heart of the matter. Tautologies play a decisive role in SL because they enable us to state a *criterion of validity* for SL arguments and argument forms.

A preliminary step in establishing this criterion is to define the corresponding conditional of an SL argument form. The corresponding conditional of an argument (see §18) is a conditional sentence whose antecedent is the conjunction of the premises of that argument and whose consequent is the conclusion. Similarly, the corresponding conditional of an SL argument form is a conditional SL sentence form obtained by taking as the antecedent the conjunction of the SL sentence forms that serve as the premises of the argument form, and as the consequent the SL sentence form that serves as the conclusion of the argument form. Thus

(1) $P \rightarrow Q$
         P
         Therefore Q

is an SL argument form.   A substitution instance of it is

(1′)   If Perkins publishes, Perkins is promoted.
         Perkins publishes.
         Therefore Perkins is promoted.

The corresponding conditional of (1) is

(2) $[(P \rightarrow Q) \& P] \rightarrow Q$.

THE CRITERION OF VALIDITY

The validity criterion for SL argument forms can now be stated:

> *An SL argument form is valid if and only if its corresponding conditional is a tautology.*

Let us first illustrate how the criterion operates with respect to SL argument forms and then how it is used to tell which SL arguments are valid. Thereafter we shall relate the criterion to the notion of logical truth according to SL and to our intuitive notions about deductive validity.

Example 1

Is the following SL argument form valid?

(3) $P \lor Q$
        $\sim P$
        Therefore Q

First construct the corresponding conditional of (3):

(4) $[(P \lor Q) \& \sim P] \rightarrow Q$.

Next construct a truth table for (4), to find out whether it is a tautology. (Note that from this point on we do not repeat the truth-values of the individual sentence letters each time the letters appear in the sentence form; instead, we only list, under the connective symbols, the truth-values of the particular compounds they generate):

P	Q		$[(P$	$\lor$	$Q) \&$	$\sim P] \rightarrow Q$	
T	T			T	F	F	T
T	F			T	F	F	T
F	T			T	T	T	T
F	F			F	F	T	T

Since its truth table contains only T's under the major connective, (4) is a tautology, and (3) is therefore a valid SL argument form.

Example 2

Is the following SL argument form valid?

(5) $P \rightarrow Q$
        Q
        Therefore P

The corresponding conditional of (5) is

(6) $[(P \rightarrow Q) \& Q] \rightarrow P$

The truth table for (6) is

P	Q		$[(P$	$\rightarrow$	$Q) \&$	$Q] \rightarrow P$	
T	T			T	T	T	
T	F			F	F	T	
F	T			T	T	F	
F	F			T	F	T	

Since its truth table does *not* contain all T's under the major connective, (6) is not a tautology, and (5) is not a valid argument form.

APPLICATION TO ARGUMENTS

We can test the validity according to SL of an argument by determining whether it is a *substitution instance* of a valid SL argument *form*. For if an SL argument form is valid, as in the case of (3), then all arguments of that form will be valid; if an SL argument form is invalid, as in the case of (5), then all arguments of that form will be invalid. (Recall that by virtue of the stipulation in §25, an argument may not be a substitution instance of more than one SL argument form.) Thus the full procedure is as follows:

> 1. Determine whether a given piece of discourse expresses an SL (that is, a truth-functional) argument.
>
> 2. If so, write down its form.
>
> 3. Construct the corresponding conditional of the argument form.
>
> 4. Test this conditional to see whether it is a tautology. If the conditional is a tautology, the argument is valid. If not, it is invalid.

The following example illustrates the procedure:

> The characteristic feature of monopoly is the absence of competition. The X Corporation knows only too well that competition abounds in each industry in which it is represented.

Step 1

This passage seems to express an SL argument. If we supply its conclusion, which is understood, we can put this argument roughly as follows:

(7)   If monopoly exists in X Corporation industries, competition is absent.

Competition is not absent.

Therefore monopoly does not exist in X Corporation industries.

Step 2

The form of this argument clearly is

(7′) $P \to Q$
        $\sim Q$
        Therefore $\sim P$.

Step 3

Construct the corresponding conditional of (7′):

(8) $[(P \to Q) \ \& \ \sim Q] \to \sim P$

Step 4

Test (8) to see whether it is a tautology.

It should be evident that for steps 1 and 2 no precise set of instructions can fully supplant human ingenuity.   But steps 3 and 4 are purely mechanical and require only the accuracy and patience of a properly programmed machine.

We now have a criterion of validity for SL and procedures for deciding which SL argument forms and arguments meet this criterion.   What remains is to show how this specific SL criterion is related 1) to our intuitive notions about validity and 2) to the general validity criterion proposed in §18.

INTUITION AND THE SL VALIDITY CRITERION

Intuitive feelings about arguments vary from person to person and argument to argument.   But if there is one constant element, it is that no argument may be regarded as valid if it takes us from true premises to a false conclusion.   In other words, in a valid argument, it must be impossible for the premises all to be true and the conclusion false.

Now this is precisely what the SL criterion guarantees.   For if an SL argument form is valid, its corresponding conditional is a tautology. Hence in no case will the antecedent of this conditional (the conjunction of the premises of the argument form) take the truth-value T while the consequent (the conclusion) takes the value F.   Thus no substitution instance of a valid SL argument form will have true premises and a false conclusion.

We can express the same result in the language of Tautology Definition 2 (§26), thereby indicating the equivalence—so far as the SL validity criterion is concerned—of the two definitions of tautology.   By definition 2, all substitution instances of tautologies are true.   By the SL validity criterion, the corresponding conditional of a valid argument is a substitution instance of a tautology.   Hence the corresponding conditional of a valid SL argument must be true—that is, in no case will its antecedent (the conjunction of the premises of the argument) be true while the consequent (the conclusion) is false.

EXPLICATION OF ‘ LOGICALLY TRUE ACCORDING TO SL ’

The essential link between the SL criterion of validity and the general criterion of deductive validity is supplied by the notion of logical truth (according to SL).   This latter can be explicated by *identifying the logical truths according to SL with the substitution instances of tautologies.*   For example,

(9) $P \lor \sim P$

as was seen above, is a tautology.   A substitution instance of (9) is

(9')   It is raining or it is not raining.

Thus (9') is a logical truth according to SL.   Again

(10) $[(P \to Q) \& P] \to Q$

is a tautology.   A substitution instance of (10) is

(10')   If [(if Perkins publishes, Perkins is promoted), and Perkins publishes], then Perkins is promoted.

Thus (10') too is a logical truth according to SL.

(A word of caution.   It is only the logical truths *according to SL* that are here identified with the substitution instances of tautologies.   A broader set of logical truths that includes those of SL will be defined in a later chapter.)

Now in §18, a general criterion of deductive validity was formulated as follows:

(11)   An argument is valid if and only if its corresponding conditional is a logical truth.

The specific criterion of validity for SL is

(12)

> *An SL argument form is valid if and only if its corresponding conditional is a tautology.*

Since all substitution instances of valid SL argument forms are valid arguments and have corresponding conditionals that are substitution instances of tautologies, (12) can then be written as

(12')

> *An argument is valid according to SL if and only if its corresponding conditional is a substitution instance of a tautology.*

By substitution, this formulation becomes

(12″)

> *An argument is valid according to SL if and only if its corresponding conditional is logically true according to SL.*

Thus when 'logical truth according to SL' is explicated as 'substitution instance of a tautology', the SL criterion of validity is clearly seen to be a special case of the general criterion of validity.

LOGICAL IMPLICATION, LOGICAL EQUIVALENCE

The term 'implies' is highly controversial in logic.   Our purpose will be served if we define it for SL in terms of two notions: SL conditional and tautology.   The definition reads: if A and B are SL sentence forms, then ' A implies B' is to mean the same as '$A \rightarrow B$ is a tautology '.

Applying this definition to specific SL sentence forms, we have

(13)   'P & Q' implies 'P'

means the same as

(14)   '$(P$ & $Q) \rightarrow P$' is a tautology.

Logical Implication and the SL Conditional

Warning: Do not confuse ' $\rightarrow$ ' and 'implies'.   The former is an *SL connective symbol* and generates an SL compound sentence form when placed between SL sentence forms, as in

(15) $(P$ & $Q) \rightarrow P$.

On the other hand, 'implies' is not an SL connective symbol but a *verb*, and when written between the *names* of sentence forms, as in (13) above, it states a certain relation between those sentence forms.   In sum, SL conditionals *are* SL sentence forms or instances thereof, whereas implications are statements *about* (in this case) SL sentence forms or *about* their instances.

We shall use the word 'implies' freely in the sense defined.   Thus if an SL argument form, say,

A
Therefore B,

is valid, we shall express this fact by saying either '*A* implies *B*' or '*A* → *B* is a tautology '.

Logical Equivalence and the SL Biconditional

If *A* and *B* are SL sentence forms, then '*A* is equivalent to *B*' is defined as '*A* ↔ *B* is a tautology '. Thus *A* implies *B* iff *A* → *B* is a tautology; and *A* is equivalent to *B* iff *A* ↔ *B* is a tautology.

Note that *A* ↔ *B* is true iff *A* and *B* have the same truth-value. Hence if *A* and *B* are *equivalent*, they *always* have the same truth-value and hence have identical truth tables. They can therefore be put in place of one another without altering the truth-value of any SL sentence form in which they may occur.

TAUTOLOGY AND SOME TRADITIONAL LAWS OF LOGIC

No explication of logical truth according to SL can be regarded as successful unless it accounts for various long-accepted laws of logic and argument forms. Some of these go back to the Stoics, some to the Middle Ages; all antedate Frege. Our explication in terms of tautology does meet the test; the following laws and forms of argument, among others, can easily be shown either to be, or to be based on, tautologies. (In stating these principles and forms, we use '*A* ', '*B* ', and '*C*' as variables over SL sentence forms.)

Some Equivalences

1. Laws for the SL Conditional
$$(A \rightarrow B) \leftrightarrow (\sim A \lor B)$$
$$(A \rightarrow B) \leftrightarrow \sim (A \mathbin{\&} \sim B)$$

2. Law of Double Negation
$$A \leftrightarrow \sim \sim A$$

3. Law of Contraposition
$$(A \rightarrow B) \leftrightarrow (\sim B \rightarrow \sim A)$$

4. Law of Exportation
$$[(A \mathbin{\&} B) \rightarrow C] \leftrightarrow [A \rightarrow (B \rightarrow C)]$$

5. De Morgan's Laws
$$\sim (A \lor B) \leftrightarrow (\sim A \mathbin{\&} \sim B)$$
$$\sim (A \mathbin{\&} B) \leftrightarrow (\sim A \lor \sim B)$$

The laws under 5) had been known to medieval logicians, but were later rediscovered and attributed to Augustus De Morgan (1806–1871). They relate negation, disjunction, and conjunction, and they follow directly from the definitions of these SL connectives: a disjunction takes the value F *only if both* of its disjuncts take F, and a conjunction takes the value F if either or both of its conjuncts take F. Hence the negation of a disjunction of two SL sentence forms will have the same truth table as the conjunction of their negations, and the negation of their conjunction will have the same truth table as the disjunction of their negations.

Noncategorical Syllogisms

Perhaps the most familiar valid SL argument forms are *modus ponens* and *modus tollens*.

Modus ponens (*affirming the antecedent*):

$A \to B$
A
Therefore B

Modus tollens (*denying the consequent*):

$A \to B$
$\sim B$
Therefore $\sim A$

These valid forms are to be distinguished from the two following *invalid* forms

$A \to B$ $A \to B$
B $\sim A$
Therefore A Therefore $\sim B$

known respectively as the *formal* fallacies of *affirming the consequent* and *denying the antecedent*.

Other frequently used SL argument forms are the disjunctive syllogism and the chain syllogism.

The disjunctive syllogism:

$A \lor B$
$\sim A$
Therefore B

The chain syllogism:

$A \to B$
$B \to C$
Therefore $A \to C$

Dilemmas

There are several kinds of dilemma, one of which is called the constructive dilemma:

$A \to B$
$C \to D$
$A \lor C$
Therefore $B \lor D$

Reductio ad Absurdum

The phrase 'reductio ad absurdum' covers the two different argument forms listed below. Examples of both will be found in the exercises. Form 2 is the basis for the method of Indirect Proof, widely applied in mathematics. An early instance is Euclid's proof that $\sqrt{2}$ is irrational.

    1. $A \rightarrow \sim A$
        Therefore $\sim A$

    2. $A \rightarrow (B \ \& \ \sim B)$
        Therefore $\sim A$

The "Three Laws of Thought"

The so-called three laws of thought, which go back to Aristotle, are the principles of identity, of contradiction, and of the excluded middle. Under one interpretation, they may be regarded as laws of logic, and in standard sentence logic they may be stated as follows:

Principle of Identity	$A \rightarrow A$
Principle of Contradiction	$\sim(A \ \& \ \sim A)$
Principle of the Excluded Middle	$A \lor \sim A$

So expressed, the principles are clearly tautologies. Notice, in passing, that with the aid of the Laws for the SL Conditional

    $A \rightarrow A$

can be rewritten as

    $\sim(A \ \& \ \sim A)$.

By De Morgan's Laws, this becomes

    $\sim A \lor \sim \sim A$

and by Double Negation

    $\sim A \lor A$

or, since ' $\lor$ ' is commutative,

    $A \lor \sim A$.

SHORTCUT TRUTH-TABLE TESTS

Since the construction of truth tables, like any mechanical task, is tedious, we naturally look for some shortcuts. An obvious one is to test for *in*validity rather than validity. An SL argument form will be invalid if its corresponding conditional is *not* a tautology—that is, if the conditional comes out F on at least one row of its truth table. And it will come out F on any row that makes the premisses of the argument form T and the conclusion F. The point then is to find out if there is such an invalidating row.

The full procedure is illustrated first for the simple case of

(16) $P \to Q$
         $\sim P$
         Therefore $\sim Q$.

As shown below, the first two rows of the corresponding truth table do not invalidate (16). But if F is assigned to 'P' and T to 'Q', both premisses of (16) will be T, the conclusion F, and the corresponding conditional, therefore, F:

Row	Letters P Q	First Premiss $P \to Q$	Second Premiss $\sim P$	Con-clusion $\sim Q$	Corresponding Conditional $[(P \to Q) \,\&\, \sim P] \to \sim Q$
1	T T	T	F	F	T
2	T F	F	F	T	T
3	F T	T	T	F	F

Thus the third row invalidates the argument form (16).

The search for an invalidating row can be speeded up and used as a general method if we conduct it as follows: 1) eliminate all rows that do not make the conclusion F; 2) eliminate all rows that do not make all the premisses T. Then if any row remains, the form is invalid. But if no row remains, the form is valid, for there is then no row that makes the premisses all T and the conclusion F. What the method amounts to is doing truth tables "in our heads," as we do simple sums.

Let us now apply the method to a more complicated SL argument form, one that involves four sentence letters and a sixteen-row table:

(17) $(P \,\&\, Q) \to R$
         $P \to S$
         Therefore $(S \,\&\, Q) \to R$.

First eliminate all rows that do not make the conclusion F. Now '$(S \,\&\, Q) \to R$' is F only if '$S \,\&\, Q$' is T and 'R' is F; '$S \,\&\, Q$' is T only if '*S*' is T and '*Q*' is T. Thus all of the sixteen rows can be discarded except these two:

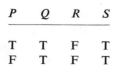

P	*Q*	*R*	*S*
T	T	F	T
F	T	F	T

Next eliminate any row that does not also make all premisses T. Now if '*P*' is T, the first premiss will be F because '*Q*' is T and '*R*' is F. We are left therefore with just one row:

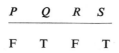

P	*Q*	*R*	*S*
F	T	F	T

Since on this row '*P*' is F, the second premiss '*P* → *S*' is T. Thus there is a row that makes the conclusion F and all the premisses T, and hence *invalidates* (17).

What happens in the case of a *valid* SL argument form? Consider

(18)   (*P* & *Q*) → *R*
        S → *P*
        Therefore (*S* & *Q*) → *R*.

As before, if the conclusion is to be F, then '*R*' must be F, and '*S*' and '*Q*' both T. Under these conditions, if the first premiss is to be T, then '*P*' must be F. But for the second premiss also to be T, since '*S*' is T, '*P*' would have to be T. But '*P*' is F. Therefore the second premiss cannot be T if the first premiss is T. Under the same conditions, any assignment of truth-values that makes the second premiss T will make the first premiss F. Thus *no* row can be found that makes the conclusion false and the premisses all true. Hence (18) is valid.

SUMMARY

This account of SL is now essentially complete. We have described how SL accomplishes, for the sentences it considers, the three tasks that a deductive logic sets itself:

1. To analyze the *forms* of a specified class of sentences. Here, *true-false sentences* and *their truth-functional compounds* have been analyzed.

2. To formulate for arguments (or argument forms) composed of such sentences (or sentence forms) a *criterion* of validity. *An SL argument form is valid iff its corresponding conditional is a tautology; an argument*

is valid according to SL iff its corresponding conditional is a substitution instance of a tautology—that is, is logically true according to SL.

3.   To devise a *procedure* for determining which arguments (argument forms) satisfy the criterion.   *Truth tables constitute a mechanical procedure for deciding just which SL sentence forms are tautologies, and hence just which arguments (argument forms) are valid according to SL.*

At this point, we could end the discussion of SL and go on to other portions of logic.   There are two reasons why we do not.

First, it is desirable to consider alternatives to truth tables as a way of doing SL.   Even with shortcuts, truth tables can be quite cumbersome.   For example, the argument form

(19) $P \rightarrow Q$
          $Q \rightarrow R$
          $R \rightarrow S$
          $P \vee U$
          $\sim S$
          Therefore U,

a textbook favorite, involves a table with 2^5, or 32, rows.   Moreover, truth tables do not reflect the mode of reasoning that seems most "natural" in such extended arguments as (19).   Nor are the tables fully applicable beyond SL, whereas the alternative procedures to be described in the next section (§28) and in Chapter 7 can be extended to elementary logic as a whole.

Second, more should be said about some of the difficulties encountered in applying SL to ordinary-language arguments (see Chapter 8).   In particular, some *non*-truth-functional uses of 'if-then' should be reviewed and distinguished more clearly from the truth-functional use.   We also need to pay our respects to the so-called paradoxes of "material implication."

EXERCISES

27.1.   For each of these SL argument forms, use the truth table of its corresponding conditional to determine whether it is valid or invalid.

a. $P \vee (\sim P \ \& \ Q)$
     Q
     Therefore $\sim P$

b. $P \rightarrow \sim Q$
     Q
     Therefore $\sim P$

c. $P \ \& \ (Q \rightarrow P)$
     $\sim P \vee Q$
     Therefore Q

d. $P \to Q$
    $R \lor \sim Q$
    $\sim R$
    Therefore $\sim P$

e. $P \lor Q$
    $\sim P \lor \sim Q$
    Therefore $(P \& \sim Q) \lor (\sim P \& Q)$

f. $(P \lor Q) \to (P \& \sim Q)$
    $\sim Q \to R$
    Therefore $P \to R$

g. $P \& Q$
    $(Q \& R) \to P$
    Therefore R

h. $P \& Q$
    $(Q \& R) \to \sim P$
    Therefore $\sim R$

i. $(P \leftrightarrow Q) \to (P \leftrightarrow R)$
    $Q \to P$
    Therefore $P \to R$

j. $(P \leftrightarrow Q) \to (P \to R)$
    $P \to Q$
    $Q \to P$
    Therefore $P \to R$

27.2.   Determine the validity of each of these arguments by determining through truth tables the validity of the SL argument form of which it is a substitution instance.

a.   If Frege was correct, sense differs from reference.
Sense does differ from reference.
Therefore Frege was correct.

b.   You will understand Kant only if you understand Hume.
Therefore if you don't understand Hume, you won't understand Kant.

c.   If the Democrats adopt a good program, they will name Canavan.
If they name Canavan, they will win.
Therefore if the Democrats adopt a good program, they will win.

d.   If Rogers earns 120 credits and completes a major, he graduates.

Hence if he earns 120 credits, he graduates if he completes a major.

e. Unless Perkins completes his dissertation and it is accepted, he will not be reappointed.
If he completes his dissertation, it will be accepted.
Hence if he completes his dissertation, he will be reappointed.

f. If Perkins is reappointed iff his dissertation is accepted, then he is reappointed iff his dissertation makes a contribution to scholarship.
If Perkins's dissertation is accepted, he is reappointed.
Therefore if Perkins is reappointed, his dissertation makes a contribution to scholarship.
(Compare *f* with *i* in Exercise 27.1.)

27.3. The following passages, some from earlier exercises, may be interpreted as containing SL arguments. For each such argument, 1) write the premisses and conclusion of the argument, 2) write the SL argument form of which the argument is a substitution instance, and 3) test the corresponding conditional of that SL argument form to see if the conditional is a tautology, and hence if the argument is valid. (Remember that you may have to supply premisses or conclusions from the context.)

a. "If we can go fusion for Lindsay," the Liberal Party source said, "then there's a contest. If we can't go fusion for Lindsay, it becomes a one-way affair. So if we go independent or take a Democrat, the election is over right now." [*New York Post*, April 14, 1969]

b. Dr. Urey, reached by telephone last evening, said that it should have been obvious that the bombardment that has so heavily cratered the moon took place early in its lifetime. If the moon and earth had been subjected to a uniform rate of impacts up to the present, there would be far more evidence of cratering on the earth. [*The New York Times*, August 25, 1969]

c. "I don't think you can conclude that the United States, by not sending an ambassador, is saying that it does not approve of the Government of Sweden," Mr. Palme said. "To argue this is to argue that the United States does approve of the Governments in Greece, South Africa, Spain and Bulgaria, where it does have ambassadors." [Olof Palme, then Premier-designate of Sweden, quoted in *The New York Times*, October 2, 1969]

d. Either Thieu implements the Paris agreements and loses, or he refuses to implement them and he loses. [A North Vietnamese, quoted in *The New York Times*, February 18, 1974]

e. As for instance: "If you had borrowed and not paid, you owe me money; but you have not borrowed and not paid; therefore you do not owe me money." [*The Discourses of Epictetus*, Ch. VIII]

f. Let me get this straight. In order to be grounded I have to be crazy. And I must be crazy to keep flying. But if I ask to be grounded—that means I'm not crazy and I have to keep flying. [Yossarian, in the Joseph Heller book and movie, *Catch 22*, quoted from *The New York Times Magazine*, March 16, 1969]

27.4. Exercise on logical equivalence. Here are pairs of SL sentence forms. Determine by truth tables which (if any) are pairs of *equivalent* sentence forms.

    a. $\sim(P \ \& \ Q), \ \sim P \ \lor \ \sim Q$

    b. $\sim P \to \sim Q, \ Q \to P$

    c. $(P \ \& \ Q) \to R, \ P \ \& \ (Q \to R)$

    d. $(P \ \& \ Q) \to R, \ P \to (Q \to R)$

    e. $P \to (Q \to R), \ (P \to Q) \to R$

27.5. For each of the following logical "principles" write an ordinary-language sentence (or argument) to illustrate the principle (see §27):

    a. Law of the Excluded Middle.

    b. Laws for the Conditional.

    c. Law of Contraposition.

    d. Law of Exportation.

    e. De Morgan's Laws.

    f. *Reductio ad absurdum* (two forms).

For example: Law of Double Negation $A \leftrightarrow \sim \sim A$

   Illustration: It is raining iff it is not the case that it is not raining.

27.6. Use the shortcut test for *in*validity to determine whether the SL argument forms in Exercises 27.1 and 27.2 are valid or invalid.

§28   *Validity: Truth-Tree Test*

This section will deal with the first of two alternatives to truth tables as a way of testing the validity of SL argument forms. This alternative employs what are called "*truth trees.*" The second, which is discussed in Chapter 7, is known as *natural deduction* and makes use of a system of rules of inference.

Each method has its advantages, each its advocates. Truth trees are no doubt simpler to manage and hence easier to master. On the other hand, a natural deduction system conveys a clearer notion of the whole process of deductive inference and reasoning.

TRUTH TREES[2]

The idea behind truth trees is one with which we are already familiar. It underlies the shortcut test for *in*validity described just above. To test for invalidity, we see if we can assign truth-values to the sentence letters of an SL argument form in such a manner that the premisses all come out T and the conclusion F. If an assignment of this sort is possible, we then have a *counterexample* to the claim that the argument form is valid. For in a valid argument form it is *impossible* for the premisses all to take T while the conclusion takes F. Truth trees, as we shall see, are essentially a device to *organize* the search for a counterexample.

In the truth-tree procedure we begin by *assuming* that the argument form is *invalid*. To express this assumption, we assign the truth-value T both to the premisses of the argument form and to the *negation* of its conclusion. We then develop the consequences of this assumption. If the assumption of invalidity leads to *contradiction*, then the argument form is *valid*. If not, we have a *counterexample*, and the argument form is shown to be *invalid*.

Suppose we are asked to test the validity of the argument form

(1) $P \rightarrow Q$
        $Q \rightarrow R$
        Therefore $P \rightarrow R$.

The first step is to list the premisses together with the *negation* of the conclusion:

---

[2]   This account of the truth-tree procedure for SL is adapted from Richard C. Jeffrey, *Formal Logic: Its Scope and Limits* (New York: McGraw-Hill, 1967), pp. 64–74.

1. $P \to Q$

2. $Q \to R$

3. $\sim(P \to R)$

These make up the "trunk" of the "tree."

Note: In the truth-tree method, to list a sentence form is to assign it the truth-value T.   Thus to list the premises of (1) and the negation of its conclusion is to *assume* that it is possible for the premises all to take T while the conclusion takes F.

We then set about unpacking the information contained in the trunk. This is done by listing, one below the other, the items obtained from each of the initial sentence forms.   As this information is entered, the tree grows—downward.   Once a sentence form is unpacked, it is checked off.

Let us start the process with line 3.   By the truth tables for the connective symbols ' $\sim$ ' and ' $\to$ ', the sentence form ' $\sim(P \to R)$ ' takes the truth-value T iff ' P ' takes the value T *and* ' R ' the value F (that is, if ' $\sim R$ ' takes T).   We enter the information thus obtained on lines 4 and 5 and check off ' $\sim(P \to R)$ ':

3. ✓ $\sim(P \to R)$

4. P

5. $\sim R$

Next we unpack the sentence form on line 2.   Here the tree *branches*. For ' $Q \to R$ ' takes the value T iff ' $\sim Q$ ' takes the value T *or* ' R ' takes the value T (where the 'or' is *non*exclusive).   This information is then entered on line 6 in the following manner:

2. ✓ $(Q \to R)$

3. ✓ $\sim(P \to R)$

4. P

5. $\sim R$

6. $\sim Q$ R

Now observe that the path going down from the trunk through ' P ', ' $\sim R$ ', and ' R ' contains *contradictory information*—a sentence letter *and* its negation.   Any such path is closed off at once with an X, thus:

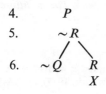

4. P

5. $\sim R$

6. $\sim Q$ R

                X

The construction is finished when we unpack '$P \to Q$' on line 1. For a tree is complete when *all* occurrences of the *binary* connective symbols ('$\to$', '$\vee$', '$\&$', '$\leftrightarrow$') are eliminated in favor of sentence letters or their negations.   Since '$P \to Q$' takes T iff '$\sim P$' takes T *or* 'Q' takes T, the tree branches again and we have the finished tree:

1.	$\checkmark P \to Q$	Premiss
2.	$\checkmark Q \to R$	Premiss
3.	$\checkmark \sim(P \to R)$	Negation of the conclusion
4.	P	From line 3
5.	$\sim R$	From line 3
6.	$\sim Q \quad R$	From line 2
	$\quad\quad X$	
7.	$\sim P \quad Q$	From line 1
	$X \quad X$	

Notice that now every path has been closed off with X's.   Each contains contradictory information.   Thus the assumption that the argument form is *in*valid has led to contradiction, and we have proved that the argument form is *valid*.

In contrast, consider a case in which at least one path in a completed tree remains open.   Take, for example, the argument form

(2) $P \to Q$
         Q
         Therefore P

Its truth tree is

1.	$\checkmark P \to Q$	Premiss
2.	Q	Premiss
3.	$\sim P$	Negation of the conclusion
4.	$\sim P \quad Q$	

Here both paths remain open.   Now an *open* path in a completed tree signifies that *no* contradictory information is to be found along that path. Thus it is indeed possible—without generating a contradiction—to assign the truth-value T to all the premisses of the argument form *and* to the negation of its conclusion.   In short, the original assumption of *invalidity* is sustained, and we have a *counterexample* to the claim of validity.

The Truth-Tree Rules

The rules that govern the unpacking process are based on the truth-table definitions of the SL connective symbols. They may be formulated as follows (where *A* and *B* are *any* SL sentence forms):

RULE 1:   Since $A \rightarrow B$ takes the truth-value T iff $\sim A$ takes the value T *or B* takes the value T, it is unpacked as

RULE 2:   Since $A \vee B$ takes T iff *A* takes T *or B* takes T, it is unpacked as

RULE 3:   Since A & B takes T iff *A* takes T *and B* takes T, it is unpacked as

RULE 4:   Since $A \leftrightarrow B$ takes T iff *A* and *B* both take T *or* $\sim A$ and $\sim B$ both take T, it is unpacked as

RULE 5:   Since $\sim(A \rightarrow B)$ takes T iff *A* takes T *and* $\sim B$ takes T, it is unpacked as

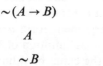

RULE 6:   Since $\sim(A \lor B)$ takes T iff $\sim A$ takes T *and* $\sim B$ takes T, it is unpacked as

$$\sim(A \lor B)$$
$$\sim A$$
$$\sim B$$

RULE 7:   Since $\sim(A \& B)$ takes T iff $\sim A$ takes T *or* $\sim B$ takes T, it is unpacked as

RULE 8:   Since $\sim(A \leftrightarrow B)$ takes T iff A and $\sim B$ both take T *or* $\sim A$ and B both take T, it is unpacked as

$$\sim(A \leftrightarrow B)$$

$$A \quad \sim A$$

$$\sim B \quad\quad B$$

RULE 9:   Write A wherever $\sim\sim A$ appears.   (This is the Cancellation Law for negation.)

Note that of the eight rules for binary connective symbols, five are *branching* rules and three are not.   Observe, too, that an unpacking rule will branch if and only if the corresponding sentence form has more than one T in its truth table.

TRUTH TREES VERSUS TRUTH TABLES

Truth trees have several advantages over truth tables as a means of testing the validity of argument forms.   For one thing, they may be applied not only in SL but also in elementary logic as a whole (see Chapter 9), whereas truth tables can be used generally only in SL.   For another, they are more economical.   This difference becomes quite obvious when we are asked to test the validity of argument forms that involve more than two or three distinct sentence letters.

Consider, for example, the SL argument form

(3) $P \to \sim Q$
          $\sim Q \to R$
          $\sim R \lor S$
          $(S \lor T) \to U$
          Therefore $P \to U$

A truth-table test for the validity of (3) would require a table with $2^6 =$ 64 rows! It is much easier—if still somewhat tedious—to use a truth tree as follows:

1.	$\checkmark P \rightarrow \sim Q$	Premiss
2.	$\checkmark \sim Q \rightarrow R$	Premiss
3.	$\checkmark \sim R \vee S$	Premiss
4.	$\checkmark (S \vee T) \rightarrow U$	Premiss
5.	$\checkmark \sim (P \rightarrow U)$	$\sim$ (conclusion)
6.	P	From 5 Rule 5 $\sim (\rightarrow)$
7.	$\sim U$	From 5 Rule 5 $\sim (\rightarrow)$
8.	$\checkmark \sim (S \vee T)$ U / X	From 4 Rule 1 $(\rightarrow)$
9.	$\sim S$	From 8 Rule 6 $\sim (\vee)$
10.	$\sim T$	From 8 Rule 6 $\sim (\vee)$
11.	$\sim R$ S / X	From 3 Rule 2 $(\vee)$
12.	Q R / X	From 2 Rule 1 $(\rightarrow)$
13.	$\sim P$ $\sim Q$ / X X	From 1 Rule 1 $(\rightarrow)$

Notice that at line 12 we used the Cancellation Law for negation: we wrote 'Q' in place of '$\sim \sim Q$'.

TIPS AND CAUTIONS ON THE USE OF TRUTH TREES

In constructing truth trees, we can save ourselves a lot of trouble if we bear in mind the following points:

First, although the unpacking order is arbitrary, it is usually good economy to apply the *non*branching rules *first*, if possible. Otherwise the trees thicken needlessly, since the results of later applications of the unpacking rules must be entered on each branch (see Example 1).

Second, the unpacking process is complete only when *every* binary connective symbol has been eliminated in favor of sentence letters and their negations. Hence SL sentence forms with two or more occurrences of binary connective symbols will require a series of unpackings (see Example 2).

Third, the unpacking rules may be applied only to whole sentence forms, not to parts of sentence forms (see Example 3).

Example 1

Let us go back to the argument form (1) with which we began. But this time we apply a *branching* rule first. Line 1 is unpacked, producing the branches shown in line 4. The branches produced by unpacking line 2 must then be shown in line 5 under each branch that appears in line 4. The information obtained from line 3 must now be entered three times—once for each branch that still remains open on line 6.

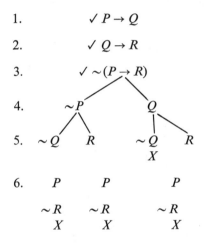

1.	✓ $P \to Q$
2.	✓ $Q \to R$
3.	✓ $\sim(P \to R)$

The tree, of course, still shows (1) to be valid. But by using a branching rule first (to produce lines 4 and 5), we have needlessly added to our labors. The earlier tree for (1) has six occurrences of 'Ps' 'Qs' and 'Rs' on lines 4 through 7, whereas the present version requires twelve.

Example 2

The truth tree for the following argument form illustrates how truth-tree rules are applied to sentence forms with two or more occurrences of binary connective symbols.

(4) $P \to (Q \to R)$
       Therefore $(P \to Q) \to (P \to R)$

The truth tree for (4) is

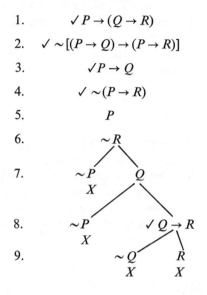

1. $\checkmark P \rightarrow (Q \rightarrow R)$
2. $\checkmark \sim[(P \rightarrow Q) \rightarrow (P \rightarrow R)]$
3. $\checkmark P \rightarrow Q$
4. $\checkmark \sim(P \rightarrow R)$
5. P
6. $\sim R$
7. $\sim P$ Q
               X
8. $\sim P$ $\checkmark Q \rightarrow R$
               X
9. $\sim Q$ R
                   X X

Thus (4) is valid.   Notice that the unpacking process was continued until *every* binary connective symbol was eliminated.

Example 3

The error of applying an unpacking rule to part of a sentence form is illustrated by an attempt to determine whether the following argument form is valid:

(5) $\sim[(P \rightarrow Q) \; \& \; (Q \rightarrow P)]$
        P
        Therefore $\sim Q$

It is incorrect to construct the truth tree for (5) as

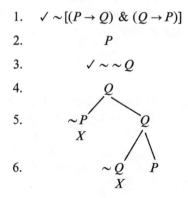

1. $\checkmark \sim[(P \rightarrow Q) \; \& \; (Q \rightarrow P)]$
2. P
3. $\checkmark \sim \sim Q$
4. Q
5. $\sim P$ Q
               X
6. $\sim Q$ P
                   X

Unpacking rule for $A \rightarrow B$ mis-applied to '$P \rightarrow Q$', which is only a *part* of line 1. The mistake is repeated for '$Q \rightarrow P$'

The proper tree for (5) is

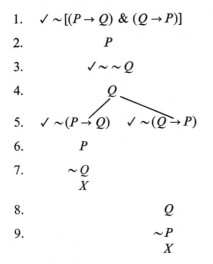

1.   ✓ ~[(P → Q) & (Q → P)]
2.   P
3.   ✓ ~ ~ Q
4.   Q
5.   ✓ ~(P → Q)   ✓ ~(Q → P)
6.   P
7.   ~Q
          X

8.   Q
9.   ~P
                           X

in which all paths close.

THE TRUTH-TREE TEST FOR TAUTOLOGY

An SL sentence form is a tautology iff its negation is a contradiction. Hence to determine whether an SL sentence form is a tautology, we simply construct a truth tree for its negation. If all paths close, then the sentence form is a tautology, otherwise it is not. Some examples follow.

Example 4

Determine whether the SL sentence form

(6)   P → (Q → P)

is a tautology.   Its truth tree is

1.   ✓ ~[P → (Q → P)]
2.   P
3.   ✓ ~(Q → P)
4.   Q
5.   ~P
             X

The single path closes; hence (6) is a tautology.

Example 5

Consider now the sentence form

(7) $P \rightarrow (P \rightarrow Q)$

Its truth tree is

1.   ✓ $\sim[P \rightarrow (P \rightarrow Q)]$

2. P

3.   ✓ $\sim(P \rightarrow Q)$

4. P

5. $\sim Q$

The path fails to close; hence (7) is not a tautology.

Example 6

Determine whether the SL sentence form

(8) $[(P \rightarrow Q) \,\&\, (Q \rightarrow R)] \rightarrow (P \rightarrow R)$

is a tautology.   Its truth tree is

1.   ✓ $\sim\{[(P \rightarrow Q) \,\&\, (Q \rightarrow R)] \rightarrow (P \rightarrow R)\}$

2.   ✓ $(P \rightarrow Q) \,\&\, (Q \rightarrow R)$

3.   ✓ $\sim(P \rightarrow R)$

4. P

5. $\sim R$

6.   ✓ $P \rightarrow Q$

7.   ✓ $Q \rightarrow R$

8. $\sim Q$ R
                           X

9. $\sim P$ Q
        X X

Thus (8) is a tautology.

   Now an argument form is *valid according to SL* iff its corresponding conditional is a *tautology*. Hence since (8) is the corresponding conditional of the argument form (1), the tree for (8) also tests the validity of (1).

EXERCISES

28.1. Determine by truth trees which of these SL argument forms are valid.

a–j.
  Argument forms *a* through *j* from Exercise 27.1.

k. $P \to (Q \to R)$
  Q
  Therefore $\sim R \to \sim P$

l. $R \lor (S \,\&\, \sim T)$
  $(R \lor S) \to (U \lor \sim T)$
  Therefore $T \to U$

m. $[(P \lor Q) \,\&\, (R \lor S)] \to T$
  $\sim P \,\&\, \sim R$
  Therefore $Q \to T$

n. $(P \,\&\, \sim Q) \to [(R \lor S) \to (T \to U)]$
  $P \,\&\, (R \lor S)$
  Therefore $\sim Q \to (T \to U)$

o. $N \to M$
  $M \to D$
  $M \to P$
  $\sim P$
  $M \lor N$
  Therefore D

28.2. Here is a set of SL argument forms that you are also to test for validity by the truth-tree method. Notice that *a* differs from *c*, and *b* differs from *d*, only in their first premisses; and that *a* differs from *b*, and *c* differs from *d*, only in their second premisses. See if you can explain why the tests result as they do.

a. $(P \,\&\, Q) \to R$
  $S \to P$
  Therefore $(S \,\&\, Q) \to R$

b. $(P \,\&\, Q) \to R$
  $P \to S$
  Therefore $(S \,\&\, Q) \to R$

c. $(P \to Q) \to R$
  $S \to P$
  Therefore $(S \,\&\, Q) \to R$

    d. $(P \rightarrow Q) \rightarrow R$
        $P \rightarrow S$
        Therefore $(S \ \& \ Q) \rightarrow R$

    e. $(P \rightarrow Q) \rightarrow R$
        Therefore $(S \ \& \ Q) \rightarrow R$

28.3. Determine by truth trees whether these SL sentence forms are tautologies:

    a. $(P \rightarrow Q) \rightarrow (\sim Q \rightarrow \sim P)$

    b. $[P \rightarrow (Q \ \& \ \sim Q)] \rightarrow \sim P$

    c. $(P \rightarrow \sim P) \rightarrow P$

    d. $(P \ \lor \ \sim P) \lor (R \ \& \ S)$

    e. $[(P \ \& \ Q) \rightarrow R] \rightarrow [P \ \& \ (Q \rightarrow R)]$

    f. $[P \ \& \ (Q \rightarrow R)] \rightarrow [(P \ \& \ Q) \rightarrow R]$

    g. $[(P \ \& \ Q) \rightarrow R] \leftrightarrow [P \rightarrow (Q \rightarrow R)]$

    h. $[P \rightarrow (Q \rightarrow R)] \leftrightarrow [(P \rightarrow Q) \rightarrow R]$

    i. $(P \ \& \ \sim P) \ \& \ (Q \ \lor \ R)$

    j. $[(P \rightarrow Q) \ \& \ (Q \rightarrow R)] \rightarrow (P \rightarrow R)$ For *j* use only the rules for $\sim(A \rightarrow B)$, $A \rightarrow B$, and the Cancellation Law for negation.

28.4. Use truth trees to test the validity of the SL argument forms of which the following arguments are substitution instances.

    a. Argument *a* from Exercise 27.3.

    b. If the college admits a substantial number of nontraditionally prepared students, it will fail in its obligation to these students unless it assures them supplemental instruction.
The college cannot assure them supplemental instruction.
Hence if the college is not to fail in its obligation to these students, it must deny them admission.

    c. If the college admits a substantial number of nontraditionally prepared students, it will fail in its obligation to these students unless it assures them supplemental instruction.
The college will not fail in its obligation to these students.
Hence the college must deny them admission.

d. If the college admits a substantial number of nontraditionally prepared students, it will fail in its obligation to these students unless it assures them supplemental instruction.
The college will (has a duty to) admit a substantial number of nontraditionally prepared students.
The college will not fail in its obligation to these students.
Hence the college must assure them supplemental instruction.

e. If the Democrats name Johnson or Walton and the Republicans name Rockwell, then the Democrats will not win even if they adopt a good program.
The Democrats will adopt a good program.
The Republicans will name Rockwell.
Therefore if the Democrats name Johnson or Walton, they will not win.

f. If the Democrats adopt a good program and name Canavan and the Republicans name Firth or Rawlings, the Democrats will win.
The Democrats will adopt a good program.
The Republicans will name Firth or Rawlings.
Therefore if the Democrats name Canavan, they will win.

g. If the Democrats name Johnson or Walton and the Republicans name Firth or Rawlings, a third candidate will enter the field.
The Democrats will not name Walton.
The Republicans will not name Rawlings.
Therefore if the Democrats name Johnson and the Republicans name Rawlings, a third candidate will enter the field.

h. If the gods exist, and they do not declare to men beforehand what future events will be, then either they do not love men, or they do not know what future events will be, or they judge that it is of no importance to men to know what the future will be, or they think it is not consonant with their dignity to preannounce to men what future events will be, or the gods, though they be gods, cannot reveal what future events will be. But it is not the case that they do not love us, for they are beneficent friends of the human race; nor is it the case that they are ignorant of the things which they themselves form and design; nor is it of no importance for us to know those things which will happen in the future, for we shall be more careful if we know; nor does giving signs of the future comport badly with their dignity, for there is nothing more excellent than kindness; nor is it the case that they cannot reveal what future events will be. Therefore it is not true that there are gods and that they do not give signs of future events. But there are gods.   Therefore it is not the case that they do not give signs (i.e., they do give signs).   [Chrysippus, *ca.* 279–206 B.C., quoted in Josiah B. Gould, *The Philosophy of Chrysippus*, 1970, p. 86]

Hint: The SL argument form for *h* requires seven distinct sentence letters.

7

Sentence Logic Argument Forms and Their Validity: Derivations

The second alternative to truth tables as a way of doing sentence logic makes use of a *set of rules* that specify which SL sentence forms may be *inferred* from which others. An SL *argument form* will then be valid if it is possible, applying just these rules, to construct a *derivation* of its conclusion from its premisses.

Systems made up entirely of such sets of inference rules are called *natural deduction systems*. They were first proposed for SL and other areas of logic in 1934 in separate publications by the logicians Stanislaw Jaskowski and Gerhard Gentzen. The earlier systems of deduction for SL, such as those of Gottlob Frege and Bertrand Russell, had relied on a combination of logical "axioms" and rules of inference.

§29   Natural Deduction Derivations in General

Suppose we are asked to determine the validity of an SL argument form with a number of premisses, such as

(1) $P \rightarrow Q$
$Q \rightarrow R$
$R \rightarrow S$
$P \vee U$
$\sim S$
Therefore U.

We could, of course, construct a thirty-two-row truth table and test the corresponding conditional of (1) to see if it is a tautology.   More economically, we could fashion a truth tree.

But another and perhaps more "natural" alternative is to proceed as follows: From the first two premisses '$P \rightarrow Q$' and '$Q \rightarrow R$', we obtain the conclusion '$P \rightarrow R$', because the SL argument form

(a)
_____

$P \rightarrow Q$
$Q \rightarrow R$
Therefore $P \rightarrow R$

is valid,   Likewise, we obtain '$P \rightarrow S$' because

$P \rightarrow R$
$R \rightarrow S$
Therefore $P \rightarrow S$

is valid.   Now consider '$P \rightarrow S$' and '$\sim S$'.   Since the argument form

(b)
_____

$P \rightarrow S$
$\sim S$
Therefore $\sim P$

is valid, we now have '$\sim P$'.   Finally, the premisses '$\sim P$' and '$P \vee U$', by virtue of the valid argument form

----

(c)

$P \lor U$
$\sim P$
Therefore U,

give us ' U '.   We thus conclude that the SL argument form (1) is valid.

Let us now see exactly what we did.   First, how was the validity of (1) established?   This was done not by truth trees or by truth tables, but by deriving the conclusion step by step from the premisses, just as a theorem in a geometry is deduced from the axioms and postulates.   Thus we made use of a different criterion of validity for SL—one defined in terms not of *tautological conditionals* but of *derivations*.   And this is indeed the first essential idea in natural deduction: *that an argument form is to count as valid if and only if its conclusion can be obtained in a specified way from its premisses.*

Second, how was the conclusion ' U ' obtained?   In effect, (1) was broken down into a sequence of simple argument forms, each of which served to sanction a step in the derivation.   But we were still thinking of the validity of these simple argument forms as being determined by truth tables.   In order to complete the transition to natural deduction, we must now replace these elementary *valid argument forms*, such as

(2) $P \lor U$
          $\sim P$
         Therefore U,

with corresponding *rules of inference*.   In the case of (2) the rule will be

         from ' $P \lor U$ ' and ' $\sim P$ '
         to infer ' U ',

or, where A and B are *any* SL sentence forms,

         from $A \lor B$ and $\sim A$
         to infer B.

Here we reach the second essential idea of natural deduction: *that the steps allowed in a derivation are just those provided for by a specified set of inference rules.*

INFERENCE RULES AND ARGUMENT FORMS

Let us dwell for a moment on the relationship between

(3) $A \to B$
          A
         Therefore B,

which represents a class of SL argument forms, and

(4)   from $A \rightarrow B$ and A
       to infer B,

which is a rule sanctioning a class of inferences.   To adopt inference rule (4) is to declare valid the instances of (3); conversely, to establish that the instances of (3) are valid is in effect to adopt inference rule (4). Although the relationship between (3) and (4) is very close, it is not one of identity.   An argument form is a sequence of sentence forms that becomes an argument when suitable substitutions are made; a rule of inference is a "license" that allows us to draw conclusions of a certain form when we have prem-isses of a certain form.   Gilbert Ryle has compared the difference between inference rule and argument form to the difference between a ticket and a trip.[1]   For instance, a ticket from Berkeley, California, to Cambridge, Massachusetts, does not put us on bus or plane, but it does entitle us to take the trip.   Similarly, an inference rule does not supply us with premises, but it does entitle us, *if* we have the premises, to draw appropriate conclusions.

SYSTEMS OF INFERENCE RULES: SOUNDNESS AND COMPLETENESS

If inference rules are to constitute a system serving as an alternative to truth tables and truth trees, then certain conditions should be satisfied. First, the system must be *sound*—that is, the rules must be so chosen that they *never* take us from true premises to false conclusions.   Second, the system should be *complete*—that is, the rules should be so chosen that they take us from true premises to all the true conclusions that follow. Thus a rules system that is sound and complete will give us *all* and *only* the true conclusions that follow from any given set of true premises.

EXERCISES

29.1.   Using only the three rules corresponding to the elementary valid argument forms (*a*), (*b*), and (*c*) introduced at the beginning of this section, show that the following SL argument forms are valid:

a. $P \rightarrow Q$
     $R \vee \sim Q$
     $\sim R$
     Therefore $\sim P$

---

[1]   Gilbert Ryle, "'If', 'So', and 'Because'," in *Philosophical Analysis*, edited by Max Black (New York: Prentice-Hall, 1950), pp. 307 ff.

b. $P \rightarrow Q$
$Q \rightarrow (R \lor S)$
Therefore $P \rightarrow (R \lor S)$

c. $P \lor (Q \rightarrow R)$
$Q \lor \sim P$
$\sim Q$
Therefore $Q \rightarrow R$

d. $R \rightarrow Q$
$Q \rightarrow P$
$P \rightarrow S$
$\sim S$
Therefore $\sim R$

e. $P \rightarrow Q$
$Q \rightarrow R$
$P \lor \sim S$
$\sim R$
Therefore $\sim S$

---

§30   *Validity, Derivation, and Derivability-in-SN*

In natural deduction systems the validity of an argument form is defined in terms of derivation.   Now let SN be a list of inference rules constituting a natural deduction system for sentence logic.   We shall define the notions of validity, derivation, and derivability relative to the system SN.

VALIDITY

In SN, the criterion of validity for SL argument forms takes the form

(1)

> *An SL argument form is valid if and only if there is a derivation in SN of its conclusion from its premisses.*

DERIVATION

Let $A_1, \ldots, A_n, B$ be SL sentence forms.   Then a derivation in SN of B from the set of premisses $\{A_1, \ldots, A_n\}^2$ is a column of SL sentence forms such that

> 1.   Each entry in the column is either a premiss or may be inferred from preceding entries in the column by virtue of one of the inference rules of SN.

> 2.   The last entry in the column is B.

Derivability-in-SN

To say that an SL sentence form B is derivable-in-SN from a set of SL sentence forms $\{A_1, \ldots, A_n\}$ is to say that there exists a derivation in SN of B from the set $\{A_1, \ldots, A_n\}$, or in abbreviated form,

(2) $\{A_1, \ldots, A_n\} \vdash_{SN} B$.

The "turnstile" symbol '$\vdash$' is to be read 'is derivable-in- $\cdots$ from'; thus (2) says that B is derivable-in-SN from $\{A_1, \ldots, A_n\}$.

Example of a Derivation

To see what a derivation looks like, let us construct one for the SL argument form (1) in §29.   Assume that our natural deduction system includes among its rules of inference

> (a)   from $A \to B$ and $B \to C$
> to infer $A \to C$,

> (b)   from $A \to B$ and $\sim B$
> to infer $\sim A$,

> (c)   from $A \lor B$ and $\sim A$
> to infer B.

Then the following column of SL sentence forms, with the authority for each entry written beside it, is a derivation in our system of 'U' from the premisses of (1) in §29:

1.	$P \to Q$	Premiss
2.	$Q \to R$	Premiss
3.	$R \to S$	Premiss
4.	$P \lor U$	Premiss
5.	$\sim S$	Premiss

---

2   Braces, '$\{\cdots\}$', are the usual symbol for a set; thus $\{A_1, \ldots, A_n\}$ is the set whose elements or members are the SL sentence forms $A_1, \ldots, A_n$.

6. $P \rightarrow R$ From lines 1 and 2 by Rule (*a*)

7. $P \rightarrow S$ From lines 6 and 3 by Rule (*a*)

8. $\sim P$ From lines 7 and 5 by Rule (*b*)

9. U From lines 4 and 8 by Rule (*c*)

---

§31   *The Natural Deduction System SN'*

We turn now to a specific natural deduction system for SL.   There are many combinations of inference rules that can serve as satisfactory systems.   The one we shall use—we call it SN'—turns up with minor variations in a number of textbooks.   Its list of inference rules is overlong, but this redundancy enables us to shorten and simplify some of the derivations.

There is little point in trying to memorize the list of rules we are about to consider.   For one thing, the reader can always look them up in the book.   For another, the reader will find that by doing a reasonable number of exercises, he or she will succeed in memorizing the most important rules without really trying.

GROUP A RULES

The first group consists of rules that permit us to infer one SL sentence form from one or more other SL sentence forms ($A, B, C, D, \ldots$ being any SL sentence forms).

RULE 1.   *Modus Ponens* (MP): from $A \rightarrow B$ and A, to infer B

RULE 2.   *Modus Tollens* (MT): from $A \rightarrow B$ and $\sim B$, to infer $\sim A$

RULE 3.   Hypothetical Syllogism (HS): from $A \rightarrow B$ and $B \rightarrow C$, to infer $A \rightarrow C$

RULE 4.   Disjunctive Syllogism (DS): from $A \lor B$ and $\sim A$, to infer B

RULE 5.   Addition (Add.): from A, to infer $A \lor B$

RULE 6.   Simplification (Simp.): from $A \& B$, to infer A

RULE 7.   Adjunction (Adj.): from A and B, to infer $A \& B$

RULE 8.   Constructive Dilemma (CD): from $(A \rightarrow B) \& (C \rightarrow D)$ and $A \lor C$, to infer $B \lor D$

GROUP B RULES

The second group of rules permit us to interchange with one another certain SL sentence forms or parts of SL sentence forms.

RULE 9.   Double Negation (DN): A is interchangeable with $\sim\sim A$

RULE 10.   Transposition (Trans.): $A \rightarrow B$ is interchangeable with

$\sim B \rightarrow \sim A$

RULE 11.   Commutation (Com.):

$A \vee B$ is interchangeable with $B \vee A$
$A \,\&\, B$ is interchangeable with $B \,\&\, A$

RULE 12.   Association (Assoc.):

$A \vee (B \vee C)$ is interchangeable with $(A \vee B) \vee C$
$A \,\&\, (B \,\&\, C)$ is interchangeable with $(A \,\&\, B) \,\&\, C$

RULE 13.   Distribution (Dist.):

$A \,\&\, (B \vee C)$ is interchangeable with $(A \,\&\, B) \vee (A \,\&\, C)$
$A \vee (B \,\&\, C)$ is interchangeable with $(A \vee B) \,\&\, (A \vee C)$

RULE 14.   De Morgan's Laws (DeM):

$\sim(A \,\&\, B)$ is interchangeable with $\sim A \vee \sim B$
$\sim(A \vee B)$ is interchangeable with $\sim A \,\&\, \sim B$

RULE 15.   The Conditional (Con.): $A \rightarrow B$ is interchangeable with

$\sim A \vee B$

RULE 16.   The Biconditional (Bicon.): $A \leftrightarrow B$ is interchangeable with

$(A \rightarrow B) \,\&\, (B \rightarrow A)$

RULE 17.   Exportation (Exp.): $(A \,\&\, B) \rightarrow C$ is interchangeable with

$A \rightarrow (B \rightarrow C)$

RULE 18.   Absorption (Abs.): $A \rightarrow B$ is interchangeable with

$A \rightarrow (A \,\&\, B)$

RULE 19.   Tautology (Taut.):

> *A* is interchangeable with *A* ∨ *A*
> *A* is interchangeable with *A* & *A*

Note that the rules in Group B serve as two-way inference rules.   That is, each of the interchange rules can be expressed as a pair of inference rules.   For example, Rule 9,

> *A* is interchangeable with ∼ ∼ *A* ,

can be written as

> from *A*, to infer ∼ ∼ *A*
> from ∼ ∼ *A*, to infer *A* .

Note also that in general the rules constituting our system SN' are counterparts to familiar valid SL argument forms and equivalences, such as those listed in §27 under "Tautology and Some Traditional Laws of Logic."   Indeed, each rule—as the reader may verify—is associated with a class of SL argument forms whose corresponding conditionals or bi-conditionals are tautologies.   Thus Rule 10 (Transposition) says

> *A* → *B* is interchangeable with ∼*B* → ∼*A* .

For one of the associated argument forms, the corresponding conditional would be

$$(P \rightarrow Q) \rightarrow (\sim Q \rightarrow \sim P),$$

which, as the usual truth-table test shows, is a tautology.

DERIVATIONS IN SN'

The following samples illustrate the construction of derivations in SN.

First Sample

The SL argument form is

(1) $(P \ \& \ Q) \rightarrow R$
          $S \rightarrow P$
          Therefore $(S \ \& \ Q) \rightarrow R$.

The derivation is

(1')	1.	$(P \ \& \ Q) \to R$	Premiss
	2.	$S \to P$	Premiss
	3.	$P \to (Q \to R)$	From line 1 by Exportation (Exp.)
	4.	$S \to (Q \to R)$	From lines 2 and 3 by Hypothetical Syllogism (HS)
	5.	$(S \ \& \ Q) \to R$	From line 4 by Exp.

Second Sample

The SL argument form is

(2) $P \to Q$
       $\sim(\sim R \ \& \ \sim P)$
       $\sim R$
       Therefore Q.

The derivation is

(2')	1.	$P \to Q$	Premiss
	2.	$\sim(\sim R \ \& \ \sim P)$	Premiss
	3.	$\sim R$	Premiss
	4.	$\sim\sim R \ \lor \ \sim\sim P$	From 2 by De Morgan's Laws (DeM)
	5.	$R \ \lor \ \sim\sim P$	From 4 by Double Negation (DN)
	6.	$R \ \lor \ P$	From 5 by DN
	7.	P	From 6 and 3 by Disjunctive Syllogism (DS)
	8.	Q	From 1 and 7 by *Modus Ponens* (MP)

Before moving to the next sample, we add a new piece of machinery: a column on the left that shows for each entry in the derivation exactly which *set* of the original premisses the particular entry is based upon. Each premiss is identified by its *premiss number*—the number of the line on which that premiss first makes its appearance in the derivation. Note that every premiss is to be regarded as being inferred from itself—that is, *we now explicitly add to our rules the following*:

from A, to infer A.

Thus (2') in full dress becomes

{1}	1.	$P \to Q$	Premiss
{2}	2.	$\sim(\sim R \ \& \ \sim P)$	Premiss
{3}	3.	$\sim R$	Premiss
{2}	4.	$\sim\sim R \ \lor \ \sim\sim P$	From 2 by De Morgan's Laws (DeM)

{2}	5.	$R \lor \sim \sim P$	From 4 by Double Negation (DN)
{2}	6.	$R \lor P$	From 5 by DN
{2, 3}	7.	P	From 6 and 3 by Disjunctive Syllogism (DS)
{1, 2, 3}	8.	Q	From 1 and 7 by *Modus Ponens* (MP)

Note that all three premisses were required to derive the conclusion 'Q'. This is not always the case; sometimes an argument form may contain superfluous premisses.

Third Sample

Derive 'U' from the indicated premisses:

(3)				
	{1}	1.	$\sim Q \to \sim P$	Premiss
	{2}	2.	$Q \to (R \lor S)$	Premiss
	{3}	3.	$R \to T$	Premiss
	{4}	4.	$T \to U$	Premiss
	{5}	5.	$S \to Y$	Premiss
	{6}	6.	P	Premiss
	{7}	7.	$\sim Y$	Premiss
	{1}	8.	$P \to Q$	From 1 by Transposition (Trans.)
	{1, 2}	9.	$P \to (R \lor S)$	From 8 and 2 by Hypothetical Syllogism (HS)
	{1, 2, 6}	10.	$R \lor S$	From 9 and 6 by *Modus Ponens* (MP)
	{5, 7}	11.	$\sim S$	From 5 and 7 by *Modus Tollens* (MT)
	{1, 2, 5, 6, 7}	12.	R	From 10 and 11 by Disjunctive Syllogism (DS)
	{3, 4}	13.	$R \to U$	From 3 and 4 by HS
	{1, 2, 3, 4, 5, 6, 7}	14.	U	From 13 and 12 by MP

Note: Between steps 10 and 11, we omit as obvious an application of the Rule for Commutation (Com.) to '$R \lor S$' to obtain '$S \lor R$'.

Derivation Strategy

Our ability to find a derivation, if one exists, depends on two factors. The first is familiarity with the moves that the rules allow, and this only practice can breed.   The second is facility in putting together the required combinations of moves, and this only reflection on practice can develop. Some points are obvious.   We should take careful note of *all* the premisses.   We should make full use of the interchange rules—Transposition, De Morgan's, Double Negation, and the like—to express premisses or other entries in a form to which appropriate rules of inference can be applied. Other ideas will occur to anyone who works through the exercises.

It is often good strategy to start with the conclusion and look for a path back to the premisses. For example, in (3) the desired conclusion 'U' is part of premiss 4, which with premiss 3 yields '$R \rightarrow U$'. Thus if 'R' can be obtained, the problem is solved. Now 'R' occurs in premiss 2 disjoined with 'S'; and '$\sim S$' may be obtained from premisses 5 and 7. Hence if '$R \vee S$' is obtainable, so is 'R' (by DS). If we transpose premiss 1, apply HS to it and premiss 2, then bring in premiss 6, we have '$R \vee S$', therefore 'R', and therefore 'U'.

EXERCISES

31.1. The following are derivations in SN' of the conclusion (last line) from the premisses indicated. Complete the first and last columns.

a. {1}   1. $(Q \vee R) \rightarrow P$ Premiss
    {2}   2. $\sim R \rightarrow S$ Premiss
    {3}   3. $\sim S$ Premiss
          4. $\sim \sim R$
          5. R
          6. $R \vee Q$
          7. $Q \vee R$
          8. P

b. {1}   1. $(P \mathbin{\&} Q) \rightarrow R$ Premiss
    {2}   2. $S \rightarrow Q$ Premiss
    {3}   3. $P \vee \sim S$ Premiss
    {4}   4. S Premiss
          5. Q
          6. $\sim S \vee P$
          7. $\sim \sim S$
          8. P
          9. $P \mathbin{\&} Q$
         10. R

c. {1}   1. $P \leftrightarrow Q$ Premiss
    {2}   2. $\sim P$ Premiss
    {3}   3. $Q \vee R$ Premiss
    {4}   4. $R \rightarrow S$ Premiss
          5. $(P \rightarrow Q) \mathbin{\&} (Q \rightarrow P)$
          6. $Q \rightarrow P$
          7. $\sim Q$
          8. R
          9. S

d.   {1}   1. $(P \lor Q) \to R$ Premiss
     {2}   2. $(Q \lor \sim R) \to S$ Premiss
     {3}   3. $\sim R \lor \sim S$ Premiss
              4. $\sim R \to \sim (P \lor Q)$
              5. $\sim S \to \sim (Q \lor \sim R)$
              6. $[\sim R \to \sim (P \lor Q)]$
                  $\& [\sim S \to \sim (Q \lor \sim R)]$
              7. $\sim (P \lor Q) \lor \sim (Q \lor \sim R)$
              8. $(\sim P \& \sim Q) \lor (\sim Q \& \sim \sim R)$
              9. $(\sim P \& \sim Q) \lor (\sim Q \& R)$
             10. $(\sim Q \& \sim P) \lor (\sim Q \& R)$
             11. $\sim Q \& (\sim P \lor R)$
             12. $\sim Q \& (P \to R)$

31.2. Using the rules for SN', show that the following SL argument forms are valid:

a. $(P \& Q) \to R$
     $\sim P \lor Q$
     P
     Therefore R

b. $(P \lor Q) \to R$
     $P \lor S$
     $\sim S$
     Therefore R

c. $P \to Q$
     $R \to S$
     $(Q \lor S) \to T$
     $P \lor R$
     Therefore T

d. $P \to R$
     $Q \to \sim R$
     $Q \lor S$
     $S \to \sim P$
     Therefore $\sim P$

e. $P \to (Q \& R)$
     $Q \to S$
     $\sim S$
     Therefore $\sim P$

f. $P \to Q$
     $R \to S$
     $\sim P \to T$
     $\sim T$
     Therefore $Q \lor S$

    g. $P \rightarrow (Q \lor R)$
        $\sim P \rightarrow S$
        $\sim T \rightarrow \sim S$
        $\sim T \lor U$
        $\sim U$
        Therefore $Q \lor R$

    h. $P \rightarrow (Q \rightarrow R)$
        $\sim Q \rightarrow \sim S$
        $S \lor T$
        $\sim T \lor U$
        $\sim U$
        Therefore $P \rightarrow R$

31.3. These arguments are all substitution instances of valid SL argument forms. For each argument form, construct a derivation in SN′ of the conclusion from the premises.

    a. Argument *b* from Exercise 28.4.

    b. Argument *d* from Exercise 28.4.

    c. If the Democrats name Johnson, they will lose the peace vote and a third candidate will enter the race. If a third candidate enters the race, the Democrats will lose. The Democrats will not lose. Therefore they will not name Johnson.

    d. If the Democrats name Canavan and he accepts Walton as his running mate, the liberals will leave Canavan. If the liberals leave Canavan, a third candidate will enter the race. If a third candidate enters the race, the Democrats will lose the election to the Republicans. The Democrats will not lose the election to the Republicans. Therefore if the Democrats name Canavan, he will not accept Walton as his running mate.

    e. If the Democrats adopt a liberal program and yet name Walton, they will be caught up in an obvious contradiction. If they are caught up in an obvious contradiction, they can resolve it by repudiating their program or by repudiating their own candidate after nominating him. If they adopt a liberal program, they will not repudiate it. They will not repudiate their own candidate after nominating him. Hence if the Democrats adopt a liberal program they will not name Walton.

31.4. Which of the following arguments are valid? Which invalid? First write down the SL argument forms of which these arguments are substitution instances. Then to establish validity, show that the conclusion of the argument form is derivable in SN' from its premisses.   To establish *in*validity, find a *counterexample* to the claim of validity—that is, a substitution instance of the SL argument form that has *acknowledgedly* true premisses but an acknowledgedly false conclusion.   (Supply implicit premisses or conclusions as called for by the context.   And remember that this is an exercise in *logic*, not in economics: the truth or falsity of the premisses and conclusions does not concern us, except when we are trying to show invalidity by offering a counterexample.)

a.   If we do not reduce production, inflation will continue.   If inflation continues, total real wages will decline.   But if we reduce production, total real wages will also decline (fewer people will be working).   Either way, total real wages will decline.

b.   If inflation continues, real wages and benefits will decline. If these decline, purchasing power in general will weaken.   If purchasing power weakens, production will decline.   If production declines, inflation will not continue.   Therefore inflation will not continue.

c.   If the economists are right, then inflation is arrested if production declines.   Now production is declining and a recession is taking place.   Yet inflation is not arrested.   Therefore the economists are not right.

d.   Confidence will be restored only if inflation is arrested.   If confidence is restored, the economic situation will be stabilized and people will engage in less panic buying.   If people engage in less panic buying, pressure on prices will be less.   If pressure on prices is less, inflation will be arrested.   Hence inflation will be arrested iff people engage in less panic buying.

e.   If inflation continues, then if unemployment increases, the situation is without precedent.   If the situation is without precedent, a new economic analysis is needed if we are to develop an effective antiinflation program.   Unemployment is growing or the government figures are all wrong.   And if the government figures are all wrong, the problem is unsolvable.   But the problem is not unsolvable.   Hence if inflation continues and if we are to develop an effective antiinflation program, a new economic analysis is needed.

---

§32   *The Natural Deduction System SNS*

We take brief note of a modified natural deduction system for SL—here called SNS—presented by Patrick Suppes in his *Introduction to Logic* (1957).   Instead of specifying a list of rules of inference, this system in effect blankets in as rules *all* counterparts of tautological conditionals. For example, in addition to the nineteen rules of SN′ listed above, SNS admits

> from B, to infer $A \to B$,

since the conditionals represented by

> $B \to (A \to B)$

are tautologies.

The system SNS operates with three "rules":

> 1. RULE P: A premiss may be entered on any line of a derivation (i.e., "from A, to infer A").
>
> 2. RULE T: Any SL sentence form may be entered in a derivation if it is tautologically implied by a preceding entry or a conjunction of such entries.
>
> 3. RULE CP (CONDITIONAL PROOF): This will be discussed in §33.

The derivation procedure in SNS is like that in SN′ except for Rule T, which permits us to cite as a rule of inference *any* rule that corresponds to a tautology. The advantage gained is that with Rule T some derivations move ahead more simply. The disadvantage is that since the notion of tautology remains central, SNS is not in the full sense an *alternative* to truth tables.

---

§33 *Use of Conditional Proof and Indirect Proof*

In a conditional proof, we advance from premises to a desired conclusion with the aid of *temporary* additional premises, or hypotheses, which are introduced and then discarded once their job is done. The adoption, use, and discharge of such *conditional*, or borrowed, premises is governed by

> RULE CP: If an SL sentence form B can be derived in a system— say, SN′—from an SL sentence form A together with a set of SL sentence forms as premises, then $A \to B$ can be derived in the system from those premises alone.

We first show how Rule CP is used generally in derivations. Then we consider two particular uses that are of special interest.

Suppose we are asked to test the following argument form for validity by constructing a derivation of its conclusion from its premisses:

(1) $P \to Q$
         $Q \to R$
         $\sim P \to (S \lor T)$
         Therefore $\sim R \to (S \lor T)$.

Notice that the conclusion is a conditional. This suggests adding to the three given premisses, as a *conditional* premiss, the antecedent of the conclusion—namely, ' $\sim R$ '—*starring* it as a reminder that it is a premiss added temporarily. If with ' $\sim R$ ' as an added premiss we can derive ' $S \lor T$ ', then by Rule CP we can derive the desired conclusion ' $\sim R \to (S \lor T)$ ' from the three original premisses alone without the added premiss ' $\sim R$ ':

(1′)   {1}   1. $P \to Q$ Premiss
          {2}   2. $Q \to R$ Premiss
          {3}   3. $\sim P \to (S \lor T)$ Premiss
          {4}   4. $\sim R$ Premiss*
        {2, 4}   5. $\sim Q$ From 2 and 4 by *Modus Tollens* (MT)
      {1, 2, 4}   6. $\sim P$ From 1 and 5 by MT
    {1, 2, 3, 4}   7. $S \lor T$ From 3 and 6 by *Modus Ponens* (MP)
      {1, 2, 3}   8. $\sim R \to (S \lor T)$ From 4 through 7 by Conditional Proof (CP)

A derivation for (1) can also be constructed without using CP. This is left as an exercise for the reader.

Under what circumstances should Rule CP be used? Apart from special situations, this rule should be thought of as a possible tool whenever it is necessary to construct a derivation for a conclusion that is a conditional. A derivation using CP may not always be shorter, but it is often easier to find.

THE RULE FOR INDIRECT PROOFS

With the aid of Rule CP and the other two rules of SNS, we can obtain as a *derived rule* the procedure known as *Indirect Proof*, or Proof by Contradiction (see §27). The general idea is that if a contradiction can be derived in SNS from an SL sentence form $\sim B$ together with a set of premisses, then B is derivable in the system from the premisses alone.[3]

---

[3] See Patrick Suppes, *Introduction to Logic* (New York: Van Nostrand, 1957), pp. 38–41.

Let $\{A_1, \ldots, A_n\}$ be a set of premisses and let $C \mathbin{\&} \sim C$ be some contradiction. The derived rule then says

$$\text{If } \{A_1, \ldots, A_n, \sim B\} \vdash_{\text{SNS}} C \mathbin{\&} \sim C, \text{ then } \{A_1, \ldots, A_n\} \vdash_{\text{SNS}} B.$$

PROOF OF THE DERIVED RULE

$\{A_1, \ldots, A_n, \sim B\} \vdash_{\text{SNS}} C \mathbin{\&} \sim C$		By assumption
$\{A_1, \ldots, A_n\} \quad \vdash_{\text{SNS}} \sim B \to (C \mathbin{\&} \sim C)$		By Rule CP
$\{A_1, \ldots, A_n\} \quad \vdash_{\text{SNS}} \sim \sim B$ [i.e., B]		By DN and rules corresponding to the tautologies: $\{[A \to (B \mathbin{\&} \sim B)] \to \sim A\}$

THEOREMS OF SN

Consider the SL sentence form

(2) $P \to (P \vee Q)$.

Suppose we adopt 'P' as a conditional premiss. Then by using Rule CP we can construct the following derivation:

(2′) | | | | |
|---|---|---|---|
| $\{1\}$ | 1. | P | Premiss* |
| $\{1\}$ | 2. | $P \vee Q$ | From 1 by Addition (Add.) |
| $\wedge$ | 3. | $P \to (P \vee Q)$ | From 1 and 2 by Conditional Proof (CP) |

where the symbol '$\wedge$' stands for the empty set of premisses.

What we have done here is to use the temporary, starred premiss 'P' to obtain '$P \vee Q$' by applying Rule Add. Next we applied Rule CP to obtain '$P \to (P \vee Q)$', and in so doing, we *discharged* the borrowed 'P' as a premiss. But since 'P' was the *only* premiss that entered into the derivation, when it was discharged, the premiss set for line 3 was left empty, as shown in the derivation. Now line 3 is the SL sentence form (2). Consequently, we have shown that (2) is derivable in our system from the empty set of premisses.

An SL sentence form that is derivable in a system SN from the empty set of premisses is called a *theorem* of SN. In a more advanced study of sentence logic it is shown that an SL sentence form is a theorem in this sense if and only if it is a tautology. Here we simply take note of that fact.

This section will conclude with a second example of the derivation of an SL sentence form from the empty set of premisses. Take now the SL sentence form

(3) $[(P \to Q) \mathbin{\&} (Q \to R)] \to (P \to R)$.

Using '$P \to Q$', '$Q \to R$', and 'P' as conditional premisses, we have:

(3′)	{1}	1.	$P \to Q$	Premiss*
	{2}	2.	$Q \to R$	Premiss*
	{3}	3.	P	Premiss*
	{1, 3}	4.	Q	From 1 and 3 by *Modus Ponens* (MP)
	{1, 2, 3}	5.	R	From 2 and 4 by MP
	{1, 2}	6.	$P \to R$	From 3 through 5 by Conditional Proof (CP)
	{1}	7.	$(Q \to R) \to (P \to R)$	From 2 through 6 by CP
	$\wedge$	8.	$(P \to Q) \to [(Q \to R) \to (P \to R)]$	From 1 through 7 by CP
	$\wedge$	9.	$[(P \to Q) \,\&\, (Q \to R)] \to (P \to R)$	From 8 by Exportation (Exp.)

Thus (3) too is a theorem of our system.

EXERCISES

33.1. This is an exercise in the construction of derivations with the aid of Conditional Proof and Indirect Proof. Show that the following SL argument forms are valid, using either the system SN′ *extended* to include Conditional Proof (and Indirect Proof) or the system SNS (Rules P, T, and CP).

a. $(S \,\&\, T) \to (R \lor \sim P)$
$P \to S$
$Q \to T$
Therefore $(P \,\&\, Q) \to R$

b. $P \to S$
$Q \to \sim P$
$Q \lor (R \lor T)$
Therefore $(\sim T \,\&\, P) \to (S \,\&\, R)$

c. $P \to (Q \,\&\, S)$
$(Q \lor R) \to T$
$T \to \sim S$
Therefore $\sim(P \,\&\, R)$

d. $\sim P \to R$
$\sim Q \to T$
$T \to \sim R$
Therefore $P \lor Q$

e. $P \rightarrow (R \rightarrow T)$
    $Q \rightarrow (S \ \& \sim T)$
    Therefore $[P \ \& \ (Q \ \vee \ R)] \rightarrow (\sim T \rightarrow S)$

33.2. Using either of the systems from Exercise 33.1, construct *new* derivations with the aid of Conditional Proof and/or Indirect Proof for the SL argument forms shown to be valid in Exercises 31.2*d*, 31.2*e*, and 31.3*e*.

33.3. Prove that the following are *theorems* of SN′ (extended) or of SNS.

a. $[(P \ \vee \ Q) \ \& \ (\sim R \ \vee \ \sim Q)] \rightarrow (\sim P \rightarrow \sim R)$

b. $[(P \ \& \ Q) \ \vee \ (Q \ \& \ R)] \rightarrow (Q \ \vee \ R)$

c. $P \rightarrow \{(Q \ \vee \ R) \rightarrow [P \rightarrow (Q \ \vee \ R)]\}$

d. $[P \ \vee \ (\sim P \ \& \ Q)] \ \vee \ (\sim P \ \& \ \sim Q)$

e. $(P \ \& \ Q) \rightarrow \{\sim R \rightarrow \ \sim [P \rightarrow (Q \ \& \ R)]\}$

f. $(P \rightarrow Q) \ \vee \ (P \ \& \ \sim Q)$

8

Sentence Logic
and
Ordinary Language

Ordinary languages such as English are extremely rich in means of expression. In particular, they possess a wealth of devices for forming all sorts of compound sentences, only a small portion of which are truth-functional compounds. Thus most ordinary language compounds, as well as the arguments in which they figure, depart in one way or another from strict truth-functionality.

Sentence logic, however, limits itself to truth-functional compounds and the true-false sentences from which they are formed. It does not seek to evaluate arguments whose validity turns on anything beyond the truth-functional compounding of sentences.

Can SL have significant application to ordinary language arguments?

The answer is immediate and affirmative for one part of ordinary language: the specialized sublanguage in which mathematicians write out their proofs and their textbooks. The reader can easily verify that any compound sentence that enters into a mathematical argument either is patently truth-functional or else can be rephrased as a truth-functional compound without affecting the *validity* of the demonstration in which it appears. For example, the words 'but' and 'also' often appear in statements of mathematical proofs; but they can always be replaced by purely truth-functional occurrences of 'and'. Thus the mission of SL, while modest, is far from trivial.

Now what of SL and ordinary language in general? This is a more complex matter, and we shall touch on only a few of its aspects. First, we shall try to get a clearer view of the problem of applicability by sorting out several kinds of departures from strict truth-functionality. Second, these distinctions will be used to help point up the difference between the truth-functional connective '→' and certain *non*-truth-functional uses of 'if-then'.

§34   *The Applicability of SL to Ordinary-Language Arguments*

Only a very small class of ordinary-language compound sentences are purely truth-functional. It does not follow, however, that SL is applicable only to this quite narrow class. In the first place, not all departures from truth-functionality are essential—that is, they do not all affect the validity of arguments in which the compound appears. In the second place, not all essential departures from truth-functionality render SL inapplicable.

Take, for example, the two compound sentences

(1)   Life is short *but* art is long.

(2)   Life is short *and* art is long.

Now (1) is not a purely truth-functional compound. For the presence of 'but' (rather than 'and') gives (1) a certain element of emphasis and contrast that is absent from (2).

However, the circumstances that make (1) true or false are the same as those that make (2) true or false. The two compounds have the same *truth conditions*: each is true if and only if the two component simple sentences are both true. Thus 'and' may replace 'but' in (1) without affecting its truth-value as determined by the truth-values of its component sentences and, hence, without affecting the validity according to SL of any argument in which (1) figures. Departures from truth-functionality that leave truth-value determination and validity untouched we shall call *inessential*.[1]

A second example is

(3)   Perkins is promoted provided he publishes.

---

[1] On this point and other matters in this chapter, see Quine, *Methods of Logic* (New York: Henry Holt, 1959), §8.

As ordinarily used, (3) has exactly the same truth conditions and differs only in "flavor" from

(4)   If Perkins publishes, he is promoted.

Hence (3) also represents an inessential departure.   The same is true of

(5)   Perkins is promoted if he publishes.
(6)   Perkins is promoted in case he publishes.

These differ from (4) only in having the consequent precede the antecedent.
   Note: As was seen above in §22, when viewed truth-functionally, the sentences

(7)   Perkins publishes only if he is promoted
(8)   Perkins does not publish unless he is promoted

also have the same truth conditions as (4).   To make publishing a *sufficient* condition for Perkins's promotion—see (4)—is the same as making his promotion a *necessary* condition of his publishing, as in (7) and (8).   For '$P \rightarrow Q$' (or 'If Perkins publishes, he is promoted') is equivalent to '$\sim Q \rightarrow \sim P$' (or 'If it is not the case that Perkins is promoted, then it is not the case that he publishes').
   Even when the departure from truth-functionality is essential, often the "offending" compound is close enough in structure to truth-functionality to provide the *minimum* necessary basis for an SL evaluation of arguments in which the compound occurs.
   Consider, for example, the argument

(9)   If Perkins is a bachelor, then Perkins is unmarried.

         Perkins is a bachelor.

         Therefore Perkins is unmarried.

At first glance, it seems to be a simple instance of the valid argument form

(9') $P \rightarrow Q$
         P
         Therefore Q.

But notice the first premiss.   Is it really a truth-functional conditional?
   Let us recall that the truth-value of a truth-functional compound is determined in all cases solely by the truth-values of its component sentences, and *not* by their content, the context, or *any relation of dependency*

between the truth-values of these components themselves. Now assume that the conditional

(10)   If Perkins is a bachelor, then Perkins is unmarried

is strictly truth-functional.   It will then have a truth table with the usual assignments of truth-values to its component sentences, as follows:

Perkins is a bachelor	Perkins is unmarried	Perkins is a bachelor $\rightarrow$ Perkins is unmarried
T	T	T
T	F	F
F	T	T
F	F	T

Now line 2 assigns T to 'Perkins is a bachelor' and F to 'Perkins is unmarried'.   But here no such assignment is possible!   Because of the definition of 'bachelor', there is a *relation of dependency* between the truth-values of 'Perkins is a bachelor' and 'Perkins is unmarried': if the first sentence is true, the second *must* be true.   Thus the occurrence of 'if-then' in (10) is not truth-functional, and the departure from truth-functionality is an essential one.   It is therefore necessary to distinguish between (9) and instances of (9′) such as

(11)   If Perkins publishes, he will be promoted.

Perkins publishes.

Therefore Perkins will be promoted.

In (11) the compound premiss is purely truth-functional.

Yet the distinctive feature of (9)—the definitional character of its first premiss—does not altogether remove it from the scope of SL.   For (9) is close enough to a truth-functional structure to provide the minimum basis for applying the SL criterion of validity.   From the standpoint of SL, then, it may be treated like (11) as just another instance of the truth-functionally valid argument form (9′).

Thus the range of application of SL to ordinary language arguments is not confined to those that are obviously truth-functional.   Even arguments marked by essential departures from truth-functionality may nonetheless be open to evaluation by SL.   Additional examples of such arguments will be cited when ordinary language conditionals are considered in detail; others will be found in the exercises.

EXERCISES

34.1. The following compound sentences all exhibit departures from pure truth-functionality. Some of these departures are *inessential*. Show this, in each such case, by recasting the original sentence into a purely truth-functional compound with the *same* truth conditions as the original sentence.

a. The Democrats named Canavan for President, yet chose Walton to run with her for Vice-President.

b. Perkins seeks neither fame nor fortune.

c. Nero fiddled while Rome burned.

d. Unless certain measures are taken, inflation will not be checked.

e. If 6 is even, then 6 is divisible by 2.

f. Rogers will not graduate even though he has 120 credits.

g. Algebra is useful whether or not you are a mathematician.

h. The chairman asked for volunteers, whereupon one hand went up.

i. Perkins will vacation in the Poconos or else he will stay home all summer.

j. Quincy's argument, though valid, is nevertheless not sound.

k. The Supreme Court handed down a decision, which pleased no one.

l. The Supreme Court handed down a decision that pleased no one.

---

§35 *'If-Then', '→', and the So-called Paradoxes of "Material Implication"*

Most controversy over SL and ordinary language focuses on the conditional—and with good reason. Despite ample warning, we often assume that the truth-functional connective ' → ' is meant to fit *all* uses of 'if-then' in ordinary language. We soon find out, of course, that this cannot be so, that the ordinary language conditional serves a number of clearly *non*-truth-functional purposes. The result is perplexity and confusion.[2]

Some of the confusion can be cleared away if we list and characterize briefly the more important kinds of non-truth-functional conditionals found in ordinary discourse, noting at the same time to what extent truth-functional considerations may still be applied to arguments in which they appear.

Definitional conditionals. These are conditionals that express partial definitions. They depart from truth-functionality in that the truth of the consequent *depends* on the truth of the antecedent. One example was given in §34 in (10); another is

(1)   If the book is blue, the book is colored.

In general, as we have seen, definitional conditionals lie within the range of applicability of SL despite their departure from truth-functionality.

Counterfactual conditionals. These are conditionals whose antecedent makes a statement known to be contrary to the facts, or false. An example is

(2)   If Hitler had invaded England, the Third Reich would have won World War II.

Now a counterfactual conditional such as (2) cannot be truth-functional. For suppose it were. Then, since its antecedent is admittedly false (Hitler did not invade England), the conditional itself would of course be true. But if the falsity of its antecedent sufficed to make a counterfactual conditional true, then *all* such conditionals would automatically be true (since by definition they all have false antecedents). There would then be no point in debating their truth or falsity—indeed, no point in uttering them at all. Hence counterfactual conditionals cannot be truth-functional.

Note that this departure from truth-functionality is such that SL is not even minimally applicable. An analysis of counterfactual conditionals clearly lies beyond the reach of SL.

Incomplete conditionals. These are conditionals with the characteristic feature that they are addressed only to the possibility that the antecedent

---

[2] For a recent discussion of 'if-then', see C. L. Stevenson, "If-ficulties," *Philosophy of Science* 37 (1970), pp. 27–49. Professor Stevenson blames "current logical pedagogy" for the fact that students take '→' and the English 'if' as being "intertranslatable." He argues that if SL is to help us with ordinary language arguments it must be supplemented with additional symbols and concepts "that will preserve the meanings of our various if's with greater accuracy."

is *true*. They are *incomplete* in the sense that they are inoperative if the antecedent is *false* (in contrast to counterfactual conditionals, which by definition *must* have false antecedents). It has been argued that most of our everyday conditionals are of this kind.

Consider the conditional

(3)   If Perkins finishes writing his logic text in May, he will take the summer off.

Now (3) is counted as true if its antecedent and consequent are both true, and false if the antecedent is true and the consequent false. To that extent, (3) coincides with the truth-functional conditional. But suppose Perkins does not finish his text in May. As ordinarily used, (3) is silent on this possibility. Thus if we were to write a truth table for (3), it would have only two lines instead of four:

Antecedent	Consequent	Conditional
T	T	T
T	F	F

Therefore (3) is an incomplete conditional, and it is in this respect that it departs from truth-functionality.

Nonetheless, we may in general still treat an incomplete conditional as if it were truth-functional. That is, it is usually possible to fill out its table along truth-functional lines without doing violence to the conditional or its context. Thus SL is minimally applicable to arguments that have incomplete conditionals among their premises.

Generalized conditionals. These are conditionals that involve the element of *generality*. For example, compare the two conditionals

(4)   If Perkins publishes, then Perkins is promoted.

(5)   If anyone publishes, then that person is promoted.

The first is an ordinary truth-functional conditional with the usual truth table, and it may serve as a premiss in SL arguments, such as

(6)   If Perkins publishes, then Perkins is promoted.

Perkins publishes.

Therefore Perkins is promoted.

But as the presence of the word 'anyone' indicates, (5) is a *generalized* conditional.   Obviously, it cannot serve in the same way as (4) as a premiss in an SL argument.   The "argument"

(7)   If anyone publishes, then that person is promoted

Anyone publishes

Therefore that person is promoted

does not make sense.

This is not to say, however, that generalized conditionals cannot appear as premisses in *any* argument.   Take the following case:

(8)   If anyone publishes, then that person is promoted.

Perkins publishes.

Therefore Perkins is promoted.

This argument is surely valid, even though its validity cannot be certified by the means available to SL.   Arguments such as (8) lie beyond the scope of SL.   They require a logic of *generality*, and this will be discussed in the next chapter.

Implicational conditionals.   These are conditionals with the distinctive property that their consequent is *implied by*, or can be validly inferred from, their antecedent.   An example is

(9)   If Perkins publishes or Perkins perishes and Perkins does not publish, then Perkins perishes.

This is an instance of the SL sentence form

(9′) $[(P \lor Q) \mathbin{\&} \sim P] \to Q$.

If we write its antecedent as two premisses and its consequent as the conclusion, then (9) becomes the argument

(10)   Perkins publishes or Perkins perishes.

Perkins does not publish.

Therefore Perkins perishes.

This is an instance of the valid argument form

(10′) $P \lor Q$

$\sim P$

Therefore Q.

An implicational conditional, then, is simply the corresponding conditional of a valid argument—in this case, valid according to SL. Our criterion of validity may thus be restated as follows: an argument is valid if and only if its corresponding conditional is an implicational conditional.

Notice that in an implicational conditional, 'if-then' has the force of 'since-therefore':

(11)   Since Perkins publishes or Perkins perishes and Perkins does not publish, therefore Perkins perishes.

Notice too that since

> *A* logically implies *B*

means the same (in SL) as

> *A* → *B* is a tautology,

therefore the *two* notions used in defining 'logical implication'—'→' and tautology—are both *truth-functional*. Hence those implicational conditionals whose consequents are implied by their antecedents *according to SL* come fully within the jurisdiction of SL.

But not all implicational conditionals are of this sort. Consider this one:

(12)   If all men are mortal and all mortals live under uncertainty, then all men live under uncertainty.

This too is an implicational conditional. But the argument of which it is the corresponding conditional involves the element of *generality*. Here SL alone is once again not even minimally applicable.

At this point, we break off our listing of uses of 'if-then', although there are many others. Thus we have omitted what might be called "conditionals of emphasis," such as

> If that's music, then I'm Beethoven.
>
> If Smith is reelected, then I'm taking the next trip to the moon.
>
> I'm darned if I can understand one word the guy is saying.

These express disbelief, dismay, disgust—attitudes that do not enter into our discussion of SL.

This review of ordinary language conditionals has shown some of the reasons why the relation between '→' and 'if-then' presents so much difficulty. We turn now to certain confusions that have added to this difficulty.

"PARADOXES OF MATERIAL IMPLICATION"

The term 'material implication' was formerly used to designate the truth-functional conditional.   At that time it was held—as it sometimes still is—that certain paradoxes attach to the notion of material implication.

In §22 it was noted that the truth-functional conditional does have what at first sight seem to be bizarre consequences.   For by the definition of '→', this conditional is *true* if its *antecedent* is *false*, regardless of whether its consequent is true or false; and it is *true* if its *consequent* is *true*, regardless of whether its antecedent is true or false.   Hence such truth-functional conditionals as

> If Perkins is President of the United States, then $2 + 2 = 4$
>
> If Perkins is President of the United States, then $2 + 2 = 5$

are both true, and so are

> If Ford is President of the United States, then $2 + 2 = 4$.
>
> If Agnew is President of the United States, then $2 + 2 = 4$.

But as has been said before, if these consequences strike us as odd, it is only because we forget that a truth-functional conditional, like any other truth-functional compound, simply expresses a certain relation between the *truth-values* of the compound and the *truth-values* of the component sentences.   The latter need not be related to each other at all in *content*.

The bizarre, however, is transformed into the paradoxical if we mistake the truth-functional conditional (*material* implication) for *logical* implication.   For thereby '→' is given the meaning of 'since-therefore'. Antecedents are thus changed into premisses and consequents into conclusions, so that

> If the antecedent is false, the conditional is true, no matter what the consequent

and

> If the consequent is true, the conditional is true, no matter what the antecedent

are changed into

> If the premiss is false, it *logically implies any* conclusion

and

> If the conclusion is true, it is *implied by any* premiss.

On this basis, the *argument*

(13)   Perkins is President of the United States
       Therefore $2 + 2 = 4$,

for example, would have to be declared *valid* according to SL.   But this would indeed result in a paradox.   For (13) is an instance of the argument form

(13′)   *P*
      Therefore *Q*,

which obviously is *not* a valid SL argument form.   Hence by the SL criterion of validity, (13) is in fact *invalid* according to SL.   Paradox!

But this sort of paradox appears only if the truth-functional conditional is confused with logical implication, '→' with 'since-therefore'.   As for the so-called paradoxes of material implication, they simply vanish once this confusion is erased.

"PARADOXES OF VALIDITY"

At this point, however, it might seem that the element of paradox has been eliminated from the truth-functional conditional only to reappear in the form of "paradoxes" of logical implication, or validity.   For now we confront the following:

> 1.   *Any* sentence is logically implied by or can be validly inferred from contradictory premises.
>
> 2.   A logically true sentence (in SL, an instance of a tautology) is logically implied by or can be validly inferred from *any* premisses.

That both 1 and 2 are consequences of our SL criterion of validity may be shown *schematically* by using an *n*-line truth table to represent the truth-values of the conjoined premisses, the conclusion, and the corresponding conditional.   In the case of consequence 1, we have

1′	Conjoined Premisses	Conclusion	Conjoined Premisses → Conclusion
1.	F	T	T
2.	F	F	T
3.	F	⋮	T
⋮	⋮	F	⋮
n.	F	T	T

The same result can be had by using the method of derivation. We prove that from contradictory premisses—say, A and $\sim A$—we can derive in SNS (see §32) *any* conclusion B, as follows:

$\{1\}$	1.	A	Premiss
$\{1\}$	2.	$A \vee B$	Rule T—A tautologically implies $(A \vee B)$
$\{3\}$	3.	$\sim A$	Premiss
$\{1, 3\}$	4.	B	Rule T—$[(A \vee B)\ \&\ \sim A]$ tautologically implies B

In the case of consequence 2, we have

2′

	Conjoined Premisses	Conclusion	Conjoined Premisses $\rightarrow$ Conclusion
1.	T	T	T
2.	F	T	T
3.	⋮	T	T
⋮	F	⋮	⋮
n.	T	T	T

In the language of derivations, consequence 2 states that a logically true sentence can be derived from *any* set of premisses. Now it is known from the fact cited above (near the end of §33) that any tautology—hence any sentence that is logically true according to SL—is derivable in SN from the empty set of premisses; that is to say, it needs no premisses. But if a sentence needs no premisses, then whatever premisses there may be are redundant; such a sentence is then "derivable" from any set of premisses. Hence a sentence that is logically true according to SL is derivable in SN from any set of premisses.

Thus we have shown that consequences 1 and 2 do indeed follow from our general criterion of validity. But these consequences are not as upsetting as one might suppose.

Consider consequence 1, that any argument with contradictory premisses is valid. There is an air of paradox about it, but only if we conflate (fail to distinguish between) *validity* and *soundness*. Now our practical concern with arguments centers on their soundness, and it would certainly be paradoxical if there were a *sound* argument from contradictory premisses. But this is clearly impossible. A sound argument must not only be valid; it must also have premisses that are all true. This latter condition obviously cannot be fulfilled if the premisses are contradictory. Thus if we distinguish carefully between a valid argument and a sound argument, the "paradox" loses much of its force. An argument from contradictory premisses may be technically valid, but it is of necessity *unsound*.

Now consider consequence 2, that any argument with a logically true conclusion is valid.   Here the sense of paradox is very much weakened if we note that the practical objective in offering an argument at all is to present premisses to support a conclusion.   But if the conclusion is logically true (in the case of SL, a substitution instance of a tautology), it obviously needs no such support.   Hence arguments with logical truths as conclusions, while technically valid, are quite *unnecessary*.

On this reassuring note, we conclude our informal account of sentence logic and move on to a more powerful, and more difficult, logical theory.

EXERCISES

35.1.   The examples below contain occurrences of 'if-then' (or of an idiomatic variant).   Which of these occurrences, in your opinion, involve *essential* departures from strict truth-functionality?   Explain your answers.

a.   If the Democrats name Johnson, then the liberals will be unhappy, but the conservatives will rejoice.

b.   If the Democrats hadn't nominated Davis for President in 1924, then La Follette would not have run on a third ticket.

c.   If it rains, it pours.

d.   If Quincy has a sibling, then she has a brother or a sister.

e.   Inflation will be checked even temporarily only if price controls are established.

f.   If all teachers are underpaid and overworked and Perkins is a teacher, then Perkins is underpaid and overworked.

g.   If $2 + 2 = 4$, then Hemingway wrote *The Great Gatsby*.

h.   If horses are animals, then the head of a horse is the head of an animal.

9

Predicate Logic Sentence Forms

Sentence logic provides a clear and simple criterion of validity for a particular class of arguments—those whose validity turns *solely* on the truth-functional compounding of whole, unanalyzed sentences. But this is a very narrow class.

It is easy to show that there are valid arguments whose validity cannot be certified by the use of the SL criterion. Consider, for example, the following argument:

(1)   All men are mortal.

All members of the French Academy are men.

Therefore all members of the French Academy are mortal.

Obviously this argument is perfectly valid. Yet what happens when we subject it to the SL criterion? In terms of sentence logic, (1) consists of three *distinct* simple (noncompound) sentences, and its form is

(1')   *P*

Q

Therefore *R*.

The corresponding conditional of (1′) is

$$(P \ \& \ Q) \rightarrow R.$$

Now an assignment of the truth-values T to 'P', T to 'Q', and F to 'R' makes this conditional take the value F.   Hence the conditional is not a tautology, and (1) is not valid according to SL!

Thus not all arguments depend for their validity only on how sentences are combined.   On the contrary, in most cases—and (1) is among them —validity depends also on the *internal* structure or form of the simple sentences that appear in the arguments.   The criteria of validity for such arguments cannot fall within the scope of SL, since SL does not look inside the noncompound sentence.

To locate the desired criteria, we need broader theories that not only incorporate the sentential fragment, but also extend the scope of logic by analyzing the internal structure of simple sentences.   Modern logic supplies a sequence of such theories, of which the most elementary—and yet in many respects the most important—is called first-order predicate logic, or simply first-order logic.

First-order predicate logic (PL-1) may be defined as that part of modern logic which 1) considers certain forms of simple (noncompound) sentences —specifically, singular and some general sentences—and 2) constructs a theory of inference for all arguments whose validity rests on the internal structure of such sentences and on how they are combined truth-functionally.

As in SL, so in PL-1, there are two fundamental notions.   In SL these were *truth-functionality* and *tautology*.   In PL-1 the basic concepts are *quantification* (hence the practice of calling predicate logic "quantification theory") and *valid sentence form* (the analogue in PL-1 of tautology in SL, and not to be confused with valid argument or valid argument form).

A word on "first order."   Modern logic employs "quantifiers"—for example, 'all', 'some', and the like—to express generality, as in

(2)   All men are mortal.

All perfect numbers are even.

Some sophomores are perspicacious.

Some numbers are odd.

A logic that uses such quantifiers in connection *only* with individual objects or elements is called a *first-order* logic.   Logics of higher order may be introduced if one wishes to consider "all" or "some" *sets*, or classes, of individuals, sets of sets, and so on.

The procedure in this discussion of PL-1 will parallel that used in the account of SL.   The first thing that must be done is to get quite clear about the forms of sentences considered by first-order logic.   This means that we need to look in some detail into the *internal* structure of certain kinds of noncompound sentences, so as to obtain a reasonably rigorous definition of *PL-1 sentence form*.   The second step is to formulate a PL-1 *theory of inference*: a criterion of validity for argument forms composed of PL-1 sentence forms, and with it a set of simple procedures for determining just which PL-1 argument forms meet this criterion.

---

§36   *Singular and Open (Incomplete) Sentences and Their Forms*

Our analysis of the internal structure of simple sentences begins with the simplest type: the noncompound singular sentence.   We then examine what have come to be known as *open*, or *incomplete*, sentences.

SINGULAR SENTENCES AND THEIR FORMS

A singular sentence is one that makes a statement to the effect that a named individual object or element has a certain property or that two or more named individuals stand in a certain relation to one another. Examples of singular sentences are

(1)   Socrates is human.

Johnson defeated Goldwater.

5 is between 4 and 6.

Names and Predicates

In (1) 'Socrates', 'Johnson', 'Goldwater', '5', '4', and '6' desig-nate individual objects or elements; these words and numerals are called *names*.   And 'is human', 'defeated', and 'is between . . . and . . .' express the property or relation that is being attributed to the in-dividuals named; such expressions we call *predicates*.

(Note that we may also uniquely refer to individuals in other ways than by naming them.   Thus 'the even prime' picks out but does not name the number 2; 'the President of the United States on July 1, 1973' picks out but does not name Richard M. Nixon.   Modes of reference other than naming are quite important, but they do not enter into an account of PL-1.)

Kinds of Singular Sentences

A simple singular sentence contains a single predicate.   Now predicates may be classified according to the number of names required to fill them out into sentences.   We may then speak of one-place predicates ('is human'), two-place predicates ('defeated'), three-place predicates ('is between . . . and . . .'), . . . , *n*-place predicates. The forms or kinds of singular sentences can be differentiated according to the number of places called for by their respective predicates.

Symbolizing the Forms of Singular Sentences

The forms of singular sentences can be expressed by means of two banks of symbols: *predicate letters* and *individual constants*.

Predicate letters. These are symbols that serve as *place-holders* for the actual *predicates* belonging to ordinary language. For this purpose we use Latin capitals, beginning with the letter '*F*':

$$F \quad G \quad H \cdots$$

If very large numbers of predicate letters are needed, we may attach numerical subscripts to one of these capitals—for example, 'F_1', 'F_2', 'F_3', . . .—to produce the required number of predicate letters.

Individual constants. These are symbols that serve as *arbitrary names* and stand in place of actual names of *particular individuals*. For this purpose we use the small Latin letters

$$a \quad b \quad c \cdots w$$

Again, if very large numbers of individual constants are required, we may use one of these letters—say, '*a*'—with numerical subscripts: 'a_1', 'a_2', 'a_3', . . .

The forms of the sentences in (1) can now be symbolized as, respectively,

(1')   *Fa*
          Fab
          Fabc

In (1') the '*F*'s are place-holders respectively for one-place, two-place, and three-place predicates, and '*a*', '*b*', and '*c*' are individual constants standing in place of the names that occur in the sentence whose form is being expressed.

The reader will recall that in SL, besides using the sentence letters '*P*', '*Q*', '*R*', . . . as *place-holders* for *any* sentence, we sometimes employed miscellaneous Latin capitals as *abbreviations* for *specific* sentences. Similarly, we may at times find it convenient in PL-1 to abbreviate predicates and names.   Thus

(2)   Bob loves Jane

might be written as

   Lbj .

OPEN SENTENCES

The notion of an open sentence has become standard fare in grade school. Yet this notion is so essential to the analysis of PL-1 sentence forms that knowledge of it had better not be taken for granted.   We shall therefore illustrate and define it in some detail.

   Suppose we write

(3)   Caligula is infamous.

This is an ordinary sentence that can be used to make a statement that counts as true if what it says is so and false if what it says is not so.

   Now suppose we write

(4)   _____ is infamous.

The '_____' marks an open place.   Clearly (4) as it stands cannot be used to make a statement, since it is open.   But except for the open place, (4) is like (3), and in fact it becomes a complete sentence that can be used to make a true or false statement if we insert some name in the open place. Thus if for '_____' we put the name 'Caligula', (4) becomes (3), a sentence that can be used to make the true statement that Caligula is infamous; if for '_____' we put 'Virgil', we get a sentence that can be used to make the false statement that Virgil is infamous.

Definition of Open Sentence

We may now define an open or incomplete "sentence" as an expression that

> 1. Is like a sentence except that it contains at least one open place instead of a name.
>
> 2. Becomes a statement-making sentence if "appropriate" names are inserted in the open places.

   A name may be regarded as appropriate if its insertion results in a sentence that can be used to make a meaningful (but not necessarily *true*) statement.   Thus it would not be appropriate to insert 'Socrates' in '_____ is a prime number'; but it would be appropriate to insert '6', even though the resulting sentence would of course make a false statement.

Now we can represent open sentences that contain one-place, two-place, ..., *n*-place predicates by writing

(5)   _____ is human.

_____ defeated ✳✳✳.

_____ is between ✳✳✳ and ///.

But the representation is much more perspicuous if (5) is written as

(6)   *x* is human.

x defeated *y*.

x is between *y* and *z*.

Accordingly, in order to represent open sentences, we add a third bank of symbols, called *individual variables*.

Individual variables.   These are symbols that serve, as in (6), to mark open places where appropriate names may be inserted.   For this purpose we select the small Latin letters

$$x \qquad y \qquad z$$

If more individual variables are needed, numerical subscripts can be attached to one of the letters—e.g., 'x_1', 'x_2', 'x_3', ...

Utilizing this notion of individual variable, we now amend our definition of 'open sentence' to read as follows: an *open sentence* is an expression that 1) is like a sentence except that it contains *at least one individual variable free* (in a sense of 'free' to be defined below) and 2) becomes a statement-making sentence either if appropriate names are put in place of the variables or if *all occurrences of the variables are bound* (in a sense of 'bound' to be defined below).

Symbolizing the Forms of Open Sentences

With the three banks of symbols available—predicate letters, individual constants, and individual variables—we have the means to express the forms of open sentences.   Thus the open sentences in (6) have respectively the following forms:

(6′)   *Fx*

Fxy

Fxyz

Notice, too, that the following expressions are by definition open sentences, since they contain *at least one* individual variable free:

(7)   *x* defeated Goldwater.

         5 is between *y* and 6.

Their forms are expressed by

(7′)   *Fxa*

         Fayb

EXERCISES

Exercises for §36 are combined with those for §37.

---

§37   *General Sentences and Their Forms : Quantification*

Analysis of the internal structure of simple sentences yields a second type besides singular sentences.   How this comes about is best understood if we observe that there are two ways—not just one—to obtain a sentence from an open sentence, say,

(1)   *x* is human.

   One way is to insert for '*x*' an appropriate name—say, 'Aristotle'—and thus obtain the true singular sentence

(2)   Aristotle is human.

Such a sentence, we say, has been obtained from (1) by *instantiation*.

GENERAL SENTENCES AS GENERALIZATIONS
OF OPEN SENTENCES .

But there is a second way to obtain sentences from open sentences.   Consider the following:

(3)   Everything is human.

         Something is human.

Clearly, these expressions are sentences, for they may be used to make statements (the first one presumably false, the second of course true). Moreover, they are simple sentences, since they contain no proper parts that are sentences. And they are nonsingular, since they contain no names or descriptions. What kind of sentences are they? Suppose (3) is rewritten as

(4)   For every individual object x, x is human.

        For some (*at least one*) object x, x is human.

Notice that these expressions, even though ' x ' occurs in them, are nevertheless sentences. For although quite clumsy, they too can be used to make statements—in fact the very statements we normally use (3) to make.

It therefore seems natural to regard (4) as made up of (1) plus either one of the two prefixes, which may be simplified as

(5)   For all x, ...

        There is an x such that ...

It is now plain that the two sentences

(6)   For all x, x is human

        There is an x such that x is human

are indeed obtained from (1) by prefixing one of the two expressions in (5). These sentences, we say, have been obtained from (1) by *generalization*, and we call them *general* sentences.

SYMBOLIZING THE FORMS OF GENERAL SENTENCES

The symbolic counterparts of the two generalizing prefixes are called *quantifiers*, and the process of attaching them to open sentences is called *quantification*. The general theory of quantifiers, developed chiefly by Gottlob Frege, is known as quantification theory.

We shall symbolize 'for all x' as

$$(x).$$

This is the *universal* quantifier, and the sentence it forms is called the universal generalization of the open sentence to which it is prefixed.

For 'there is an x such that' we shall use

$$(\exists x).$$

This is known as the *existential* quantifier, and it is said to form the existential generalization of the open sentence to which it is prefixed. It bears the name "existential" because *one* way of rewriting a sentence that states existence, such as

(7)   Human beings exist,

is by using the existential quantifier, as follows:

(8)   There is an x such that x is human.

We now have a fourth group of symbols—the two quantifiers. With their aid we can symbolize the forms of simple general sentences. Thus the two sentences in (6) have the forms

(6′) $(x)Fx$
        $(\exists x)Fx$.

Alternative Notations

There are a number of other ways of writing the quantifiers. Some of these are

Universal Quantifier	(x)	$\wedge x$	$\forall x$	Πx
Existential Quantifier	(Ex)	$\vee x$	$\exists x$	Σx

COMPOUND GENERAL SENTENCES AND OPEN SENTENCES

Compound sentences—singular, general, mixed—and compound open sentences can be formed by means of the SL connective symbols. These, together with a supply of parentheses for punctuation, can now be incorporated into the PL-1 stock of symbols.

Examples of singular, general, and mixed compound sentences are

(9)   Sylvia is fair or Sylvia is wise.

       Some numbers are perfect and some numbers are odd.

       If someone is famous, then Aristotle is famous.

It is not difficult to determine that their forms are

(9′) $Fa \vee Ga$
        $(\exists x)Fx \ \& \ (\exists x)Gx$
        $(\exists x)Fx \to Fa$

So much for compound general sentences. What of compound open sentences? Let us call an *open* sentence *compound* if it contains at least one counterpart to an SL connective symbol. Thus the following expressions are examples of compound open sentences:

(10)   *x* is fair or *x* is wise.

       x is odd and *x* is perfect.

       If *x* is human, then *x* is mortal.

       If *x* is fair, then Sylvia is wise.

Their forms are, respectively,

(10′) $Fx \lor Gx$

        $Fx \mathbin{\&} Gx$

        $Fx \to Gx$

        $Fx \to Ga$

We are not yet done with general sentences. Consider the sentence

(11)   All human beings are mortal.

Clearly, it is a general sentence. And as it stands, it is a simple one, in the sense that it does not contain a proper part that by itself is a sentence. Now let us rewrite it in roughly equivalent idioms:

       All that is human is mortal.

       Whatever is human is mortal.

       If anything is human, then it is mortal.

Let us express the last of these as

(12)   For all *x*, if *x* is human, then *x* is mortal.

This sentence may be obtained from the third example in (10) by prefixing 'for all *x*'. Its form is then

(12′) $(x)(Fx \to Gx)$.

The second pair of parentheses helps indicate the *scope* (to be defined shortly) of the quantifier.

    Notice that although (12) contains an SL connective, it does not have a proper part that, standing alone, is a sentence. This is a particular type of general sentence, and its characteristic feature is that it is obtained by generalization from a *compound* open sentence.

Accordingly, we may distinguish three types of general sentences:

1. Simple general sentences (with no SL connectives) obtained by generalization from *simple* open sentences—see (6).

2. Simple general sentences (containing one or more SL connectives) obtained by generalization from *compound* open sentences—see (12).

3. Compound general sentences obtained with the use of SL connectives from one or more simple general sentences, or from these and singular sentences—see (9).

One further illustration of the distinction between compound general sentences and simple general sentences containing SL connectives may be helpful.   Consider the sentence:

(13)   Some perfect numbers are odd.[1]

There are numerous idiomatic variants of this sentence, such as

> Some numbers that are perfect are odd.
> Some things that are perfect numbers are odd numbers.
> There is at least one thing that is a perfect number and is an odd number.

Now let the individual variable 'x' range over whole numbers, and rewrite the last variant as

(14)   There is an x such that x is perfect and x is odd.

Compare this with the following:

(15)   Some numbers are perfect and some numbers are odd.

Sentence (15) says that there is at least one perfect number *and* there is at least one odd number, and the sentence is obviously true.   But (14) says there is at least one number that is *both* perfect and odd—a statement the truth or falsity of which is still undetermined.   The two sentences are therefore quite different.

------

[1]   A number is said to be *perfect* if it is equal to the sum of its divisors, including the number 1 but excluding itself.   Thus 6 is a perfect number because $6 = 1 + 2 + 3$; but 8 is not a perfect number, since $8 \neq 1 + 2 + 4$.   All known perfect numbers are even, and it has been shown that there is no odd perfect number smaller than 10^{36}.   But it is still not known if there are any odd perfect numbers. (See *Scientific American*, June 1971, p. 56.)

Sentence (15) is formed by conjoining two existential generalizations of *simple* open sentences; hence it is a compound general sentence (type 3 above). But (14) is formed by existentially generalizing a *compound* open sentence (itself a conjunction of two simple open sentences); hence it is a simple general sentence that contains at least one SL connective (type 2 above). The difference between these two types of sentences is reflected in their forms:

(14') $(\exists x)(Fx \ \& \ Gx)$

(15') $(\exists x)Fx \ \& \ (\exists x)Gx$

The second pair of parentheses in (14') again helps to indicate the scope of the quantifier.

BOUND AND FREE VARIABLES

Earlier an *open* sentence was defined as an expression that contains at least one individual variable. Later we saw that individual variables also occur in certain (closed) sentences—namely, generalizations of open sentences. It is therefore necessary to draw a distinction between these two kinds of occurrences of individual variables, and for this there is an official terminology.

A *variable* is said to be *free* in an expression if it has a free occurrence in that expression; it is said to be *bound* in an expression if it has a bound occurrence in that expression. An *occurrence* of a variable is said to be *free* if that occurrence does not fall within the scope of a quantifier using that variable; it is said to be *bound* if it falls within the scope of such a quantifier. Finally, the *scope* of a quantifier includes the quantifier itself *and* the open sentence(s) or open sentence form(s) that it quantifies.

On this terminology, since the individual variable '*x*' occurs free in the open expressions

    x is famous Fx ,

it is therefore said to be free in them. Since '*x*' occurs bound (twice) in the closed expressions

    There is an *x* such that *x* is famous $(\exists x)Fx$,

'*x*' is said to be bound in them.

Where needed to show the scope of a quantifier, parentheses are used to delimit the extent of the expression to which the quantifier is applied. Thus in the form

(16) $(\exists x)Fx \ \& \ Gx$

the quantifier is understood to apply only to the simple sentence form '*Fx*', not to '*Gx*', whereas in

(17) $(\exists x)(Fx \ \& \ Gx)$

the quantifier is applied to the compound open sentence '*Fx & Gx*'. In words, we might express the difference between (16) and (17) thus:

(16)   There is an *x* such that *it* is *F*, and *x* is *G*   (The form of an open sentence)

(17)   There is an *x* such that *it* is *F* and *it* is *G*   (The form of a general sentence)

As an exercise in free and bound occurrences of variables, let us check occurrences of '*x*' in the following forms:

(18)   (*a*) $(x)Fx$
       (*b*) $Fx \rightarrow Gx$
       (*c*) $(x)Fx \rightarrow Gx$
       (*d*) $(x)(Fx \rightarrow Gx)$

In (*a*) both occurrences of '*x*' are bound; in (*b*) both are free; in (*c*) the first two occurrences are bound and the third is free; in (*d*) all three occurrences of '*x*' are bound. Notice that the difference between the last two of these forms may be expressed in words as

(18*c*)   If everything is *F*, then *x* is *G*   (The form of an open sentence)

(18*d*)   If anything is *F*, then *it* is *G*   (The form of a general sentence)

Notice too that in (18*c*) the variable '*x*' has both free and bound occurrences. Thus by our definition a variable can be both free and bound in the same expression.

n-PLACE PREDICATES AND *n*-ADIC QUANTIFICATION

There is one last piece of machinery to install before we move on. So far we have considered the application of quantifiers only to expressions with one-place predicates. This is called *monadic* quantification. Now a preliminary word should be said about *polyadic* quantification: the application of quantifiers to expressions containing two-place, three-place, ..., *n*-place predicates.

Let the two-place predicate 'loves' serve as the illustration. The corresponding open sentence is

(19)   *x* loves *y*,

and its form or structure is

(19')   *Fxy*.

Since (19) contains two individual variables, two generalizing prefixes must be applied if a general sentence is to be obtained from it. For example, the universal generalization of (19) is

(20)   For all *x* and for all *y*, *x* loves *y*,

and its form is

(20')   *(x)(y)Fxy*.

When we quantify simple expressions with one-place predicates, only two distinct structures are possible: '*(x)Fx*' and '*(∃x)Fx*'. The number increases for expressions with two-place predicates. Consider the following sentences:

(21)   (*a*)   Everyone loves everyone.
         (*b*)   Someone loves someone.
         (*c*)   Everyone loves someone.
         (*d*)   Someone loves everyone.

If '*x*' and '*y*' are allowed to range over the set of persons, then the sentences of (21) have the following forms, as the reader may verify:

(21')   (*a*)   *(x)(y)Fxy*
         (*b*)   *(∃x)(∃y)Fxy*
         (*c*)   *(x)(∃y)Fxy*
         (*d*)   *(∃x)(y)Fxy*

Notice that when the expression contains one universal and one existential quantifier, the order in which the quantifiers appear may make a difference. In fact, that is just the difference between (21'*c*) and (21'*d*).

The number of distinct structures obtained by quantifying simple expressions grows rapidly for expressions with three- and higher-place predicates. Happily, we shall have little or no occasion to study predicates with more than two places, although we shall need to consider various expressions containing three or more distinct variables. One example is

> For all *x*, for all *y*, for all *z*, if *x* is taller than *y* and *y* is taller than *z*, then *x* is taller than *z*.

Its form, if we let the variables '*x*', '*y*', and '*z*' range over the set of persons, is

$$(x)(y)(z)[(Fxy \ \& \ Fyz) \rightarrow (Fxz)]$$

PL-1 SYMBOLS

We collect here the four groups of symbols that, together with the SL connective symbols and parentheses for punctuation, are required *in PL-1* to express the internal structure, or form, of simple and compound singular, general, and open sentences.

Group 1	Predicate Letters	$F\ G\ H \cdots$	
Group 2	Individual Constants	$a\ b\ c \cdots w$	$a_1\ a_2 \cdots$
Group 3	Individual Variables	$x\ y\ z$	$x_1\ x_2 \cdots$
Group 4	Quantifiers	$(x)\,(y)\,(z) \cdots$	$(\exists x)\,(\exists y)(\exists z) \cdots$

EXERCISES

37.1.   Symbolize the forms, according to PL-1, of these *singular* sentences:

    a.   Aristotle is not infallible.

    b.   Pisces and Leo are signs of the Zodiac.

    c.   Eleanor and Franklin are cousins.

    d.   Anthony William Amo is an eighteenth-century African philosopher.

    e.   Roosevelt was the Democratic nominee and defeated Hoover.

    f.   The dean reports not to the president but to the provost.

    g.   Kantian philosophy is a synthesis of rationalism and empiricism.

    h.   Gonzales teamed with Laver to play Ashe and Smith.

37.2.   Symbolize the forms, according to PL-1, of these *general* sentences:

    a.   All teachers are fallible.

    b.   Some students are not career-oriented.

    c.   There are philosophers and there are cellists and some people are both.

    d.   No one heckled Churchill.

e. Some exercises are more difficult than others.

f. Everyone relies on someone.

g. If Russell cannot understand Wittgenstein, then no one can.

h. Every country has the government it deserves. [Joseph DeMaistre (1753–1821)]

37.3. Symbolize the forms, according to PL-1, of the following expressions. Indicate which are singular sentences, which general, which open.

a. Some people hated FDR but no one questioned his courage.

b. Coolidge succeeded Harding and Hoover succeeded Coolidge.

c. If x is larger than y and y is larger than z, then x is larger than z.

d. Gertrude Stein introduced Hemingway to Fitzgerald.

e. No exercise is interesting if it is easy.

f. There is no greatest integer.

g. What x wants, x gets.

h. Things which are equal to the same thing are equal to each other. [Euclid, *The Elements*, Axiom 1]

37.4. For each of these symbolic expressions, write a sentence whose form is given by that symbolic expression:

a. $Fa \vee {\sim}Fb$

b. ${\sim}Fa \mathbin{\&} Ga$

c. $Fa \rightarrow Gb$

d. $Fx \rightarrow Gb$

e. $(\exists x)Fx \rightarrow Gb$

f. $(x)Fx \rightarrow Gx$

g. $(\exists x) {\sim} Fxab$

h. $(x)Fxx$

i. $(\exists x)(y)Fxy \rightarrow (y)(\exists x)Fxy$

j. $(x)(y)(Fxy \rightarrow {\sim}Fyx)$

k. $(x)Fx \vee {\sim}Fx$

l. $(x)Fx \vee {\sim}(x)Fx$

m $(x)Fx \vee (x) \sim Fx$

n. $(x)(Fx \vee \sim Fx)$

37.5. This is an exercise on *free* and *bound variables*. For those expressions in Exercise 37.4 that have occurrences of variables, indicate whether the occurrences are free or bound.

37.6. This is an exercise on the *scope of quantifiers*. Express in words the difference between

a.   '$(x)Fx \rightarrow Ga$' and '$(x)(Fx \rightarrow Ga)$'

b.   '$(\exists x)Fx \rightarrow Ga$' and '$(\exists x)(Fx \rightarrow Ga)$'

c.   '$(x)Fx \vee (x) \sim Fx$' and '$(x)(Fx \vee \sim Fx)$'

---

§38   *Quantifiers and Ordinary-Language Counterparts*

Ordinary language has many different ways of saying 'all' and 'some'. But just as SL cannot be expected to capture all the devices used in ordinary language to form *compound* sentences, so too PL-1 cannot be expected to capture all the devices used in ordinary language to form *general* sentences. It is enough if the PL-1 quantifiers enable us to account formally for at least some of the important quantifying idioms of everyday discourse.

Even this modest task is not without its complications. We shall touch on a few of these here—the multiplicity of quantifying idioms, negation and general sentences, and a puzzle about 'all' and 'any'. In §50 there will be a discussion of some of the more general problems we run into in "translating" the general sentences of ordinary language into the "language" of PL-1.

THE QUANTIFYING IDIOMS OF ORDINARY LANGUAGE

The first problem in determining the form according to PL-1 of general sentences is the multiplicity of quantifier idioms in ordinary discourse. Here, for example, are some of the ways in which a universal generalization can be formed:

(1)   All tigers are predacious.

Every tiger is predacious.

Each tiger is predacious.

> Any tiger is predacious.
>
> The tiger is predacious.
>
> Whatever is a tiger is predacious.
>
> If anything is a tiger, it is predacious.

Now all of these are expressed formally in PL-1 by

(1') $(x)(Fx \rightarrow Gx)$.

That is, whatever differences may exist among the sentences—are there any, beyond matters of style and emphasis?—are ignored by PL-1 as *non-structural*.   This is how the problem of multiple idioms is treated.   But the list in (1) is not complete, nor is there any mechanical formula for completing it.   Hence determining the form of ordinary-language generalizations will always require a certain amount of informed ingenuity.

In principle, the situation is the same in the case of the existential quantifier.   There is the added complication, however, that the word 'some' has a rather long list of uses.   Two that especially concern us and that are sometimes confused are 'some' as 'some, *possibly* all', and 'some' as 'some, but *not* all'.   The quantifier '$(\exists x)$' is *always* taken in the first of these senses.   Thus the sentence

(2)   Someone (possibly everyone) is happy

is of the form

(2') $(\exists x)Hx$.

The second sense, however, can also be expressed formally in PL-1.   Thus

(3)   Someone (but not everyone) is happy

means the same as

> Someone is happy and it is not the case that everyone is happy

which is of the form

(3') $(\exists x)Hx \ \& \sim(x)Hx$.

Some of the quantifying idioms for existential generalization are

(4)   Some sophomores are perspicacious.

At least one sophomore is perspicacious.

A sophomore is perspicacious.

Something that is a sophomore is also perspicacious.

There is something such that it is a sophomore and it is perspicacious.

All of these are expressed formally in PL-1 by

(4') $(\exists x)(Fx \ \& \ Gx)$.

NEGATIONS OF GENERAL SENTENCES

We negate general sentences in ordinary language pretty much as we negate other sentences. But there are certain pitfalls to avoid. Consider, for example, the sentence

(5)   All men are mortal (i.e., if anything is a man, then it is mortal).

This is of the form

(5') $(x)(Fx \rightarrow Gx)$.

What is its negation?   We might at first suppose that it is

(6)   No men are mortal (i.e., if anything is a man, then it is not mortal).

This is of the form

(6') $(x)(Fx \rightarrow \sim Gx)$.

But if we recall earlier warnings (§22) about applying negation in ordinary discourse, we will write the negation as

(7)   *It is not the case that* all men are mortal (i.e., not all men are mortal)

or

(8)   Some men are not mortal.

These are of the forms, respectively,

(7') $\sim(x)(Fx \rightarrow Gx)$

(8') $(\exists x)(Fx \ \& \sim Gx)$

Notice that (6) cannot be the negation of (5), since both of them may be false (namely, if some men are mortal and some are not).   But if (5) is false, then (7)/(8) must be true, and vice versa.   In other words, (5) and (6) are contraries, not contradictories.

There are other difficulties.   Some expressions seem to form negations, but really do not; others do form negations, but not the expected ones. For example, the sentence

(9)   No one but a six-footer plays basketball today

may seem to be a negation, because the expression 'no one' occurs in it. Actually, it is not, since it can be rewritten as

None but the six-footer plays basketball today.

Only six-footers play basketball today (i.e., if any person plays basketball today, then that person is a six-footer).

Thus (9) is not a negation; it is simply another way of saying

(10)   All basketball players are six-footers

and its form is expressed by

(10′) $(x)(Fx \rightarrow Gx)$.

Finally, the sentence

(11)   All sophomores are not perspicacious

is clearly a negation.   But which negation is it?   In some contexts, it may be intended as

(12)   No sophomores are perspicacious.

In most cases, however, it is better to read it as

(13)   Not all sophomores are perspicacious (i.e., some sophomores are not perspicacious).

A NOTE ON 'ANY' AND 'ALL'

There are contexts in which 'any' means the same as 'all'.   An example is

(14)   All roads lead to Rome.
         Any road leads to Rome.

But this is not always the case, as is shown by the following illustration, adapted from Quine.[2]

(15)   Perkins can outrun all the men on the team.

(16)   Perkins can outrun any man on the team.

(17)   Perkins cannot outrun all the men on the team.   *at least one he can't beat*

(18)   Perkins cannot outrun any man on the team.

The first two—(15) and (16)—are equivalent, and their form is given by

(15′)/(16′)

$$(x)(Tx \rightarrow Sx)$$

(where 'T' abbreviates the predicate 'is a member of the team' and 'S' abbreviates the predicate 'Perkins can outrun'). Now (17) is the negation of (15). It is of the form

(17′) $\sim(x)(Tx \rightarrow Sx)$.

But (18) is *not* the negation of (16), and hence it is not the equivalent of (17). On the contrary, it is of the form

(18′) $(x)(Tx \rightarrow \sim Sx)$.

Thus the interchangeability of 'any' and 'all' fails for negations of universal generalizations. Another example would be

(19)   Doctors don't know everything (i.e., all things).

Doctors don't know anything.

As mentioned earlier, in §50 we shall consider again the relationship between PL-1 and ordinary language. That section will include further discussion of 'any' and 'all' and of 'all' and 'each'. It will also include comments on ordinary-language quantifying expressions other than 'all' and 'some'.

important

EXERCISES

38.1. An exercise on *quantifier idioms*: Here are some sentences in which the words 'some' and 'all' do *not* appear. Yet all of these

---

sentences are general sentences. How would you symbolize them, according to PL-1? Remember: You may paraphrase the sentence—while retaining the sense—if this helps you obtain a suitable symbolic expression. For example, a natural paraphrase of *a* below would be: "For all (people) *x*, if *x* helps himself or herself, then God helps *x*."

a.   God helps those who help themselves.

b.   Economists exist who are mathematicians, but not every economist is.

c.   Any valid argument that is not sound has a false premiss.

d.   Only Ph.D.'s are being hired.

e.   There is no candidate in the field who has a good program and a good chance to win.

f.   Contemporary philosophers are either existentialists or "analysts."

g.   There is at least one person in whom everyone has confidence.

h.   If everyone is sending and no one is receiving, then no one is communicating with anyone.

i.   In June, if ever, come perfect days.

j.   If anything can go wrong, it will.

38.2. An exercise on *negations* of general sentences: Symbolize each of these sentences; then write a sentence that is a negation of the original sentence; then symbolize the negation.

a.   All faculty members are effective teachers.

b.   No faculty member is an effective teacher.

c.   Some faculty members are effective teachers.

d.   Some faculty members are not effective teachers.

e.   Not all faculty members are effective teachers.

f.   None but faculty members are effective teachers.

§39   *Definition of PL-1 Sentence Form*

The notion of a PL-1 sentence form spells out for PL-1 the general notion of the logical form of a sentence (see §17).   The definition is fairly precise and somewhat formidable.

We shall first define a *PL-1 expression* as any (finite) sequence, or string of symbols, made up exclusively of predicate letters, individual constants, individual variables, quantifiers, sentence letters, truth-functional connective symbols, and punctuation symbols.

Having defined a PL-1 expression, we may formulate a definition of a *PL-1 sentence form.*

> *A PL-1 sentence form is any PL-1 expression that becomes a true-false sentence or else an open sentence when we uniformly replace sentence letters by true-false sentences, n-place predicate letters by ordinary-language n-place predicates, individual constants by the names of particular individuals belonging to a specified set, and quantifiers and truth-functional connective symbols by their ordinary-language counterparts.*

Thus PL-1 sentence forms may be of any of the following four types:

1.   Sentence letters.

2.   *n*-place predicate letters followed by *n* individual symbols (individual constants and/or individual variables).

3.   Universal or existential generalizations of type 1, 2, 3 itself, or 4.

4.   Truth-functional compounds of type 1, 2, 3, or 4 itself.

Any sentence or open sentence obtained from a PL-1 sentence form by substitutions made in accordance with the definition is called a *substitution instance* of that PL-1 sentence form.[3]

---

[3]   It is understood that in obtaining substitution instances from PL-1 sentence forms, we need to make suitable adjustments with respect to word order and idiom.   This should be clear from the examples that appear later in this and the following section.

THE DEFINITION ILLUSTRATED

The following are examples of PL-1 expressions that are PL-1 sentence forms:

Type 1	*P*	*Q*	*R*	*S*
Type 2	*Fa*	*Fx*	*Fax*	*Fxy*
Type 3	*(x)P*	*(x)Fx*	*(x)(∃y)Fxy*	*(x)(Fx & Gx)*
Type 4	*P* ∨ *Q*	*Fx* → *Gx*	*(x)Fx* ↔ *Ga*	*(x)(Fx* → *Gx)* → *(Fa* → *Ga)*

The following are examples of PL-1 expressions that are *not* PL-1 sentence forms:

(a)Fa   Fx &   Fa ∼ ∨ (x)Gx   (∃F)Fb

The following are examples of expressions that are not PL-1 expressions:

a ∈ S   (A)Fx   P % Fy

Comments on the Definition

The definition shows clearly that PL-1 absorbs the SL fragment. If types 2 and 3 are eliminated, together with the PL-1 sentence forms that can be constructed from them, what remain are sentence letters and their truth-functional compounds. These are just the SL sentence forms.

Notice too that the definition covers both *open* and *closed* sentence forms: an open PL-1 sentence form is one in which there is at least one free occurrence of a variable; a closed PL-1 sentence form is one in which no variable occurs free. Closed PL-1 sentence forms are sometimes called *symbolic* sentences, since all of their substitution instances are true-false sentences.

VARIABLES OVER PL-1 EXPRESSIONS

We shall find it useful, in talking about PL-1 expressions and PL-1 sentence forms, to employ variables that range over the set of PL-1 expressions. For this purpose, we reintroduce the letters

A   *B*   *C* · · ·

used earlier as variables over SL expressions.

EXERCISES

39.1. Which of the following expressions are *not* PL-1 expressions?

    a. *abcd*

    b. $(x)[(Fx + Gx) \rightarrow Hx]$

    c. $(F)Gx$

    d. $[(x)$

    e. $(x) - (y)$

    f. $(\exists A)Fa$

39.2. Which of the following PL-1 expressions are *not* PL-1 sentence forms?

    a. $(\exists a)Ga$

    b. $\sim(x)(y)Fxy \lor \sim Ga$

    c. $Fa \rightarrow (\sim x)Fx$

    d. $(y)(Fa \rightarrow Gy)$

    e. $Fa \lor (Gx \ \& \ Hx)$

    f. $(x)(Fx\sim \ \lor \ Fx)$

---

§40   *More on Quantification*

There are many more things that could be said about quantification, but only three will be mentioned briefly.

THE INTERDEFINABILITY OF '(x)' AND '$(\exists x)$'

In standard PL-1, the universal and existential quantifiers are interdefinable in the presence of negation. Thus 'Everyone is happy' means the same as 'It is not the case that someone is not happy'; or expressed formally,

(1)   '$(x)Fx$' may be defined as '$\sim(\exists x) \sim Fx$'.

Likewise,

(2)   '$(\exists x)Fx$' may be defined as '$\sim(x) \sim Fx$'.

Notice also that if we negate both sides of (1), we obtain

(3)   '$\sim(x)Fx$' may be defined as '$\sim \sim (\exists x) \sim Fx$',

which, since standard PL-1 accepts the principle of double negation, gives us

'$\sim(x)Fx$' may be defined as '$(\exists x) \sim Fx$'.

TRUTH-FUNCTIONAL EXPANSIONS OF
GENERAL SENTENCE FORMS

Consider the PL-1 sentence form

(4) $(x)Fx$

and assume that 'x' ranges over a finite set of n objects whose names are 'a_1', 'a_2', ..., 'a_n'. Now (4) is a universal generalization; thus it affirms the predicate 'F' of *all* the values of 'x'. Hence (4) can be expressed as the finite conjunction

(4*) $Fa_1 \ \& \ Fa_2 \ \& \cdots \& \ Fa_n$.

Similarly, the PL-1 sentence form

(5) $(\exists x)Fx$

is an existential generalization, and thus affirms the predicate 'F' of *at least one* value of 'x'. Hence (5) can be expressed as the finite disjunction

(5*) $Fa_1 \ \lor \ Fa_2 \ \lor \cdots \lor \ Fa_n$.

We call (4*) and (5*) the *truth-functional expansions* of, respectively, (4) and (5).

DOMAINS

To introduce a variable, we must specify the set of objects over which the variable ranges. This set is usually called the *domain*, or domain of interpretation, of the variable. (In our discussion, we shall assume that all variables range over or are defined for *all* objects in their domains.)

Choosing a Domain

The choice of domain depends on the problem or exercise we are faced with. If nothing is said to the contrary, the domain is understood to be the *set of all objects*, or the universe (*U*).   Often, however, it is more economical to pick a *restricted* domain.   Suppose, for example, we wish to express formally the sentence

(6)   All positive integers are odd or even.

We have two choices.   The first procedure is to take *U* as the domain; in that case, we have to introduce predicate letters to stand in place not only of 'is odd' and 'is even', but also of 'is a positive integer'.   We then write

(6′) $(x)[Ix \rightarrow (Ox \vee Ex)]$,

that is,

　　　　For all *x*, if *x* is a positive integer, then *x* is odd or *x* is even.

The second, and easier, procedure is to take as the domain the set of positive integers.   Then (6) can be written simply as

(6″) $(x)(Ox \vee Ex)$.

　As a second example, consider the sentence

(7)   All the world loves a lover.

If *U* is taken as the domain, the form of (7) may be represented as

(7′) $(x)\{[Px \ \& \ (\exists y)(Py \ \& \ Lxy)] \rightarrow (z)(Pz \rightarrow Lzx)\}$,

where '*P*' stands in place of 'is a person' and '*L*' in place of 'loves'. But if *people* is taken as the domain, it suffices to write

(7″) $(x)[(\exists y)Lxy \rightarrow (z)Lzx]$.

Domains Finite and Infinite

It was shown above that universal or existential generalizations over *finite* domains can be expressed truth-functionally as finite conjunctions or disjunctions.   But not all domains are finite.   In (6″), for example, where the domain is the set of positive integers, we quantify over an *infinite* domain.   It is obvious that a generalization over such a domain as, for instance,

(8)   There is no odd perfect integer

cannot be expressed by a finite truth-functional expansion.

A NOTE ON MONADIC PREDICATE LOGIC

Various partial first-order logics can be defined if certain restrictions are imposed on the range of PL-1 sentence forms under consideration. For example, if we stipulate that only *one-place predicates* be allowed, we obtain what is called *monadic* first-order predicate logic.

This portion of PL-1 has a number of interesting features. One is that Aristotle's logic of the syllogism may be treated as itself a fragment of monadic predicate logic. The four basic forms of categorical propositions studied by Aristotle are

> All S are P (the A proposition)
>
> No S are P (the E proposition)
>
> Some S are P (the I proposition)
>
> Some S are not P (the O proposition)

These may be expressed in monadic PL-1 as

> $(x)(Sx \rightarrow Px)$
> $(x)(Sx \rightarrow \sim Px)$
> $(\exists x)(Sx \ \& \ Px)$
> $(\exists x)(Sx \ \& \sim Px)$

Many of the examples of PL-1 argument forms that we shall use will be the monadic PL-1 equivalents of Aristotle's syllogisms.[4]

EXERCISES

40.1. Write out the truth-functional expansions for

   a. $(x)(Fx \ \lor \ \sim Fx)$

   b. $(\exists x)(Fx \ \& \sim Ga_1)$

where 'x' ranges over a finite set.

40.2. Which of the following are pairs of equivalent PL-1 sentence forms?

   a. $(x)[(\exists y)Fxy \ \& \ Gy]$
      $(x)(\exists y)(Fxy \ \& \ Gy)$

   b. $(\exists x)[(y)Fxy \ \& \ Gx]$
      $(\exists x)(y)Fxy \ \& \ (\exists x)Gx$

find example that makes one true + one false

---

[4]   See the Appendix on Aristotelian logic.

   c. $(x) \sim Gx$ & $(y)(Gy \lor \sim Gy)$
        $\sim(\exists x)Gx$ & $(y)(Gy \rightarrow Gy)$

   d. $Fab \rightarrow (x) \sim Fxx$
        $Fab \rightarrow \sim(\exists x)Fxx$

   e. $(x)(Fax \rightarrow Gx)$
        $(x)Fax \rightarrow (x)Gx$

   f. $(x)[Fax \rightarrow (\exists y)Fyx]$
        $\sim(\exists x)[Fax$ & $(y) \sim Fyx]$

   g. $(\exists x)[Fx$ & $(y)(Gy \rightarrow Hxy)]$
        $\sim(x) \sim [Fx$ & $(y)(Gy \rightarrow Hxy)]$

40.3. This is an exercise on domains. Here are some more sentences to symbolize. Notice that each one says something about two or more *different* sorts of objects (e.g., people and contests, questions and answers). Hence to symbolize these sentences according to PL-1, we take as the *domain* not one particular sort of object—say, *people*—but the *universe*, or the *universal domain*. And we use predicates—such as 'is a person'— to pick out the different *sorts* of objects we are talking about.

    Consider, for example, the sentence

> You can't win them all (i.e., no one can win all the contests in which he or she participates).

Here two sorts of objects are involved—*people* and *contests*. Hence we take as our domain the *universe*. The predicates we need for distinguishing the two sorts of objects are 'is a person' and 'is a contest', which we symbolize respectively by '*F*' and '*G*'. We also need the two-place predicates 'participates in' and 'win', which we symbolize respectively by the predicate letters '*H*' and '*I*'. We then have

$$\sim(\exists x)\{Fx \ \& \ (y)[(Gy \ \& \ Hxy) \rightarrow Ixy]\}$$

or

> It is not the case that there is an object x such that x is a person and such that for any object y, if y is a contest and x participates in y, then x wins y.

  One further point: Remember that generally there are several different but equivalent symbolizations of a sentence. Thus if we utilize the interdefinability of quantifiers in the presence of negation, we may also symbolize our sentence as follows:

$$(x) \sim \{Fx \ \& \ (y)[(Gy \ \& \ Hxy) \rightarrow Ixy]\}.$$

And if we make use of the truth-functional equivalence of $\sim(A$ & $B)$ and $A \rightarrow \sim B$, we may symbolize the sentence as

$$(x)\{Fx \rightarrow \sim(y)[(Gy \ \& \ Hxy) \rightarrow Ixy]\}.$$

a.   Everyone answered some of the questions.

b.   No one answered none of the questions.

c.   Some questions have no answers.

d.   Someone asked a question that no one answered.

e.   Every day in every way we are getting better.

f.   Everybody reads a newspaper every day.

g.   There is a newspaper that everybody reads every day.

h.   You can't tell the players without a scorecard (i.e., no one can identify the players unless he or she has a scorecard).

i.   Everyone learns something every day.

j.   When a great truth once gets abroad in the world, no power on earth can imprison it, or prescribe its limits, or suppress it. [Frederick Douglass (1817?–1895)]

40.4.   Now try your hand at symbolizing the following long, but not difficult, sentence. (Hint: Use '*x*' with numerical subscripts as your variables, since you may need four or five of them.   Also, it may help you keep track of things if you use abbreviation letters as predicate letters— thus '*I*' for 'is an instructor', '*S*' for 'is a student', '*C*' for 'have confidence in', and the like.)

> There are instructors in whom all students have confidence, and all the examinations or marks that such instructors give are fair, and such instructors neither patronize nor hector students, but instead respect and assist them.

do this chp.
~~chpt~~ 246 - 256
do it ↗

10

Validity of Predicate Logic Argument Forms: Truth Trees

Having described the various kinds of sentences and sentence forms considered in first-order predicate logic (PL-1), we turn now to the arguments and argument forms in which they appear. How are we to determine just which of these argument forms are *valid according to PL-1*, and which are not?

To answer this question, we require two things. First, we must have a *criterion of validity* for PL-1 argument forms. Second, there must be some *procedure* by which we can find out which PL-1 argument forms (hence which PL-1 arguments) fulfill this criterion.

Such a criterion is introduced and explained in the present chapter, together with two complementary procedures for applying it: the *method of interpretation* and the *truth-tree method*. An alternative procedure—the *method of derivations*, or natural deduction—is taken up in the following chapter.

§41   *Definition of PL-1 Argument Form*

The notion of a PL-1 argument form runs parallel to that of an SL argument form.   It spells out for PL-1 the general notion of the logical form of an argument.   The definition is

> *A PL-1 argument form is a sequence of closed PL-1 sentence forms such that when we uniformly replace n-place predicate letters with ordinary-language n-place predicates, individual constants with the names of particular individuals belonging to a specified set, sentence letters with true-false sentences, and quantifiers and truth-functional connective symbols with their ordinary-language counterparts, the result is a deductive argument, valid or invalid.*

Any argument obtained by making these substitutions in a PL-1 argument form is called a *substitution instance* of that PL-1 argument form. Thus

(1) $(x)(Fx \rightarrow Gx)$
         Fa
         Therefore *Ga*

is a PL-1 argument form. The sentence forms that make up (1) are all closed PL-1 sentence forms (see the definition, §39).   And when the indicated substitutions are made in these sentence forms, the outcome is an argument—for instance

(2)   All members of the French Academy are mortal.
         René Clair is a member of the French Academy.
         Therefore René Clair is mortal.

On the other hand,

(3) $Fa \rightarrow 5 > 2$
         Fa
         Therefore $5 > 2$

and

(4) $(x)(Fx \rightarrow Gx)$
         Ga

are not PL-1 argument forms, because (3) is not a sequence of PL-1 sentence forms and (4), although it is such a sequence, does not yield an argument when the appropriate substitutions are made.

Note that by definition, the set of PL-1 argument forms includes the set of SL argument forms as a proper subset.

---

§42   *Valid PL-1 Sentence Forms and Argument Forms*

Just as the notion of *tautology* is the key to the theory of inferences valid according to SL, so the notion of a *valid PL-1 sentence form* is the key to the theory of inferences valid according to PL-1. (Notice that the word 'valid' is now being used in *two* distinct senses. In the first, it is applied to PL-1 *argument forms* and *arguments*; in the second, it is applied to PL-1 *sentence forms*. The relationship between the two uses will emerge shortly.)

The notion of a valid PL-1 sentence form is not too difficult, but it must be approached in stages. We first consider two notions on which it rests —*interpretation* and *truth under an interpretation*. To simplify the discussion of these matters, we confine ourselves to *closed* PL-1 sentence forms —that is, those in which no variables occur free. The question of "truth" and "validity" for *all* PL-1 sentence forms, open and closed, is better left to a formal account of PL-1.

INTERPRETATION RELATIVE TO A DOMAIN

Let us first explain what is to be understood by the phrase '*interpreting* a PL-1 sentence form *relative to a domain of objects or individuals*'. This notion of interpretation can then be extended from single PL-1 sentence forms to *sets* of PL-1 sentence forms.

> *To interpret a closed PL-1 sentence form A relative to a domain of individuals D is to obtain from A an ordinary language sentence S by*
>
> 1. *Replacing the predicate letters of A (if any) with ordinary language predicates defined for the individuals of D.*
> 2. *Replacing the individual constants of A (if any) with the names of particular individuals of D.*
> 3. *Replacing the quantifier symbols and connective symbols of A (if any) with their ordinary-language counterparts.*
> 4. *Replacing the sentence letters of A (if any) with true-false sentences.*

For example, the sentence

(1)   Aristotle is fallible

may be regarded as the result of interpreting the PL-1 sentence form

(1')   *Fa*

relative to the domain of people.   For (1) can be obtained from (1') by replacing the predicate letter '*F*' with the ordinary-language predicate 'is fallible', which is defined for the domain of people, and replacing the individual constant '*a*' with the name of an individual person, Aristotle.
   A second example is the sentence

(2)   All perfect numbers are even (i.e., if anything is a perfect positive integer, it is even).

This sentence may be regarded as the result of interpreting the PL-1 sentence form

(2') $(x)(Fx \rightarrow Gx)$

relative to the domain of positive integers.   For (2) can be obtained from (2') by replacing the predicate letters '*F*' and '*G*' with the predicate 'is perfect' and 'is even' respectively, which are defined for positive integers, and replacing the connective symbol '$\rightarrow$' and the universal quantifier '(x)' with their ordinary-language counterparts 'if-then' and 'anything'.
   Obviously, the same PL-1 sentence form may be given different interpretations relative to the same domain and, of course, different interpretations relative to different domains.   Thus the sentences

> Aristotle is famous
> Aeschylus is Greek

can be obtained under different interpretations of (1') relative to the same domain (people) used in (1).   And the sentences

> 9 is odd
> Mars is uninhabited

can be obtained under different interpretations of (1') relative to different domains (integers, planets).
   It is also clear that the notion of interpretation-relative-to-a-domain can be extended from a *single* PL-1 sentence form to *sets* of PL-1 sentence forms.   All we need do is require that the domain be the same for all the

sentence forms in the set and that the replacements—of predicate letters with predicates, individual constants with names, and so forth—be uniform throughout the set.   For example, from the set of sentence forms

(3′)   *Fa*
         $(x)(Fx \lor Gx)$

interpreted relative to the domain *integers*, we could obtain, say, the set of sentences

(3)   1 is odd
           All integers are odd or even.

TRUTH UNDER AN INTERPRETATION

We now define what it means to say that a closed PL-1 sentence form is *true under an interpretation*.   The definition is

> *A closed PL-1 sentence form A is said to be true under an interpretation I iff the sentence S obtained from A under that interpretation is true.*

Here, as in the preceding chapter, we shall be content to say that a statement-making sentence *S* is true iff what it says is so; for example, the sentence

          Aristotle is Greek

is true iff Aristotle is indeed Greek.

VALID (CLOSED) PL-1 SENTENCE FORM DEFINED

With the aid of the two preceding definitions, we may now formulate the following one:

> *A closed PL-1 sentence form is valid iff it is true under* every *interpretation in* every *nonempty domain.*

Let us illustrate the definition first with a negative example.   Take '*Fa*' again.   This is a PL-1 sentence form that is not valid.   For let the domain be *people*, and let '*F*' be replaced by 'is French' and '*a*' by 'Aristotle'. Under this interpretation of '*Fa*' we obtain the sentence:

Aristotle is French.

This sentence is not true, since it is not the case that Aristotle is French. (Notice that a PL-1 sentence form can be *proved* to be *not* valid if we can find a counterexample—that is, an interpretation under which the sentence form is *not* true.)

Let us turn now to a positive example. Consider the PL-1 sentence form

(4') $(x)Fx \rightarrow Fa$.

Again let the domain be *people*, and let '*F*' be replaced by 'is French' and '*a*' by 'Aristotle'. Under this interpretation of (4') we obtain

(4a)   If everyone is French, then Aristotle is French.

This, of course, is a true sentence. Choose next any other domain—say, *integers*; let '*F*' be replaced by 'is even' and '*a*' by '1'. We then have

(4b)   If every integer is even, then 1 is even,

which is also a true sentence. Thus we can see (although we have not proved) that (4') is a valid PL-1 sentence form: it comes out true under every interpretation in every nonempty domain.

Remarks: We pause briefly for three remarks on PL-1 sentence forms and their domains of interpretation.

First, while all tautologies are valid PL-1 sentence forms, not all valid PL-1 sentence forms are tautologies. Remember that tautologies such as

(5') $P \vee \sim P$

are PL-1 sentence forms (see the definition, §39). They are also valid. For if we replace the sentence connectives with their ordinary-language counterparts, then no matter what true-false sentences we (uniformly) put in place of the sentence letters, we obtain a true sentence, such as

(5)   Socrates is a philosopher or Socrates is not a philosopher.

Not all valid PL-1 sentence forms are tautologies, however. Take, for example, (4'). It is a valid PL-1 sentence form. But clearly it is not a tautology. For its truth table is the same as that for '$P \rightarrow Q$', unless we quite arbitrarily limit its interpretations to those with finite domains and then replace it with its truth-functional expansion.   In that case, we would have

(4″) $(Fa_1 \ \& \ Fa_2 \ \& \ \cdots \ \& \ Fa_n) \rightarrow Fa_1$

for some finite number n, and this obviously can be shown to be a tautology.

Second, the definition of a valid PL-1 sentence form bars the empty set as a domain.   This limitation is purely a matter of technical convenience. For instance, if the empty domain is admitted, the sentence form

(6′) $(x)Fx \rightarrow (\exists x)Fx$

cannot be accepted as valid.   For let the domain be *female ex-Presidents of the United States* and let '*F*' be replaced by 'is famous'.   Then although it is (vacuously) true that all members of the domain are famous, it is not true that there *is* a member that is famous, since the domain has no members.   Thus (6′) is not true under this interpretation and hence is not valid.   Contrariwise, if only nonempty domains are admitted, then (6′) will be valid, a result that will simplify the system of inference rules we shall consider later in this chapter.

Third, PL-1 sentence forms that are valid in the *universal* sense defined above should be distinguished from those that are valid in the *restricted* sense that they come out true under every interpretation relative to a *particular* domain or set of domains.   For example, let the domain be *even primes* (2 is the only one), and let '*F*' be replaced by the one-place predicate 'is less than 3'.   Under this interpretation, the PL-1 sentence form

(7′) $(\exists x)Fx \rightarrow (x)Fx$

will be true.   For if there is a member of the domain that is less than 3, then each member of the domain is less than 3, since the domain has only one member.   Indeed, (7′) will be true under every interpretation in any domain with just one member and is thus valid for single-member domains. But clearly it is not valid.   For let the domain be *integers* and let '*F*' again be replaced by 'is less than 3'.   Under this interpretation of the sentence form (7′), we obtain

(7)   If there is an integer less than 3, then each integer is less than 3,

which of course is not true.

Theorems on Valid PL-1 Sentence Forms

Three simple theorems follow directly from our definitions.   (The proofs are left to the reader.)   Let '*A*' and '*B*' be variables ranging over PL-1 sentence forms.   Then

THEOREM 1:   If A is valid, so is $A \lor B$.

THEOREM 2:   If B is valid, so is $A \to B$.

THEOREM 3:   If A and $A \to B$ are valid, so is B.

A CRITERION OF VALIDITY FOR PL-1 ARGUMENT FORMS

Valid *sentence* forms play the same crucial role in PL-1 as that played by tautologies in SL.   They enable us to formulate a simple *criterion of validity* for PL-1 *argument* forms.   This criterion is at the same time a criterion of validity for PL-1 arguments, since in PL-1, as in SL, inference is formal: if an argument form is valid, so are all the arguments that are its substitution instances.

The Criterion Stated

(8)

> *A PL-1 argument form is valid iff its corresponding conditional is a valid PL-1 sentence form.*

Note that the criterion in effect reduces the validity problem for PL-1 *argument* forms to the validity problem for PL-1 *sentence* forms.   (Here we see the relationship, referred to at the beginning of this section, between the two uses of ' valid ': one as applied to argument forms and the other as applied to sentence forms.)

The Criterion Illustrated

The PL-1 argument form

(9′) $(x)(Fx \to Gx)$
       Fa
       Therefore Ga

is valid iff its corresponding conditional

$$[(x)(Fx \to Gx) \;\&\; Fa] \to Ga$$

is a valid PL-1 sentence form.

Similarly, a PL-1 argument, say

(9)   All who publish are promoted
       Perkins publishes
       Therefore Perkins is promoted

is valid if the PL-1 argument form of which it is a substitution instance, namely (9'), is valid.

VALIDITY AND LOGICAL TRUTH IN PL-1

We now explicate the notion of logical truth in PL-1 as follows: a sentence *S* is a *logical truth according to PL-1* iff it is a substitution instance of a valid PL-1 sentence form.   For example,

(10') $(x)Fx \rightarrow Fa$,

as was seen above, is a valid PL-1 sentence form.   A substitution instance of (10') is

(10)   If everyone is fallible, Aristotle is fallible.

Hence (10) is a logical truth according to PL-1.

Since all substitution instances of valid PL-1 argument forms are valid PL-1 arguments and have corresponding conditionals that are substitution instances of valid PL-1 sentence forms, our criterion of validity (8) may be rewritten as follows:

(8')

> *An argument is valid according to PL-1 iff its corresponding conditional is a substitution instance of a valid PL-1 sentence form—i.e., iff its corresponding conditional is logically true according to PL-1.*

Thus (8') is seen to be a special case of the general criterion of deductive validity suggested in §18 :

> *An argument is valid iff its corresponding conditional is a logical truth.*

VALIDITY, AND IMPLICATION AND EQUIVALENCE, IN PL-1

The parallel with SL continues.   In SL (logical) *implication* and (logical) *equivalence* were defined as the *tautologicality* of the conditional and the biconditional respectively.   In PL-1 they are defined as the *validity* of the conditional and the biconditional respectively.

Thus in PL-1, if *A* and *B* are PL-1 sentence forms, then *A* implies *B* iff the conditional

$A \rightarrow B$

is a valid PL-1 sentence form; and A is equivalent to B iff the biconditional

$$A \leftrightarrow B$$

is a valid PL-1 sentence form.   For example, '$[(x)(Fx \to Gx)$ & $Fa]$' implies 'Ga' iff the conditional

$$[(x)(Fx \to Gx) \ \& \ Fa] \to Ga$$

is a valid PL-1 sentence form.

EXERCISES

42.1.   Show that each of the following PL-1 sentence forms is *not valid* by finding a *counterexample*—that is, an *interpretation* under which the sentence form is acknowledgedly *false*.   Specify the domain (D) of interpretation in each case.

    a. $(x)Fx \lor (x) \sim Fx$

    b. $(\exists x)Fx \to (x)Fx$

    c. $Fa \lor (\sim Fa \ \& \ Ga)$

    d. $(x)(Fx \to Gx) \to (x)(Gx \to Fx)$

    e. $(\exists x)(Fx \ \& \sim Gx) \to (\exists x)(Gx \ \& \sim Fx)$

    f. $(x)(y)(Fxy \to \sim Fyx)$

    g. $(x)(y)(z)[(Fxy \ \& \ Fyz) \to Fxz]$

    h. $(x) \sim Fx \lor \sim (\exists x)Fx$

42.2.   Which of these PL-1 sentence forms would you regard as valid? Which would *not* come out true under any interpretation in any nonempty domain?

    a. $\sim(x) \sim Fx \ \& \sim (\exists x)Fx$

    b. $(x) \sim Fx \lor (\exists x)Fx$

    c. $(x)(Fx \to Gx) \to (\exists x)Fx$

    d. $(x)[Fx \lor (\sim Fx \lor Ga)]$

    e. $(\exists x)[(Fx \ \& \ Gx) \ \& \ (\sim Fx \lor \sim Gx)]$

    f. $\sim Fa \lor (x)Fx$

    g. $(\exists x)(Fx \to Gx) \lor (\exists x) \sim Gx$

    h. $[(x)(Fx \to Gx) \ \& \ Fa] \to \sim Ga$

42.3.   Prove the following theorems about *valid PL-1 sentence forms:*

    a.   If B is valid, so is $A \rightarrow B$.

    b.   If $A \rightarrow B$ and A are valid, so is B.

---

§43   *Testing the Validity of PL-1 Argument Forms: Method of Interpretation*

In Chapter 9 we analyzed the *internal structure* of certain simple sentences, singular and general.   In §42 we formulated a *criterion of validity* for arguments composed of such sentences or their truth-functional compounds.   Our task now is to devise a simple, economic *procedure* for finding out if any given PL-1 argument or argument form meets that criterion.

Here the parallel with SL is interrupted, for truth tables cannot fully serve our purpose.   An alternative procedure is therefore not merely a convenience in PL-1 but a necessity.

This section will present the first of several such alternatives: the *method of interpretation*.   While simple and direct, it is *not* general in scope.   It enables us to prove *only* that a PL-1 argument form is *in*valid. Hence it should be used only when invalidity is suspected.

The two other procedures that will be considered are *truth trees* and *natural deduction*, or *derivations*—both extended so as to be applicable to PL-1.   Here the parallel with SL resumes.   These two methods enable us to determine validity *or* invalidity, and are thus quite general in scope. They can be used either to complement or to replace the method of interpretation.

In PL-1, truth trees (with an exception to be entered later) retain the virtue of simplicity and can be described briefly.   But natural deduction in PL-1 runs into complications and will invite an unhurried view.

THE METHOD OF INTERPRETATION: FINDING A COUNTEREXAMPLE

According to our criterion of validity, a PL-1 argument form is *invalid* if its corresponding conditional is not a valid sentence form.   A PL-1 *sentence form* in turn is not valid if there is an interpretation under which it comes out false.   Thus if we can find an interpretation under which a corresponding conditional is *not* true (a counterexample), we shall then have shown that the argument form to which it corresponds is invalid.

Example 1

The PL-1 argument form

(1) $(\exists x)Fx$
          $(\exists x)Gx$
          Therefore $(\exists x)(Fx \ \& \ Gx)$

is valid iff its corresponding conditional

(2) $[(\exists x)Fx \ \& \ (\exists x)Gx] \rightarrow (\exists x)(Fx \ \& \ Gx)$

is a valid PL-1 sentence form.   But is (2) valid?
    Consider a counterexample.   Let the domain be *integers*, and let '*F*' be replaced by 'is odd' and '*G*' by 'is even'.   Under this interpretation of (2) we obtain

(2′)   If some integers are odd and some integers are even, then some
          integers are odd and even,

which of course is false.   Hence (2) is not valid.   But (2) is the corresponding conditional of (1); therefore (1) is invalid.
    Here we have proved (1) invalid by locating an interpretation under which the corresponding conditional comes out false.   But a corresponding conditional turns out false under an interpretation iff the argument form, under that interpretation, yields a substitution instance that is *invalid*.   Hence we could just as well have proved (1) invalid by showing that there is an interpretation under which it yields an invalid substitution instance—that is, an argument with true premisses and a false conclusion.

Example 2

PL-1 Argument Form

          $(x)(Fx \rightarrow Gx)$
          $(x)(Fx \rightarrow Hx)$
          Therefore $(x)(Gx \rightarrow Hx)$

Counterexample.   Let the domain be *arguments*, and let '*F*' be replaced by 'is sound', '*G*' by 'is valid', and '*H*' by 'has true premisses'.   Under this interpretation, we obtain the argument

          Any sound argument is valid.
          Any sound argument has true premisses.
          Therefore any valid argument has true premisses.

This argument is invalid, since its premisses are all true and its conclusion false.

Example 3

PL-1 ARGUMENT FORM

> $(y)(\exists x)Fxy$
> Therefore $(\exists x)(y)Fxy$

Counterexample.   Let the domain be *integers*, and let ' F ' be replaced by the two-place predicate 'is greater than'.   We then have

> For any integer there is a greater integer.
>
> Therefore there is an integer that is greater than any integer (i.e., there is a greatest integer).

But this argument is invalid, since its premiss is true and its conclusion false.

Warning: Although the method of interpretation is simple—a single counterexample suffices to show that a PL-1 argument form is invalid—it is not error-proof.   The construction of counterexamples can go wrong in many ways.   Two cautions are in order.   First, be sure—paying special heed to the proper choice of domain—that the argument you offer as a counterexample really is a substitution instance of the argument form under attack.   Second, be sure—mindful that intuitions about validity may mislead—that the substitution instance you offer really is invalid.   The next example illustrates the first caution.

Example 4

A counterexample is sought to the PL-1 argument form

(3) $(x)(\exists y)Fxy$
       Therefore $(\exists y)(x)Fxy$

The following argument is offered:

(3′)   Everyone loves someone.

        Therefore there is someone whom everyone loves.

Now (3′) is a substitution instance of (3) obtained under the interpretation in which the domain is *people* and ' F ' is replaced by 'loves'. Moreover, (3′) is invalid: its conclusion may be false even if the premiss is true.   Hence it is a proper counterexample to (3).

Suppose, however, that instead of (3'), the following argument is offered as a counterexample to (3).

look at # 4
there is a
mistake

(4')   Everyone answered some question.

Therefore there is some question that everyone answered.

Clearly (4') is invalid. But is it a substitution instance of (3)? We can, of course, take 'answered' as replacing '*F*'. But what shall we choose as the domain of interpretation? *People? Questions?* Obviously it cannot be either alone, nor can it be both. Thus (3), as it stands, cannot have (4') as a substitution instance. Hence (4') is not a proper counter-example to (3).

In fact, (4') is an instance of a different PL-1 argument form. For let the domain be *the universe*, and let 'answered' be the replacement of '*F*'. Then if we treat 'is a person' and 'is a question' as predicates and think of them as having replaced the predicate letters '*G*' and '*H*' respectively, we see that (4') is the instance yielded under this interpre-tation by

(4) $(x)(\exists y)[(Gx \ \& \ Hy) \rightarrow Fxy]$

Therefore $(\exists y)(x)[(Gx \ \& \ Hy) \rightarrow Fxy]$

And since (4') is invalid, it is a counterexample to (4).

A final example illustrates the second caution.

Example 5

Suppose we suspect that the following PL-1 argument form is invalid:

(5) $(x)[(\exists y)Lxy \rightarrow (z)Lzx]$

$\sim Lbj$

Therefore $\sim Ljj$

As a counterexample we offer

(5')   All the world loves a lover.

Bob does not love Jane.

Therefore Jane does not love herself.

Now (5') is indeed a substitution instance of (5); for it is obtained under an interpretation in which the domain is *people*, the two-place predicate letter '*L*' is replaced by 'loves' and the individual constants '*b*' and '*j*' by the names 'Bob' and 'Jane'. But (5') is *valid*: its. conclusion cannot be false if both of its premises are true. (Assume that the con-clusion is false—that is, assume that Jane does love herself. She is then a lover, and by the first premiss everyone loves her, including Bob, which contradicts the second premiss.)   Hence (5′) is not a proper counter-example to (5).   Nor is there one, since (5) is valid, as will be seen later.

But the question remains: Why can't the method of interpretation also be used to establish the *validity* of a PL-1 argument form?   The answer follows directly from our criterion of validity.   A PL-1 argument form is *invalid* if there is *an* interpretation under which it yields an invalid sub-stitution instance; it is *valid* only if there is *no* interpretation under which it yields an invalid instance.   We can prove that there is an interpretation that yields an invalid instance by producing one, and thus establishing invalidity.   But how can we prove—by the method of interpretation—that there is *no* such interpretation?   Proofs of *validity* require another procedure.

EXERCISES

43.1.   This is an exercise in finding counterexamples to PL-1 argument forms.   By the method of interpretation, show that the following argu-ment forms are *invalid*.   Be sure to specify domains.

a. $(x)(Gx \rightarrow Hx)$
$(x)(Fx \rightarrow \sim Gx)$
Therefore $(x)(Fx \rightarrow \sim Hx)$

b. $(\exists x)(Fx \ \& \sim Gx)$
$(\exists x)(Gx \ \& \sim Hx)$
Therefore $(\exists x)(Fx \ \& \sim Hx)$

c. $(x)(Gx \rightarrow \sim Hx)$
$(x)(Fx \rightarrow \sim Gx)$
Therefore $(x)(Fx \rightarrow \sim Hx)$

d. $(x)(Gx \rightarrow \sim Hx)$
$(\exists x)(Fx \ \& \sim Gx)$
Therefore $(\exists x)(Hx \ \& \sim Fx)$

e. $(\exists x)Fx \lor (x)Gx$
$\sim Ga$
Therefore Fa

f. $(x)(Fx \lor Gx)$
$(x)(Gx \rightarrow Hx)$
Therefore $(\exists x)(Hx \rightarrow Fx)$

g. Fab
$(x)(\exists y)Fxy$
Therefore $(\exists x)Fxa$

43.2.   For each of the following arguments, write the PL-1 argument form and supply a counterexample.   (Note that although all these arguments have true premises and true conclusions, they are invalid.)

  a.   Some musicians are concert artists.   Some violinists are musicians.   Therefore some violinists are concert artists.

  b.   Some novelists are philosophers.   Iris Murdoch is a novelist. Therefore Iris Murdoch is a philosopher.

  c.   No periodontal work is covered by Medicare.   Some work covered by Medicare is surgery.   Therefore some periodontal work is not surgery.

  d.   If one number is equal to a second, and the second to a third, then the first is equal to the third.   If one number is equal to a second, then the second is equal to the first.   Therefore every number is equal to itself.

---

§44   *Testing the Validity of PL-1 Argument Forms: Truth-Tree Method*

In PL-1, as in SL, truth trees offer a handy way of finding out whether an argument form is valid.   We need only absorb the " unpacking rules " for SL into a broader set that includes suitable rules for unpacking the closed quantified sentence forms of PL-1.

Recall (see §28) that there are three steps in a truth-tree test for the validity of an argument form.   The first step is to write down the premises of the argument form and the *negation* of its conclusion.   The second is to construct a truth tree for the set thus formed.   The third is to determine whether all paths in the tree close.   If all the paths do close, then the set is not consistent (that is, the truth of the premises is not compatible with the denial of the conclusion) and the argument form is *valid*.   If any path remains open, the argument form is invalid.

THE UNPACKING RULES FOR PL-1

The unpacking rules for PL-1 include two groups.   The first are the rules taken over from SL:

Rule 1	Rule 2	Rule 3	Rule 4
$A \rightarrow B$	$A \lor B$	$A \ \& \ B$	$A \leftrightarrow B$
$\diagdown$	$\diagdown$		$\diagdown$
$\sim A \quad B$	$A \quad B$	A	$A \quad \sim A$
		B	$B \quad \sim B$

Rule 5	Rule 6	Rule 7	Rule 8	Rule 9
$\sim(A \rightarrow B)$	$\sim(A \lor B)$	$\sim(A \,\&\, B)$	$\sim(A \leftrightarrow B)$	$\sim\sim A$
A	$\sim A$	$\sim A \quad \sim B$	$A \quad \sim A$	A
$\sim B$	$\sim B$		$\sim B \quad B$	

To these we now add three rules for dealing with universally quantified and existentially quantified sentence forms[1]:

RULE 10.   UQ: *Rule for the Universal Quantifier.*   If a universally quantified sentence form appears in an open path of a tree, we may write *any* sentence forms obtained from it by dropping the quantifier and uniformly replacing *all* occurrences of the quantified variable by occurrences of any individual constant.   Do *not* check off the universally quantified sentence form, since it may be drawn on as many times as needed.

Examples

Sentence Form	Unpacks as		
$(x)Fx$	$Fa \quad Fb$	Fc	etc.
$(x)(Fx \rightarrow Gx)$	$Fa \rightarrow Ga$	$Fb \rightarrow Gb$	etc.
$(x)(\exists y)Fxy$	$(\exists y)Fay$	$(\exists y)Fby$	etc.

But we may not write, say,

Fx
$Fa \rightarrow Gb$
$(\exists y)Fxy$

RULE 11.   EQ: *Rule for the Existential Quantifier.*   If an existentially quantified sentence form appears in an open path of a tree, we may write *some one* sentence form obtained from it by dropping the quantifier and uniformly replacing all occurrences of the quantified variable by occurrences of a *particular* individual constant—*provided that the constant we choose has not already appeared anywhere in the path.*   Then *check off* the existentially quantified sentence form, since it can be drawn on only once.

---

[1]   This discussion of the truth-tree procedure for PL-1 is adapted from Richard Jeffrey, *Formal Logic: Its Scope and Limits* (New York: McGraw-Hill, 1967), Chapter 6.

Examples

Sentence Form	Unpacks as
(∃x)Fx	Either *Fa* or *Fb* or etc.
(∃x)(Fx & Gx)	Either *Fa & Ga* or *Fb & Gb* or etc.
(∃x)(y)Fxy	Either (y)*Fay* or (y)*Fby* or etc.
(∃x)Fax	Either *Fab* or. *Fac* or etc.

RULE 12. NQ: *Rule for Negations of Quantified Sentence Forms.* If the *negation* of a *universally* quantified sentence form appears on an open path of a tree, we may *check* it and rewrite it as the *existential* quantification of the negation of the *open* sentence form that follows the universal quantifier. Similarly, if the *negation* of an *existentially* quantified sentence form appears on an open path, we may *check* it and rewrite it as the *universal* quantification of the negation of the *open* sentence form that follows the existential quantifier.

Examples

Sentence Form	Is Rewritten as
~ (x)Fx	(∃x) ~ Fx
~ (x) ~ Fx	(∃x) ~ ~ Fx [i.e., (∃x)Fx by R 9]
~ (x)(y)Fxy	(∃x) ~ (y)Fxy
~ (x)(∃y)Fxy	(∃x) ~ (∃y)Fxy
~ (∃x)Fx	(x) ~ Fx
~ (∃x) ~ Fx	(x)Fx
~ (∃x)(y)Fxy	(x) ~ (y)Fxy

With this set of unpacking rules to guide us, we can construct truth trees to determine whether any argument form is valid according to PL-1, and whether any PL-1 sentence form is a valid sentence form in PL-1.

Warnings: In constructing truth trees, we must bear in mind two warnings. *First, unpacking rules may be applied only to whole closed sentence forms and not to parts, even parts that standing alone are sentence forms.* Thus to ' (x)Fx → Fa ' we may apply not Rule UQ, but the rule for the conditional (Rule 1). We obtain

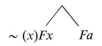

On the other hand, '$(x)(Fx \rightarrow Fa)$' is a universally quantified sentence form and therefore subject to Rule UQ.   Applying UQ, we obtain

$Fa \rightarrow Fa$
$Fb \rightarrow Fa$
$Fc \rightarrow Fa$
etc.

Second, Rules UQ and EQ may be applied only to universally or existentially quantified sentence forms, not to their negations.   Thus Rule UQ is not applicable to '$\sim (x)(Fx \rightarrow Gx)$'.   What we must do is call upon Rule NQ and obtain '$(\exists x) \sim (Fx \rightarrow Gx)$'.   We may then apply Rule EQ and obtain, say, '$\sim (Fa \rightarrow Ga)$', provided that 'a' has not already appeared anywhere in the path.   Similarly, Rule EQ is not applicable to '$\sim (\exists x)$ $(Fx \& Gx)$'.   We must again call upon Rule NQ and now obtain '$(x) \sim (Fx \& Gx)$', to which we may apply Rule UQ.

EXAMPLES OF TRUTH TREES

We turn next to a series of examples illustrating the use of truth trees in PL-1.   The first group shows how the method works for quantified sentence forms involving only one-place predicate letters.   The second group extends the procedure to quantified sentence forms with predicate letters of two or more places.   On the way, we pause to announce and illustrate a very important maxim of truth-tree construction: *always unpack existentially quantified sentence forms first.*   (See Example 4 below.)

Example 1

Determine whether the following argument form is valid:

$(x)Fx$
Therefore *Fa*

TRUTH TREE

1. $(x)Fx$ Premiss

2. $\sim Fa$ Negation of conclusion

3. Fa 1 Rule UQ
    X

Since the one path closes, this is a valid argument form.

Example 2

Determine whether the following argument form is valid:

> $(x)Fx$
> Therefore $(\exists x)Fx$

TRUTH TREE

1.	$(x)Fx$	Premiss
2.	$\checkmark \sim(\exists x)Fx$	Negation of conclusion
3.	$(x) \sim Fx$	2 NQ
4.	Fa	1 UQ
5.	$\sim Fa$	3 UQ
	X.	

Thus this argument form too is valid.

Example 3

Determine whether the following argument form is valid:

> $(x)(Fx \to Gx)$
> Fa
> Therefore Ga

TRUTH TREE

1. $(x)(Fx \to Gx)$ Premiss

2. Fa Premiss

3. $\sim Ga$ Negation of conclusion

4. $\checkmark Fa \to Ga$ 1 UQ

5. $\sim Fa$ Ga 4 →
    X   X

All paths close.   Thus it is valid.

Example 4

Now determine whether the following *argument* is valid:

> All historians are critics of times past.
> Some faculty members are historians.
> Therefore some faculty members are critics of times past.

This argument is a substitution instance of the PL-1 argument form

$(x)(Gx \rightarrow Hx)$
$(\exists x)(Fx \ \& \ Gx)$
Therefore $(\exists x)(Fx \ \& \ Hx)$

Notice that a universal quantifier appears in the first premiss and an existential quantifier in the second (and in the conclusion). Forewarned, we invoke the maxim "First eliminate existential quantifiers," which in this case bids us apply EQ (at step 5) before UQ. The tree should therefore be constructed as follows:

TRUTH TREE

1.	$(x)(Gx \rightarrow Hx)$	Premiss
2.	✓✓ $(\exists x)(Fx \ \& \ Gx)$	Premiss
3.	✓ $\sim(\exists x)(Fx \ \& \ Hx)$	Negation of conclusion
4.	$(x) \sim (Fx \ \& \ Hx)$	3 NQ
5.	✓✓ $Fa \ \& \ Ga$	2 EQ
6.	Fa	5 &
7.	Ga	5 &
8.	✓ $Ga \rightarrow Ha$	1 UQ
9.	$\sim Ga$ Ha	8 →
	X	
10.	✓ $\sim(Fa \ \& \ Ha)$	4 UQ
11.	$\sim Fa$ $\sim Ha$	$\sim(\&)$
	X X	

Thus the argument form is valid, as is the argument.

Why observe the maxim? Suppose we ignore it and apply UQ before EQ at step 5. Then our tree will look like this:

*TRUTH TREE

1.	$(x)(Gx \rightarrow Hx)$	Premiss
2.	✓ $(\exists x)(Fx \ \& \ Gx)$	Premiss
3.	✓ $\sim(\exists x)(Fx \ \& \ Hx)$	Negation of conclusion
4.	$(x) \sim (Fx \ \& \ Hx)$	3 NQ

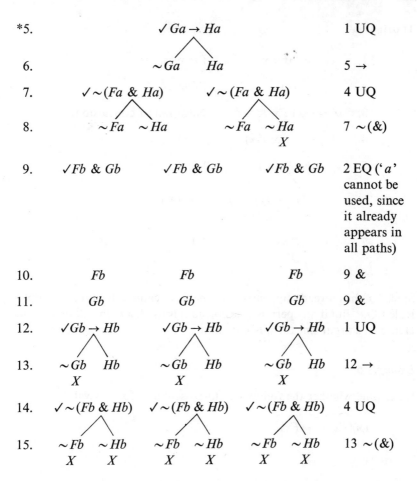

*5.   ✓ Ga → Ha   1 UQ

6.   ~ Ga   Ha   5 →

7.   ✓ ~ (Fa & Ha)   ✓ ~ (Fa & Ha)   4 UQ

8.   ~ Fa   ~ Ha   ~ Fa   ~ Ha   7 ~ (&)
                             X

9.   ✓Fb & Gb   ✓Fb & Gb   ✓Fb & Gb   2 EQ ('*a*' cannot be used, since it already appears in all paths)

10.   Fb   Fb   Fb   9 &

11.   Gb   Gb   Gb   9 &

12.   ✓Gb → Hb   ✓Gb → Hb   ✓Gb → Hb   1 UQ

13.   ~ Gb   Hb   ~ Gb   Hb   ~ Gb   Hb   12 →
      X   X   X

14.   ✓~(Fb & Hb)   ✓~(Fb & Hb)   ✓~(Fb & Hb)   4 UQ

15.   ~ Fb   ~ Hb   ~ Fb   ~ Hb   ~ Fb   ~ Hb   13 ~ (&)
    X   X   X   X   X   X

The paths all close, proving the argument valid. Thus the maxim *can* be ignored. But the result, reached after much unnecessary labor, will be a tree that is much longer and needlessly ramified. This maxim, then, is in the same category as the admonition (see §28) to apply nonbranching rules before branching rules, wherever possible. It belongs to the practice of truth-tree construction, not its theory.

The next example illustrates an error in applying EQ.

Example 5

Now test the following argument form:

(∃x)Fx
Ga
Therefore (∃x)(Fx & Gx)

TRUTH TREE

1.	✓ (∃x)Fx	Premiss
2.	Ga	Premiss
3.	✓ ~ (∃x)(Fx & Gx)	Negation of conclusion
4.	(x) ~(Fx & Gx)	3 NQ
5.	✓ ~(Fa & Ga)	4 UQ

6.   ~Fa   ~Ga   5 ~ (&)
              X

7.   Fa   1 EQ   *Wrong*
              X?

Since '*a*' has already appeared on line 2, it cannot be used in applying Rule EQ.   But if any permissible constant is used, a path will remain open. Hence this argument form is *not* valid.

Example 6

Determine whether the following closed sentence form is valid:

$(x)(Fx \lor \sim Fx)$

TRUTH TREE

1.	✓ ~(x)(Fx ∨ ~Fx)	Negation of sentence form
2.	✓ (∃x) ~ (Fx ∨ ~Fx)	1 NQ
3.	✓ ~ (Fa ∨ ~Fa)	2 EQ
4.	~Fa	3 ~(∨)
5.	~ ~Fa	3 ~(∨)
	X	

Thus Example 6 is a valid sentence form of PL-1.

Example 7

Next, determine whether the following sentence form is valid:

$(x)Fx \lor (x) \sim Fx$

TRUTH TREE

1.	$\checkmark \sim[(x)Fx \lor (x) \sim Fx]$	Negation of sentence form
2.	$\checkmark \sim(x)Fx$	$1 \sim(\lor)$
3.	$\checkmark \sim(x) \sim Fx$	$1 \sim(\lor)$
4.	$\checkmark(\exists x) \sim Fx$	2 NQ
5.	$\sim Fa$	4 EQ
6.	$\checkmark(\exists x) \sim \sim Fx$	3 NQ
7.	$\checkmark(\exists x)Fx$	6 Cancellation law for negation
8.	Fb	7 EQ (Note: 'a' has already appeared in the path)

Thus Example 7 is *not* a valid sentence form.

We come now to examples with predicate letters of two or more places.

Example 8

Determine whether the following argument form is valid:

$(\exists x)(y)Fxy$
Therefore $(y)(\exists x)Fxy$

TRUTH TREE

1.	$\checkmark(\exists x)(y)Fxy$	Premiss
2.	$\checkmark \sim(y)(\exists x)Fxy$	Negation of conclusion
3.	$\checkmark(\exists y) \sim (\exists x)Fxy$	2 NQ
4.	$\checkmark \sim(\exists x)Fxa$	3 EQ
5.	$(x) \sim Fxa$	4 NQ
6.	$(y)Fby$	1 EQ
7.	$\sim Fba$	5 UQ
8.	Fba	6 UQ
	X	

Hence Example 8 is a valid argument form.

Example 9

Now test the following argument form for validity:

$(y)(\exists x)Fxy$
Therefore $(\exists x)(y)Fxy$

TRUTH TREE

    1. $(y)(\exists x)Fxy$ Premiss

    2.   ✓ $\sim(\exists x)(y)Fxy$ Negation of conclusion

    3.   ✓ $(\exists x)Fxa$ 1 UQ

    4. Fba 3 EQ

    5. $(x) \sim (y)Fxy$ 2 NQ

    6.   ✓ $\sim(y)Fby$ 5 UQ

    7.   ✓ $(\exists y) \sim Fby$ 6 NQ

    8. $\sim Fbc$ 7 EQ   (Note: 'c' must be used, since 'a' and 'b' have already appeared)

    9.   ✓ $(\exists x)Fxb$ 1 UQ

    10. Fdb 9 EQ   (Note: 'd' must be used, since 'a', 'b', and 'c' have already appeared)

    11.   ✓ $\sim(y)Fdy$ 5 UQ

    12.   ✓ $(\exists y) \sim Fdy$ 11 NQ

    13. $\sim Fde$ 12 EQ   (Note: 'e' must be used, since 'a', 'b', 'c', and 'd' have already appeared, etc.)

             Etc.

Thus the path will not close.   Notice, however, that this tree, unlike the one in Example 7, is *incomplete*: we have not exhausted all possible moves. But clearly any further unpacking of '$(y)(\exists x)Fxy$' or '$(x) \sim (y)Fxy$' will only lengthen the path.   It will not close it (always assuming that the rules are applied correctly).   We therefore conclude that the argument form in Example 9 is *not* valid.

Example 10

Determine whether the following argument form is valid:

$(x)(y)(z)[(Fxy \ \& \ Fyz) \rightarrow Fxz]$
$(x) \sim Fxx$
Therefore $(x)(y)(Fxy \rightarrow \sim Fyx)$.

TRUTH TREE

1.	$(x)(y)(z)[(Fxy \ \& \ Fyz) \rightarrow Fxz]$	Premiss
2.	$(x) \sim Fxx$	Premiss
3.	$\checkmark \sim (x)(y)(Fxy \rightarrow \sim Fyx)$	Negation of conclusion
4.	$\checkmark (\exists x) \sim (y)(Fxy \rightarrow \sim Fyx)$	3 NQ
5.	$\checkmark \sim (y)(Fay \rightarrow \sim Fya)$	4 EQ
6.	$\checkmark (\exists y) \sim (Fay \rightarrow \sim Fya)$	5 NQ
7.	$\checkmark \sim (Fab \rightarrow \sim Fba)$	6 EQ
8.	Fab	$7 \sim (\rightarrow)$
9.	$\checkmark \sim \sim Fba$	$7 \sim (\rightarrow)$
10.	Fba	9 Cancellation law
11.	$\sim Faa$	2 UQ
12.	$(y)(z)[(Fay \ \& \ Fyz) \rightarrow Faz]$	1 UQ
13.	$(z)[(Fab \ \& \ Fbz) \rightarrow Faz]$	12 UQ
14.	$\checkmark (Fab \ \& \ Fba) \rightarrow Faa$	13 UQ

15. $\checkmark \sim (Fab \ \& \ Fba) \qquad Faa$ 14 $\rightarrow$
                                             X

16. $\sim Fab \qquad \sim Fba$ 15 $\sim (\&)$
        $X \qquad\quad X$

All paths close.   Thus this is a valid argument form.

Example 11

Now test the following argument form for validity:

$(x)(y)(z)[(Fxy \ \& \ Fyz) \rightarrow Fxz]$
$(x)(y)(Fxy \rightarrow Fyx)$
Therefore $(x)Fxx$

TRUTH TREE

1.	$(x)(y)(z)[(Fxy \ \& \ Fyz) \rightarrow Fxz]$	Premiss
2.	$(x)(y)(Fxy \rightarrow Fyx)$	Premiss
3.	$\checkmark \sim (x)Fxx$	Negation of conclusion
4.	$\checkmark (\exists x) \sim Fxx$	3 NQ

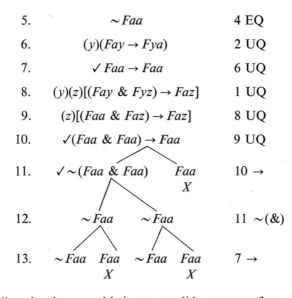

5.   ∼ *Faa*   4 EQ

6.   (*y*)(*Fay* → *Fya*)   2 UQ

7.   ✓ *Faa* → *Faa*   6 UQ

8.   (*y*)(*z*)[(*Fay* & *Fyz*) → *Faz*]   1 UQ

9.   (*z*)[(*Faa* & *Faz*) → *Faz*]   8 UQ

10.   ✓(*Faa* & *Faa*) → *Faa*   9 UQ

11.   ✓∼(*Faa* & *Faa*)   *Faa*   10 →
                                                            X

12.   ∼ *Faa*   ∼ *Faa*   11 ∼(&)

13.   ∼ *Faa*   *Faa*   ∼ *Faa*   *Faa*   7 →
                        X   *X*

Not all paths close, so this is *not* a valid argument form.

Example 12

Determine whether the following sentence form is valid:

   ∼(*x*)(∃*y*)*Fxy*.

TRUTH TREE

1.   ✓ ∼ ∼(*x*)(∃*y*)*Fxy*   Negation of sentence form

2.   (*x*)(∃*y*)*Fxy*   1 Cancellation law

3.   ✓ (∃*y*)*Fay*   2 UQ

4.   *Fab*   3 EQ   (use '*b*', since '*a*' has
                                                   appeared)

5.   ✓ (∃*y*)*Fby*   2 UQ

6.   *Fbc*   5 EQ   (use '*c*', since '*a*' and '*b*'
                                                   have appeared)

7.   ✓ (∃*y*)*Fcy*   2 UQ
           Etc.

A Note on Infinite Trees

The tree in Example 12, like the one in Example 9, illustrates a special point. In SL, as we saw, all trees are finite: we can determine in a finite number of steps whether all paths close or whether, after all possible applications of the unpacking rules have been made, one or more paths are still open. In PL-1, however, a tree may fail to close for either of two reasons: first, one or more paths may still be open at the point where no further applications of the rules are possible; second, the tree may continue to grow indefinitely, as in Example 12.

EXERCISES

44.1. Determine by truth trees whether these argument forms and sentence forms are valid:

    a. $(\exists x)Fx$
        $(x)(Fx \rightarrow Gx)$
        Therefore $(\exists x)Gx$

    b. $(x)[Fx \rightarrow (Gx \ \& \ Hx)]$
        Fa
        Therefore Ga

    c. $(\exists x)(Fx \ \lor \ Gx)$
        $(x)(Gx \rightarrow Hx)$
        Therefore $(\exists x)Hx$

    d. $(x)[Fx \ \& \ (Gx \ \lor \ \sim Hx)]$
        Ha
        Therefore $Fa \ \& \ Ga$

    e. $(x)Fx \ \lor \ Ga$
        $\sim Ga$
        Therefore $(\exists x)Fx$

    f. $(x)(Gx \rightarrow \sim Hx)$
        $(x)(Gx \rightarrow Fx)$
        Therefore $(x)(Fx \rightarrow \sim Hx)$

    g. $(x)(Gx \rightarrow \sim Hx)$
        $(x)(Fx \rightarrow Gx)$
        Therefore $(x)(Fx \rightarrow \sim Hx)$

    h. $(x)(\exists y)(Fx \ \lor \ \sim Fy)$
        $\sim Fa$
        Therefore $(\exists x)Fx$

    i. $\{[(x)Fx \ \lor \ Ga] \ \& \ \sim Ga\} \rightarrow Fa$

    j. $[(x)(Fx \rightarrow Gx) \ \& \ (\exists x)Gx] \rightarrow (\exists x)Fx$

44.2. Identify the error committed in each of these attempts at truth-tree construction:

    a. *Fa*
        Therefore $(x)Fx$

"*Truth Tree*"

1. Fa Premiss

2.   ✓ $\sim(x)Fx$ Negation of conclusion

3.   ✓ $(\exists x)\sim Fx$ 2 NQ

4. $\sim Fa$ 3 EQ
           X

should be a different variable

b. $(x)Fx \to Ga$
  Fa
  Therefore Ga

"*Truth Tree*"

1. $(x)Fx \to Ga$ Premiss

2. Fa Premiss

3. $\sim Ga$ Negation of conclusion

4.   ✓ $Fa \to Ga$ 1 UQ

5. $\sim Fa$ Ga 4 →
      X   X

used wrong rule

c. $(x)Fx \lor (x)\sim Fx$

"*Truth Tree*"

1.   ✓ $\sim[(x)Fx \lor (x)\sim Fx]$ Negation of sentence form

2.   ✓ $\sim(x)Fx$ 1 $\sim(\lor)$

3.   ✓ $\sim(x)\sim Fx$ 1 $\sim(\lor)$

4.   ✓ $(\exists x)\sim Fx$ 2 NQ

5. $\sim Fa$ 4 EQ

6.   ✓ $(\exists x)\sim\sim Fx$ 3 NQ

7.   ✓ $(\exists x)Fx$ 6 Cancellation law

8. Fa 7 EQ
              X

needed new name

d. $(x)(Fx \to Gx)$
  $(\exists x)(Gx \mathbin{\&} \sim Hx)$
  Therefore $(\exists x)(Fx \mathbin{\&} \sim Hx)$

"*Truth Tree*"

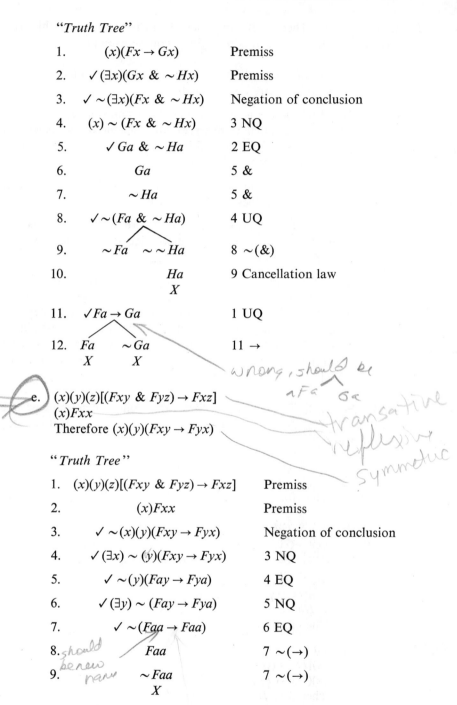

1. $(x)(Fx \rightarrow Gx)$ Premiss

2.   ✓ $(\exists x)(Gx \;\&\; \sim Hx)$ Premiss

3.   ✓ $\sim(\exists x)(Fx \;\&\; \sim Hx)$ Negation of conclusion

4. $(x) \sim (Fx \;\&\; \sim Hx)$ 3 NQ

5.   ✓ $Ga \;\&\; \sim Ha$ 2 EQ

6. Ga 5 &

7. $\sim Ha$ 5 &

8.   ✓ $\sim(Fa \;\&\; \sim Ha)$ 4 UQ

9. $\sim Fa \qquad \sim\sim Ha$ 8 $\sim(\&)$

10. Ha 9 Cancellation law
                         X

11.   ✓ $Fa \rightarrow Ga$ 1 UQ

12. $Fa \qquad \sim Ga$ 11 $\rightarrow$
      $X \qquad\; X$

wrong, should be
∧Fa   Ga
transative
reflexive
symmetric

e. $(x)(y)(z)[(Fxy \;\&\; Fyz) \rightarrow Fxz]$
    $(x)Fxx$
    Therefore $(x)(y)(Fxy \rightarrow Fyx)$

"*Truth Tree*"

1. $(x)(y)(z)[(Fxy \;\&\; Fyz) \rightarrow Fxz]$ Premiss

2. $(x)Fxx$ Premiss

3.   ✓ $\sim(x)(y)(Fxy \rightarrow Fyx)$ Negation of conclusion

4.   ✓ $(\exists x) \sim (y)(Fxy \rightarrow Fyx)$ 3 NQ

5.   ✓ $\sim(y)(Fay \rightarrow Fya)$ 4 EQ

6.   ✓ $(\exists y) \sim (Fay \rightarrow Fya)$ 5 NQ

7.   ✓ $\sim(Faa \rightarrow Faa)$ 6 EQ

8. *should* Faa 7 $\sim(\rightarrow)$
   be new
9. *name* $\sim Faa$ 7 $\sim(\rightarrow)$
                  X

44.3. For each of the following arguments, determine whether it is valid.
First, write the PL-1 argument form of which the argument is a substitu-

tion instance.   Then, if the argument form is valid, show this by constructing a truth tree; if it is not, give a counterexample.

a.   All men are rational.   Some animals are not men.   Therefore
some animals are not rational.

b.   Wittgenstein is an Austrian and a philosopher.   All philosophers are original thinkers or are influenced by Hegel.   Wittgenstein was not influenced by Hegel.   Therefore Wittgenstein is
an original thinker.

c.   All the world loves a lover.   Bob does not love Jane.
Therefore Jane does not love herself.

d.   Milton Friedman does not ignore Keynes.   Keynes is an
economist.   No economist ignores Keynes.   Therefore Milton
Friedman is an economist.

e.   "A line of argument that might be described as a silly-gism
was pursued—in all seriousness unfortunately—by the Port
Authority at a special bi-state legislative hearing yesterday.   It
went: Our agency can get involved only with self-supporting mass
transit.   Mass transit can never be self-supporting.   Therefore
we aren't getting involved."   [Editorial, *New York Post*, March 6,
1971]

44.4.   For each of the argument forms that follow, determine whether it
is valid.   If it is, show this by constructing a truth tree.   If it is not, give
a counterexample.

a.   *Ga & Ha*
$(x)[Gx \rightarrow (Fx \vee \sim Hx)]$
Therefore $(\exists x)Fx$

b.   *Ga & Fab*
$(x)(\sim Gx \vee \sim Hbx)$
Therefore $(\exists x)(Fxb \& \sim Hbx)$

c.   *Fa* $\vee$ *Gb*
$(x)[Gx \rightarrow (\sim Fa \vee Hx)]$
$\sim Hb$
Therefore $\sim Fa$

d.   *Fa*
$(x)[Fx \rightarrow (Gx \vee Hx)]$
$(x)(Hx \rightarrow Fx)$
Therefore *Ha*

e. $(x)[Fx \rightarrow (Gx \rightarrow Hx)]$
Therefore $(x)[(Fx \& Gx) \rightarrow Hx]$

f. $(x)[(Fx \rightarrow Gx) \rightarrow Hx]$
    Therefore $(x)[Fx \rightarrow (Gx \rightarrow Hx)]$

g. $(x)[Fx \rightarrow (Gx \rightarrow Hx)]$
    Therefore $(x)[(Fx \rightarrow Gx) \rightarrow Hx]$

h. $(\exists x)(y)Fxy$ & $(\exists x)Gx$
    Therefore $(\exists x)[(y)Fxy$ & $Gx]$

i. $(x)(y)(z)[(Fxy$ & $Fyz) \rightarrow Fxz]$
    $\sim (x)Fxx$
    Therefore $(x)(y)(Fxy \rightarrow \sim Fyx)$

44.5.   Determine by truth trees which pairs of PL-1 sentence forms in Exercise 40.2 are pairs of equivalent sentence forms.   (Note: Two sentence forms *A* and *B* are equivalent if they logically imply each other. Thus we may test for equivalence by constructing a pair of truth trees: one for the argument form '*A* therefore *B*' and one for the argument form '*B* therefore *A*'.   If both trees close, *A* and *B* are equivalent.)

11

Validity of Predicate Logic Argument Forms: Derivations

The *method of derivation*, also known as *natural deduction*, consists in applying a system of rules that specify which first-order predicate logic sentence forms may be derived or inferred from which others. An argument form is then said to be *valid according to PL-1* if its conclusion can be derived from its premisses, using these rules alone.

The technique of constructing derivations is already familiar to us from sentence logic (see Chapter 7). There a natural deduction system SN′ was introduced as an alternative to truth tables or truth trees. To determine *validity according to PL-1*, however, a broader, more powerful system is necessary—one that absorbs SNS (or SN′) and goes beyond it. This new system will be called PN.

---

§45   *The Natural Deduction System PN: Rules UI and EG*

As a preliminary, we define the notions of *derivation* and *derivability*, this time relative to PN:

If $A_1, \ldots, A_n$, B are PL-1 sentence forms, then a *derivation in PN* of B from the set of premisses $\{A_1, \ldots, A_n\}$ is a column of PL-1 sentence forms such that 1) each entry in the column either is a premiss or may be inferred from preceding entries by virtue of one of the inference rules of PN, and 2) the last entry in the column is B.

A PL-1 sentence form B is said to be *derivable-in-PN* from a set of PL-1 sentence forms $\{A_1, \ldots, A_n\}$ if there exists a derivation in PN of B from the set $\{A_1, \ldots, A_n\}$ or, abbreviated, if

$$\{A_1, \ldots, A_n\} \vdash_{PN} B,$$

where '$\vdash_{PN}$' signifies that the sentence form on its right is derivable-in-PN from the set of sentence forms on its left.

A satisfactory system of inference rules for PL-1, as for SL, should fulfill two conditions. First, it should be *sound*: the rules should be so chosen that they never take us from true premisses to false conclusions. Second, it should be *complete*: the rules should be so chosen that they take us from true premisses to *all* the conclusions these premisses logically imply. If these conditions are met, then a PL-1 argument form or argument will be *valid* iff there is a derivation in the system of its conclusion from its premisses.

There are many ways to formulate a suitable system. The version we select—PN—is fairly standard. Like the others, it consists of two groups of rules.

PN RULES TAKEN OVER FROM THE SYSTEM SNS

The first group is made up of rules taken over from the sentence-logic system SNS (see §32). These are

---

1. RULE P: *A premiss may be entered on any line of a derivation (i.e., "from A, to infer A").*

2. RULE T: *A PL-1 sentence form may be entered in a derivation if it is (tautologically) implied by a preceding entry or a conjunction of such entries.*

3. RULE CP (*Conditional Proof*): *If a PL-1 sentence form B can be derived in PN from a PL-1 sentence form A together with a set of PL-1 sentence forms $\{A_1, \ldots, A_n\}$, then $A \rightarrow B$ can be derived in PN from the set $\{A_1, \ldots, A_n\}$ alone, or, if $\{A_1, \ldots, A_n, A\} \vdash_{PN} B$, then $\{A_1, \ldots, A_n\} \vdash_{PN} A \rightarrow B$.*

(*Note:* As explained in §31, we may use in place of the omnibus "rule" T any appropriate list of separate SL inference rules.)   Rule P tells us how to use premisses in constructing derivations.   Rule T governs the role of truth-functional compounds.   Rule CP helps fix the relationship between derivability-in-PN ('⊢$_{PN}$') and the truth-functional conditional.

PN RULES INVOLVING QUANTIFIED SENTENCE FORMS

Now in the case of PL-1, the validity of arguments depends not only on how compound sentences are formed from simple ones, but also on the internal structure of the simple sentences themselves, general and singular. Accordingly, a *second* group of inference rules is required—one that will regulate the part played in PN derivations by the sentence forms that reflect the *internal structure* of simple sentences.

Let us work out step by step just what rules are needed to accomplish this purpose.

We begin by listing the simplest possible arguments made up of general and singular sentences.   These are one-premiss arguments such that if the premiss is general, the conclusion is singular, and vice versa.   Since there are two kinds of general sentences—universal and existential—we then have four types.   These are illustrated below, paired with their argument forms:

(1′)   Everyone is fallible.   (1) $(x)Fx$
      Therefore Perkins is fallible.   Therefore Fa

(2′)   Perkins is fallible.   (2) Fa
      Therefore someone is fallible.   Therefore $(\exists x)Fx$

(3′)   Perkins is fallible.   (3) Fa
      Therefore everyone is fallible.   Therefore $(x)Fx$

(4′)   Someone is fallible.   (4) $(\exists x)Fx$
      Therefore Perkins is fallible.   Therefore Fa

(Here 'x' ranges over *people*, 'a' names Perkins, and 'F' stands in place of 'is fallible '.)

Taking these four types as a convenient point of departure, we now ask, What do our ordinary intuitions tell us about the validity of such arguments?

THE RULE FOR UNIVERSAL INSTANTIATION (UI)

It is immediately apparent that (1′) is valid.   It rests on the commonsense principle that "what is true of all is true of any."   Hence our initial step in constituting the second group of rules is to admit a rule of inference that embodies this principle and thus validates such argument forms as (1).[1]   Accordingly, we have

---

4. RULE UI (*Universal Instantiation*):   *From a universally gener-*
alized sentence form, we may infer any *of its instantiations.*

There are numerous derivations in which, besides the rules taken over from SL, only Rule UI is required.   Here are two examples.

Example 1

> Everyone is fallible. $(x)Fx$
>
> Therefore Perkins is fallible.   Therefore Fa

DERIVATION

> {1}   1. $(x)Fx$ Rule P
>
> {1}   2. Fa 1 Rule UI

Thus Rule UI (along with Rule P) serves to validate (1).

As the reader will recall, a number appearing within braces is a *premiss* number, referring to the line on which a particular premiss was first introduced into the derivation; the number to the right of the braces is the line number in the derivation; and numbers that appear to the right of a sentence form indicate the line or lines to which the cited rule is being applied.   The set of premiss numbers on a given line tells us which premisses were used to infer the sentence form entered on that line.

Example 2

> All members of the French Academy are mortal. $(x)(Fx \rightarrow Mx)$
>
> René Clair is a member of the French Academy. Fa
>
> Therefore René Clair is mortal.   Therefore Ma

---

[1]   There is a very concise—if not immediately transparent—way to state the second group of PN inference rules. Let α (alpha) denote any individual variable, μ (mu) an individual constant, and A (as before) any PL-1 sentence form. And let $A\alpha/\mu$ denote the *result* of replacing in A each occurrence of α by an occurrence of a constant, μ. Also assume that α is the only variable occurring free in A and thus that $(\alpha)A$ and $A\alpha/\mu$ are closed PL-1 sentence forms. We may then write Rule UI as

From $(\alpha)A$, to infer $A\alpha/\mu$, for any μ.

Derivation

{1}	1.	$(x)(Fx \rightarrow Mx)$	Rule P
{2}	2.	Fa	Rule P
{1}	3.	$Fa \rightarrow Ma$	1 Rule UI
{1,2}	4.	Ma	2, 3 Rule T

Hence this argument form also is valid, since its conclusion is derivable in our system from its premisses.

In sum, Rule UI allows us to infer from a *universal generalization* any of its *instantiations*. To apply this rule is to *eliminate* the quantifier at the head of a universal generalization and to replace *all* occurrences of the variable of quantification uniformly with occurrences of an individual constant.

For example, we instantiate '$(x)Fx$' by eliminating '(x)' and replacing 'x' in 'Fx' with, say, 'a', thereby obtaining 'Fa'; likewise, when we instantiate '$(x)(Fx \rightarrow Gx)$' we obtain, say, '$Fa \rightarrow Ga$'. When we instantiate '$(x)Fxx$' we obtain, say, 'Faa'; when we instantiate '$(x)(y)Fxy$' we obtain successively, say, '$(y)Fay$' and 'Fab' (or for that matter, 'Faa', since the *same* constant may replace *different* variables).

A Warning on the Use of UI

Although Rule UI is quite simple, it is still subject to certain misuses. We illustrate three of these.

First, consider the two-line derivation

{1}	1.	$(x)Fxx$	Rule P
{1}	2.	$(x)Fxa$	1 Rule UI (!)

Surely this is a misuse of UI. For let the domain be *positive integers*, let 'a' name the integer one, and let 'F' be replaced by 'is equal to'. We then have the counterexample

> Every positive integer is equal to itself.
>
> Therefore every positive integer is equal to one.

A similar counterexample may readily be found for the argument form "'$(x)Fxx$', therefore '$(x)Fax$'."

It is an error to use UI to infer '$(x)Fxa$' from '$(x)Fxx$'. For UI can be used to infer only *instantiations* from a universal generalization, and '$(x)Fxa$' is *not* an instantiation of '$(x)Fxx$'—that is, it is not obtained from '$(x)Fxx$' by eliminating the quantifier and replacing *all* occurrences of 'x' in 'Fxx' uniformly by occurrences of the constant 'a'.

Second, consider the argument form

$$\sim(x)Fx$$
Therefore $\sim Fa$

and the corresponding derivation

{1}	1.	$\sim(x)Fx$	Rule P
{1}	2.	$\sim Fa$	1 Rule UI (!)

Obviously, this too is a misuse of UI. For let the domain be *people*, let '*a*' name Aristotle, and let '*F*' be replaced by 'is famous'. Then the resulting argument

> Not everyone is famous
>
> Therefore Aristotle is not famous

clearly provides a counterexample.

The error in this derivation is that UI is applied not to a universal generalization but to '$\sim(x)Fx$', which is the *negation* of a universal generalization.

Finally, consider the following argument and its argument form:

(5′)   All the world loves a lover.   (5) $(x)[(\exists y)Lxy \rightarrow (z)Lzx]$

Bob does not love Jane. $\sim Lbj$

Therefore Janes does not love $\sim Ljj$
herself.

This derivation is offered as a proof of their validity:

{1}	1.	$(x)[(\exists y)Lxy \rightarrow (z)Lzx]$	Rule P
{2}	2.	$\sim Lbj$	Rule P
{1}	3.	$(\exists y)Ljy \rightarrow (z)Lzj$	1 Rule UI
{1}	4.	$(\exists y)Ljy \rightarrow Lbj$	3 Rule UI (!)
{1, 2}	5.	$\sim(\exists y)Ljy$	2, 4 Rule T
{1, 2}	6.	$(y)\sim Ljy$	5 Definition
{1, 2}	7.	$\sim Ljj$	6 Rule UI

As it happens, (5) is perfectly valid, but the derivation given for it here is defective. The error lies in the use of UI to sanction the step from line 3 to line 4. Rule UI may be applied correctly only to independent universal generalizations, not to universally general components of compound sentence forms, and hence not to '$(z)Lzj$' in the sentence form '$(\exists y)Ljy \rightarrow (z)Lzj$'. Otherwise we should be compelled to accept as correct such derivations as

{1}	1.	$(x)Fx \rightarrow Ga$	Rule P
{1}	2.	$Fa \rightarrow Ga$	1 Rule UI (!)

But let the domain be *the faculty*, let 'a' name Perkins, and let 'F' be replaced by 'approves' and 'G' by 'is promoted'. We then have the counterexample

> If all the faculty members approve, then Perkins is promoted.
> Therefore if Perkins approves, then Perkins is promoted.

The validity of (5) may be established by the following derivation:

{1}	1.	$(x)[(\exists y)Lxy \rightarrow (z)Lzx]$	Rule P
{2}	2.	$\sim Lbj$	Rule P
{1}	3.	$(\exists y)Ljy \rightarrow (z)Lzj$	1 Rule UI
{4}	4.	$(\exists y)Ljy$	Rule P*
{1, 4}	5.	$(z)Lzj$	3, 4 Rule T
{1, 4}	6.	Lbj	5 Rule UI
{1}	7.	$(\exists y)Ljy \rightarrow Lbj$	4–6 Rule CP
{1, 2}	8.	$\sim (\exists y)Ljy$	2, 7 Rule T
{1, 2}	9.	$(y) \sim Ljy$	8 Definition
{1, 2}	10.	$\sim Ljj$	9 Rule UI

Note that at line 4 a "borrowed" premiss '$(\exists y)Ljy$' was introduced and later discharged with the aid of Rule CP. The purpose of this maneuver was to detach '$(z)Lzj$' from '$(\exists y)Ljy$' in '$(\exists y)Ljy \rightarrow (z)Lzj$' so that UI could be applied to '$(z)Lzj$' at line 5.

Note, too, that in order to reach line 9 we made use of the fact that in the presence of negation, the universal and existential quantifiers are interdefinable (see §37). The specific definitional equivalence employed in the above derivation is

> '$\sim (\exists y)Ljy$' may be defined as '$(y) \sim Ljy$'.

An equivalence of this sort enables us to replace the *negation* of an existential generalization with a universal generalization, and it thus makes possible an application of UI (in this instance to line 9).

THE RULE FOR EXISTENTIAL GENERALIZATION (EG)

We turn next to the second of our four types of simple PL-1 arguments:

(2')   Perkins is fallible.   (2)   *Fa*

   Therefore someone is fallible.   Therefore $(\exists x)Fx$

   Once again it is evident that the argument is valid. It rests on the notion that "what is true of a particular individual is true of some (that is, at least one) individual." We therefore admit as our next rule:[2]

---

5.   RULE EG (*Existential Generalization*): *From a sentence form containing an individual constant, we may infer any existential generalization of that sentence form.*

   The application of Rule EG consists in *introducing* an existential quantifier and replacing uniformly *some or all* occurrences of the individual constant in the sentence form by occurrences of the variable of quantification. For example, from '*Fa*' we may infer '$(\exists x)Fx$'; from '*Faa*' we may infer '$(\exists x)Fax$' or '$(\exists x)Fxa$' or '$(\exists x)Fxx$'. Similarly, from '*Fab*' we may infer '$(\exists x)Fxb$' or '$(\exists y)Fay$', and from these '$(\exists y)(\exists x)Fxy$' or its equivalent '$(\exists x)(\exists y)Fxy$'—but not '$(\exists x)Fxx$'.

Example 1

DERIVATION

   {1}   1.   *Fa*   Rule P

   {1}   2. $(\exists x)Fx$ 1 Rule EG

Thus EG validates (2).

Example 2

   Everyone is fallible. $(x)Fx$

   Therefore someone is fallible.   Therefore $(\exists x)Fx$

DERIVATION

   {1}   1. $(x)Fx$ Rule P

   {1}   2.   *Fa*   1 Rule UI

   {1}   3. $(\exists x)Fx$ 2 Rule EG

---

[2]   Using the α-μ-A symbolism introduced in footnote 1, we may write Rule EG thus:

   From $A\alpha/\mu$, to infer $(\exists\alpha)A$.

Here both UI and EG are applied, and the argument form is proved valid. Note that the application of UI assumes—as we do all along—that the domain of interpretation is *not* empty, that it has at least one member, in this case named '*a*' (see §42, under "Valid (Closed) PL-1 Sentence Form Defined").

Like UI, Rule EG is quite easy to apply. But misuses do occur—for instance, in regard to negations of singular sentences. Thus the derivation

{1}   1. $\sim Fa$ Rule P

{1}   2. $\sim(\exists x)Fx$ 1 Rule EG (!)

is clearly in error.   For an obvious counterexample is

(6)   Aristotle is not French.

          Therefore not anyone (or no one) is French.

On the other hand,

(7′)   Aristotle is not French   (7) $\sim Fa$

          Therefore someone is not French   Therefore $(\exists x)\sim Fx$

is perfectly valid.

EXERCISES

45.1.   Show that each of these argument forms is valid by deriving the conclusion from the premises (only Rules P, T, UI, and EG are required):

    a. $(x)Fx \vee Ga$
         $\sim Ga$
         Therefore $(\exists x)Fx$

    b. $(x)[Fx \rightarrow (Gx \ \& \ Hx)]$
         Fa
         Therefore Ga

    c. $(x)[Fx \ \& \ (Gx \vee \sim Hx)]$
         Ha
         Therefore $Fa \ \& \ Ga$

    d. $Ga \ \& \ Ha$
         $(x)[Gx \rightarrow (Fx \vee \sim Hx)]$
         Therefore $(\exists x)Fx$

    e. $Ga \ \& \ Fab$
         $(x)(\sim Gx \vee \sim Hbx)$
         Therefore $(\exists x)(Fxb \ \& \sim Hbx)$

f.   *Ia & Ga*
     $(x)[Gx \rightarrow (Hx \vee Fxb)]$
     $\sim Fab$
     Therefore *Ha*

g.   *Ga & Fab*
     $(x)[Fxb \rightarrow (\sim Gx \vee Fbx)]$
     Therefore $(\exists x)(\exists y)(Fxy \& Fyx)$

45.2.   Here are some *supposed* derivations.   For each of them, point out the error(s) and give a counterexample.

a. $(x)Fxx$
     Therefore $(x)Fax$

DERIVATION

{1}	1.	$(x)Fxx$	Rule P
{1}	2.	$(x)Fax$	1 UI

b.

{1}	1.	$(x)Fx \rightarrow Ga$	Rule P
{2}	2.	Fa	Rule P
{1}	3.	$Fa \rightarrow Ga$	1 UI
{1, 2}	4.	Ga	2, 3 Rule T

c.

{1}	1.	$Fb \vee Ga$	Rule P
{2}	2.	$\sim Fb$	Rule P
{1}	3.	$Fb \vee (\exists x)Gx$	1 EG
{1, 2}	4.	$(\exists x)Gx$	2, 3 Rule T

d.

{1}	1.	$(x)(Fx \rightarrow \sim Gx)$	Rule P
{2}	2.	Fa	Rule P
{1}	3.	$Fa \rightarrow \sim Ga$	1 UI
{1, 2}	4.	$\sim Ga$	2, 3 Rule T
{1, 2}	5.	$\sim (\exists x)Gx$	3 EG

45.3.   Show that each of these *arguments* is valid according to PL-1. First, write the PL-1 argument form of which the argument is a substitution instance; then derive the conclusion from the premises using only Rules P, T, UI, and EG.   (*Note:* In *each* case, one or more premises must be supplied from the context.)

a.   The economists today are at a loss, and being at a loss, are not offering many specific programs.   That is why Milton Friedman and John Kenneth Galbraith haven't too much to say.

b.   Franklin is Elliott's father and Elliott is James's brother. Therefore Franklin is James's father.

c.   Everyone who got in had a ticket or someone crashed the gate.   If anyone crashed the gate, the head usher was upset.   The head usher was not upset.   So Quincy must have had a ticket.

d.   Philadelphia is larger than Baltimore and Baltimore is larger than Newark.   But Philadelphia is not larger than Chicago, so Chicago is larger than Newark.

---

§46   *The Natural Deduction System PN: Rule UG and the EI Procedure*

To complete our account of PN, we now consider the rule for universal generalization, UG, and what we shall call the *procedure* for existential instantiation, or the "EI procedure."   These two are considerably more difficult to state than Rules UI and EG.   For if our system is to be sound, specific restrictions on their use must be built into their very formulations.

Let us turn, then, to the third type of simple PL-1 argument form [(3′) and (3) from §45]:

(1′)   Perkins is fallible.   (1)   *Fa*
          Therefore everyone is fallible.   Therefore $(x)Fx$

Plainly (1′) is invalid.   What is true of all is indeed true of any; but as (1) shows, we cannot in general accept the converse—"what is true of any is true of all."   Yet if we reflect on the matter, we discover that there are cases where the converse is quite acceptable.   What of arguments in geometry, for example, in which we reason that what is true of an arbitrary triangle is true of all triangles?   For that matter, what of the following argument?

Example 1

(2′)   All animals are mortal.

          All tigers are animals.

          Therefore all tigers are mortal.

Its argument form

(2) $(x)(Gx \rightarrow Hx)$
          $(x)(Fx \rightarrow Gx)$
          Therefore $(x)(Fx \rightarrow Hx)$

is obviously valid. Hence if our system is to be complete, the conclusion of (2) must be derivable from its premisses. Let us try.

DERIVATION

{1}	1.	$(x)(Gx \rightarrow Hx)$	Rule P
{2}	2.	$(x)(Fx \rightarrow Gx)$	Rule P
{1}	3.	$Ga \rightarrow Ha$	1 Rule UI
{2}	4.	$Fa \rightarrow Ga$	2 Rule UI
{1, 2}	5.	$Fa \rightarrow Ha$	3, 4 Rule T

But here we come to a halt. What is needed at this point is permission to go from step 5, '$Fa \rightarrow Ha$', to

| {1, 2} | 6. | $(x)(Fx \rightarrow Hx)$ | 5 Rule ____ ? |

That is, in order to complete the derivation, we must be allowed to argue that what is true of the individual named by 'a' is true of all members of the domain. In short, we must be able to *generalize universally on a constant*.

THE RULE FOR UNIVERSAL GENERALIZATION (INCOMPLETE FORM)

Clearly this cannot be done without restriction, as is shown by (1'). Our problem, then, is to formulate a rule with a suitable restriction.[3] The necessary rule may *for the moment* be stated as follows:

---

6. RULE UG (*Universal Generalization*)—Incomplete Formulation: *From a sentence form containing an individual constant, we may infer the* universal generalization *of that sentence form, so long as the constant is* arbitrary *in the sense that it does not appear in any premiss of the sentence form.*

Here by the universal generalization of a sentence form containing an individual constant is understood the sentence form obtained by replacing uniformly *all* occurrences of the constant with occurrences of a variable and prefixing to the result a universal quantifier binding all occurrences of the variable.

---

[3] Using the α-μ-A symbolism, we may write UG (*incomplete form*) as

From $A\alpha/\mu$, to infer $(\alpha)A$, provided μ does not appear in any premiss of $A\alpha/\mu$.

Thus to apply UG is to *introduce* a universal quantifier and replace uniformly *all* occurrences of the constant on which we are generalizing with occurrences of the variable of quantification. The general idea behind Rule UG is this: anything we can prove about a member of a domain by means of premisses that do not directly mention that member by name (or uniquely describe it) can then be asserted of all members of the domain.

Now if we apply UG to line 5 in Example 1, we have

$$\{1, 2\} \quad 6. \quad (x)(Fx \to Gx) \quad 5 \text{ Rule UG}$$

and this completes the derivation. The application of UG is correct, since '*a*' does not appear in any premiss of '*Fa* → *Ga*'. But UG cannot be applied correctly to (1), because there '*a*' appears in a premiss of the sentence form in which it occurs: it occurs in '*Fa*'; and '*Fa*', by Rule P, is its own premiss.

Here are some other examples of the use and misuse of UG.

Example 2

Example 2 violates the definition of 'universal generalization'.

SUPPOSED DERIVATION

$$\{1\} \quad 1. \quad (x)Fxx \quad \text{Rule P}$$

$$\{1\} \quad 2. \quad Faa \quad 1 \text{ Rule UI}$$

$$\{1\} \quad 3. \quad (x)Fax \quad 2 \text{ Rule UG (!)}$$

Counterexample. The argument form

(3) $(x)Fxx$
         Therefore $(x)Fax$

is invalid. For let the domain be *men*, and let '*F*' be replaced by 'is the worst enemy of' and '*a*' by 'Perkins'. Then

(3')   Every man is his own worst enemy
         Therefore Perkins is every man's worst enemy

is a counterexample to (3). The application of UG in the derivation is incorrect because UG can be used to infer universal generalizations *only*, and '$(x)Fax$' is not the universal generalization of '*Faa*'.

Example 3

Example 3 violates the definition of 'arbitrary'.

SUPPOSED DERIVATION

{1}	1.	$(x)Fax$	Rule P
{1}	2.	Faa	1 Rule UI
{1}	3.	$(x)Fxx$	2 Rule UG (!)

Counterexample. The argument form

(4) $(x)Fax$
          Therefore $(x)Fxx$

is invalid. For let the domain be *people*; let '*a*' be replaced by 'Per-kins' and '*F*' by 'is honest with'. Then the resulting argument

(4')   Perkins is honest with everyone

          Therefore everyone is honest with himself or herself

is a counterexample to (4). Clearly UG is misapplied in Example 3, since '*a*', the constant on which we are generalizing, does indeed appear in the premiss of '*Faa*', the sentence form to which UG is being applied.

Example 4

All voters are Democrats or Republicans.	$(x)[Fx \rightarrow (Gx \lor Hx)]$
No liberal is a Republican.	$(x)(Ix \rightarrow \sim Hx)$
Hence all liberals who vote are Democrats.	Hence $(x)[Ix \rightarrow (Fx \rightarrow Gx)]$.

DERIVATION

{1}	1.	$(x)[Fx \rightarrow (Gx \lor Hx)]$	Rule P
{2}	2.	$(x)(Ix \rightarrow \sim Hx)$	Rule P
{1}	3.	$Fa \rightarrow (Ga \lor Ha)$	1 Rule UI
{2}	4.	$Ia \rightarrow \sim Ha)$	2 Rule UI
{5}	5.	$Ia \ \& \ Fa$	Rule P*
{5}	6.	Fa	5 Rule T
{5}	7.	Ia	5 Rule T
{1, 5}	8.	$Ga \lor Ha$	3, 6 Rule T
{2, 5}	9.	$\sim Ha$	4, 7 Rule T
{1, 2, 5}	10.	Ga	8, 9 Rule T

$\{1, 2\}$	11.	$(Ia \ \& \ Fa) \to Ga$	5-10 Rule CP (premiss discharged)
$\{1, 2\}$	12.	$Ia \to (Fa \to Ga)$	11 Rule T
$\{1, 2\}$	13.	$(x)[Ix \to (Fx \to Gx)]$	12 Rule UG

The strategy used in this derivation (and in Example 1) has rather wide application. It consists in the following steps: 1) apply UI to the premisses to *eliminate* universal quantifiers; 2) then use Rule T (or a suitable set of specified SL inference rules) to extract various conclusions from the results; 3) apply Rule UG (or Rule EG) to *reintroduce* quantifiers where we desire and the rules permit.

Notice too that in this example Rule CP (Conditional Proof) was employed. The reader will recall (see §33) that Rule CP can be used to good advantage especially when the conclusion we wish to derive is a conditional.

Example 5

$$(x)(y)(z)[(Fxy \ \& \ Fyz) \to Fxz]$$
$$(x) \sim Fxx$$
$$\text{Therefore } (x)(y)(Fxy \to \ \sim Fyx)$$

DERIVATION

$\{1\}$	1.	$(x)(y)(z)[(Fxy \ \& \ Fyz) \to Fxz]$	Rule P
$\{2\}$	2.	$(x) \sim Fxx$	Rule P
$\{1\}$	3.	$(y)(z)[(Fay \ \& \ Fyz) \to Faz]$	1 Rule UI
$\{1\}$	4.	$(z)(Fab \ \& \ Fbz) \to Faz$	3 Rule UI
$\{1\}$	5.	$(Fab \ \& \ Fba) \to Faa$	4 Rule UI
$\{2\}$	6.	$\sim Faa$	2 Rule UI
$\{1, 2\}$	7.	$\sim (Fab \ \& \ Fba)$	5, 6 Rule T
$\{1, 2\}$	8.	$Fab \to \ \sim Fba$	7 Rule T
$\{1, 2\}$	9.	$(y)(Fay \to \ \sim Fya)$	8 Rule UG
$\{1, 2\}$	10.	$(x)(y)(Fxy \to \ \sim Fyx)$	9 Rule UG

We remark on three features of Example 5. First, Rule UI was successively applied to eliminate '(x)', '(y)', and '(z)'. Second, the same constant, 'a', was used in instantiating the two variables 'x' and 'z'. Third, Rule UG was applied successively to reintroduce the quantifiers '(y)' and '(x)'.

Let us now turn to the fourth and final type of simple PL-1 argument [(4′) and (4) from §45]:

(5′)   Someone is fallible.   (5) $(\exists x)Fx$

       Therefore Perkins is fallible.   Therefore Fa

This argument is obviously fallacious. Because someone is cheerful, say, it does not follow that Schopenhauer is cheerful. Plainly no sound system of inference rules can validate (5).

    Yet existential generalizations do serve as premisses in valid arguments and argument forms. Here is an illustration:

(6′)   Whoever is fallible is a security risk.   (6) $(x)(Fx \rightarrow Gx)$

       Someone is fallible. $(\exists x)Fx$

       Therefore someone is a security risk.   Therefore $(\exists x)Gx$

The second premiss is an existential generalization—indeed, the same one that appears as the premiss of (5). Nevertheless, the argument form in which it appears, (6), is clearly valid.

    Now since (6) is valid, we should be able to construct a derivation of its conclusion from its premisses. We begin with

DERIVATION

      {1}   1. $(x)(Fx \rightarrow Gx)$ Rule P

      {2}   2. $(\exists x)Fx$ Rule P

      {1}   3. $Fa \rightarrow Ga$ 1 Rule UI

      {2}   4. ?

    But here we come to a halt. We have got what we can from premiss 1. To go further, we need some way of tapping the information contained in premiss 2.

    Now suppose we had a rule of inference that allowed us, on the basis of premiss 2, to obtain

      {2}   4. Fa 2 "Rule?"

You could then complete the derivation thus

      {1, 2}   5. Ga 3, 4 Rule T

      {1, 2}   6. $(\exists x)Gx$ 5 Rule EG

and so prove (6) valid.

    Our example suggests, then, that we try the following solution. Let us round out our system with a "rule" or procedure[4] expressly designed

---

[4] Why we use the phrase '"rule" or procedure' will be explained a little further on.

to give us access to the information supplied by existentially general premisses or intermediate steps in a derivation. (A second kind of solution, based on the interdefinability of quantifiers, will be touched on later.)

THE PROCEDURE FOR EXISTENTIAL INSTANTIATION (EI)

Now what does an existential generalization tell us? Described in the idiom of interpretation, an existential generalization—say, '$(\exists x)Fx$'— informs us that some *unspecified* member of the domain has a certain property, denoted in this case by 'F'. To make use of this information, we need permission to assign a name ('a', or whatever) to the unspecified member of the domain, form the corresponding instantiation (here 'Fa'), enter it as a line of the derivation, and proceed with the construction. In short, we need a "rule" or procedure—call it EI (*Existential Instantiation*) —that allows us to "infer" an instantiation from an *existential* generalization in somewhat the way Rule UI allows us to infer *any* instantiation from a *universal* generalization.

If we do not adopt some form of EI, our rules system will be incomplete: it will fail to sanction argument forms that are obviously valid, such as (6) above.

If, on the other hand, we adopt such a "rule" or procedure without restrictions on its application, our system will be unsound: it will sanction types of argument forms that are obviously invalid. This is clear from the following examples.

Invalid Argument Form 1

(7) $(\exists x)Fx$
         Ga
         Therefore $(\exists x)(Fx \ \& \ Gx)$

Supposed Derivation

{1}	1.	$(\exists x)Fx$	Rule P
{2}	2.	Ga	Rule P
{1}	3.	Fa	1 "Rule" EI (!)
{1, 2}	4.	$Fa \ \& \ Ga$	2, 3 Rule T
{1, 2}	5.	$(\exists x)(Fx \ \& \ Gx)$	4 Rule EG

Counterexample. The argument form (7) is invalid. For let the domain be *integers*; and let 'F' be replaced by 'is odd', 'G' by 'is even', and 'a' by the numeral '6'. Then

(7′)   Some integers are odd

6 is even

Therefore some integers are odd and even

is a counterexample to (7).

To block this first type of invalid argument form, we must incorporate into the EI "rule", or procedure, the following restriction on our choice of the constant used in the instantiation:

> *EI Restriction 1:* In applying EI, do not use a constant that appears in any premiss of the desired conclusion.

Invalid Argument Form 2

(8) $(\exists x)(Fx \ \& \ Gx)$
$(\exists x)(Gx \ \& \ Hx)$
Therefore $(\exists x)(Fx \ \& \ Hx)$

SUPPOSED DERIVATION

{1}	1.	$(\exists x)(Fx \ \& \ Gx)$	Rule P
{2}	2.	$(\exists x)(Gx \ \& \ Hx)$	Rule P
{1}	3.	$Fa \ \& \ Ga$	1 "Rule" EI
{2}	4.	$Ga \ \& \ Ha$	2 "Rule" EI (!)
{1}	5.	Fa	3 Rule T
{2}	6.	Ha	4 Rule T
{1, 2}	7.	$Fa \ \& \ Ha$	5, 6 Rule T
{1, 2}	8.	$(\exists x)(Fx \ \& \ Hx)$	7 Rule EG

Counterexample.   The argument form (8) is invalid.   For let the domain be *arguments*; and let '*F*' be replaced by 'is valid', '*G*' by 'is unsound', and '*H*' by 'is invalid'.   Then the argument

(8′)   Some valid arguments are unsound

Some unsound arguments are invalid

Therefore some valid arguments are invalid

is a counterexample to (8).

To block this second type of invalid form, a further restriction is required:

> *EI Restriction 2:*   In applying EI, do not use a constant that has been introduced into the derivation by an earlier application of EI itself.

Invalid Argument Form 3

(9) $(x)(\exists y)Fxy$
       Therefore $(\exists x)Fxx$

SUPPOSED DERIVATION

{1}	1.	$(x)(\exists y)Fxy$	Rule P
{1}	2.	$(\exists y)Fay$	1 Rule UI
{1}	3.	*Faa*	2 "Rule" EI (!)
{1}	4.	$(\exists x)Fxx$	3 Rule EG

Counterexample. Let '*F*' be replaced by 'is less than' and let the domain be *integers*. Then

(9′)   Every integer is less than some integer
        Therefore some integer is less than itself

is a counterexample to (9).
   To block this third type of invalid form, we add

> *EI Restriction 3:* In applying EI, do not use a constant that appears in the existential generalization to which EI is being applied.

Invalid Argument Form 4

(10) $(\exists x)Fxx$
        Therefore $(\exists x)Fxa$

SUPPOSED DERIVATION

{1}	1.	$(\exists x)Fxx$	Rule P
{1}	2.	*Faa*	1 "Rule" EI (!)
{1}	3.	$(\exists x)Fxa$	2 Rule EG

Counterexample. Let the domain be *rational numbers*, let '*F*' be replaced by 'is the square of', and let '*a*' name 2. Then

(10′)   There is a rational number that is its own square
         Therefore there is a rational number that is the square of 2

is a counterexample to (10).

To block this last type of invalid form, we complete this series of restrictions with

> *EI Restriction 4:* In applying EI, do not use a constant that appears in the desired conclusion.

(Notice that this final restriction blocks not only (10) but also the invalid form we began with—namely, (5). For the constant used in the latter is '*a*', and '*a*' appears in the supposed conclusion, '*Fa*'.)

"RULE" EI SUMMARIZED

We may now collect the restrictions and formulate "Rule" EI as follows:

---

7. "RULE" EI (*Existential Instantiation*): *From an existential generalization, we may "infer" an instantiation of it provided that the constant so used does* not *appear 1) in any premiss of the desired conclusion, or 2) in any earlier application of EI in the same derivation, or 3) in the existential generalization to which EI is being applied, or 4) in the desired conclusion itself.*

These four restrictions may be regarded as jointly fixing the sense in which the constant used in an application of EI must be *arbitrary*. In the idiom of interpretation, a constant is arbitrary (with respect to a given derivation) if it names a member of the domain about which entries in the derivation tell us *no more* than they do about *any* member of the domain. In the idiom of linguistic expressions, the constant is arbitrary if it appears *nowhere else* in the derivation except in places where *any* constant could have been introduced in its stead.

This formulation of "Rule" EI can be greatly simplified. The only requirement need be that wherever both EI and UI are applicable and one may freely choose the order of application, EI must be applied *before UI*. For example, the derivation given for (6) was

{1}	1.	$(x)(Fx \rightarrow Gx)$	Rule P
{2}	2.	$(\exists x)Fx$	Rule P
{1}	3.	$Fa \rightarrow Ga$	1 Rule UI
{2}	4.	Fa	2 "Rule" EI
{1, 2}	5.	Ga	3, 4 Rule T
{1, 2}	6.	$(\exists x)Gx$	5 Rule EG

If we now adopt this requirement, the *correct* derivation will be

{1}	1.	$(x)(Fx \rightarrow Gx)$	Rule P
{2}	2.	$(\exists x)Fx$	Rule P
{2}	3.	Fa	2 " Rule " EI
{1}	4.	$Fa \rightarrow Ga$	1 Rule UI
{1, 2}	5.	Ga	3, 4 Rule T
{1, 2}	6.	$(\exists x)Gx$	5 Rule EG

The advantage—apart from the greater " naturalness " of applying EI before UI—is that " Rule " EI may now be stated quite briefly:

7*.   " RULE " EI (*Existential Instantiation*)—Simplified Statement: *From an existential generalization, we may " infer "*
an instantiation of it, provided that the constant so used
1) has not appeared previously in the derivation and 2) does
not appear in the desired conclusion.

EXAMPLES OF THE CORRECT USE OF EI

Example 1

(11) $(x)(Fx \rightarrow Gx)$
$(\exists x)(Hx \ \& \sim Gx)$
Therefore $(\exists x)(\sim Fx \ \& \ Hx)$

DERIVATION

{1}	1.	$(x)(Fx \rightarrow Gx)$	Rule P
{2}	2.	$(\exists x)(Hx \ \& \sim Gx)$	Rule P
{2}	3.	$Ha \ \& \sim Ga$	2 EI
{1}	4.	$Fa \rightarrow Ga$	1 Rule UI
{2}	5.	$\sim Ga$	3 Rule T
{1, 2}	6.	$\sim Fa$	4, 5 Rule T
{2}	7.	Ha	3 Rule T
{1, 2}	8.	$\sim Fa \ \& \ Ha$	6, 7 Rule T
{1, 2}	9.	$(\exists x)(\sim Fx \ \& \ Hx)$	8 Rule EG

Example 2

(12) $(x)(y)(Fxy \rightarrow \ \sim Fyx)$
$(\exists x)(\exists y)Fxy$
Therefore $(\exists x)(\exists y) \sim Fyx$

DERIVATION

{1}	1.	$(x)(y)(Fxy \rightarrow \sim Fyx)$	Rule P
{2}	2.	$(\exists x)(\exists y)Fxy$	Rule P
{2}	3.	$(\exists y)Fay$	2 EI
{2}	4.	Fab	3 EI
{1}	5.	$(y)(Fay \rightarrow \sim Fya)$	1 Rule UI
{1}	6.	$Fab \rightarrow \sim Fba$	5 Rule UI
{1, 2}	7.	$\sim Fba$	4, 6 Rule T
{1, 2}	8.	$(\exists y) \sim Fya$	7 Rule EG
{1, 2}	9.	$(\exists x)(\exists y) \sim Fyx$	8 Rule EG

Example 3

(13) $(\exists x)(y)Fxy$
           Therefore $(y)(\exists x)Fxy$

DERIVATION

{1}	1.	$(\exists x)(y)Fxy$	Rule P
{1}	2.	$(y)Fay$	1 EI
{1}	3.	Fab	2 Rule UI
{1}	4.	$(\exists x)Fxb$	3 Rule EG
{1}	5.	$(y)(\exists x)Fxy$	4 Rule UG

The three examples obey all the restrictions on EI. Also note that examples 1 and 2 illustrate a *strategy* that can often be employed in constructing PL-1 derivations. First, use UI and/or EI to strip away quantifiers from the premises. Second, apply Rule T to the sentence forms that result. Finally, use the generalization rules to restore quantifiers and obtain the desired conclusion.

Some incorrect uses of EI. The argument forms for which the following supposed derivations are offered are not valid. Indicate which of the EI restrictions they violate.

1.

{1}	1.	$(\exists x)(Fx \rightarrow Gx)$	Rule P
{2}	2.	$(\exists x)Fx$	Rule P
{1}	3.	$Fa \rightarrow Ga$	1 EI
{2}	4.	Fa	2 EI
{1, 2}	5.	Ga	3, 4 Rule T
{1, 2}	6.	$(\exists x)Gx$	5 Rule EG

2.   {1}   1. $(\exists x)Fxa$ Rule P

          {1}   2. *Faa*   1 EI

          {1}   3. $(\exists x)Fxx$ 2 Rule EG

EI: RULE OR PROCEDURE?

Recall that the fourth restriction forbids us, in applying EI, to select a constant that appears in the desired conclusion. Hence EI—unlike Rules UI, EG, and UG—can never be used to sanction the *terminal* step in a derivation.

This difference in role is quite important from a theoretical standpoint. It reflects the fact that there can be no valid inference from an existential generalization to a *particular* instantiation of it. This, of course, was what we learned from (5'): in no way can we validly obtain the conclusion "Perkins is fallible" simply from the premiss "Someone is fallible."

Thus, strictly speaking, EI is not a *rule of inference* at all. It is a derivation *procedure* that may be summarized as follows: Given an existential generalization as a premiss or as an intermediate step in a derivation, EI 1) directs us to enter a suitably chosen instantiation as a line in the derivation and 2) permits us to use this instantiation in the derivation, provided that the constant so introduced is "discharged" by a later application of *Rule EG* before the desired conclusion is reached. (The reader may verify that these features are all present in the examples above of the proper use of EI.)

If the EI procedure is correctly applied, then the system PN—made up of EI together with UI, EG, and the still-to-be-completed UG—should sanction all and only valid argument forms. PN will be complete and sound.

It was in search of completeness that we first resorted to EI. Some way of gaining access to the information contained in existentially general entries in derivations was necessary, because otherwise our system would be incomplete. It would fail to sanction clearly *valid* argument forms.

Now with EI included, the system PN can be shown to be *complete*, a proof that had best be left to a formal account of PL-1. But the inclusion of EI does raise a question about the *soundness* of PN.

Obviously, we do not want a system that sanctions *invalid* argument forms. Soundness cannot be sacrificed in order to attain completeness. Nor need it be. For in the present context, 'soundness' has two senses. A system may be called "terminally" sound if in every correctly constructed derivation the *conclusion* is a logical consequence of its premisses; a system is "line-by-line" sound if in every correctly constructed derivation each *entry* is a logical consequence of its premisses.

What then of PN? It can be shown to. be *terminally* sound. But since it includes EI, it cannot be *line-by-line* sound; for each application of EI produces an entry that is not validly inferrable from its premisses. Thus what we have had to surrender in the interest of completeness is not soundness as such, but line-by-line soundness.

An alternative still remains: to seek completeness *without* recourse to EI and EG as *primitive* rules.   Two ways to gain this end rest on the interdefinability of quantifiers.   The first dispenses with EI and EG altogether, but only at the cost of very long derivations (see below, pages 299–300).   The second, adopted by Benson Mates, uses EI and EG as *derived* rules.[5]

MORE ON RULE UG

The reader will recall that our earlier statement of Rule UG was left unfinished.   Its completion had to await the discussion of EI.   The reason for the delay is illustrated by two *incorrect* derivations.

(14) $(\exists x)Fxb$
          Therefore $(x)Fxb$

SUPPOSED DERIVATION

{1}	1.	$(\exists x)Fxb$	Rule P
{1}	2.	Fab	1 EI
{1}	3.	$(x)Fxb$	2 Rule UG (!)

Counterexample.   Let '*F*' be replaced by 'admires', '*b*' by 'Hitler'; let the domain be *people*.   Then the argument

(14′)   Someone admires Hitler.

         Therefore everyone admires Hitler.

is a counterexample to (14).
   It is a simple matter to block invalid inferences of the form (14).   We

---

[5]   *Elementary Logic*, 2d ed. (New York: Oxford University Press, 1965, 1972), pp. 120–126.   Mates's Rule EI says that, given an existential generalization, we may add (and discharge) an instantiation of it as a premiss, provided the constant we select has not yet been used in the derivation and does not appear either in any premiss added later or in the desired conclusion.   The derivation for our (6) is then:

{1}	1.	$(x)(Fx \rightarrow Gx)$	Rule P
{2}	2.	$(\exists x)Fx$	Rule P
{3}	3.	Fa	Added premiss
{1}	4.	$Fa \rightarrow Ga$	1 Rule UI
{1,3}	5.	Ga	3, 4 Rule T
{1,3}	6.	$(\exists x)Gx$	5 Rule EG
{1,2}	7.	$(\exists xGx)$	2, 3, 6 Rule EI

We give below (pp. 300–301) the derivation schemata used by him to justify EI and EG as derived rules.

need only incorporate into Rule UG the proviso that it may not be applied to a constant introduced by an application of EI.

But what of the argument form

(15) $(y)(\exists x)Fxy$
        Therefore $(\exists x)(y)Fxy$,

which is the converse of (13)?

SUPPOSED DERIVATION

{1}	1.	$(y)(\exists x)Fxy$	Rule P
{1}	2.	$(\exists x)Fxa$	1 Rule UI
{1}	3.	Fba	2 EI
{1}	4.	$(y)Fby$	3 Rule UG
{1}	5.	$(\exists x)(y)Fxy$	4 Rule EG

Counterexample.   Let the domain be *integers*, and let 'F' be replaced by 'is greater than'.   Then

(15′)   For each integer there is a greater one

        Therefore there is a greatest integer

is a counterexample to (15).

Here, in contrast to the case of (14), the constant on which we sought to generalize—namely, 'a'—was *not* introduced by EI.   Yet the derivation is clearly incorrect.   The error will be easier to locate if we write out each step of the derivation in terms of the counterexample.   We then have:

1. For each integer there is a greater one.   (True)

2. There is an integer greater than the one named by 'a'.   (True)

3. Let this greater integer be named, say, by 'b'.   (From 2 by EI)

4. The integer named by 'b' is greater than any integer.   (False)

5. There is a greatest integer.   (False)

Thus the derivation goes off the track precisely at the step from line 3 to 4 —that is, in the application of UG.

To meet this problem we must place a further restriction on UG.   Not only must we bar generalizing on a constant introduced into the derivation by an application of EI.   We must also bar generalizing on any constant that shares with a constant introduced by EI the status of being a term in the same nonmonadic (relational) sentence form or part of a sentence form.

A word of explanation about this final restriction on UG: The derivation offered for (15) goes off the track because although the constant '*a*' was obtained by UI, it is no longer "arbitrary" in the sense required by UG once it appears with '*b*' in the nonmonadic expression '*Fba*'. For '*Fba*' expresses a specific relation between the elements named by '*a*' and '*b*'. It is this new information about the element denoted by '*a*' that annuls the "arbitrary" or "generalizable" character of that constant.

The completed Rule UG may now be stated as follows:

---

6. RULE UG (*Universal Generalization*)—Completed Formulation: *From a sentence form containing an individual constant, we may infer the* universal generalization *of the sentence form, provided that the constant on which we generalize 1) does not appear in any premiss of that sentence form, 2) was not introduced into the derivation by an application of EI, and 3) does not appear in company with a constant introduced by EI, where the two are terms in the same nonmonadic part of a sentence form.*

GETTING ALONG WITHOUT EI (AND EG)

Rather than face the complications of EI, we may prefer to explore the alternative, mentioned earlier, of seeking completeness without recourse to EI. We can, by using the interdefinability of quantifiers, transform existential quantifications into universal quantifications. It then becomes possible to dispense with both EI and Rule EG altogether.

Let (6) again serve as our example. Applying the appropriate definitional equivalence to Premiss 2, we have

{2}	2.	$(\exists x)Fx$	Rule P
{2}	3.	$\sim(x)\sim Fx$	2 Definition

Once this premiss is transformed, we can construct the following derivation for (6), based simply on Rules P, T, CP, UI, and UG, together with the interdefinability of quantifiers:

{1}	1.	$(x)(Fx \rightarrow Gx)$	Rule P
{2}	2.	$(\exists x)Fx$	Rule P
{2}	3	$\sim(x) \sim Fx$	2 Definition
{1}	4.	$Fa \rightarrow Ga$	1 Rule UI

{5}	5.	$(x) \sim Gx$	Rule P* (borrowed premiss)
{5}	6.	$\sim Ga$	5 Rule UI
{1, 5}	7.	$\sim Fa$	4, 6 Rule T
{1, 5}	8.	$(x) \sim Fx$	7 Rule UG
{1}	9.	$(x) \sim Gx \rightarrow (x) \sim Fx$	5–8 Rule CP (premiss discharged)
{1, 2}	10.	$\sim (x) \sim Gx$	3, 9 Rule T
{1, 2}	11.	$(\exists x)Gx$	10 Definition

But notice that now eleven lines are required to do the work that six lines did before, in (6) above. The economy in rules has been obtained at the cost of a very much lengthened derivation.[6]

---

[6]   The penalty applies not only to (6) but generally. This is evident from the following two *derivation schemata*, adapted from Benson Mates (op. cit., pp. 120–123). Here, again, α denotes any individual variable, μ an individual constant, A a sentence form, and $A\alpha/\mu$ the result of replacing in A each occurrence of the variable α by an occurrence of the constant μ.

1. *Derivation schema for dispensing with EG.* We assume that $A\alpha/\mu$ has been obtained at line j of a derivation from a set of premisses $\{p_1, \ldots, p_n\}$. The schema shows how we may go from $A\alpha/\mu$ to its existential generalization $(\exists\alpha)A$ without recourse to Rule EG.

$\{p_1, \ldots, p_n\}$	j	$A\alpha/\mu$	
	$\vdots$		
{k}	k	$(\alpha) \sim A$	Rule P* (borrowed premiss)
{k}	$k + 1$	$\sim A\alpha/\mu$	k Rule UI
$\wedge$	$k + 2$	$(\alpha) \sim A \rightarrow \sim A\alpha/\mu$	k-$k + 1$ Rule CP (premiss discharged)
$\{p_1, \ldots, p_n\}$	$k + 3$	$\sim (\alpha) \sim A$	$j, k + 2$ Rule T
$\{p_1, \ldots, p_n\}$	$k + 4$	$(\exists\alpha)A$	$k + 3$ Definition

2.   *Derivation schema for dispensing with EI.* We assume that an existential generalization $(\exists\alpha)A$ has been obtained at line i of a derivation from a set of premisses $\{p_1, \ldots, p_m\}$. The schema shows that if we add $A\alpha/\mu$ as a *new* premiss (where μ is a constant appearing neither in any earlier entry of the derivation nor in its desired conclusion), then any PL-1 sentence form B that can be derived in PN from $A\alpha/\mu$, together with a set of premisses $\{q_1, \ldots, q_n\}$ *not* containing μ, can be derived from just these premisses *and* the premisses of $(\exists\alpha)$ A *without resort to EI.* (Notice that in the

EXERCISES

46.1. Show that each of these argument forms is valid by deriving (in PN) the conclusion from the premisses.

    a. $(x)(Fx \rightarrow Gx)$
        $(x)(Gx \rightarrow \sim Hx)$
        Therefore $(x)(Fx \rightarrow \sim Hx)$

    b. $(x)(Fx \sim Gx)$
        $(\exists x) \sim Gx$
        Therefore $(\exists x) \sim Fx$

    c. $(x)(Fx \rightarrow \sim Gx)$
        $(\exists x)(Gx \ \& \ Hx)$
        Therefore $(\exists x)(Hx \ \& \sim Fx)$

    d. $(x)(Fx \rightarrow Gx)$
        $(x)(Gx \rightarrow Hx)$
        $(x)(Hx \rightarrow \sim Ix)$
        $(\exists x)Fx$
        Therefore $(\exists x) \sim Ix$

    e. $(x)(Hx \rightarrow Gx)$
        $(x)(\exists y)(Fxy \ \lor \sim Gx)$
        Therefore $(x)(\exists y)(Fxy \ \lor \sim Hx)$

---

schema $A\alpha/\mu$ is not inferred from $(\exists \alpha)A$. It is a borrowed premiss and is discharged in the course of the derivation.)

$\{p_1, \ldots, p_m\}$	i	$(\exists \alpha)A$	——
$\vdots$	$\vdots$	$\vdots$	$\vdots$
$\{j\}$	j	$A\alpha/\mu$	Rule P* (borrowed premiss that obeys the restrictions)
$\vdots$	$\vdots$		$\vdots$
$\{q_1, \ldots, q_n, j\}$	k	B	——
$\{q_1, \ldots, q_n\}$	$k+1$	$A\alpha/\mu \rightarrow B$	j–k Rule CP (premiss discharged)
$\{k+2\}$	$k+2$	$\sim B$	Rule P* (borrowed premiss)
$\{q_1, \ldots, q_n, k+2\}$	$k+3$	$\sim A\alpha/\mu$	$k+1, k+2$ Rule T
$\{q_1, \ldots, q_n, k+2\}$	$k+4$	$(\alpha) \sim A$	$k+3$ Rule UG
$\{q_1, \ldots, q_n\}$	$k+5$	$\sim B \rightarrow (\alpha) \sim A$	$k+2$–$k+4$ Rule CP (premiss discharged)
$\{p_1, \ldots, p_m\}$	$k+6$	$\sim(\alpha) \sim A$	i Definition
$\{p_1, \ldots, p_m, q_1, \ldots, q_n\}$	$k+7$	B	$k+5, k+6$ Rule T

f. $(x)[(Fx \& Gx) \rightarrow Hx]$
    $(\exists x)Hx \rightarrow (x)(Iax \& Gx)$
    Therefore $(\exists x)(Fx \& Gx) \rightarrow (Iaa \& Ga)$

g. $(\exists x)Fx \rightarrow (x)(\sim Gx \rightarrow Fx)$
    $(\exists x)Hx \rightarrow (x)(Fx \rightarrow Hx)$
    $(\exists x)(Fx \& Hx)$
    Therefore $(x)(\sim Gx \rightarrow Hx)$

46.2. Identify the error(s) in each of these *supposed* derivations:

a. | {1} | 1. | $(x)(Fxx \rightarrow Gx)$ | Rule P |
    | {1} | 2. | $Faa \rightarrow Ga$ | 1 Rule UI |
    | {1} | 3. | $(x)(Fxa \rightarrow Gx)$ | 2 Rule UG |

b. | {1} | 1. | $(x)(Gx \rightarrow Fax)$ | Rule P |
    | {1} | 2. | $Ga \rightarrow Faa$ | 1 Rule UI |
    | {1} | 3. | $(x)(Gx \rightarrow Fxx)$ | 2 Rule UG |

c. | {1} | 1. | Fa | Rule P |
    | {2} | 2. | $(\exists x)Gx$ | Rule P |
    | {2} | 3. | Ga | 2 Rule EI |
    | {1, 2} | 4. | $Fa \& Ga$ | 1, 3 Rule T |
    | {1, 2} | 5. | $(\exists x)(Fx \& Gx)$ | 4 Rule EG |

d. | {1} | 1. | $(\exists x)Gx$ | Rule P |
    | {2} | 2. | $(x)(Gx \rightarrow Hx)$ | Rule P |
    | {1} | 3. | Ga | 1 Rule EI |
    | {2} | 4. | $Ga \rightarrow Ha$ | 2 Rule UI |
    | {1, 2} | 5. | Ha | 3, 4 Rule T |
    | {1, 2} | 6. | $(x)Hx$ | 5 Rule UG |

e. | {1} | 1. | $(\exists x)(Gx \& \sim Hx)$ | Rule P |
    | {2} | 2. | $(x)(Fx \rightarrow Gx)$ | Rule P |
    | {1} | 3. | $Ga \& \sim Ha$ | 1 Rule EI |
    | {2} | 4. | $Fa \rightarrow Ga$ | 2 Rule UI |
    | {1} | 5. | Ga | 3 Rule T |
    | {1} | 6. | $\sim Ha$ | 3 Rule T |
    | {1, 2} | 7. | Fa | 4, 5 Rule T |

| {1, 2} | 8. | *Fa & ~ Ha* | 7, 6 Rule T |
| {1, 2} | 9. | $(\exists x)(Fx \ \& \sim Hx)$ | 8 Rule EG |

f.

{1}	1.	$(x)(\exists y)Fxy$	Rule P
{2}	2.	*Ga*	Rule P
{1}	3.	$(\exists y)Fay$	1 Rule UI
{1}	4.	*Fab*	3 Rule EI
{1}	5.	$(x)Fax$	4 Rule UG
{1, 2}	6.	*Ga & (x)Fax*	2, 5 Rule T
{1, 2}	7.	$(\exists y)[Gy \ \& \ (x)Fyx]$	6 Rule EG

g.

{1}	1.	$(x)(y)(z)[(Fxy \ \& \ Fyz) \to Fxz]$	Rule P
{2}	2.	$\sim (x)Fxx$	Rule P
{2}	3.	$(\exists x) \sim Fxx$	2 Definition
{2}	4.	$\sim Faa$	3 Rule EI
{1}	5.	$(Fab \ \& \ Fba) \to Faa$	1 Rule UI (three times)
{1, 2}	6.	$\sim (Fab \ \& \ Fba)$	5, 4 Rule T
{1, 2}	7.	$Fab \to \sim Fba$	6 Rule T
{1, 2}	8.	$(y)(Fay \to \sim Fya)$	7 Rule UG
{1, 2}	9.	$(x)(y)(Fxy \to \sim Fyx)$	8 Rule UG

46.3. "The philosopher Chrysippus . . . used to propound arguments such as the following: If anyone is in Megara, he is not in Athens; now there is a man in Megara; therefore there is not a man in Athens." [Diogenes Laertius, third century A.D. ?, *Lives of the Philosophers*, Vol. 2, pp. 295, 297, tr. by R. P. Hicks]. Consider the following derivation offered as proof of the validity of the argument:

{1}	1.	$(x)(Mx \to \sim Ax)$	Rule P
{2}	2.	$(\exists x)Mx$	Rule P
{2}	3.	*Ma*	2 Rule EI
{1}	4.	$Ma \to \sim Aa$	1 Rule UI
{1, 2}	5.	$\sim Aa$	4, 3 Rule T
{1, 2}	6.	$\sim (\exists x)Ax$	5 Rule EG

What error does the derivation contain?

46.4. Determine whether the following arguments are valid. First, write the PL-1 argument form of which the argument is a substitution instance. Then if the argument form is valid, show this by deriving (in PN) the conclusion from the premisses. If it is not valid, give a counter-example.

a.   Descartes is a French philosopher.   There are German philosophers.   Therefore there are French and German philosophers.

b.   A poet is an artist.   Some artists are temperamental.   Therefore some poets are temperamental.

c.   Some plays are not comedies.   No comedies are tragedies. Therefore some plays are not tragedies.

d.   Everyone is an introvert or an extrovert.   And all extroverts are happy.   But some people are not happy.   So there must be some introverts.

e.   If any PL-1 sentence form is equivalent to a second one and the second is equivalent to a third, then the first is equivalent to the third.   If a PL-1 sentence form is equivalent to a second one, then the second is equivalent to the first.   Therefore every PL-1 sentence form is equivalent to itself.

---

§47   Theorems of PN

In §33 a *theorem of SN* was defined as an SL sentence form that is derivable in SN from the empty set of premisses.   The definition of a *theorem of PN* is identical except that PL-1 replaces SL and PN replaces SN.
    For example,

(1) $(x)Fx \rightarrow Fa$

is a theorem of PN.   For take '$(x)Fx$' as a *conditional* premiss.   Then

$$
\begin{array}{llll}
\{1\} & 1. & (x)Fx & \text{Rule P* (borrowed premiss)} \\
\{1\} & 2. & Fa & \text{1 Rule UI} \\
\wedge & 3. & (x)Fx \rightarrow Fa & \text{1--2 Rule CP}
\end{array}
$$

is a derivation of (1) from the empty set of premisses $\wedge$.
    Another example is

(2) $(x)(Fx \rightarrow Gx) \rightarrow [(\exists x)Fx \rightarrow (\exists x)Gx]$

Here take '$(x)(Fx \rightarrow Gx)$' and '$(\exists x)Fx$' as conditional premisses.   Then

{1}	1.	$(x)(Fx \rightarrow Gx)$	Rule P*
{2}	2.	$(\exists x)Fx$	Rule P*
{2}	3.	Fa	2 EI
{1}	4.	$Fa \rightarrow Ga$	1 Rule UI
{1, 2}	5.	Ga	3, 4 Rule T
{1, 2}	6.	$(\exists x)Gx$	5 Rule EG
{1}	7.	$(\exists x)Fx \rightarrow (\exists x)Gx$	2–6 Rule CP
$\wedge$	8.	$(x)(Fx \rightarrow Gx) \rightarrow [(\exists x)Fx \rightarrow (\exists x)Gx]$	1–7 Rule CP

is a derivation of (2) from the empty set of premisses.

In determining whether a PL-1 sentence form is a theorem of PN, it is often, but not always, advantageous to use the method of *indirect proof*. In using this method, we take the *negation* of the desired theorem as a conditional premiss and see if we can develop a contradiction.   If we succeed, then by Rule T we have proved the theorem.   For example, an indirect proof that

(3) $(x)[(Fx \,\&\, Gx) \rightarrow (Fx \vee Gx)]$

is a theorem can be had as follows:

{1}	1.	$\sim (x)[(Fx \,\&\, Gx) \rightarrow (Fx \vee Gx)]$	Rule P*
{1}	2.	$(\exists x) \sim [(Fx \,\&\, Gx) \rightarrow (Fx \vee Gx)]$	1 Definition
{1}	3.	$\sim [(Fa \,\&\, Ga) \rightarrow (Fa \vee Ga)]$	2 EI
{1}	4.	$Fa \,\&\, Ga$	3 Rule T
{1}	5.	$\sim (Fa \vee Ga)$	3 Rule T
{1}	6.	$\sim Fa$	5 Rule T
{1}	7.	Fa	4 Rule T
{1}	8.	$Fa \,\&\, \sim Fa$	6, 7 Rule T
$\wedge$	9.	$\sim (x)[(Fx \,\&\, Gx) \rightarrow (Fx \vee Gx)] \rightarrow (Fa \,\&\, \sim Fa)$	1–8 Rule CP
$\wedge$	10.	$\sim \sim (x)[(Fx \,\&\, Gx) \rightarrow (Fx \vee Gx)]$	9 Rule T
$\wedge$	11.	$(x)[(Fx \,\&\, Gx) \rightarrow (Fx \vee Gx)]$	10 Rule T

An indirect proof of (1), on the other hand, would be rather wasteful. It would require eight lines instead of three:

{1}	1.	$\sim[(x)Fx \rightarrow Fa]$	Rule P*
{1}	2.	$(x)Fx$	1 Rule T
{1}	3.	$\sim Fa$	1 Rule T
{1}	4.	Fa	2 Rule UI
{1}	5.	$Fa \& \sim Fa$	3, 4 Rule T
$\wedge$	6.	$\sim[(x)Fx \rightarrow Fa] \rightarrow (Fa \& \sim Fa)$	1–5 Rule CP
$\wedge$	7.	$\sim\sim[(x)Fx \rightarrow Fa]$	6 Rule T
$\wedge$	8.	$(x)Fx \rightarrow Fa$	7 Rule T

A formal treatment of PL-1 would include a proof that a PL-1 sentence form is a *theorem* if and only if it is a *valid* sentence form. Here we merely record that fact.

EXERCISES

47.1.   Prove that each of the following PL-1 sentence forms is a theorem of PN. Use whichever approach seems most effective. Two approaches have been discussed above, "direct" proof and indirect proof. A third approach employs *singular* assumptions to prove generalized conditionals. An example is this proof of (3), which is much shorter than the one in the text:

(3) $(x)[(Fx \& Gx) \rightarrow (Fx \vee Gx)]$

Proof:	{1}	1.	$Fa \& Ga$	Rule P*
	{1}	2.	Fa	1 Rule T
	{1}	3.	$Fa \vee Ga$	2 Rule T
	$\wedge$	4.	$(Fa \& Ga) \rightarrow (Fa \vee Ga)$	1–3 Rule CP
	$\wedge$	5.	$(x)[(Fx \& Gx) \rightarrow (Fx \vee Gx)]$	4 Rule UG

Note: UG is used *correctly* here. The constant generalized on—'*a*'—does appear in the borrowed premiss, but *not* in any premiss of the sentence form to which UG is applied. Indeed, that sentence form—'$(Fa \& Ga)$ $\rightarrow (Fa \vee Ga)$'—*has no premisses*.

a. $(\exists x)(Fx \& Gx) \rightarrow [(\exists x)Fx \& (\exists x)Gx]$

b. $(x)(Fx \vee Gx) \rightarrow [(\exists x)Fx \vee (\exists x)Gx]$

c. $(\exists x)[(y)Fxy \ \& \ Gx] \rightarrow [(\exists x)(y)Fxy \ \& \ (\exists x)Gx]$ (cf., Exercise 44.5)

d. $(x)(\exists y)(Fx \ \& \ Gy) \rightarrow [(\exists x) \sim Gx \rightarrow (\exists x)Gx]$

e. $(x) \sim Fx \lor (\exists x)Fx$ (Hint: Use indirect proof.)

f. $(\exists x)[(\exists y)Fy \rightarrow Fx]$

g. $(\exists x)(Fx \lor Gx) \leftrightarrow [(\exists x)Fx \lor (\exists x)Gx]$

h. $(x)\{[(Fx \ \& \ Gx) \rightarrow Hx] \rightarrow [Fx \rightarrow (Gx \rightarrow Hx)]\}$ (Hint: Use singular assumption.)

i. $(x)\{[Fx \rightarrow (Gx \rightarrow Hx)] \rightarrow [(Fx \ \& \ Gx) \rightarrow Hx]\}$

j. $(x)((Fx \ \& \ Gx) \rightarrow \{(y)[Hy \rightarrow (\sim Gy \lor \sim Fy)] \rightarrow \sim Hx\})$

k. $(x)(Fx \rightarrow Gx) \rightarrow (x)[(\exists y)(Fy \ \& \ Hxy) \rightarrow (\exists y)(Gy \ \& \ Hxy)]$

l. $(\exists x)[(\exists y)Fy \rightarrow Gx] \leftrightarrow [(\exists y)Fy \rightarrow (\exists x)Gx]$

---

§48   *Some Useful Tools in Working with Quantifiers*

There are a number of results on quantifiers that specify when and where one is permitted to change their order, scope, and type. Such results may be used as *derived* rules of inference to simplify the construction of derivations.

Take, for example, the sentence form

$$(\exists x)Fx \rightarrow P.$$

Though it is not immediately obvious, we may derive from it the following universally quantified sentence form:

$$(x)(Fx \rightarrow P).$$

Indeed, the two are equivalent—that is, interderivable—as the following two derivations show:

{1}	1.	$(\exists x)Fx \rightarrow P$	Rule P
{2}	2.	$\sim P$	Rule P*
{1, 2}	3.	$\sim(\exists x)Fx$	1, 2 Rule T

$\{1, 2\}$ 4. $(x) \sim Fx$ 3 Definition

$\{1, 2\}$ 5. $\sim Fa$ 4 Rule UI

$\{1\}$ 6. $\sim P \rightarrow \sim Fa$ 2–5 Rule CP

$\{1\}$ 7. $Fa \rightarrow P$ 6 Rule T

$\{1\}$ 8. $(x)(Fx \rightarrow P)$ 7 Rule UG

and

$\{1\}$ 1. $(x)(Fx \rightarrow P)$ Rule P

$\{2\}$ 2. $(\exists x)Fx$ Rule P*

$\{2\}$ 3. Fa 2 Rule EI

$\{1\}$ 4. $Fa \rightarrow P$ 1 Rule UI

$\{1, 2\}$ 5. P 4, 3 Rule T

$\{1\}$ 6. $(\exists x)Fx \rightarrow P$ 2–5 Rule CP

Our result may be expressed thus:

From '$(x)(Fx \rightarrow P)$', to infer '$(\exists x)Fx \rightarrow P$', and conversely.

This is an instance of a *derived* rule.[7]   Other derived rules, expressed in terms of typical applications, include the following:

1.   From '$(x)(y)Fxy$', to infer '$(y)(x)Fxy$', and conversely.

2.   From '$(\exists x)(\exists y)Fxy$', to infer '$(\exists y)(\exists x)Fxy$', and conversely.

3.   From '$(\exists x)(y)Fxy$', to infer '$(y)(\exists x)Fxy$', but *not* conversely.

4.   From '$(x)(Fx \,\&\, Gx)$', to infer '$(x)Fx \,\&\, (x)Gx$', and conversely.

5.   From '$(\exists x)(Fx \lor Gx)$', to infer '$(\exists x)Fx \lor (\exists x)Gx$', and conversely.

6.   From '$(\exists x)(Fx \,\&\, Gx)$', to infer '$(\exists x)Fx \,\&\, (\exists x)Gx$', but *not* conversely.

---

[7]   This rule may be formulated in the α-μ-A symbolism as

From $(\alpha)(A \rightarrow B)$, to infer $(\exists \alpha)A \rightarrow B$, and conversely (where α is *not* free in B).

7. From '$(x)(Fx \rightarrow Gx)$', to infer '$(x)Fx \rightarrow (x)Gx$', but *not* conversely.

8. From '$(x)Fx \lor (x)Gx$', to infer '$(x)(Fx \lor Gx)$', but *not* conversely.[8]

---

§49 *Summary of the System PN*

A soundness proof for PN assures us that if the conclusion of a PL-1 argument form is derivable in PN from its premisses, then the argument form is valid. Conversely, a completeness proof for PN assures us that if a PL-1 argument form is valid, its conclusion is derivable in PN from its premisses.

But while the completeness proof for PN guarantees that for a valid argument form the desired derivation *exists*, it does not tell us how to find it. It does not supply a general search procedure.

Now in SL, if we fail to find a derivation, we can always fall back on truth tables. These provide a general mechanical procedure for deciding whether SL argument forms are valid. We can therefore entrust SL to the diligence of a well-programmed machine.

For PL-1, however, it has been shown that no *general* decision procedure of this type can exist (Alonzo Church, 1936). Accordingly, if after a reasonable length of time we fail to find a derivation, we shall never

---

[8] In the α-μ-A symbolism, we list additional derived rules on the scope and type of quantifiers (it is understood that α is *not* free in A):

1. From $(\alpha)(A \lor B)$, to infer $A \lor (\alpha)B$, and conversely.
2. From $(\exists\alpha)(A \lor B)$, to infer $A \lor (\exists\alpha)B$, and conversely.
3. From $(\alpha)(A \& B)$, to infer $A \& (\alpha)B$, and conversely.
4. From $(\exists\alpha)(A \& B)$, to infer $A \& (\exists\alpha)B$, and conversely.
5. From $(\alpha)(A \rightarrow B)$, to infer $A \rightarrow (\alpha)B$, and conversely.
6. From $(\exists\alpha)(A \rightarrow B)$, to infer $A \rightarrow (\exists\alpha)B$, and conversely.
7. From $(\alpha)(B \rightarrow A)$, to infer $(\exists\alpha)B \rightarrow A$, and conversely (see our example above).
8. From $(\exists\alpha)(B \rightarrow A)$, to infer $(\alpha)B \rightarrow A$, and conversely.

For example, Rule 7 tells us that

$$(x)[Fxb \rightarrow (\exists y)Gy]$$

and

$$(\exists x)Fxb \rightarrow (\exists y)Gy$$

are equivalent and hence may replace each other in derivations. On the other hand, Rule 7 does not sanction replacing, say, '$(x)(Fxb \rightarrow Gx)$' with '$(\exists x)Fxb \rightarrow Gx$', because since '$x$' is free in '$Gx$', this would violate the understanding that α *not* be free in A.

know whether it is because there is none—that is, because the argument form is invalid—or because we simply have not looked hard enough.

We now collect and restate the rules and procedure that make up the system PN.

GROUP A

1.   RULE P: A premiss may be entered on any line of a derivation.

2.   RULE T: A PL-1 sentence form may be entered in a derivation if it is (tautologically) implied by a preceding entry or conjunction of such entries.

3.   RULE CP (Conditional Proof): If a PL-1 sentence form B can be derived in PN from a PL-1 sentence form A together with a set of PL-1 sentence forms $\{A_1, \ldots, A_n\}$, then the sentence form $A \rightarrow B$ can be derived in PN from the set $\{A_1, \ldots, A_n\}$ alone, *or*

$$\text{If } \{A_1, \ldots, A_n, A\} \vdash_{PN} B, \text{ then } \{A_1, \ldots, A_n\} \vdash_{PN} A \rightarrow B.$$

GROUP B

4.   RULE UI (Universal Instantiation): From a universal generalization, we may infer *any* of its instantiations.   For example,

From '$(x)Fx$' we may infer, say, 'Fa'.

5.   RULE EG (Existential Generalization): From a sentence form containing an individual constant, we may infer any existential generalization of that sentence form.   For example,

From 'Fa', say, we may infer '$(\exists x)Fx$'.

6.   RULE UG (Universal Generalization): From a sentence form containing an individual constant, we may infer the universal generalization of the sentence form, provided that the constant on which we generalize 1) does not appear in any premiss of that sentence form, 2) was not introduced into the derivation by an application of EI, and 3) does not appear in company with a constant introduced by EI, where the two constants are terms in the same nonmonadic part of a sentence form.   For example,

From 'Fa', say, we may infer '$(x)Fx$', provided that 'a' is a constant that meets the conditions stated in the rule.

7.   THE EI PROCEDURE (Existential Instantiation)—*Simplified Statement, with EI to Be Used Before UI Wherever the Order Is*

Open to Choice: Given an existential generalization, we may enter and use an instantiation of it, provided that the constant so introduced 1) has not appeared previously in the derivation and 2) does not appear in the desired conclusion. For example,

> Given '$(\exists x)Fx$', we may enter and use, say, 'Fa', provided that 'a' is a constant that fulfills the conditions stated in the procedure.

EXERCISES

49.1. Determine whether each of these argument forms is valid. If it is valid, show this by deriving in PN the conclusion from the premises. If it is not valid, give a counterexample.

a. $(\exists x)(Fx \mathrel{\&} Gx)$
    $(x)(Hx \rightarrow \sim Gx)$
    $(\exists x)Hx$
    Therefore $(\exists x)Gx \mathrel{\&} (\exists x) \sim Gx$

b. $(\exists x)(Fx \lor Gx)$
    $(x)(Gx \rightarrow Hx)$
    Therefore $(\exists x)Hx$

c. $Fa \lor Gb$
    $[(\exists x)Fx \lor (\exists x)Gx] \rightarrow (x)(Fx \lor Gx)$
    $(\exists x) \sim Gx$
    Therefore $(\exists x)Fx$

d. $(x)[(Fx \lor Gx) \rightarrow Hx]$
    $(\exists x) \sim (Fx \lor Gx)$
    Therefore $(\exists x) \sim Hx$

e. $(x)(Fx \lor Gx)$
    $(x)\{Gx \rightarrow [Hx \mathrel{\&} (\exists y)Ixy]\}$
    Therefore $(x)(\sim Hx \rightarrow Fx)$

f. $(x)(y)(z)[(Fxy \mathrel{\&} Fyz) \rightarrow Fxz]$
    $(x)(y)(Fxy \rightarrow \sim Fyx)$
    Therefore $(x) \sim Fxx$

g. $(x)(y)(z)[(Fxy \mathrel{\&} Fyz) \rightarrow Fxz]$
    $(x)(y)(Fxy \mathrel{\&} Fyx)$
    Therefore $(x)Fxx$

h. $(x)(y)(\exists z)[Fxyz \mathrel{\&} (Gx \lor Gy)]$
    $(x)(y)(z)(Fyzx \rightarrow \sim Gx)$
    Therefore $\sim (\exists x)Fxxx$

12

More on Predicate Logic and Ordinary Language

"If you've seen one slum, you've seen them all."

How do we "translate" this ordinary-language sentence (of a former Vice President) into the formal language of first-order predicate logic?

When we set out to express the structure of such a sentence in the notation of PL-1, we run into a number of difficulties. Several of these we touch on below. We then call attention to some amphibolous general sentences, add a word on 'any' and 'all', and conclude with a brief look beyond 'all' and 'some'.

---

§50 *Problems in "Translating" from Ordinary Language into PL-1*

In SL we agreed to write out sentence forms in terms of their sentence letters, thus exhibiting SL structures *in full*. By this stipulation, we ensured that to each truth-functional sentence, for instance,

> If Jones or Smith wins the nomination, the Republicans will win the election,

there would correspond a *single* SL sentence form. In this case, it is

$$(P \vee Q) \rightarrow R.$$

But in the case of PL-1, we are unable to formulate an analogous requirement because of the complications associated with quantification and predication in ordinary language. Hence we cannot speak of *the* PL-1 form of an ordinary-language sentence. The best we can do is to explore the structure of the sentence in as much depth as the situation calls for and as our analysis of PL-1 forms permits.

KINDS OF PROBLEMS IN "TRANSLATION"

What kinds of problems are we likely to encounter in "translating" English sentences into symbolic sentences? Among the most important kinds are the following:

1. What should we take as *predicates*?

2. Which *quantifiers* should we choose?

3. What should we take as the *domain*?

4. What *scope* should we assign the quantifiers?

5. Which *connectives should we use with which quantifiers*?

We shall illustrate and discuss each of these in turn. Note that generally it will be necessary to recast the English sentence into some idiomatic equivalent in order to obtain an appropriate symbolic counterpart.

What To Take as Predicates

Consider the sentence

(1)   Only fools make the same mistake twice.

We could, of course, represent its structure as

(1') $(x)Fx$,

where the domain is *people* and where 'F' is taken as replacing the "predicate" expressed by the words 'is a fool if he or she makes the same mistake twice'. But obviously (1') does not reproduce as much of the structure of (1) as we would ordinarily want to have. We obtain more of the structure (and enough for our purposes) if we let 'F' stand in place of 'makes the same mistake twice' and '*G*' in place of 'is a fool'. We then have

(1″) $(x)(Fx \rightarrow Gx)$.

Which Quantifiers To Choose

Now consider the sentence

(2)   If you can't stand the heat, you should keep out of the kitchen.

One might at first be inclined to write the form of (2) as

(2′) $(\exists x)(\sim Hx \rightarrow Kx)$,

where again the domain is *people*, '*H*' replaces 'can stand the heat', and '*K*' replaces 'should keep out of the kitchen'. But a moment's thought makes clear that what (2′) reproduces is the form of

> There is at least one person such that if he or she cannot stand the heat, he or she should keep out of the kitchen.

In other words, the 'you' in (2) has the sense not of 'someone' but of 'anyone' or 'whoever'. Hence the quantifier we want here is not the existential but the universal:

(2″) $(x)(\sim Hx \rightarrow Kx)$.

Note that even the word 'some' may on occasion have the force of 'any'. Take, for instance, the sentence

> Any course that is more interesting than some course is easier than that course.

Its form, as the reader may verify, is expressed by

> $(x)(y)(Fxy \rightarrow Gxy)$

(where the domain is *courses*, '*F*' replaces 'is more interesting than', and '*G*' replaces 'is easier than'), and not by, say,

> $(x)(\exists y)(Fxy \rightarrow Gxy)$.

What To Select as the Domain

(3)   No one has all the answers (i.e., answers all questions).

A person who ignored the problem of domains might be tempted to express the form of (3) as

(3′) $\sim(\exists x)(y)Axy$,

where 'A' is the stand-in for the two-place predicate 'answers'. But this would be quite wrong. For (3′) represents (3) as saying

> There is no object that answers all objects,

which makes no sense at all.

The point is that we want to use 'x' to talk about *persons* and 'y' to talk about *questions*. The simplest way to accomplish this is to take the *universe* as the domain and to put 'H' for the predicate 'is human' and 'Q' for 'is a question', while retaining 'A' for 'answers'. We can then express the form of (3) as

(3″) $\sim(\exists x)[Hx \ \& \ (y)(Qy \to Axy)]$,

that is,

> There is no object such that it is human *and* whatever is a question, it answers the question.

What Scope To Assign the Quantifiers

(4)   Smith, if anyone, admires Jones.

Let 'A' be put for the two-place predicate 'admires'; let the domain be *people*, with 'j' naming Jones and 's' naming Smith. It may seem plausible to represent the form of (4) as

(4′) $(\exists x)(Axj \to Asj)$.

(Notice that in *this* context, 'anyone' has the force of 'someone' and is therefore replaced by the *existential* quantifier rather than the universal quantifier.)

But could we not also write the form of (4) as

(4″) $(\exists x)Axj \to Asj$,

that is, with the *scope* of the quantifier limited to 'Axj'? And is there actually a difference between (4′) and (4″)?

Now (4′) represents (4) as saying

> There is at least one person such that if that person admires Jones then Smith admires Jones.

On the other hand, (4″) represents (4) as saying

> If any (at least one) person admires Jones then Smith admires Jones.

Doesn't (4″) come closer to what (4) says than (4′)?

Which Connective to Use with Which Quantifiers

By way of preliminary, recall that in PL-1 we write the two forms of universal propositions of Aristotelian logic

> A   All *S* are *P*
> E   No *S* are *P*

as the universally quantified *conditionals*

> $(x)(Sx \rightarrow Px)$
> $(x)(Sx \rightarrow \sim Px)$,

or in words,

> Everything is such that *if* it is *S, then* it is *P* (i.e., if anything is *S*, then it is *P*).
> Everything is such that *if* it is *S, then* it is not *P* (i.e., if anything is *S*, then it is not *P*).

And we write the two forms of particular propositions

> I   Some *S* are *P*
> O   Some *S* are not *P*

as the existentially quantified *conjunctions*

> $(\exists x)(Sx \ \& \ Px)$
> $(\exists x)(Sx \ \& \ \sim Px)$,

or in words,

> Something is such that it is *S and* it is *P* (i.e., something is *S* and *P*).
> Something is such that it is *S and* it is not *P* (i.e., something is *S* and not *P*).

(*Caution:* Do not confuse '$(\exists x)(Sx \ \& \ Px)$' with the existentially quantified *conditional* '$(\exists x)(Sx \rightarrow Px)$', which we read as

> There is something such that *if* it is *S, then* it is *P*.)

It is this pairing of the universal quantifier with the '→' and of the existential quantifier with the '&' that we wish to explore further, particularly in quantified compounds with two or more quantifiers.

Let us look back for a moment to

(3)　　No one has all the answers.

We saw above that its form is correctly represented as

(3″)　　$\sim(\exists x)[Hx \, \& \, (y)(Qy \to Axy)]$

or, equivalently,

(3‴)　　$\sim(\exists x)(y)[Hx \, \& \, (Qy \to Axy)]$.

Notice that these are quantified *conjunctions*. Now in an earlier manuscript version of this book, the form of (3) was mistakenly represented as the quantified *conditional*

(3XXX)　$\sim(\exists x)(y)[(Hx \, \& \, Qy) \to Axy]$,

which in words is

> It is not the case that there is something such that *if* it is human and anything is a question, *then* it answers the question.

This was an error! For although (3XXX) implies (3‴), the converse does not hold. Thus (3XXX) is not equivalent to (3‴) and hence fails to reproduce the form of (3) accurately.

In sum: if a sentence has the form of a multiply quantified *compound*, then

> 1. If the initial quantifier in the corresponding sentence form is *existential*, then the proper *major* connective will usually be the '&'—that is, the sentence has the form of a quantified conjunction.

> 2. If the initial quantifier in the corresponding sentence form is *universal*, then the proper major connective will usually be the '→'—that is, the sentence has the form of a quantified conditional.

Note: This is not to say that '(x)' never takes anything but '→' as the major connective—what of '$(x)[(Fx \to Gx) \, \& \, (Gx \to Fx)]$'?—

or that '$(\exists x)$' never takes anything but '&' as the major connective. Such cases are rare, however.   A moment's reflection suggests why.

The expression

$$(x)(Fx \ \& \ Gx)$$

represents the form of sentences to the effect that *all* members of the domain have *both* of two properties.   And

$$(\exists x)(Fx \rightarrow Gx)$$

represents the form of sentences to the effect that *some* members of the domain are such that *if* they have a certain property, *then* they have a certain other property.

Now surely we have less occasion to use sentences of these two kinds than sentences whose forms are represented by the expressions

$$(x)(Fx \rightarrow Gx)$$

and

$$(\exists x)(Fx \ \& \ Gx)$$

—that is, sentences to the effect, respectively, that *those members* of the domain having a certain property also have a certain other property and that *some* members of the domain have *both* of two properties.

In any event, we must be careful not to confuse an existentially quantified conjunction with an existentially quantified conditional; or a universally quantified conditional with a universally quantified conjunction.

Summary of the "Translation" Problems

We return now to

(5)   If you've seen one slum, you've seen them all.

This sentence will serve to illustrate the whole ensemble of problems that we have considered.

First, what do we take as predicates?   It won't do to settle on such "predicates" as 'have seen one slum' and 'have seen them all'.   For then the form of (5) would be expressed by

$$(\text{quantifier})(Fx \rightarrow Gx),$$

which hardly begins to represent the structure of (5). We do better if we consider using the one-place predicates 'is human' and 'is a slum' and the two-place predicate 'has seen'.

Second, which quantifiers do we pick? Here, as in (2), 'you' is to be understood in the sense of 'anyone' or 'whoever'. Hence for our initial quantifier we want

$$(x)$$

with the entire expression as its scope. But we shall need additional quantifiers with limited scope, as indicated below.

Third, the domain we need is the *universe*. Then we can single out *people* and *slums* from the other objects in the universe by using the predicates 'is human' and 'is a slum'. And if we take 'one' to mean the same as 'at least one', we can write the form of the antecedent of (5) as

$$(x)[(Hx \ \& \ (\exists y)(Sy \ \& \ Vxy)],$$

where 'H' is put for 'is human', 'S' for 'is a slum', and 'V' for 'has seen'; the existential quantifier '$(\exists y)$' replaces 'at least one object such that'.

Fourth, we need a final quantifier whose scope is the consequent of (5), so that we can express the form of 'have seen them all (i.e., all slums)'

$$(z)(Sz \rightarrow Vxz)$$

Lastly, the connectives that come into play are the conjunction and the conditional, with the conditional required as the *major* connective. The complete expression then reads

(5') $(x)\{[Hx \ \& \ (\exists y)(Sy \ \& \ Vxy)] \rightarrow (z)(Sz \rightarrow Vxz)\}$.

Notice that the quantifier '(x)' includes within its scope the two quantifiers '$(\exists y)$' and '(z)'.

What error is committed if the form of (5) is written as

(5") $(x)\{[Hx \ \& \ (\exists y)Sy \ \& \ Vxy] \rightarrow (z)(Sz \rightarrow Vxz)\}$?

AMPHIBOLOUS GENERAL SENTENCES

Amphibolies are ambiguities that attach to whole sentences. The quantificational idioms of ordinary language supply many examples. Here is one:

(6)   You can fool all the people some of the time,

which may be paraphrased as

All the people can be fooled some of the time.

Now (6) is amphibolous, since it admits of two readings:

(6*a*)   Each person can be fooled at some time (or other).

(6*b*)   There is some (at least one) time such that all people can be fooled at that time.

If we take (6) as (6*a*), its form is expressed by

(6*a'*) $(x)[Hx \rightarrow (\exists y)(Ty \ \& \ Fxy)]$,

where the domain is the *universe* and '*H*' is put for 'is human', '*T*' for 'is a time' and '*F*' for the two-place predicate 'can be fooled at'. But if we take (6) as (6*b*), its form is expressed by

(6*b'*) $(\exists y)(x)[Ty \ \& \ (Hx \rightarrow Fxy)]$.

We see that (6*a*) and (6*b*) differ in structure.   Thus formal analysis, by exhibiting this difference, serves to disambiguate (6).

Notice again that the initial universal quantifier is associated with the ' $\rightarrow$ ' as major connective, and the existential quantifier with the ' $\&$ ' as major connective.

A FURTHER WORD ON 'EACH' AND 'ALL', 'ANY' AND 'ALL'[1]

We observed earlier (in §38) that ordinary language has many ways of expressing generality, not all of which are captured by first-order logic. But what of those that remain at liberty?   Are they all merely *stylistic* variants of those in captivity and hence of no interest *logically*?   Or do some of them perhaps represent elements of *structure* in ordinary-language quantifying expressions that elude the PL-1 quantifiers?

Consider, for example, 'each' and 'all'.   In many contexts their uses agree, but in some they differ.   Thus we say

(7)   All of the little pigs went to market.

---

[1]   For further discussion of what follows, see Zeno Vendler, "Any and All," in *The Encyclopedia of Philosophy*, ed. Paul Edwards (New York: Macmillan, 1967), Vol. 1, pp. 131–133.

We can just as well say

(8)   Each of the little pigs went to market.

But although we say of a puzzle

(9)   All of the pieces fit together,

we really cannot say

(10)   Each of the pieces fits together.

This divergent behavior reflects the fact that there are *two* sorts of universal generality—*distributive* and *collective*—and that ordinary language is capable of expressing both. 'All' may express either sort: distributive, as in (7), or collective, as in (9). By contrast, 'each' is available only for distributive use, as in (8).

In PL-1, on the other hand, the universal quantifier can express only *one* sort of generality, for it can be used only *distributively*. Since it is not possible to turn a sentence expressing distributive generality into one expressing collective generality (or vice versa) simply by quantifier paraphrase, the difference between the two is one of structure, not merely one of style. Collective generality is an element of structure that cannot be captured by the universal quantifier of standard first-order logic.

Now take 'any' and 'all'. As we saw earlier (§38), the two are interchangeable in some contexts, but not in others. Thus

(11)   All contributions are gratefully accepted

differs only in style—and overtones—from

(12)   Any contribution is gratefully accepted.

But consider the following examples:

(13)   Perkins was not able to answer all the questions the students asked.

(14)   Perkins was not able to answer any question the students asked.

Sentences (13) and (14) illustrate that in negative contexts the behavior of 'any' and 'all' diverges, and this divergence is associated with a difference in structure.

For let the domain be the *universe*; let 'p' name Perkins; and put 'S' for 'is a student', 'Q' for 'is a question', 'A' for 'asked', and 'R'

for 'was able to answer'.   Notice, too, that (14) may be paraphrased as

(14*a*)   Perkins was able to answer no question the students asked.

Then the form of (13) is expressed by

(13′) $\sim(x)(y)[(Sx \ \& \ Qy \ \& \ Axy) \to Rpy]$,

whereas the form of (14*a*) is expressed by

(14a′) $(x)(y)[(Sx \ \& \ Qy \ \& \ Axy) \to \sim Rpy]$.

Obviously (13) and (14*a*) differ structurally.

Notice that in this case, however, PL-1 is quite capable of expressing the difference in structure.

The interchangeability of 'any' and 'all' fails elsewhere, too—for instance, in interrogative contexts.   To the question

(15)   Are all the flowers gone?

we may answer

(16)   Yes, all the flowers are gone.

But to the question

(17)   Has any stone been left unturned?

it makes no sense to reply

(18)   Yes, any stone has been left unturned.

But this difference in the behavior of 'any' and 'all' lies outside the confines of our discussion.   For PL-1 considers only sentences that we use to make statements.   The examination of question-asking sentences is left to other logics.

EXERCISES

50.1.   Show that the expression

$$\sim(\exists x)(y)[Hx \ \& \ (Qy \to Axy)]$$

is equivalent to (3″) in §50?   (Hint: see §48.)

In what way does the expression

$$\sim(\exists x)(y)[Hx \ \& \ (Qy \ \& \ Axy)]$$

fail to reproduce the form of (3)?

50.2. Show that

$$(x)(Axj \rightarrow Asj)$$

is equivalent to (4″) in §50.   (Again, see §48.)

50.3. Consider the sentences

1. No president is universally admired.

2. Not all presidents are universally admired.

Let the domain be *people,* and put 'P' for 'is president' and 'A' for the two-place predicate 'admires'.   Which of the following sentence forms express the form of sentence 1?   Which express the form of sentence 2?

    a. $\sim(\exists x)(y)(Px \ \& \ Ayx)$

    b. $\sim(x)(y)(Px \rightarrow Ayx)$

    c. $(\exists x) \sim (y)(Px \ \& \ Ayx)$

    d. $(x) \sim (y)(Px \rightarrow Ayx)$

    e. $(x) \sim (y)(Px \ \& \ Ayx)$

    f. $(\exists x) \sim (y)(Px \rightarrow Ayx)$

    g. $\sim(\exists x)(y)(Px \rightarrow Ayx)$

    h. $\sim(x)(y)(Px \ \& \ Ayx)$

    i. $(x)(y)(Px \rightarrow \sim Ayx)$

    j. $(\exists x)(y)(Px \rightarrow \sim Ayx)$

    k. $(x)(y)(Px \ \& \sim Ayx)$

    l. $(\exists x)(y)(Px \ \& \sim Ayx)$

Write out in words each of *a* through *l.*

§51   *A Brief Look Beyond 'All' and 'Some'*

Despite its limitations, PL-1 does cover a very important range of quantificational situations.   More than that, it provides the necessary founda-
tion for extending the analysis of logical structure to additional areas of
ordinary discourse.   An illustration follows.

In PL-1 we express the form of

(1)   There is at least one even prime

as

(1′) $(\exists x)(Ex \ \& \ Px)$,

where the domain is *integers*, '*E*' is put in place of 'is even', and '*P*' is
put in place of 'is prime'.   But in order to express the form of

(2)   There is just one even prime,

we need an additional predicate letter.   For (2) is equivalent to the conjunction of (1) and

(3)   There is at most one even prime,

and to render the sense of (3) we require the predicate 'is identical with'.
If in place of this predicate we put the predicate letter '*I*', then for our
present purposes we may express the form of (3) as

(3′) $(x)(y)[(Ex \ \& \ Px \ \& \ Ey \ \& \ Py) \rightarrow Ixy]$,

that is

> If x and y are even primes, then x is identical with y (or, there is
> at most one even prime).

And we can then express the form of (2) as

(2′) $(\exists x)(Ex \ \& \ Px) \ \& \ (x)(y)[(Ex \ \& \ Px \ \& \ Ey \ \& \ Py) \rightarrow Ixy]$,

that is

> There is at least one integer x that is an even prime, and if any
> integers x and y are even primes, then x is identical with y.

Notice that (2) asserts the existence of a unique integer—*the* even prime.   Phrases of the type '*the* so-and-so' and their idiomatic variants are called singular descriptions.   Their logical structure was first studied by Bertrand Russell in his celebrated essay "On Denoting."[2]

Russell pointed out that there are two ways of referring to an individual object.   We may name it, as in

(4)   Plato is Greek,

or we may describe it uniquely, as in

(5)   The author of *The Republic* is Greek.

Now the form of (4) is simply

(4′)   *Ga*

where '*a*' names Plato and '*G*' is put in place of 'is Greek'.   What is the form of (5)?   Is it the same as that of (4)?   Can it be written as

(5′)   *Gb*

where '*b*' stands in place of 'the author of *The Republic*'?   In other words, can *descriptions* be treated formally as if they were *names*?

Let us suppose that they can be.   Consider then, with Russell, the following sentence:

(6)   The present King of France is bald.

Its form would be expressed by

(6′)   *Ba*,

where '*a*' stands in place of 'the present King of France' and '*B*' is put for 'is bald'.   Since there is no present King of France, our first impulse might then be to count (6) as false.   In that case, however, its negation

(7)   The present King of France is not bald

with the form

(7′) $\sim Ba$

---

[2] The essay was first published in *Mind*, Vol. 14, 1905, pp. 479–493. It has been reprinted in numerous anthologies.

would have to be true. This, of course, is absurd. Therefore, we must reject the assumption that descriptions may be treated formally as if they were names.

According to Russell, a proper analysis of descriptions and hence of (6) must be sought along different lines. The sentence (6) is to be paraphrased as the triple conjunction

(6a)   There is at least one object x such that x is now King of France, and there is at most one object x such that x is now King of France, and this object x is bald.

The form of (6a) may then be expressed as

(6a') $(\exists x)[Kx \ \& \ (y)(Ky \rightarrow Ixy) \ \& \ Bx]$

and that of (7), similarly paraphrased, as

(7a') $(\exists x)[Kx \ \& \ (y)(Ky \rightarrow Ixy) \ \& \ \sim Bx]$,

where the domain is *men* and 'K' is put for the predicate 'is now King of France', 'B' for 'is bald', and 'I' for 'is identical with'.

Hence on Russell's analysis of '*the* so-and-so', (6) and (7) are *not* simply singular sentences, the second of which is the negation of the first. On the contrary, they are existentially generalized compound open sentences. They agree in asserting that there is just one male such that he is now King of France; they differ on whether he is bald. Since (7) is not the negation of (6), it does not follow that if (6) is false, (7) must be true. Instead, both may be false. And indeed, on this analysis, they both are, since no one is now King of France; thus the problem vanishes.

Singular descriptions—and referring expressions generally—are still a subject of lively controversy. Russell's theory of '*the*', however, remains a brilliant illustration of how first-order logic may be used to analyze the structure of key elements in ordinary language.

III

Nondeductive Arguments

The celebrated Monsieur Leibniz has observed it to be a defect in the common systems of logic that they are very copious when they explain the operations of the understanding in the forming of demonstrations, but are too concise when they treat of probabilities and those other measures of evidence on which life and action depend, and which are our guides even in most of our philosophical speculations.

David Hume, *An Abstract of a Treatise of Human Nature*

13

Nondeductive ("Inductive") Arguments

The study of nondeductive arguments is beset with problems from the very beginning. Those who undertake it must abandon all hope of finding in this area anything like the settled criteria and procedures of standard deductive logic. Indeed, the experts are not even in full agreement on what a nondeductive argument is, much less on whether there is, or can be, an actual *logic* of such arguments—an "inductive" logic.

The firmest ground to start from, perhaps, is the commonsense notion of a nondeductive argument given in §3. The present chapter considers various arguments of this sort, warns against some of the fallacies that attend their use, and poses the problem of seeking an appropriate means by which such arguments may be evaluated. Chapter 14 takes up certain patterns of nondeductive reasoning that figure largely in any systematic effort to *describe* what is so, to *explain* why it is so, and to *determine* what can—or should—be done about it.

§52   *What Is a Nondeductive Argument?*

An argument, as we saw in §2, is a sequence of sentences together with the claim that one of these, the conclusion, follows from the others, the premisses.   An argument is *deductive* (§3) if the claim is that the conclusion follows from the premisses in the sense that it is *impossible* for the conclusion to be false if all the premisses are true.   An argument is *nondeductive* if the claim is that, given the truth of the premisses, it is *improbable* that the conclusion is false.[1]

What distinguishes a deductive argument from a nondeductive one is not some property of the premisses or of the conclusion, but the kind of relationship held to exist between the premisses and the conclusion. The deductive claim is that the premisses and conclusion are so related that the truth of the premisses guarantees the truth of the conclusion. The nondeductive claim is that premisses and conclusion are so related that the truth of the premisses, rather than ensuring the truth of the conclusion, only makes it more or less improbable that the conclusion will be false.

Consider, for example, these two arguments:

(1)   All members of the French Academy are men.

René Clair is a member of the French Academy.

Therefore René Clair is a man.

(2)   Professor Able's logic text is easy.

Professor Baker's logic text is easy.

Professor Charles's logic text is easy.

Therefore all logic texts are easy.

On our definitions, (1) clearly qualifies as a deductive argument, (2) as nondeductive.   For the sequence of sentences in (1) is associated with the strong claim that if the two premisses are true, the conclusion *cannot possibly* be false.   On the other hand, the sequence in (2) is associated with the weaker claim that, granted the truth of the premisses, it is at best *improbable* (but *not* impossible) that the conclusion will be false.

It is sometimes supposed that deductive reasoning always proceeds from universals to particular instances and that nondeductive reasoning simply reverses the process.   But this view is wrong on two counts.

---

[1]   See Brian Skyrms, *Choice and Chance* (Encino, Calif.: Dickenson, 1966), Chapter 1. This book is an instructive and spirited introduction to "inductive logic."

First, it is not true that every nondeductive argument proceeds from premisses that state particular instances ("Professor Able's logic text is easy," etc.) to a conclusion that is a generalization from these instances ("All logic texts are easy"). We need only consider the following nondeductive argument:

(3)   The recession of 1948–49 was moderate.

          The recession of 1953–54 was moderate.

          The recession of 1957–58 was moderate.

          The recession of 1969–70 was moderate.

          Therefore, the recession of 1973–? will be moderate.

This argument moves from particular instances not to a generalization, but to another instance.

Second, not every deductive argument proceeds from a premiss set that contains at least one universally generalized sentence ("All members of the French Academy are men") to a singular conclusion ("René Clair is a man"). An obvious counterexample is the deductive argument

(4)   Hypatia is a philosopher or Hipparchus is a philosopher.

          Hipparchus is not a philosopher.

          Therefore Hypatia is a philosopher.

The notion that "inductive" arguments are limited to reasoning from particular instances to a universal conclusion is especially persistent. That is why it has seemed better to classify arguments not as deductive or *inductive*, but as deductive or *nondeductive*.[2]

---

§53 *Some Common Varieties of Nondeductive Arguments*

We are constantly exposed, in the ordinary business of living, to nondeductive reasoning. Some of the more familiar kinds—and the varieties of nondeductive arguments embedded in them—are illustrated and described below.

1. "Every time I go to Maxim's I get a good meal; so Maxim's always serves good meals."

---

[2] On this matter, see S. F. Barker, "Must Every Inference Be Either Deductive or Inductive?" in *Philosophy in America*, ed. M. Black (Ithaca, N.Y.: Cornell University Press, 1965).

Here the premisses say that *all observed* things of a certain kind (Maxim's meals) have a certain property (goodness); the (probable) conclusion says that *all* things of that kind have that property.   Thus the argument proceeds from premisses that state particular instances to a conclusion that is a universal generalization.   This variety of nondeductive argument, already illustrated by (2) in §52, is known as *enumerative generalization*.

2.   "Each Mike Nichols film I've gone to has been worth seeing; so I expect the next one will be, too."

Again the premisses say that all observed things of a certain kind have a certain property.   This time, however, the (probable) conclusion is not a universal generalization but a specific prediction—namely, that the *next* thing of that kind encountered will also have that property.   Thus the argument proceeds from premisses that state particular instances to a conclusion that simply states an additional instance.   This variety of nondeductive argument, illustrated by (3) in §52, has been termed *eduction*.

3.   "We know that Princeton and Harvard have strong programs in physics, history, and philosophy, and that Princeton has a strong program in political science as well; so the chances are that Harvard also has a strong program in political science."

In this case, the premisses say that two things of a certain kind have *several properties* in common and that one of the two has an *additional* property; the (probable) conclusion predicts that the other will *also* be found to have that property.   Thus the argument proceeds from premisses that attribute like properties to two particular things (or to two kinds of things) to a conclusion that attributes an additional property to one of these things when the other already is known to have that property.   This variety of nondeductive argument is generally called *argument by analogy*.

The claim, in all three cases, is the same: granted the truth of the premisses, it is more or less improbable (not *impossible*) that the conclusion will be false—that Maxim's will serve me a bad meal, that the next Mike Nichols film won't be worth seeing, that Harvard will turn out to have a weak program in political science.   Thus these are indeed varieties of nondeductive arguments.   They are also perhaps the most common ones, although they are not to be thought of as the only ones.

ENUMERATIVE GENERALIZATION

The first variety of nondeductive argument, enumerative generalization, can be represented by the following schema:

A_1 is B (or is a B)
A_2 is B
$\vdots$
A_n is B
Therefore all As are B,

where the *A*s denote individual things of a certain kind—swans, emeralds, etc.—and *B* denotes some property (or class).

A further example of this type of argument is

(1)   Thirty spokes will converge
         In the hub of a wheel;
         But the use of the cart
         Will depend on the part
         Of the hub that is void

         With a wall all around
         A clay bowl is molded;
         But the use of the bowl
         Will depend on the part
         Of the bowl that is void

         Cut out windows and doors
         In the house as you build;
         But the use of the house
         Will depend on the space
         In the walls that is void

         So advantage is had
         From whatever is there;
         But usefulness rises
         From whatever is not.[3]

Warning: In a nondeductive enumerative generalization, the conclusion must cover *more* instances than are enumerated in the premisses. If the enumeration is *exhaustive*, as in

      The integer 3 is prime

      The integer 5 is prime

      The integer 7 is prime

      Therefore all odd integers between 2 and 8 are prime,

the argument is of course deductive, not nondeductive.   For the truth of the premisses obviously guarantees the truth of the conclusion.

---

[3]   From Lao Tzu, *The Way of Life*, tr. R. B. Blakney (New York: New American Library, 1955).

EDUCTION

The second variety of nondeductive argument, eduction, may be schematized as

A_1 is B
A_2 is B
$\vdots$
A_n is B
Therefore A_{n+1} is B.

A further example of this type of argument is

(2)   The first emerald inspected was green.

The second emerald inspected was green.

$\vdots$

The nth emerald inspected was green.

Therefore the next emerald inspected will be green.

ARGUMENT BY ANALOGY

A schema for argument by analogy is

Two things A and B are alike in respect to $p_1, \ldots, p_n$

A has property p_{n+1}

Therefore B will have property p_{n+1}.

A further example of this type of nondeductive argument is

(3)   The Democratic and Republican parties are national parties, hold national conventions in presidential election years, adopt national platforms, and nominate candidates for national offices.

The Democratic party held an off-year national convention.

Therefore the Republican party will hold an off-year national convention.

These and other varieties of nondeductive arguments differ among themselves in many respects.   But they all have one feature in common: the conclusions convey information (about unobserved instances, predicted properties, and so forth) *not* contained in the premisses.   That is, the conclusions " go beyond " the premisses.

Note: There is a species of argument sometimes mistaken for nondeductive.   It is illustrated by the following bit of reasoning:

(4)   Beginning instructors usually overprepare their first classes; so Mary, when she starts off, will probably do so too.

Here the combination of universal premiss and particular conclusion suggests that the argument is deductive. But the word 'probably' in the conclusion seems to signal a nondeductive argument. The difficulty, however, disappears when we take a closer look at the universal premiss. It *is* a generalization, but of a special kind: a *statistical* or *probabilistic* generalization. It does not say that all things of a certain kind have a certain property. What it says is that the *chances are* that any thing of that kind has that property. From such a premiss, together with the premiss that a particular thing (Mary) is a thing of that kind, it then follows *deductively* that the *chances are* that that thing also has that property. Replacing 'probably' (and 'usually') with 'the chances are', we may then rephrase (4) as follows:

(4')   For any beginning instructor, the chances are that he or she will overprepare his or her first classes.

Mary is a beginning instructor.

Therefore the chances are that Mary will overprepare her first classes.

Put this way, (4) is clearly intended as deductive. For what is "probabilistic" here is not the *relationship* between premisses and conclusion, but the first premiss itself (and of course the conclusion). Thus (4) is a deductive argument: if the premisses are both true, it is impossible for the conclusion to be false.

---

§54   *What Is a Good Nondeductive Argument?*

From description we pass on to evaluation. How are we to determine whether a nondeductive argument is good or bad?

In commonsense terms, a good argument (see §4) is expected to satisfy two conditions: first, the conclusion must follow from the premisses in the sense claimed; second, the premisses must be true. (Logic itself is concerned only with the first of these.) While the two conditions apply to both deductive and nondeductive arguments, the application in each case is quite different.

Consider the first condition. In the case of a *deductive* argument, the claim is that the premisses and conclusion are so related that *if* the premisses are all true, it is *impossible* for the conclusion to be false. If this claim is sustained, the argument is *valid*. (If, in addition, the premisses are all true, the argument is *sound*.) Now impossibility is an either-or affair: either the truth of the premisses guarantees the truth of the conclusion or it does not. Deductive logic provides certain formal criteria for determining which is the case. Thus for wide classes of arguments we may obtain precise yes-or-no answers to the question of deductive validity.

In the case of a *nondeductive* argument, the claim is that the premises and the conclusion are so related that, *given* the truth of the premises, it is *improbable* that the conclusion will be false. If this claim is sustained, we may say that the argument is "good." But how can we verify that the claim is sustained? Improbability, unlike impossibility, is a matter of degree, of more or less. Hence to evaluate a nondeductive claim, we must have some way of determining 1) *how much support* is claimed for the conclusion on the basis of the premises, and 2) whether that amount of support is actually forthcoming. This done, one may then say that a nondeductive argument is *strong* or *weak* depending on whether it promises and provides a degree of support appropriate to the purposes for which the argument is being offered.

In sum, while deductive arguments are valid or invalid, nondeductive arguments are strong or weak.

But how are we to *measure* the strength of evidential relationships between premises and conclusion? On this matter, since the experts are at odds, we take refuge once more in common sense. There we do find some rough and ready ways to estimate—and augment, if need be— the strength of the more familiar types of nondeductive arguments.

EVALUATING ENUMERATIVE GENERALIZATIONS

In the ordinary affairs of life, no variety of argument is used more widely than enumerative generalization. We distinguish two types.

First, there are the *simple enumerative generalizations*. In judging their strength, we are guided by such simple criteria as the number and varied character of the instances on which they rest. For example, the nondeductive argument

(1)   Einstein loved music

Sommerfeld loved music

Heisenberg loves music

Therefore all physicists love music

would surely count as relatively weak. Granted that the premises are all true, the instances they report are few and unvaried—only German physicists of the twentieth century. Of course, the argument could be fortified somewhat if more, and more varied, instances were added— that is, if a larger and more diversified evidential base was developed. Further strength would accrue if it was determined that no negative instances had been observed, and still further strength if care was taken to ensure that our stock of instances constituted in some sense a "fair sample" of the entire population of physicists.

Often the generalizations we employ, especially in matters of social policy, are of the second kind: *statistical generalizations*.   Consider, for example, the question of how students who lack traditional preparation fare in college.   Suppose that the following premisses are true:

(2)   John of Newark lacked traditional preparation but was able to graduate from college.

Jane of Waterbury lacked traditional preparation but was able to graduate from college.

Luis of the Bronx lacked traditional preparation but was able to graduate from college.

Debra of Brooklyn lacked traditional preparation but was able to graduate from college.

Were we then to conclude

Therefore all students who lack traditional preparation can graduate from college,

we would be offering an obviously weak nondeductive argument.   And merely adding more instances and varying the geography would not change things appreciably.

Clearly, the appropriate type of nondeductive argument in this case is not one that has as its conclusion a simple generalization (" all ").   Rather, it is one that leads to a statistical generalization—something to the effect that a *certain percentage* of such students *will be able* (under certain conditions) to graduate from college.   And the appropriate premiss states the *actual percentage* of sampled students who *proved able* (under certain conditions) to graduate from college.   The argument then looks like this:

(3)   Of a sample of n students who lacked traditional preparation, m were able, with the aid of certain types of support services, to graduate from college.

Therefore something in the neighborhood of m/n students lacking traditional preparation will be able, under similar conditions, to graduate from college.

In (3) we generalize not from single instances but from a sample; and our conclusion is not that all such students will be able, under certain conditions, to graduate from college, but that a certain percentage will.   Thus this second type of enumerative generalization argues from what is true statistically of a sample to what is true statistically of the whole population under consideration.   The strength of this type of nondeductive argument of course depends, among other things, upon the representative character of the sample. Such matters are the province of the statisticians, who have developed highly sophisticated techniques for refining their predictions.

Still there is always the danger that a sample, even a very big one, will for some reason turn out to be unrepresentative. An example is the famous *Literary Digest* poll of 1936, which predicted a victory for the Republican presidential candidate, Alfred M. Landon. But Franklin Roosevelt won in a landslide, and the *Digest* soon after ceased publication.

EVALUATING EDUCTIONS

In judging the strength of eductions, we follow pretty much the same criteria as in the case of enumerative generalizations. Indeed, common sense tends to think of an eduction as reducing to a combination of two arguments: an enumerative generalization and a (predictive) deductive instantiation.

To illustrate, suppose it is true that

(4)   The first time Perkins took the campus bus, it was late.

The second time Perkins took the campus bus, it was late.

$\vdots$

The nth time Perkins took the campus bus, it was late.

The eductive conclusion is then

Therefore the next time Perkins takes the campus bus, it will be late.

Now the premisses listed in (4) may also be taken as evidence for an enumerative generalization with the conclusion

Therefore any time Perkins takes the campus bus, it is late.

This conclusion, in turn, may serve as the premiss for a deductive instantiation that yields the conclusion

Therefore the next time Perkins takes the campus bus, it will be late,

which is the eductive conclusion drawn above from the premisses (4).

Whether this treatment of eduction is plausible or not, the criteria applied in judging the strength of such an argument will again include 1) the number and variety of instances cited and 2) the character of the background information (the weather, the state of repair of the vehicles, the incentives for drivers to maintain schedules, and so forth), as well as 3) some assurances that there are no known accidental circumstances that would make "the next time" an exceptional instance.

An eduction from *instances* to a next instance should not be confused with an eduction from one *sample* to another sample.[4]   For example, a Stanford University study of shyness in college students (reported in *The New York Times*, May 10, 1975) gives this preliminary result:

(5)   Of a national sample of 1000 students, 40 percent were found to be shy.

Taking (5) as a true premiss for an *enumerative induction*, we obtain the conclusion

> Therefore somewhere in the neighborhood of 40 percent of all college students are shy.

Using (5) as a true premiss for an *eduction*, we obtain as a conclusion, say,

> Therefore somewhere in the neighborhood of 40 percent of the students at State College are shy.

The strength of an eduction of this kind is appraised with the help of various statistical techniques and in the light of relevant background information.

EVALUATING ARGUMENTS BY ANALOGY

We argue by analogy almost as often as we generalize from instances or from samples.   But the evaluation of such arguments is complicated by the fact that "there is no word used more loosely, or in a greater variety of senses, than Analogy."[5]   Nonetheless, common sense does supply rough guidelines for appraising arguments that rely on analogy.

Consider these two examples:

(6)   Britain bore the relationship to its American colonists that a mother bears to her children.

Children owe obedience to their mother.

Hence the American colonists owed obedience to Britain.

---

[4]   See the article "Induction" by Max Black, in *The Encyclopedia of Philosophy*, ed. Paul Edwards (New York: Macmillan, 1967).

[5]   John Stuart Mill, *A System of Logic*, 8th ed. (London: Longmans, 1872) Book III, Chapter 20.   Example (6) is adapted from Mill.

(7)   Colleges, like industrial enterprises, hire employees, rent or buy land and buildings, purchase materials and equipment, and sell products or services.

Industrial enterprises must be held accountable for the quality of their products, reject defective ones, and drop unprofitable lines.

Therefore so must colleges.

Surely common sense, with little or no hesitation, would count these arguments by analogy as *bad*.

On the other hand, the two following examples would count as *good* (or at least better):

(8)   A pastor is to a congregation as a shepherd is to a flock.

A shepherd is responsible for the welfare of all the flock, the weak and the strong.

Hence a pastor is responsible for the welfare of all the congregation, the weak and the strong.

(9)   Belle DePart and Ben Suerte are Democratic members of Congress from the urban East, elected on a platform of peace and social legislation.

Belle DePart has endorsed a federal health plan.

Therefore Ben Suerte will do so too.

Now why is the first pair bad and the second good? A common-sense answer would be: (6) is bad because whatever similarity there may be between the mother-child relationship and the motherland-colony relationship (first premiss), it is not *relevantly connected* to the relationship (obedience) that figures in the conclusion. And (7) is bad because there is no *relevant connection* between the properties alleged to be common to colleges and industrial enterprises (first premiss) and the properties then ascribed to colleges in the conclusion.

In general, where little or no connection may be supposed to exist between the premissed similarity of relations or properties and the inferred similarity, common sense says that the analogy is "false," "limps," "breaks down," and that the corresponding *argument by analogy* is bad, or *weak*. Contrariwise, if the connection is well established, we say that the corresponding argument is good, or *strong*. But even in the case of very good arguments by analogy, common sense warns against "pressing the analogy too far."

This commonsense criterion will perhaps appear in sharper focus, if we consider briefly another way of looking at the structure of arguments by

analogy. Such arguments, according to our account above (§53), are of
the form

> Two things A and B are alike in respect to $p_1, \ldots, p_n$
>
> A has property p_{n+1}
>
> Therefore B will have property p_{n+1}.

In the alternative account, the first premiss asserts *explicitly* the general
connection of similarities to which the argument by analogy makes
implicit appeal.[6] The form then is

(10)   All things that have properties $p_1, \ldots, p_n$ also have property p_{n+1}

> B has been found to have properties $p_1, \ldots, p_n$
>
> Therefore B will have property p_{n+1}.

Notice that in (10) the first premiss is a universal generalization: it says
that *all* things that have properties $p_1, \ldots, p_n$ in common also have
property p_{n+1} in common. Notice, too, that (10) itself is a universal
instantiation: it simply asserts of B what holds for all things. Thus the
alternative account in effect transforms each analogy argument into a
corresponding and obviously valid *deductive* argument. For example,
the analogy argument (7) now becomes

(7′)   All establishments that hire employees, rent or buy land and
buildings, purchase materials and equipment, and sell products
or services must also be held accountable for the quality of their
products, reject defective ones, and drop unprofitable lines.

Colleges hire employees, rent or buy land and buildings, purchase
materials and equipment, and sell products or services.

Therefore colleges also will have to be held responsible for the
quality of their products, reject defective ones, and drop unprofitable lines.

By the same token, the problem of appraising the *strength* of an argument by analogy is transformed into the problem of appraising the
soundness (not the validity!) of the corresponding deductive argument.
For the first premiss of the deductive argument affirms universally the
same connection of similarities on which the analogy argument relies.
But such a premiss (unless it is itself *deducible* from true premisses) can
be accepted as "true" only if it is well supported by the evidence—that
is, only if it is the (nondeductive) conclusion of a strong enumerative

---

6   See "Fallacies" by J. L. Mackie, in *The Encyclopedia of Philosophy*, Vol. 3, p. 175.

generalization. Thus the problem of evaluating the soundness of the corresponding deductive argument becomes, in turn, the problem of evaluating the *strength of the enumerative generalization* whose conclusion is the first premiss of that deductive argument.

In sum, to say that an argument by analogy is weak or strong is, on the alternative account, simply to say that there is little or much (nondeductive) evidence to support the first premiss of the corresponding deductive argument. The commonsense criteria used to measure such support include the number and variety of the instances cited, the absence of known negative instances, and the character of the background information. These were touched on earlier in this section.

---

§55 Some Fallacies in the Use of Nondeductive Arguments

Fallacies are typical errors, and fallacies in argument are typical errors in argument. This notion of fallacy in argument (see §11) may be applied to nondeductive as well as to deductive arguments. But of course the mere fact that the conclusion of even a *strong* nondeductive argument may turn out to be false does not in itself convict the argument of fallacy. Otherwise, *all* nondeductive arguments would by definition be fallacious.

A fallacy in deduction is a typical error in which an *invalid* form of argument is mistaken for a *valid* one. Similarly, a fallacy in nondeductive reasoning is a typical error in which a *weak* nondeductive argument is mistaken for a *strong* one. Now a nondeductive argument is strong if its true premisses lend its conclusion the degree of support suited to the purposes for which the argument is being offered. Hence a fallacy in nondeductive reasoning is a typical error in which true premisses that in fact lend little or only trivial support to a conclusion are mistakenly thought to lend it significant support.

Each of the three varieties of nondeductive arguments enumerated in §53 can go wrong in typical ways. We end this chapter by touching briefly on some of them.

FALLACIES IN THE USE OF ENUMERATIVE GENERALIZATIONS

In an enumerative generalization we argue from true premisses that cite instances to a conclusion that covers these instances and more. The most common error made in this connection is to rely on too few or on "unrepresentative" instances. This typical error is known as the *fallacy of hasty generalization*.

Generalize we must. But too often we do so in haste—from a few instances or even from just one.   Thus, having had a bad experience with, say, a Problems of Philosophy course, one might conclude—without bothering to find out whether that course is really representative of its kind—that all Problems of Philosophy courses or indeed that all philosophy courses are just as unrewarding as the one observed.

Depressingly familiar examples of the fallacy of hasty generalization are the many racial and ethnic stereotypes that still rule the thought and direct the action of so many of us.   We observe, or fancy we observe, or are told that one or two or several ////'s are ****; we then conclude that all ////'s are ****.   (It is only too easy to fill in the blanks.)

There is no vaccine that confers immunity from hasty generalizing. But a respect for carefully observed facts and a willingness to withhold judgment increase our powers of resistance, just as prejudice and a propensity to ignore the negative instance lower them.

Certain subvarieties of hasty generalization have special names.   One such is the *converse fallacy of accident*.   (For the fallacy of accident, see §11.)   This fallacy is committed when we generalize not merely from a single instance but from a single instance that happens to have exceptional features.   An example is

Franklin Delano Roosevelt was reelected President three times.

So any President can be reelected three times.

Here the exceptional feature is not only the extraordinary prestige of Roosevelt but the absence in his time of any constitutional bar to serving three or more full presidential terms.

Other typical errors in generalizing include the group known as *sampling fallacies*.   These occur in connection with statistical generalizations (for example, public opinion polls), in which we argue from what is true of a *sample* to what is true of the sampled *whole*.   Error enters if the sample is unrepresentative, typical error if the sample fails in some typical way to be representative.

There are several kinds of sampling fallacies.   One consists in using samples too small to bear the burden of inference placed upon them.   A tool-kit of devices to minimize sampling errors of this kind may be found in any standard introduction to mathematical statistics.

But even a very large sample may be *unfair*.   Undetected bias may have been introduced by the very way in which the sample was chosen.   Thus the 1936 *Literary Digest* presidential election poll, referred to in §54, used a very large sample indeed: more than ten million ballots were mailed out, and the response rate was better than one out of five.   The mailing lists, however, were compiled from telephone directories and rosters of magazine subscribers and automobile owners—a procedure that could not possibly produce a fair sample of the 1936 American population.

Only a careful analysis of the selection procedure can protect the sample from such contamination. And only a rich background knowledge of the traits of the group or population under study can provide a standard by which to judge whether a sample—however large—is fair.[7]

Finally, there is a form of hasty generalization that may be called the *fallacy of anecdotal evidence.* It is to be found especially in those areas, such as history and the social sciences, in which well-supported generalizations are very hard to come by and the temptation to substitute illustrative examples for hard evidence often proves too difficult to resist.[8]

For instance, some historians have contended that American Populists in the 1890s were anti-Semitic. The evidence cited in support of the contention is largely anecdotal. It consists in the main of references in Populist writing and oratory to "Shylock" and "the Rothschilds of London." But there is no showing that the Populists ever adopted or pursued a *policy* of anti-Semitism. Thus the so-called evidence here at most illustrates the contention; it scarcely establishes it.

FALLACIES IN THE USE OF EDUCTIONS

In eduction we argue from true premises that cite instances (or report the results of a sampling) to a conclusion that covers a *new* instance (or new sample). Fallacies in eduction are not too different, at the level of common sense, from the fallacies that crop up in the use of enumerative generalizations. Most forms of hasty generalization—reliance on too few instances or on unrepresentative samples or on impressionistic evidence—have their eductive analogues. An exception, of course, is the converse fallacy of accident, which consists in generalizing from one exceptional instance.

FALLACIES IN THE USE OF ARGUMENTS BY ANALOGY

In an argument by analogy we reason that two things, or two kinds of things, that are known to be similar in certain respects are also similar in one or more other respects. An argument by analogy is strong only if there is a relevant connection between the similarities we know and the one or more we infer. Hence fallacies in arguing by analogy represent typical ways in which we misjudge this connection.

Two sorts of errors stand out. First, we may suppose or even insist that there is a revelant connection when none in fact exists. We then have the fallacy of "false analogy." Second, even when a relevant

---

[7]   A great number of fallacies in nondeductive reasoning, including sampling fallacies, are plentifully illustrated in David Hackett Fischer's *Historians' Fallacies* (New York: Harper and Row, 1970).

[8]   See M. I. Finley, *The Ancient Economy* (Berkeley and Los Angeles: University of California Press, 1973), p. 25.

connection does exist, we may extend it beyond its actual reach.   We then have the fallacy of " pressing an analogy too far."

There is no dearth of examples of the first sort.   Thus when we use the phrase " Good Neighbor Policy," we falsely liken the political and economic relations between countries to the social relations between families on the block.   When we espouse the " domino theory," we falsely liken the impact of political changes in one country upon the politics of other countries to the impact of one falling domino upon others standing in a row.

There is also an abundance of examples of the second sort.   Thus the following argument is often heard:

> The Democratic and Republican parties nationally are alike in containing conservatives and liberals, rich and poor, voters from varied ethnic and religious backgrounds, and rival groups of ambitious politicians.
>
> The Republican party is unresponsive to the demands of labor and minority groups.
>
> Therefore the Democratic party also will be unresponsive to the demands of labor and minority groups.

But surely this is carrying the analogy too far—as matters stand today.

Many times, of course, analogy is employed not as an argument to prove a point, but as a metaphor to embellish it.   In such cases, of course, there is no question of fallacy.   Hegel, for example, held that philosophy comes late upon the scene; it can only interpret the world, it cannot instruct it.   When he likened philosophy to the Owl of Minerva, which spreads its wings only at dusk, he was illuminating his conception of the role of philosophy, not arguing it.   His argument was his entire work.

14

Nondeductive Arguments in Science and in Social Policy

Science is a systematic attempt to find out *what is the case* and *why*. As such, its aim is to provide well-confirmed universal *descriptions* of what is so, and well-confirmed (often "causal") *explanations* of just why it is so.

Social policy seeks to determine *what can* or *should be done about what is so*. At its best, the making of social policy consists essentially in the application of a scientifically schooled, politically sophisticated, and morally responsive common sense to the solution of social problems.

Like science, social policy making is thus an extension of common sense. And like science, it both shares and refines the reliance that common sense places on nondeductive—more exactly, on an *interweaving of deductive* and *nondeductive*—reasoning.

The present chapter first briefly examines this interweaving in connection with description and explanation in science. Some standard lore is included from the past century (John Stuart Mill's "canons"), and some influential material from the present (Carl Hempel's analysis of scientific explanation). The discussion then turns to some of the patterns of argument found in social policy making, which are illustrated with the aid of several contemporary examples.

§56 *Argument and the Confirmation of Descriptive Hypotheses*

Description and explanation of course differ: it is one thing to describe poverty, another to determine its causes (and still another to decide what to do about it).   In general, however, we describe in order to explain, just as we explain in order to predict.   The separation of scientific description from scientific explanation is a matter of analytic convenience.   It should not be carried too far.

SCIENTIFIC DESCRIPTIONS

The universal descriptions sought by empirical science vary in kind and source.   The simplest, perhaps, are of the form

> All *A*s are *B*s (or, all *A*s have property *p*).

An example is

> All cordates are renates (that is, all creatures with hearts are creatures with kidneys).

Such descriptions answer questions of the form

(1)   Are all *A*s also *B*s? (or, Do all *A*s have property *p*?)

But there are other kinds, among them those that answer questions of the form

(2)   Are there *A*s? (or, Is there an *A*?)

SIMPLE UNIVERSAL DESCRIPTIONS

Well-confirmed answers to questions of kind (1) come from either of two sources.   Some are obtained by *deduction* from well-confirmed universal descriptions already at hand.   An example is

(3)   All whales are warm-blooded.

This follows deductively from the premisses

(4)   All mammals are warm-blooded.
        Whales are mammals.

Others can be obtained only as conclusions of *nondeductive* arguments —in particular, of enumerative generalizations (see §53).   Such conclusions count as well confirmed or ill confirmed—and the arguments as strong or weak—depending on the amount and quality of the support lent them by their true premises.   An example to consider is

(5)   All human societies use language.

Now (5) is supported by numerous true premises setting forth positive instances; there are no known negative instances; and there is a mass of background information.   Thus (5), although it is not deduced from well-confirmed universal descriptions, is itself a well-confirmed universal description.

Nonetheless (5), as the conclusion of a nondeductive argument, may still turn out to be false even though all of its premises are true.   It is therefore open to correction; it is a tentative general description, a *hypothesis*.

Similar considerations apply to well-confirmed *statistical* descriptions, such as

Some 40 percent of black youths are officially unemployed (spring 1975).

The only difference is that in the case of statistical descriptions, the strong confirming evidence consists in carefully drawn samples, rather than in individual instances.

UNIVERSAL DESCRIPTIONS AS CONFIRMED HYPOTHESES

The main steps in confirming hypotheses—hence in confirming descriptions viewed as hypotheses—are often outlined as follows:[1]

First, we deduce one or more consequences of our hypothesis, *H*.

Second, we determine by observation or experiment whether what these consequences express is indeed the case.

Third, depending on the outcome, we draw the appropriate conclusion regarding *H*.

To illustrate, let us select (5) as our hypothesis, *H*.   Our first step is to *deduce* one or more consequences from *H*: for example, that if in the

---

[1]   For this account of the confirmation of hypotheses, see Carl G. Hempel, *Philosophy of Science* (Englewood Cliffs, N.J.: Prentice-Hall, 1966), Chapters 3 and 4.

Philippine rain forest there is a human society hitherto unknown to anthropologists, it, too, uses language.   Our deduction has the form

> *H*
> Therefore if *I*, then *J*.

Assume that the deduction is valid—that is, that the hypothesis does imply the consequence we have deduced from it.   We list the corresponding conditional of the deduction as our first premiss in what follows.   It is of the form

> If *H*, then (if *I*, then *J*).

The next step is to determine whether *I* is true.   Suppose it is—suppose, in our example, that we go to the rain forest and find a human society, the Tasadays, hitherto not known to anthropologists.   Now we have two true premisses of the form

> If *H*, then (if *I*, then *J*)
> *I*.

We then distinguish two cases: either the Tasadays do not use language or they do.

Case One

Suppose they do not.   We then have another premiss and with it a complete *deductive* argument of the form

> (6)   If *H*, then (if *I*, then *J*)
>   *I*
>   Not-*J*
>   Therefore not-H.

Exit hypothesis!   For (6) is a *valid* deductive argument form; it is a variant of the familiar *modus tollens*.   Hence arguments of that form are valid and, if their premisses are all true, sound.

Case Two

Suppose the Tasadays do use language.   We then have an argument of the form

> (7)   If *H*, then (if *I*, then *J*)
>   *I*
>   *J*
>   Therefore *H*   (?)

Now (7), if offered as a *deductive* argument form, must be rejected as obviously invalid. We cannot deduce *H* from the premisses of (7). To do so would be to commit the formal fallacy of *affirming the consequent*.

Yet the finding that the Tasadays likewise use language is clearly a new piece of evidence in support of (5). In fact, the second and third premisses of (7) represent the form of a *new* confirming instance. Thus (7) contributes to the confirmation of *H* and should be interpreted as part of the nondeductive reasoning on which *H* rests. The nondeductive argument itself may be stated as follows:

(8)   The first human society observed uses language.
        The second human society observed uses language.
        $\vdots$
        The *n*th human society observed uses language.
        The Tasadays, a newly observed human society, use language.
        Therefore all human societies use language.

Notice that (5), as the conclusion of the nondeductive argument (8), may be false even if all of its premisses, including the newly added one, are true. It remains a hypothesis. And on this analysis of the confirmation of hypotheses, it can in principle only be either *disproved*—as in (6)—or *confirmed*—as in (7)—but never *proved*.

Notice, too, that the confirmation procedure outlined here illustrates the *interweaving* of deductive and nondeductive reasoning mentioned at the beginning of this chapter. It is a characteristic feature of what some philosophers have called "the logic of empirical science."

Caution: The discussion of confirmation underlines the importance of determining whether an argument is being offered as deductive or nondeductive. Often we cannot tell this from its structure alone. Thus an argument of the form (7) is formally invalid if offered as a deductive argument, and yet it may make a positive contribution to confirmation when offered as part of a nondeductive argument. If we are to avoid the danger of conflating *invalid* deductive arguments and *useful* nondeductive arguments, we must pay heed to the contexts and idioms in which arguments appear.

EXISTENCE DESCRIPTIONS

In addition to answering questions of kind (1), empirical science is often called upon to answer questions about existence—that is, questions of the form

(2)   Are there *A*s? (or, Is there an *A*?)

Examples from the history of science are: Do molecules exist? Is there an (electromagnetic) ether? Examples from contemporary science are: Is there extraterrestrial life? Are there gravitational waves?

Descriptions that answer questions of existence are in general also to be regarded as hypotheses, hence open to either confirmation or disproof. The procedure on the whole is the same as that discussed above in connection with the confirmation of simple descriptive hypotheses. But the deducing of consequences of the form 'If I, then J' from the hypothesis H is usually a rather complicated affair, involving many intermediate steps; the setting up of the experimental or observational conditions specified in I often presents great difficulties; and even the carrying out of the observation reported by J may turn out to be a quite arduous task.

An example of a description answering a question of existence is the hypothesis that there is an ether relative to which the earth moves. This hypothesis was *disproved* by the Michelson-Morley experiment in 1887 (though interpretations of the outcome varied at the time). Accepting the hypothesis that an ether exists, the experimenters deduced the following consequence: if the velocity of light is measured in each of two perpendicular directions in a reference frame "moving through the ether," the measured velocities will differ. To their surprise, however, no difference was detected.

A more recent example pointing up some of the perils encountered in confirming existence hypotheses is the case of Water II, or "polywater."[2] Several years ago a team of Soviet physical chemists reported the discovery of samples of water that exhibited strange properties, among them a density nearly one and a half times the established density of water. They concluded that there exists a superdense form of water, which they called *Water II*. Their (nondeductive) argument was of the familiar form

If H_1, then (if I, then J)
I
J
Therefore H_1 (is confirmed)

where H_1, the "confirmed" hypothesis, was "Water II exists."

Later studies, however, indicated that these strange properties are exhibited when and only when the samples contain impurities—that is,

If H_2, then (if I, then J)
I
J
Therefore H_2 (is confirmed)

where H_2, the confirmed hypothesis, is "The water samples used contain impurities."

The Soviet scientists, employing new and improved techniques, re-

---

[2]   See "Exit Polywater," *Scientific American*, September 1973, p. 66.

analyzed their samples and reported in 1973 that all of their samples contained some impurities.   As a result, we were left with the following *deductive* argument:

> If H_1', then (if I, then J)
> I
> Not-J
> Therefore not-H_1'

where H_1', the *disproved* hypothesis, is "There is an impurity-free, superdense form of water, Water II."

OTHER KINDS OF DESCRIPTIVE HYPOTHESES

Sometimes hypotheses that answer questions of the forms

(9)   Where do As come from?

and

(10)   What are As?

are also regarded as requests for descriptions of As.

But questions of the form (9) ask about *origins*; an example is the question "Where did life on earth come from?"   And it seems more appropriate that such questions be interpreted as requests for a certain kind of explanation than for a certain kind of description.   We shall return to them in the next section.

Questions of the form (10)—an example is "What are pulsars?"—are ambiguous.   A question of this form may be intended merely as a request for a *definition of the word 'A'*.   In that case, it is readily answered with the aid of a suitable dictionary or textbook.   On the other hand, it may be intended as a request for an account of what As are, for a *theory about As*.   In that case, it is clearly a plea for an explanation of As.   These questions, too, we leave for the next section.

For that matter, even existence questions often require us to step over the uncertain line that separates description from explanation.   Thus in discussing the "polywater" hypothesis, we quite naturally found ourselves saying that it was the presence of impurities that accounted for, or "explained," the strange properties exhibited by certain samples of water.

---

§57   *Argument and Explanatory Hypotheses*

Explanations in empirical science, because they are open-ended generalizations and thus go beyond the data at hand, are always to be counted as tentative.   Like scientific descriptions, they are hypotheses; and their confirmation involves a similar interweaving of deductive and nondeductive reasoning.

Explanatory hypotheses are of different types, corresponding to the different senses attached to the word 'explain'. Consider, for example, the following questions:

(1)   Why are there rainbows in the sky?

(2)   Why do people commit suicide?

(3)   Why do fish have gills?

(4)   Why is there life on earth?

All of these are requests for explanations. But in the case of (1), to explain is to give the *cause* or causes of phenomena of a certain kind; in (2), the *reason* or reasons for human actions of a certain kind; in (3), the *purpose* served by objects of a certain kind; and in (4), the *origin* of processes of a certain kind.

This enumeration is of course not intended to cover *all* types of explanations. For instance, some philosophers seek an answer to the following question:

(5)   Why is there something rather than nothing?

But since scientists evidently do not include this question among their concerns, we too shall put it aside.[3]

CAUSAL EXPLANATORY HYPOTHESES: MILL'S CANONS

Causes have long been credited with playing a leading explanatory role both in science and in everyday life. The Roman poet Virgil (70–19 B.C.) rated as happy that person who is able to gain a knowledge of the causes of things.[4] And the philosopher of science John Stuart Mill (1806–1873) proposed five rules to guide us in acquiring such knowledge. These rules are known as Mill's Canons, or Methods of Induction. (A canon is simply the principle regulating the use of the corresponding method.) Mill's Canons have become a tradition in logic texts, and we present them in his own words.[5]

Note that for Mill an inquiry into the laws of phenomena, or events, has a twofold character: to determine the cause of a given effect or to

---

[3] Anyone who wishes to pursue this question further should read P. L. Heath, "Nothing," and Paul Edwards, "Why," both in *The Encyclopedia of Philosophy* (New York: Macmillan, 1967).

[4] *Felix qui potuit rerum cognoscere causas* (*Georgics*, II, 490).

[5] *System of Logic*, 8th ed. (London, 1872), Book III, Chapters 8 through 10. Also see J. L. Mackie, "Mill's Methods of Induction," in *The Encyclopedia of Philosophy*.

determine the effect of a given cause. Mill's Canons are intended to cover both efforts.

First Canon: Method of Agreement

> *If two or more instances of the phenomenon under investigation have only one circumstance in common, the circumstance in which alone all the instances agree is the cause (or the effect) of the given phenomenon.*

To illustrate, suppose that on a certain day Professors Perkins, Quincy, and Rogers all come down with food poisoning after eating at the underfunded faculty cafeteria.   Suppose further that all three are committed to two-sandwich luncheons, and that on the day in question

> 1.   Perkins had for his lunch a chicken salad sandwich, a tuna salad sandwich, and coffee.
>
> 2.   Quincy had for her lunch a chicken salad sandwich, a ham salad sandwich, and tea.
>
> 3.   Rogers had for his lunch a chicken salad sandwich, an egg salad sandwich, and milk.

Now the one "circumstance" common to the instances of food poisoning is the ingestion of a chicken salad sandwich.   Thus according to the Method of Agreement, we may conclude

(6)   Ingesting a chicken salad sandwich is the cause of the food poisoning.

The form of the argument embodied in this illustration may be represented by the following schema:

> A, B, and C are accompanied by a and other circumstances b and c.
>
> A, D, and E are accompanied by a and other circumstances d and e.
>
> A, F, and G are accompanied by a and other circumstances f and g.
>
> Therefore A is the cause of a (or a is the effect of A).

Here, with Mill, we have put the capital letters *A, B, C*, ... for what he calls "causes," or "antecedents," and the small letters *a, b, c*, ... for the "effects," or "consequents," that accompany them.

Clearly, the Method of Agreement incorporates a nondeductive form of argument, specifically enumerative generalization (see §53). But in this case there are two distinctive features: first, the premises report two or more instances of a phenomenon that have only one antecedent circumstance in common; second, the conclusion is a general statement to the effect that occurrences of events of one kind (the common antecedent) are the *causes* of occurrences of events of another kind (the phenomenon) or that occurrences of events of the second kind are *effects* of occurrences of events of the first kind.

Notice that (6), as the conclusion of a nondeductive argument, may be false even if all of its premises are true. (The professors may have shared a can of tainted vichyssoise just before lunch.) Notice also that (6), since it goes beyond the data or instances at hand, is a hypothesis, hence still subject to confirmation or disproof.

Second Canon: Method of Difference

> *If an instance in which the phenomenon under investigation occurs, and an instance in which it does not occur, have every circumstance in common save one, that one occurring only in the former; the circumstance in which alone the two instances differ is the effect, or the cause, or an indispensable part of the cause, of the phenomenon.*

To illustrate this method, suppose that on a certain day Professor Quincy lunches with a friend at the faculty cafeteria. Quincy has a chicken salad sandwich, a ham salad sandwich, and tea; her friend is content with just a ham salad sandwich and tea. Suppose further that Quincy comes down with food poisoning, but her friend does not. The Method of Difference then tells us that the cause (" or an indispensable part of the cause") of the food poisoning is the one antecedent circumstance—the eating of a chicken salad sandwich—that is *present* when the phenomenon occurs and *absent* when it does not.

The form of the argument embodied in this illustration may be represented by the following schema:

A, B, and *C* are accompanied by *a* and other circumstances *b* and *c.*

B and *C* are accompanied by circumstances *b* and *c* but *not* by *a*.

Therefore *A* is the cause or an indispensable part of the cause of *a*.

Again we have a nondeductive form of argument, and the conclusion is a hypothesis.

Notice that in determining the cause of a phenomenon, the Method of Difference relies on paired positive and negative instances that *differ* in just one antecedent circumstance. The Method of Agreement relies on positive instances that *agree* in just one antecedent circumstance.

Third Canon: Joint Method of Agreement and Difference

> *If two or more instances in which the phenomenon occurs have only one circumstance in common, while two or more instances in which it does not occur have nothing in common save the absence of that circumstance, the circumstance in which alone the two sets of instances differ is the effect, or the cause, or an indispensable part of the cause, of the phenomenon.*

Now suppose that Professors Perkins and Quincy lunch at the faculty cafeteria one day with their colleagues Professors Rogers and Stasi. Perkins has a chicken salad sandwich, a tuna salad sandwich, and coffee, while Quincy has a chicken salad sandwich, a ham salad sandwich, and tea; Rogers makes do with a tuna salad sandwich and coffee, and Stasi with a ham salad sandwich and tea. Suppose further that Perkins and Quincy come down with food poisoning, but Rogers and Stasi do not. According to the Joint Method of Agreement and Difference, we may then conclude that eating a chicken salad sandwich—the only circumstance that is present in each positive instance and absent in each negative instance— is the cause or an indispensable part of the cause of the food poisoning.

Here the form of the argument may be represented by the schema

A, *B*, and *C* are accompanied by *a* and other circumstances *b* and *c*.

A, *D*, and *E* are accompanied by *a* and other circumstances *d* and *e*.

B and *C* are accompanied by circumstances *b* and *c* but not by *a*.

D and *E* are accompanied by circumstances *d* and *e* but not by *a*.

Therefore *A* is the cause or an indispensable part of the cause of *a*.

Notice that the expression 'Joint Method of Agreement and Difference' is something of a misnomer. Indeed, as Mill is quick to point out, this Method really "consists in a double employment of the Method of Agreement." For it relies on 1) a set of two or more positive instances that *agree* only in the presence of a certain antecedent circumstance and 2) a set of two or more negative instances that *agree* only in the absence of that same circumstance.

Fourth Canon: Method of Residues

> *Subduct from any phenomenon such part as is known by previous inductions to be the effect of certain antecedents, and the residue of the phenomenon is the effect of the remaining antecedents.*

This method, Mill notes, is simply the Method of Difference applied to the special case of "residual phenomena." An example he gives is planetary motion. The observed paths of the planets differ from those that may be "calculated in a consideration solely of their gravitation toward the sun." This difference or residue is due to the remaining antecedents: "the disturbing effects mutually produced by the earth and the planets upon each other's motions."

Fifth Canon: Method of Concomitant Variations

> *Whatever phenomenon varies in any manner whenever another phenomenon varies in some particular manner, is either a cause or an effect of the phenomenon, or is connected with it through some fact of causation.*

This final method cannot be reduced to any of the preceding four. These latter can be used only where we are able to exclude an antecedent altogether. But often, remarks Mill, this is not possible. Suppose, for example, we wish to study the effect of heat on bodies. Since "we are unable to exhaust a body of the whole of its heat," we cannot exclude the antecedent (in this case heat) altogether. But we can still ascertain whether *changes* in the antecedent short of total removal are always followed by changes in some consequent (say, the dimensions of the body). To this sort of case the only method applicable is the Method of Concomitant Variations.

COMMENTS ON THE CANONS

Mill's Methods of Induction, together with his discussion of them, are usually criticized as simplistic. No doubt they are. Certainly the neat arrays of "antecedents" and "consequents," of sequences with "only one circumstance in common" or with "every circumstance in common save one," cannot do full justice to the complex realities of causal inquiry. Nor was Mill himself entirely unaware of this deficiency: "Unfortunately it is hardly ever possible to ascertain all the antecedents, unless the phenomenon is one which we can produce artificially. Even then, the difficulty is merely lightened, not removed."

Yet it would be wrong to dismiss the methods as useless. For one thing, the Method of Difference is widely invoked in testing hypotheses in such important areas as biomedical research. For example, studies of verbal learning in older men show a decline in performance with advancing age. The hypothesis was put forward that this decline is not due solely to structural changes in the central nervous system that accompany aging. Rather, the impaired performance stems, at least in part, from heightened arousal of the autonomic nervous system in older persons engaged in a learning task. (That is, under these circumstances they become tense.) An experiment was devised to test this hypothesis. Propranolol, an agent that partially blocks the effects of autonomic arousal, was given to one group of subjects ranging in age from sixty to seventy-eight—the "drug group"—and an inert drug was given to a similar group—the "control" or "placebo group." The result was improved performance in a rote learning task by the "drug group."[6]

Now let *A* be the blocking effect of the drug, not-*A* the *absence* of that effect in the placebo group, and *a* the improved learning performance. Then the structure of this inquiry into causes may be represented as

> *A*, *B*, *C*, ... are accompanied by *a* and other circumstances *b*, *c*, ...
>
> Not-*A*, *B*, *C*, ... are accompanied by circumstances *b*, *c*, ... but not by *a*.
>
> Therefore *A* is the cause or an indispensable part of the cause of *a*.

---

[6] See a report by Carl Eisdorfer, John Nowlin, and Frances Wilkie in *Science*, December 18, 1970, pp. 1327–1329.

Thus this experiment and "control group" experiments in general may be thought of as applications of the Method of Difference.

It should be added that Mill's Methods of Induction can be refined so as to give them a wider range of application. Suppose that, with J. L. Mackie, we make some such assumptions as the following:

> 1.   The *conclusions* obtained by applying the Methods of Agreement and of Difference are to have the form: "Such and such is a cause of such-and-such kind of event or phenomenon."
>
> 2.   A *cause* is to be regarded as a *necessary and sufficient condition*—that is, ' X is a cause of Y' is to mean the same as ' X is present where and only where Y is present'. (In some cases, a cause may be regarded simply as a *sufficient* condition—'Wherever X is present, so is Y'—in some as a necessary condition—'Wherever Y is present, so is X'.)
>
> 3.   Background knowledge would supply us with manageable lists of *possible causal factors* (Mill's "antecedents").
>
> 4.   A phenomenon may have *multiple* causes.

Given these or similar assumptions, it is then possible to apply the basic Methods of Agreement and of Difference, or more sophisticated variants thereof, so as to *eliminate* candidates from a list of possible causes, and move toward some positive conclusion.[7]

Such a conclusion would still be tentative, subject to confirmation or disproof. (How could we be certain that our list included *all* the possible causal factors?) But that the conclusion is only a hypothesis would not, of course, be counted a defect in Mill's Methods.

This is not to say that oversimplification is the only shortcoming from which the methods suffer. On the contrary, there are serious difficulties with the notions of *cause* and *scientific explanation* on which Mill's account relies.

First, Mill identifies cause with "invariable antecedent." He is then hard put to distinguish between those "invariable" sequences that are causal and those—such as the sequence of day and night—that are not. Surely, as Mill notes, we do not want to say that day causes night, or vice versa.   He would confine the term 'cause' to those "invariable" sequences that are "unconditional."   But what then is meant by 'unconditional'? As a matter of fact, even if Mill's idea is replaced by the somewhat less vague notion of cause as *uniform*, or *regular, antecedent* (cause as necessary and sufficient condition), the problem remains.   Any theory of causality as *regularity* is still vulnerable, for example, to the

---

[7]   J. L. Mackie, op. cit.

familiar fallacy of *post hoc ergo propter hoc* (*Y* follows *X*; therefore *X* is a cause of *Y*). Thus because there is a heavy incidence of poverty among the aged, are we to conclude that age is a cause of poverty? The question that really ought to be asked is, What are the factors in our society that account for the high incidence of poverty among certain groups in the population, such as the aged?[8] Clearly, Mill's notion of cause as "invariable antecedent" requires at least some further refinement and clarification.

Second, even if Mill's idea of cause were adequate, we should still have to question his assumption that in science to *explain an event* is always, or for that matter primarily, to *find its cause*. In science there are different *levels* of explanation and different *kinds* of explanation. Thus in physics, talk of causes (at the experimental level) gives way at the *theoretical* level to talk of *functional dependencies*. Galileo's law of free fall expresses a functional relationship between the distance traversed by a freely falling body and the time during which it falls. In the human sciences it becomes advantageous to distinguish between *causes* of behavior and *reasons* for actions. Causal explanations are no doubt extremely useful in commonsense situations and in certain types of scientific research. But we cannot simply identify scientific explanation with causal explanation.

EXPLANATORY HYPOTHESES IN GENERAL: HEMPEL'S VIEW

The general nature of scientific explanation has long been a matter of central concern to philosophers of science. One of the most influential explications of this concept is the so-called *covering-law theory*. While other scholars, such as Ernest Nagel and Sir Karl Popper, have made major contributions, the theory is associated above all with the name of Carl G. Hempel.[9]

As a preliminary step, Hempel distinguishes between scientific and nonscientific explanations. The former must meet two requirements: they must have "explanatory relevance" and they must be "testable." Consider an example from radio astronomy: Why do radio stars, like visible stars, twinkle? To account for this phenomenon as a manifestation of some otherwise undefinable "cosmic rhythm" would be to indulge in a nonscientific explanation. For such an account has no explanatory relevance, nor can it be tested in any way. On the other hand, to show that the phenomenon is due to the presence of plasma clouds in the ionosphere is to offer a scientific explanation.[10] Or take a more familiar

---

[8] See David Hamilton, *A Primer on the Economics of Poverty* (New York: Random House, 1970).
[9] See Carl G. Hempel, *Philosophy of Natural Science* (Englewood Cliffs, N.J.: Prentice-Hall, 1966), Chapters 5 and 6.
[10] See A. Hewish's Nobel lecture, "Pulsars and High Density Physics," *Science*, June 13, 1975, pp. 1079 ff.

example. Why are there rainbows in the sky? The scientific explanation attributes events of this kind not to "nature's artistic impulses," but to the reflection and refraction of the sun's light in droplets of water.

Hempel then moves to the essential point in his analysis: To explain a phenomenon is simply to show that its occurrence is to be expected, given certain scientific laws and certain appropriate conditions. More exactly, a scientific explanation of a phenomenon is to be regarded as an *argument*. Its conclusion is the sentence that describes the phenomenon (the *explanandum sentence*); its premisses (the *explanans sentences*) include, in addition to sentences stating particular facts, one or more scientific laws. These latter, in this context, are called covering laws. Hence this analysis is often referred to as the covering-law theory of scientific explanation.

The theory recognizes two different forms or models of explanation: 1) the *deductive* model, in which the covering laws are universal generalizations and the explanandum sentence follows *deductively* from the premisses; 2) the *probabilistic* model, in which the covering laws are statistical in character and the explanandum sentence follows *nondeductively* from its premisses.

Explanation: The Deductive Model

In Hempel's deductive model, a scientific explanation is a deductive argument, one or more premisses of which must be general scientific laws. Consequently, he calls explanations of this form *deductive-nomological*, abbreviated as D-N. ('Nomological' is derived from '*nomos*', the Greek word for law.)

Now let E be the sentence describing the phenomenon that is to be explained; $L_1, L_2, \ldots, L_m$, universal generalizations that state scientific laws; and $C_1, C_2, \ldots, C_n$, singular sentences that state particular facts, the "initial conditions." Then the form of a D-N explanation, according to Hempel, may be shown by the following schema:

$$\left.\begin{array}{l} L_1, L_2, \ldots, L_m \\ C_1, C_2, \ldots, C_n \end{array}\right\} \quad \text{Explanans sentences}$$

Therefore E Explanandum sentence

Let us illustrate this schema with the example of the rainbow. Here the explanans sentences that state scientific laws may be summed up very roughly as

(L)   Whenever a spray or mist or cloud of spherical water droplets is illuminated by a strong white light behind the observer, the light is broken down into the visible spectrum (the "rainbow effect") in accordance with the optical laws of reflection and refraction.

The explanans sentences that state the initial conditions may be brought together approximately as follows:

(C)   At place *p* and at time *t* a cloud was illuminated by sunlight behind the observer.

From these premises we then deduce the explanandum sentence

(E)   A rainbow appeared in the sky at place *p* and at time *t*.

By deducing *E*, we explain the event that it describes.

Hempel adds that the phenomenon to be explained need not be only an occurrence of a particular event of a certain kind, such as the free fall of a specific piece of chalk that slips from Professor Quincy's hand at place *p* and at time *t*. It may also be an empirical regularity, such as the behavior of freely falling bodies in general expressed in Galileo's formula. Of course, if the explanandum sentence itself is a law, such as Galileo's, then the explanans sentences from which it is to be deduced must include laws or theories of broader scope, such as Newton's laws of motion and of gravitation.

Notice that D-N explanations are deductive arguments that must number among their premises one or more general scientific laws. But laws of this type, as universal generalizations, are always hypotheses subject to confirmation or disproof. Clearly, for a D-N explanation to be *good*, it is not enough that the corresponding deductive argument be *valid*. It is also necessary that the general laws among its premises be *well-confirmed*. Since confirmation, as we saw in §56, rests on a combination of deductive and nondeductive reasoning, the same is true, by extension, of D-N explanations.

Explanation: The Probabilistic Model

A probabilistic explanation differs from a deductive-nomological explanation in two basic respects. First, the explanans sentences include at least one *probabilistic* or *statistical* law—that is, a law that expresses a probable or statistical regularity rather than a universal one. Second, the explanandum sentence follows from its premises *non*deductively—that is, granted the truth of the premises, it is improbable (not impossible) that the conclusion will be false.

Hempel introduces his account of the probabilistic model with the following example:

> The probability for persons exposed to
> the measles to catch the disease is high. ⎤ Premisses
> Jim was exposed to the measles. ⎦
>
>   *Makes highly probable*
> Jim caught the measles.   Conclusion

This is a very simple type of probabilistic explanation, and its form may be represented by the schema

> $p(O, R)$ is close to 1
> i is a case of R
>
> *Makes highly probable*
>
> i is a case of O

Here by $p(O, R)$ is meant the statistical probability that an observation or experiment R will have outcome O.   Or, very roughly, it is the proportion of cases with outcome O in a long series of performances of R.

Comments on Hempel's View

The covering-law theory has come to dominate discussion of scientific explanation in contemporary philosophy of science.   Hempel's view, in particular, has given rise to a considerable body of literature—much of it critical.   Here in capsule form are some of the objections.[11]

The theory is too broad.   It admits as explanations certain arguments that are not really explanations.   An example is

> Sodium emits a yellow light when optically excited.
> This specimen of sodium did not emit yellow light.
> Therefore it was not optically excited.

This is a deductive argument and includes among its premises a general law.   Yet intuitively we would surely not count it an explanation of why this specimen of sodium was not optically excited.

The theory is too narrow.   It excludes as explanations certain genuine explanations that are not arguments.   For example, a paleontologist explains the fossil prints of prehistoric animals by describing in detail the creatures whose tracks they are.   This is a recital, not an argument; yet intuitively we regard it as an explanation.

The theory is systematically mistaken in identifying explanation with argument.   To explain is not to offer an argument, but to provide a model, a mechanism, a way of *understanding* how something operates—how, for example, life evolved from nonliving matter.

---

[11]   For a fuller account of the objections, and of replies by covering-law theorists, see Jaegwon Kim, "Explanation in Science," *The Encyclopedia of Philosophy*.

The theory assumes that the primary business of science is to explain.
But this is not so.   The primary business of the sciences is to answer
"why" questions.   And answers to such questions differ in structure
from covering-law explanations.

The theory makes the false assumption that basically there is just *one*
kind of explanation in science, that found in the physical sciences.   But
the biological and social sciences exhibit varied patterns of explanation.
Some of these—in particular, explanations in terms of reasons, purposes,
and origins—do not conform to the covering-law requirement.   Philosophers of history are especially insistent on the point that the covering-law
theory, whatever its merits, cannot satisfy the needs of historical explanation.[12]

Covering-law theorists are not at a loss to respond to these and other
objections.   Generally, their replies take the line that opponents 1) leave
out of consideration *implicit* premises and 2) fail to recognize that
reasonable qualifications must of course be attached to the application of
the theory in certain situations.   Philosophers continue to debate the
question.   Still, the issues have been clarified, and thus the discussion has
proved to be philosophically useful.

NONCAUSAL EXPLANATIONS

Not all explanations in science are obviously causal.   Among those often
held to be noncausal are explanations that give *reasons*, state *purposes*, or
describe *origins*.   Some, perhaps all, of them may eventually prove to be
causal in character or "reducible" to causal explanations; it may also
turn out that, on this or some other ground, they can all be brought under
the covering-law theory.[13]   In any event, noncausal explanations are of
interest in their own right, not least because of the philosophical perplexi-
ties that surround them.   We shall conclude this section with brief comments on a few of these.

Explanation by Reasons

In recent years a number of philosophers have sought to distinguish
between reasons and causes, and thus between explanation by reasons
and explanation by causes.   What seems to have motivated them espe-

---

[12]   See William Dray, *Laws and Explanation in History* (London: Oxford University
Press, 1957); and Arthur Danto, *Analytical Philosophy of History* (Cambridge, England:
Cambridge University Press, 1965), Chapter 10.

[13]   A detailed discussion of these types of explanation and their relationship to the
covering-law theory is in Carl G. Hempel, *Aspects of Scientific Explanation* (New York:
Free Press, 1965).   For explanation by reasons, see pp. 463–487; by purposes (functional
explanation), pp. 297–330; by origins (genetic explanations), pp. 447–453.   Also see
Ernest Nagel, *The Structure of Science* (New York: Harcourt, Brace and World, 1961).

cially was the need to clarify the concept of human behavior involved in such traditional philosophical problems as free action and determinism.   But the enterprise has turned out to be extremely difficult, and the distinction remains in controversy.

Consider an example.   Suppose that today in Professor Perkins's logic class Marie's hand goes up.   We then ask

(7)   Why did Marie's hand go up?

Two kinds of answers may be offered to (7):

(8)   Marie's hand went up because her arm and shoulder muscles contracted, etc.

(9)   Marie's hand went up because she wanted to ask a question about distinguishing reasons from causes.

Roughly speaking, (8) tells simply what physiological events or mechanisms *caused* Marie's hand to go up.   But (9) tells us what motives, intentions, or purposes *prompted* her to raise her hand.   Thus (8) is part of an explanation by causes of the *behavioral event* of her hand going up; (9) is an explanation by reasons of her *action* in raising her hand.   Now of course her action in raising her hand involves the behavioral event of her hand going up.   But the two are not identical.   The behavioral event has only causes, the action has reasons.

A second example is

(10)   Why do people continue smoking?

Here, again, two kinds of answers may be offered.   The first would include only certain physiological events or states (the "craving") that *cause* a smoker to continue smoking.   The second would cite certain reasons (desire for peer approval, false bravado in the face of health warnings) that might *prompt* a person to continue smoking.

The distinction between cause and reason should not be confused with the distinction between what *happens to* a person and what a person *does*.   It is the latter distinction that is expressed, for example, when a newspaper reports that someone *fell or jumped* from a tall building.   Falling from a building is an event that happens to a person; it is caused by slipping, sudden giddiness, or the like.   Jumping from a building is an action that a person performs.   To explain it requires reasons.

It is plausible to conclude that we can distinguish reasons from causes, at least as concerns human action.   But views as to the precise nature of this distinction still vary widely.   At one extreme are those who maintain that reasons and causes differ totally and that a purely causal account of human behavior misses what is distinctive about human action.   At the other are those who hold that reasons are simply a species of the genus *cause* associated in particular with explanations of human actions in terms of motives, intentions, purposes, and the like.[14]   On the first view, explanations by reasons are necessarily noncausal; on the second, they are a particular variety of causal explanations.

Explanation by Purposes (Functional Explanation)

According to a very old tradition, questions of the type

(11)   Why do fish have gills?

are answered not by giving causes in the sense of Mill's antecedent circumstances, but by stating *purposes* or *ends*.   Thus fish have gills because gills enable them to extract from water the oxygen they need to exist.   Such explanations are called *teleological*, from '*telos*', the Greek word for end or purpose.

Teleological explanations have long been suspect in science.   For one thing, the terms 'end' and 'purpose' are both notoriously ambiguous. For another, explanations in terms of "purposes" are too often fanciful and untestable.   But if purpose is taken as *function performed*, the result is *functional explanation*—a type widely used in such sciences as biology and anthropology.

Consider, for example, the question

(12)   Why has sexual reproduction evolved?

A functional explanation offered by George C. Williams rests on the hypothesis that "sexual reproduction evolves because it permits each parent to diversify its own offspring and thus overcome unpredictable changes in the environment encountered from one generation to the next."[15]   (In sexual reproduction each parent contributes one-half the genes, so a sexual population can combine favorable mutations through matings among its various members.   This is not possible in asexual populations, where all the genes come from a single parent.)

Returning to (11), suppose we are asked to explain the occurrence of an item *i* (having gills) in a system *s* (a fish) in a setting of kind *c* (water).   A

---

[14]   For an example of the first view, see A. I. Melden, *Free Action* (London: Routledge and Kegan Paul, 1961); for an example of the second, see Donald Davidson, "Actions, Reasons, and Causes," *The Journal of Philosophy* 60 (1963), pp. 685–700.

[15]   The hypothesis is stated by Edward O. Wilson in his review of George C. Williams, *Sex and Evolution* (1975), *Science*, April 11, 1975, p. 139.

functional account, Hempel suggests, might have the following argument structure:

1.   *s* functions adequately in *c*.

2.   *s* functions adequately in *c* only if a certain necessary condition, or "need," *n* (a supply of oxygen) is satisfied.

3.   If item *i* were present in *s* then, as an effect, *n* would be satisfied.

Therefore *i* is present in the system *s*.

But as Hempel indicates, this argument is not deductively valid, for it commits the fallacy of affirming the consequent in connection with premiss 3.   Several possible repairs are discussed.   One consists in strengthening premiss 3 to

3'.   *Only if i* were present would *n*, as an effect, be satisfied.

The argument would then be valid, but 3' is a very difficult premiss to establish.   Another consists in weakening the explanandum as follows:

3".   *I* is the class of empirically sufficient conditions for *n* in the context determined by *s* and *c*, and *I* is nonempty.

Therefore some one of the members of *I* is present in *s*.

On these and related grounds, Hempel concludes that in general, functional analysis has quite limited explanatory import.[16]

Explanation by Origins (Genetic Explanation)

In some cases, to explain a phenomenon is to describe its origins.   Consider, for example, the question

(13)   Why is there life on earth?

Science interprets (13) as a request for an account of how life originated on earth, where by 'life' is meant systems possessing "the capacity for self-duplication with mutation."[17]   (The notion that life came to the earth from another planet is no longer widely held.)   The answer to (13), then, is a description of how such systems evolved from nonliving systems. Now clearly this description must be hypothetical; it is a reconstruction

---

[16]   Hempel, *Aspects of Scientific Explanation*, especially pp. 303–314.
[17]   See *Biology and the Future of Man*, ed. Philip Handler (New York: Oxford University Press, 1970), Chapter 5.

that relies on theories of prebiotic and biotic evolution drawn especially from cosmology, geochemistry, molecular genetics, and developmental biology. Yet there is no doubt that such a reconstruction, if well-confirmed, makes a unique contribution to our understanding of life.

An account in terms of origins is called a *genetic explanation*. Hempel characterizes it as follows:

> [I]t presents the phenomenon under study as the final stage of a developmental sequence, and accordingly accounts for the phenomenon by describing the successive stages of that sequence.[18]

So defined, genetic explanations 1) apply only to phenomena *with a history*, 2) rely on *explanatory hypotheses* furnished by various sciences, 3) are thus themselves *hypothetical* in nature, and 4) are widely accepted as contributing significantly to our *understanding* of phenomena.

On Multiple Explanations

In closing, we remark that an understanding of complex phenomena with a history is often advanced by the joint application of what we have been regarding as different kinds of explanation.

Consider, for example, the question

(14)   Why did capitalism develop?

A full answer would surely require a study of the causes, functions, and origins of capitalism—perhaps even of the " reasons " why people oppose it or support it. Such a study would seek to determine

> 1. What were the causes of capitalism, in the sense of the *antecedent conditions necessary* for it to come into being (say, the existence of large masses of wealth and of propertyless people).
>
> 2. What functions were or are performed by capitalism (such as fostering the growth at a given time and place of the forces of production).
>
> 3. What were the successive stages by which the capitalist system developed out of precapitalist economies.

This seems to have been the line of inquiry undertaken by such students of capitalism as Karl Marx in the past century and Fernand Braudel in the present.[19]

---

[18]   Hempel, *Aspects of Scientific Explanation*, p. 447.
[19]   For Marx, see the three volumes of *Capital*; for Braudel, see his *Civilisation matérielle et capitalisme* (Paris: Armand Colin), vol. 1 (1967).

§58   *Argument and Social Policy Making*

Having some knowledge of what is the case, and why, may indeed be a necessary condition for sensible policy making, but obviously it cannot be a sufficient one.   The choice of a proper course of action—individual or social—with respect to a given situation involves more than describing or explaining that situation.   It must also involve *evaluating* it, determining in some fashion whether it is *good* or *bad* and thus whether it ought to be maintained or changed.

How does evaluation differ from description?   What are values?   What is a moral judgment?   What is the relationship between " ought " and " is "?   More particularly, can sentences that state what *ought to be* ever be validly deduced from sentences that merely state what *is*?

Questions of this sort have long been debated by philosophers.[20]   But everyday life, though it profits from these debates more than is sometimes realized, cannot wait for their outcome.   So in practice we resolve these questions as best we can by subscribing to one or another " value system," not always explicitly defined, which we apply, not always consistently, to the various situations, conditions, or actions that we feel called upon to evaluate.

Our discussion here of the patterns of argument in policy making cannot and need not explore the basic issues in value theory and ethics.   As a preliminary, however, we take brief note of two points about values.

The first is the distinction between end-values and means-values, between things being *good* (or bad) and things being *good-for* (or bad-for). As an example, assume that physical well-being is a good thing, that it has positive end-value.   Then moderate exercise is something that is good-for that good thing, just as smoking is something that is bad-for that good thing.   Or assume that capital punishment is a bad thing.   Then a guillotine, which is good-for decapitating people, is good-for a bad thing, just as a defective hangman's noose is bad-for a bad thing.   Notice that a thing may be a means in one context and an end in another.   Thus physical well-being is an end relative to moderate exercise.   But suppose we introduce " peace of mind " as an end; then relative to it, physical well-being becomes a means.   Thus the means-end relation may be used as a kind of ordering principle to fit at least some values into a means-ends hierarchy.

The second point is the distinction between *good* and *better* (bad and worse), and between *good-for* and *better-for* (bad-for and worse-for). Even though the comparison of values raises complicated theoretical

---

[20]   See *Theories of Ethics*, ed. Philippa Foot (New York: Oxford University Press, 1967), especially Ms. Foot's introduction.   The collection also includes a paper by John R. Searle entitled "How to Derive 'Ought' from 'Is'."

issues, we do seem able to attach a reasonably clear sense to 'better-for' and, derivatively, to 'best-for'. We do regularly compare means. Indeed, the most familiar type of policy-making problem is precisely that of choosing the *best* means or combination of means to some desired end. For example, let the agreed-upon end be quality education for all. The question then is to determine which means or combination of means— curriculum enrichment, improved teaching methods, increased parent involvement, community control, desegregation by busing if necessary, and the like—will best accomplish that end. And a means is best if it 1) fully achieves the end and 2) does so with a maximum of economy and a minimum of negative consequences.

On the other hand, comparing *ends* is distinctly more problematic. What are we saying when we say that one end is *better* than some other in a given context? Is scholarly research better than teaching? Is the comfort of social conformity better than the discomfort of social dissent? The difficulty becomes most acute when a person is compelled to decide between "conflicting values" located far up in her or his means-ends hierarchy. Thus Antigone must choose between defying the laws of the king and defying those of the gods; the young draft resister must choose between violating the laws of the land and violating those of conscience. This is tragedy in the classic sense—from which there is no escape short of changing the whole context of choice.

THE PATTERN OF ARGUMENT IN POLICY MAKING

By a 'policy' we shall mean something that ought to be done, a course of action that should be undertaken. By 'policy making' we shall mean the process of adopting or agreeing upon a policy. We shall think of policies as being expressed by sentences, and of policy making as the construction of nondeductive arguments whose conclusions express policies.

What distinguishes this type of nondeductive argument from others is not only the presence in its conclusion of the word 'ought', but also the character of its premises. Specifically, the premises in the case of a policy-making argument must include one or more from each of the following categories:

1. *Generalized descriptions* of a situation s_1 (juvenile crimes of violence have increased).

2. *Evaluations*, negative or positive, of s_1 (the increase in juvenile crimes of violence is bad).

3. *Explanatory hypotheses* giving the cause or causes $c_1, \ldots, c_n$ of s_1 either in the sense that
   a. One or more of $c_1, \ldots, c_n$ are sufficient conditions of s_1 or in the sense that

b.   One or more of $c_1, \ldots, c_n$ are necessary and sufficient conditions of s_1

(The cause or causes of the increase in juvenile crimes of violence are rising unemployment among young people, and/or worsened urban housing, and/or more violence on TV, and/or a greater availability of handguns, and/or an increase in the number of juveniles, and/or more permissiveness, and/or "human nature," and/or ...)

4.   *Predictive causal hypotheses* specifying courses of action $a_1, \ldots,$ a_m such that if one or more of them are undertaken, then one or more of the causes $c_1, \ldots, c_n$ may or will cease to operate, and hence the (bad) situation s_1 may or will be changed. (For example, if Congress adopts legislation guaranteeing schooling or jobs for all the young people, then unemployment will decrease and hence juvenile crimes of violence may or will also decrease.)

5.   *Other predictive causal hypotheses* to the effect that if one or more of the courses of action $a_1, \ldots, a_m$ were undertaken, this would not or probably would not bring about a situation s_2 that is as bad as or worse than s_1. (For example, if young people were guaranteed schooling or jobs, this action would not or probably would not bankrupt the economy, destroy youthful initiative, and the like.)

With suitable sentences from each of these categories as premises, we then have a *nondeductive* argument that goes like this: Given that all these premises are true or well-confirmed, it is more or less improbable that the conclusion

Therefore one or more of the courses of action $a_1, \ldots, a_m$ *ought* to be undertaken

will be false.

The premises needed for social and individual policy-making arguments come from various sources. Generalized descriptions, explanatory hypotheses, and predictive hypotheses are often based on the findings of the sciences, especially the social sciences, with some help from everyday experience. Evaluations have an origin that is more difficult to trace. They reflect the diverse and changing value systems of the individual; the family; educational, church, or other institutions; ethnic groups; the nation.

The "logical form" of policy-making arguments may be represented by the following rough schema, in which, for simplicity, consideration is limited to the case of a single cause c and a single course of action a:

1. s_1 is the case.

2. s_1 is bad (good).

3a.   If c occurs, then s_1 occurs

　　　or

3b. s_1 occurs iff c occurs.

4.   If a is undertaken, then c will *not* occur.

5.   If a is undertaken, this will not result in a situation s_2 with a negative value equal to or greater than that of s_1.

Therefore a ought to be undertaken.

Notice how the difference between 3a and 3b affects the course and the outcome of the argument. If 3b is available, then with 4 we have the premises

3b. s_1 occurs iff c occurs

4.   If a is undertaken, then c will not occur

that lead by a valid *deductive* subargument to the conclusion

(1)　　Therefore if a is undertaken, s_1 will not occur

and thence with 1, 2, and 5 nondeductively to

(2)　　Therefore a ought to be undertaken,

the conclusion of the argument as a whole.

On the other hand, if just the weaker premiss 3a is available, we have

3a.   If c occurs, then s_1 occurs.

4.   If a is undertaken, then c will not occur.

These provide at best only the most modest nondeductive evidential support for (1) and thus for (2).

Notice also that the two senses of 'cause' that give rise to 3a and 3b—cause as sufficient condition, and cause as necessary and sufficient condition—likewise apply in regard to causal premises 4 and 5. Hence a more complete schema would include alternative formulations 4a and 4b for 4, and 5a and 5b for 5.

THE APPRAISAL OF POLICY-MAKING ARGUMENTS

In appraising the usual social policy-making argument, we face at least two questions. The first concerns the *nondeductive strength* of the argument: the degree of evidential support that accrues to its conclusion, granted that all of its premises are true or well-confirmed.   The second relates to the *degree of confirmation* of the premises.

Now most controversies over policy seem to center not around the first question, but around the second.   The usual dispute is not whether the premises, once granted, give the "appropriate" degree of evidential support to the conclusion; lacking an agreed-upon way of measuring such support, we generally follow the rough, intuitive guidelines of common sense.   Rather, what is most often at issue is whether the premises themselves—the generalized descriptions, the evaluations, the explanatory and predictive hypotheses—are sufficiently well confirmed to merit being granted.

Disagreements about social policy premises run the gamut.   We shall describe five types, using the example of juvenile crime as a running illustration.

First, people may disagree about the description of the situation under consideration.   Thus some might hold that juvenile crime has not increased; it is merely being reported more fully.

Second, there may be agreement on the description of the situation, but disagreement about its evaluation.   Thus conceivably someone might maintain that although juvenile crime has increased, this is a natural form of self-expression and, hence, cannot be judged good or bad.

Third, there may be agreement on the description and evaluation of the situation, but disagreement about its causes.   Thus it might be held that although increased juvenile crime is bad, the cause is not unemployment or bad housing, but fear on the part of judges to enforce the law, or "permissiveness," or "human nature."

Fourth, agreement may extend to the description, evaluation, and causes of the situation, and yet there may be disagreement as to whether a specified course of action—or indeed any course of action—would eliminate the causes.   Thus it might be contended that a federal guarantee of schooling or jobs would not help, because the funds would be dissipated long before they reached the unemployed youth.   Or it might be held that since human nature is the cause of increased juvenile crime and "you can't change human nature," nothing can be done about the situation.

Finally, even if it is agreed that a certain course of action would eliminate the causes of the bad situation, there may still be disagreement on whether such action might not produce a situation worse than the one under consideration.   Thus it might be argued that although a federal guarantee of schooling or jobs would reduce juvenile crime, it would undermine the economy and stifle youthful initiative, and that this would be worse than increased juvenile crime.

AN EXAMPLE OF SOCIAL POLICY MAKING

Policy making, as we suggested earlier, may be thought of as the construction of nondeductive arguments whose conclusions state what ought to be done.   For a closing illustration of social policy making, we turn to another current problem: how to assure quality education for all. To develop a suitable argument, we proceed as follows:

First, we assemble an accurate *description* of the situation. This is not difficult. Public and private studies of education in the United States fully document the existence of pervasive inequalities and, in particular, of disparities between the quality and quantity of education furnished to whites and that provided for blacks and certain other ethnic minorities. Thus official data for 1973 show 1) that 85 percent of whites between the ages of twenty and twenty-four have completed high school, but only 71 percent of blacks; and 2) that 25 percent of whites between the ages of eighteen and twenty-four are enrolled in colleges, but only 16 percent of blacks.[21] Other figures disclose the large gap in quality between the education available to blacks in the segregated schools of the cities and that available to whites in various suburban schools.

Second, we *evaluate* the situation. This too, in principle, is not difficult. Unequal access—based on race—to quality education is not only unconstitutional; it is also immoral, and would be so judged by anyone who is not an outright racist. The evil is all the more obvious if account is taken of the economic correlates of inequality in education: in 1973, 31.4 percent of blacks were officially classified as poor, as against 8.4 percent of whites; the median income of black families was little more than half—58 percent—of that of white families; 8.9 percent of black workers were unemployed, 4.3 percent of white workers.

Third, we examine the possible *causes* of the bad situation. There are a number of explanatory hypotheses to consider, some competing, some overlapping: inequities in per-pupil outlay, especially underfunding in areas of ethnic concentration; white racism permeating textbooks, curricula, and the attitudes of teaching and administrative staffs; inadequate community involvement; racially segregated schools; so-called racial inferiority. These and similar hypotheses must be properly weighed on the basis of evidence that confirms or disproves them. (We leave aside the complications introduced by the two senses of 'cause'.)

Fourth, we consider *courses of action* that would change the situation by eliminating its causes. Suppose we find that the prime cause is the racially segregated school as such. We might then propose such countermeasures as rezoning, the merger of urban and suburban school districts, or even busing, as the means of assuring quality education for all. Or suppose we find that the prime cause is underfunding. We might propose federal *educare* (and *educaid*) legislation to remove inequities in school-district financing and to provide catch-up moneys for districts long underfunded—as part of a broader program that would also include community involvement and measures to end racist practices.

---

[21]   All figures used in this illustration are from *The Social and Economic Status of the Black Population in the United States, 1973*, U.S. Bureau of the Census, Current Population Reports, 1974.

Fifth, we determine whether the course of action we propose might not create a situation *as bad as* or *worse than* the one we seek to change. For example, assume that the action proposed is to desegregate the schools, and that this requires court-ordered busing. It may then be argued that such busing promotes the " white flight " from the cities and hence worsens the very situation we are trying to better.[22] Or assume that the action proposed is the adoption of a federal educare-educaid program. It might be objected that such a program would result in financial crisis, chaos in school administration, and widespread corruption. It is thus essential to determine just what negative consequences, if any, a proposed course of action is likely to have.

Finally, on the basis of the premisses thus obtained, we may formulate such appropriate *policy* conclusions as

> Therefore all measures necessary to ensure desegregated schools *should be* undertaken

> Therefore a federal educare-educaid program *should be* undertaken

and the like.

We should add, however, that one factor that also influences the choice of a policy on this matter is a fundamental difference in outlook that divides opponents of racial discrimination into two groups: those who believe that the road to equality lies through integration and those who hold that the road to integration lies through equality.

---

[22] This seems to be the conclusion reached by Dr. James S. Coleman, whose findings have been challenged by Professors Robert L. Green and Thomas F. Pettigrew (*The New York Times*, June 14, 1975).

Appendix

Traditional Logic: The Aristotelian Syllogism

People argued before there was a logic, just as they counted before there was an arithmetic and measured before there was a geometry. It remained for the Greek philosopher Aristotle (384–322 B.C.) to establish deductive logic as a scientific discipline.

Aristotle laid the foundations for the discipline by formulating the notion of a *deductive argument*, distinguishing between the *validity* and the *soundness* of an argument, and basing validity upon the *forms*—not the subject matter, or content—of the sentences that make up the argument (see Chapter 1). In addition, he created the first actual body of deductive logic, including a logic of *categorical sentences and syllogisms*. This portion, elaborated later by *traditional logic*, dominated the discipline till late in the nineteenth century.

Modern logicians have gone far beyond Aristotle. Yet traditional logic (hereafter abbreviated as TL) still has several claims on our attention. First, it has played a major role in the history of world thought. Second, many forms of argument from TL appear to this day in the discussions, debates, and controversies of ordinary life. Finally, because of its simple structure, TL is widely regarded as a helpful starting point in a study of other deductive logics.

377

Like any deductive logic, TL has these tasks: 1) to specify the range of *sentence forms* it intends to consider and 2) to set up a *criterion* of validity for arguments or inferences whose premises and conclusions are sentences of those forms.   All that remains then is to indicate suitable *procedures* for finding out which of these arguments or inferences conform to the criterion and thus are valid.   What follows is a brief account of how TL fulfills its tasks.

TL SENTENCE FORMS

Traditional logic is concerned with just *four* forms of sentences.   These are known, respectively, as the A, E, I, and O forms and are represented as follows:

> A: All *S* are *P*
> E: No *S* are *P*
> I: Some *S* are *P*
> O: Some *S* are not *P*

Here '*S*' and '*P*' are symbols that stand in place of *terms*—that is, of words (such as 'persons' or 'pacifists') that stand for *classes* of things. And the word 'some' has the sense not of 'some but not all', but of 'at least one' or 'some, possibly all'.

Sentences of these forms are called *categorical* sentences.   Some examples are

> A: All statespersons are politicians.
> E: No statespersons are politicians.
> I: Some statespersons are politicians.
> O: Some statespersons are not politicians.

Notice that a categorical sentence consists of only *two* terms, a subject term and a predicate term, joined by the copula 'are'.

Quality and Quantity

Each categorical sentence or sentence form has a *quality* and a *quantity*. A sentence form (or a sentence) may be *affirmative* or *negative* in quality, *universal* or *particular* in quantity.   Quality is expressed by the presence or absence of a negating word, 'no' or 'not'; quantity is expressed by the presence of one of the two quantifiers, 'all' or 'some'.

Now according to TL, categorical sentence forms differ in just these two respects.   Hence the A, E, I, and O are the *only* possible forms of categorical sentences:

A:	All *S* are *P*	Universal affirmative
E:	No *S* are *P*	Universal negative
I:	Some *S* are *P*	Particular affirmative
O:	Some *S* are not *P*	Particular negative

(The affirmative forms are called A and I, from the first two vowels in '*affirmo*', the Latin word for *I affirm*; the negative forms are called E and O, from the two vowels in '*nego*', the Latin word for *I deny*.)

Distribution

The notion of *distribution* plays a pivotal role in TL.   However, it presents certain difficulties, which cannot be treated fully or precisely in this brief summary.   For our purposes, we shall be content to define it as follows:

> *A term is said to be* distributed in a given sentence *if that sentence, as ordinarily used, says something about* (*does not merely refer to*) all *of the class denoted by the term.*

Notice 1) that what is distributed is a *term*, not a sentence; 2) a term is distributed *in* a sentence; 3) whether a term is distributed or undistributed depends solely on the *form* of the sentence in which it occurs, not on the subject matter.

Using this definition, let us now find out which terms in the four forms of sentences are distributed and which are not.   Take first a sentence of form A:

(1)   All socialists are pacifists.

Obviously, the subject term in (1) is distributed, since (1) says something about *all* socialists.   The predicate term, on the other hand, is *not* distributed: (1) says only that all socialists are pacifists, not that all socialists are *all* the pacifists.

Consider next a sentence of form E:

(2)   No squares are pentagons.

In this case, what is said is that two *entire* classes—squares and pentagons—have no member in common; they are mutually exclusive.   Hence in (2) *both* terms are distributed.

Now apply the definition to a sentence of form I:

(3)   Some sophomores are philosophy majors.

Here the subject term is obviously *un*distributed: (3) does not say something about all sophomores, but only about *some*.   Nor does it say that some sophomores are *all* the philosophy majors.   Hence in (3) both terms are undistributed.

Finally, take a sentence of form O:

(4)   Some senior citizens are not parents.

The subject term is of course undistributed.   But what of the predicate term?   Now (4) says that at least one senior citizen is not a member of the class of parents—that is, cannot be found anywhere in the *entire* class of parents.   Hence the predicate term is to be counted as distributed.

We may summarize these results as follows:

	S	P
A	D	U
E	D	D
I	U	U
O	U	D

where 'D' and 'U' are abbreviations for 'distributed' and 'undistributed'. As the summary shows, the *subject terms* of *universal* sentences and the *predicate terms* of *negative* sentences are distributed.   The remaining terms are all undistributed.

Opposition

Two TL sentence forms or sentences are said to be *opposed* if they differ in quality or in quantity or in both.   Thus A and E differ only in quality: they are called *contraries*.   Likewise, I and O differ only in quality: they are called *subcontraries*.   On the other hand, A and I, and E and O differ only in quantity: A and E are called the *superalterns* of I and O, respectively, while I and O are called the *subalterns* of A and E, respectively.   Finally, sentence forms or sentences that differ in both quality and quantity are called *contradictories*.

These relations are shown in the Traditional Square of Opposition:

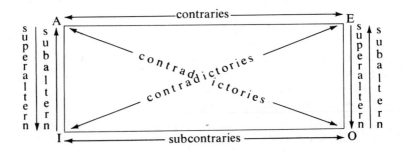

Note that of two contraries, both may be false but both cannot be true. Of two subcontraries, both may be true but both cannot be false. Of two contradictories, if one is true, the other must be false; and if the first is false, the second must be true.

VENN DIAGRAMS FOR TL SENTENCE FORMS

Before we discuss inference and argument in TL, we pause to introduce a device for depicting TL sentence forms. It is called the Venn Diagram, after the English logician John Venn (1834–1923).

There are two steps in the construction of a Venn Diagram. First, we erect a framework by drawing within a rectangle a pair of overlapping circles and assigning one to *S* and the other to *P*:

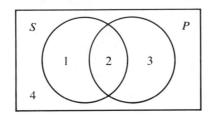

For ease of reference, we number the regions thus formed: region 1 is inside of circle *S* and outside of circle *P*; region 3 is inside of *P* and outside of *S*; region 2 is inside of both; region 4 is outside of both.

Second, we adopt a method of representing within this framework just what the sentence form says about the classes *S* and *P*. For example, the A form—'All *S* are *P*'—says that whatever *S*s there are belong to the *class P*. In the language of circles, this means that there are no *S*s outside the *circle P*—that is, region 1 is *empty*. We show this by shading out region 1:

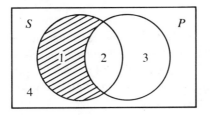

All *S* are *P*

The I form—'Some *S* are *P*'—says that some members of class *S* are also members of class *P*, that there is at least one thing that belongs to *S* and belongs to *P*. In terms of circles, this means that region 2, the area common to circles *S* and *P*, is *not* empty.   This we show by placing an X in region 2:

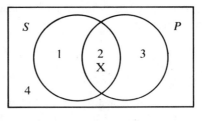

Some *S* are *P*

Following the same procedure with E and O forms, we obtain

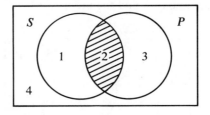

No *S* are *P*

and

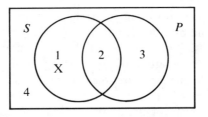

Some *S* are not *P*

ARGUMENT AND INFERENCE IN TL

It is customary in TL to divide the treatment of inference and argument into two parts.   The first is called *immediate inference*, and it is limited to arguments with a *single* premiss.   The second is called *mediate inference*, and it includes arguments with more than one premiss, most notably the Aristotelian syllogism.

IMMEDIATE INFERENCE: CONVERSION

There are several kinds of immediate inference.   One of them, conversion, we shall describe in detail.   Others, such as obversion and contraposition, will only be mentioned.

Conversion consists in interchanging subject and predicate terms, leaving all else untouched. Thus the converses of the four Aristotelian sentence forms are

> A: All *P* are *S*
>
> E: No *P* are *S*
>
> I: Some *P* are *S*
>
> O: Some *P* are not *S*

And the four forms of *argument by conversion* are

> A: All *S* are *P*   Therefore all *P* are *S*
>
> E: No *S* are *P*   Therefore no *P* are *S*
>
> I: Some *S* are *P*   Therefore some *P* are *S*
>
> O: Some *S* are not *P*   Therefore some *P* are not *S*

VALIDITY OF IMMEDIATE INFERENCE

With conversion as our continuing example, we turn now to the question of validity. Which of the four forms of argument by conversion are valid? We shall test them by two methods: by the TL rule or criterion for valid immediate inference, and by Venn Diagrams.

The TL Test for Validity

The TL criterion of validity for immediate inference centers on the notion of *distribution*. It will help us understand how to use this criterion if we first list again the four forms of argument by conversion, noting this time which terms in the premisses and conclusions are distributed and which are undistributed:

>   D   U   D   U
>
> A: All *S* are *P*   Therefore all *P* are *S*
>
>   D   D   D   D
>
> E: No *S* are *P*   Therefore no *P* are *S*
>
>   U   U   U   U
>
> I: Some *S* are *P*   Therefore some *P* are *S*
>
>   U   D   U   D
>
> O: Some *S* are not *P*   Therefore some *P* are not *S*

The *TL rule for immediate inference* reads as follows:

> *In a valid argument, no term may be distributed in the conclusion unless it was distributed in the premiss.*

Applying this rule, we find that the conversions of the E and I forms are valid. In E both terms are distributed, and in I both are undistributed; hence interchanging *S* and *P* cannot violate the rule.   The conversions of A and O, however, are invalid.   For when we convert A, the *P*-term is distributed in the conclusion but not in the premiss; when we convert O, the *S*-term is distributed in the conclusion but not in the premiss.

The TL test and the commonsense test.   These results agree fully with the findings of common sense.   According to common sense, an argument is valid only if it is *impossible* for the conclusion to be false when the premisses are true.   On this criterion, conversion is *invalid* for the A and O forms, as these two examples prove:

(5)   All freshmen are students.

Therefore all students are freshmen.

(6)   Some Europeans are not Belgians.

Therefore some Belgians are not Europeans.

In both (5) and (6), the premisses are true, yet the conclusions are false. But for E and I, conversion is valid, as the following examples illustrate:

(7)   No freshmen are sophomores.

Therefore no sophomores are freshmen.

(8)   Some sophomores are philosophy majors.

Therefore some philosophy majors are sophomores.

In (7) and (8), it is impossible for the conclusion to be false when the premisses are true.

The problem with the commonsense criterion is its vagueness.   We do not have a clear notion of what is meant by 'impossible'.   The progression from the commonsense criterion to the TL criterion is an illustration of the refining of common sense into early science.

The basis for the TL rule.   Recall that a term is distributed in a given sentence if that sentence, as ordinarily used, says something about *all* of the class denoted by the term.   Thus the TL rule, by forbidding us to distribute a term in the conclusion unless it was distributed in the premiss, bars us from saying *more* about a class in the conclusion than we said about it in the premiss.   (We may, of course, say the same or less.)   This prohibition is characteristic of deductive logic: the conclusion of a valid deductive argument must not "go beyond" the premisses.

The Venn Diagram Test for Validity

Venn Diagrams provide a simple, graphic means of testing the validity of immediate inferences.   Consider these four pairs of diagrams:

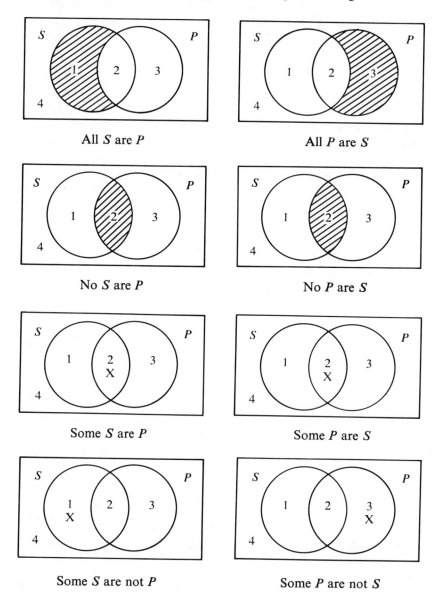

All *S* are *P*	All *P* are *S*
No *S* are *P*	No *P* are *S*
Some *S* are *P*	Some *P* are *S*
Some *S* are not *P*	Some *P* are not *S*

Now let us formulate the following "*diagram rule*" *for immediate inference*:

> *An argument is valid iff the diagram of the conclusion does not contain any* more *information—shown by shading out a region or inserting an X—than is already present in the diagram of the premiss.* (*It may, of course, contain the same information or less.*)

If we apply this rule to the pairs of diagrams, we see at once that the conversions of the A and O forms are invalid, those of the E and I forms valid. Thus the correspondence between classes and circles, between what sentences say about classes and what the diagrams show about the regions formed by the circles, also extends to the validity of arguments. The correspondence *preserves validity*: immediate inferences—with certain exceptions to be noted later—are valid by the diagram rule iff they are valid by the TL rule.

Immediate Inference: Obversion and Contraposition

Obversion consists in changing the *quality* of the sentence or sentence form and negating the P-term. We have

A:	All S are P	Therefore no S are non-P
E:	No S are P	Therefore all S are non-P
I:	Some S are P	Therefore some S are not non-P
O:	Some S are not P	Therefore some S are non-P

All of these inferences are valid, as may be verified by constructing Venn Diagrams. (Do not confuse 'not' and 'non'. 'Not' negates a sentence or a sentence form, 'non' negates a term; thus 'non-P' stands for the class consisting of everything *outside of* the class P.)

Contraposition consists in interchanging the S-term and the P-term and negating each. We then have

A:	All S are P	Therefore all non-P are non-S	(Valid)
E:	No S are P	Therefore no non-P are non-S	(Invalid)
I:	Some S are P	Therefore some non-P are non-S	(Invalid)
O:	Some S are not P	Therefore some non-P are not non-S	(Valid)

That contraposition is invalid for the E and I forms is proved by the following examples:

(9)   No sophomores are freshmen.

Therefore no nonfreshmen are nonsophomores.

(10)   Some entities are humans.

Therefore some nonhumans are nonentities.

In each case it is obviously possible for the premiss to be true and the conclusion false.

Contraposition may also be described as consisting in the sequence obversion-conversion-obversion. Thus 'All *S* are *P*' by obversion becomes 'No *S* are non-*P*', which by conversion becomes 'No non-*P* are *S*', which by obversion becomes 'All non-*P* are non-*S*'. Notice that contraposition is invalid for the E form because this involves converting an A form; it is invalid for the I form because this involves converting an O form.

MEDIATE INFERENCE: THE CATEGORICAL SYLLOGISM

We come now to the centerpiece of TL, the Aristotelian *categorical syllogism*. The full definition and accompanying terminology are as follows:

> *A syllogism is an argument consisting of* three categorical sentences—two premisses and a conclusion —*and* containing just three distinct terms, *each of which appears in two of the sentences. The term that appears in both premisses is called the* middle term, *and the conclusion contains the other two terms. The premiss in which the predicate term of the conclusion appears is called the* major *premiss, and it is written first; the premiss in which the subject term of the conclusion appears is called the* minor *premiss.*

Examples of syllogisms are

(11)   All men are mortal.

All members of the French Academy are men.

Therefore all members of the French Academy are mortal.

(12)   No men are infallible.

All past Presidents of the United States are men.

Therefore no past Presidents of the United States are infallible.

The corresponding *syllogistic forms* are

(11')   All *M* are *P*

All *S* are *M*

Therefore all *S* are *P*

(12')   No *M* are *P*

All *S* are *M*

Therefore no *S* are *P*

In (11') and (12'), '*S*' is a place-holder for the term that appears as the subject of the conclusion, '*P*' for the term that appears as the predicate of the conclusion, and '*M*' for the middle term—the term that appears in both premisses.

Mood and Figure

Two important formal properties of syllogisms are mood and figure. The *mood* of a syllogism is determined by the quality and quantity of the sentences that make up the syllogism. For example, (11) is a syllogism in the mood AAA—that is, the two premisses and the conclusion are all sentences of the A form; (12) is a syllogism in the mood EAE.

Since there are four different sentence forms and each syllogistic form consists of three sentence forms, there are exactly 4^3, or 64 *possible* syllogistic moods. Thus for each of A, E, I, or O as the form of the major premiss, there are 16 syllogistic moods. In the case of A, these are

AAA	AEA	AIA	AOA
AAE	AEE	AIE	AOE
AAI	AEI	AII	AOI
AAO	AEO	AIO	AOO

The *figure* of a syllogism is determined by the position of the middle term. There are just four such positions:

1		2		3		4	
M	*P*	*P*	*M*	*M*	*P*	*P*	*M*
S	*M*	*S*	*M*	*M*	*S*	*M*	*S*
S	*P*	*S*	*P*	*S*	*P*	*S*	*P*

Since each syllogistic mood may occur in each of the four figures, there are exactly 4 × 64, or 256, *possible* syllogistic forms, when account is taken of both mood and figure.   For example, the syllogism (11) is in the mood AAA in the first figure, or AAA-1, for short.   The syllogism (12) is in EAE-1.

Of course, not all 256 syllogistic forms are *valid*.   Thus syllogisms in AII-4 are invalid, as is proved by this example:

(13)   All Belgians are Europeans.

Some Europeans are Italians.

Therefore some Italians are Belgians.

The premisses are both true, but the conclusion is false.

VALIDITY OF SYLLOGISTIC FORMS

Our task now is to determine which syllogistic forms—hence which syllogisms—are valid.   As in the case of immediate inference, we shall employ two methods: the Traditional Rules for Valid Syllogisms, and Venn Diagrams.

The Traditional Rules for Valid Syllogisms

In TL the criterion of validity for syllogisms is expressed in the following set of rules:

> 1.   In a valid syllogism the middle term must be distributed at least once.
>
> 2.   In a valid syllogism no term may be distributed in the conclusion unless it was distributed in a premiss (but a term may be distributed in a premiss and not be distributed in the conclusion).
>
> 3.   No syllogism with two negative premisses is valid.
>
> 4.   In a valid syllogism, a) if one premiss is negative, the conclusion must be negative, and b) if the conclusion is negative, one premiss must be negative.

Jointly, these rules make up a system that is sound and complete: it admits as valid *all* and *only* those syllogisms that meet the commonsense or intuitive criterion of validity.   Some writers begin their list with a " zeroth " rule: a valid syllogism may contain three and only three terms.   But this requirement is really part of the definition of syllogism.   A syllogism with an ambiguously used middle term actually contains four terms, not three, and hence is said to commit the " fallacy of four terms."   Syllogistic forms that violate Rule 1 are said to commit the " fallacy of the undistributed middle."

It is a simple, if tedious, matter to apply these rules.   We first determine the form of the syllogism and then see if this form complies with all the rules.   For example, the syllogism (13), which is in AII-4, is not valid because it violates Rule 1: the middle term, 'Europeans', is undistributed in both premisses.   On the other hand, syllogisms (11) and (12), which are in AAA-1 and EAE-1, are both valid: they obey all the rules.

Valid syllogistic moods and figures.   Using the TL rules, we can now ascertain which of the 256 possible syllogistic forms are valid.   The first step is to determine the valid moods; the second is to see in which figures these valid moods are valid.

We begin by listing all 64 moods, citing for those that are invalid the rule or rules they violate:

AAA	valid	EAA	4a	IAA	1 or 2	OAA	4a
AAE	4b; 1 or 2	EAE	valid	IAE	4b; 2	OAE	1 or 2
AAI	valid	EAI	4a	IAI	valid	OAI	4a
AAO	4b	EAO	valid	IAO	4b; 2	OAO	valid
AEA	4a	EEA	3	IEA	4a	OEA	3
AEE	valid	EEE	3	IEE	2	OEE	3
AEI	4a	EEI	3	IEI	4a	OEI	3
AEO	valid	EEO	3	IEO	2	OEO	3
AIA	2	EIA	4a; 2	IIA	1	OIA	4a; 2
AIE	4b; 2	EIE	2	IIE	1	OIE	2
AII	valid	EII	4a	III	1	OII	4a
AIO	4b; 1 or 2	EIO	valid	IIO	1	OIO	1 or 2
AOA	4a	EOA	3	IOA	4a	OOA	3
AOE	1 or 2	EOE	3	IOE	2	OOE	3
AOI	4a	EOI	3	IOI	4a	OOI	3
AOO	valid	EOO	3	IOO	2	OOO	3

Notice that some moods violate Rule 1 *or* Rule 2.   For example, AOE is invalid because the premisses A and O together contain only two distributed terms, whereas three are needed: the middle term and the subject and predicate terms of the conclusion E.   Hence AOE is bound to violate either Rule 1 or Rule 2.

Thus of the 64 possible moods, only the following 11 are valid:

AAA	AEO	EAE	IAI
AAI	AII	EAO	OAO
AEE	AOO	EIO	

Since each of these 11 moods may occur in each of the four figures, we have 4 × 11 or 44 survivors of the 256 possible syllogistic forms.   Now we have to determine in which figures the 11 moods are valid. For ex-ample, here are the four figures for AAA:

1	2	3	4
All *M* are *P*	All *P* are *M*	All *M* are *P*	All *P* are *M*
All *S* are *M*	All *S* are *M*	All *M* are *S*	All *M* are *S*
Hence all *S* are *P*	Hence all *S* are *P*	Hence all *S* are *P*	Hence all *S* are *P*

Applying the TL rules, we find that AAA-2 violates Rule 1, AAA-3 and AAA-4 both violate Rule 2, and AAA-1 alone is valid. When we per-form the same operation on the remaining 10 moods, we obtain as the complete list of valid syllogistic forms the following

First figure: AAA, EAE, AII, EIO, (AAI), (EAO)

Second figure: EAE, AEE, EIO, AOO, (EAO), (AEO)

Third figure: AAI, IAI, AII, EAO, OAO, EIO

Fourth figure: AAI, AEE, IAI, EAO, EIO, (AEO)

or a total of 24. Of these, the five in parentheses are known as "weak-ened" forms. They are called weakened because their conclusions are simply the *subalterns* of—hence, according to TL, say less than—the conclusions of the valid syllogistic forms whose premisses they share. For example, AAI-1 is a weakened form of AAA-1 and in TL must be valid if AAA-1 is.

Proving derived rules for valid syllogisms. From the TL rules for valid syllogisms we may obtain certain *derived* rules. For example,

No syllogism with two particular premisses is valid

is not one of the four original TL rules. But we can prove it from those rules.

PROOF

First list all possible cases of syllogistic forms with two particular prem-isses. These are

O	I	I	O
O	I	O	I

Second, show that all four cases are barred by the original rules:

Case 1: OO.   Syllogistic forms with two negative premisses violate Rule 3.

Case 2: II.   Syllogistic forms with two particular affirmative premisses fail to distribute the middle term and hence are invalid by Rule 1.

Cases 3 and 4: IO and OI.   In each case the pair of premisses contains only one distributed term.   But to obtain a conclusion, we require two distributed terms.   First, by Rule 1 the middle term must be distributed at least once.   Second, with a negative premiss, the conclusion by Rule 4a must be negative and so must distribute the *P*-term, which by Rule 2 must then already have been distributed in a premiss.   Thus syllogistic forms with IO or OI as premisses must violate either Rule 1 or Rule 2.

Using a similar procedure, we can prove other derived rules—for example, that in a valid syllogism if one premiss is particular, the conclusion must be particular.

It is also possible to prove that each original rule is independent, that it cannot be derived from the remaining original rules.   Here is the proof for Rule 4b:

PROOF

To prove that a rule is independent, it is enough to cite at least one syllogistic form that is barred by the rule, violates no other original rule, and yet is intuitively invalid.   For 4b, such a form is AAO-4:

(14′)   All *P* are *M*

All *M* are *S*

Therefore some *S* are not *P*

Clearly, AAO-4 violates Rule 4b; it complies with each of the other original rules; yet it is intuitively invalid, as this syllogism in AAO-4 shows:

(14)   All students with 120 credits and a major are graduating students.

All graduating students are diploma recipients.

Therefore some diploma recipients are not students with 120 credits and a major.

Here both premisses are true, yet the conclusion is (or should be) false.

Thus Rule 4b is independent of the other rules.   If it were dropped from the original TL set, the TL system would become *unsound*.   For it would admit as valid certain syllogisms that are intuitively invalid.

Testing the Validity of Syllogisms by Venn Diagrams

Since syllogisms contain three distinct terms, Venn Diagrams for testing the validity of syllogisms require systems of *three* overlapping circles:

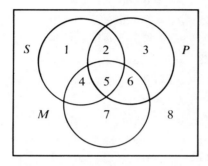

The eight regions formed by the circles are numbered for convenience.

A suitable "diagram rule" for the validity of syllogisms and syllogistic forms may be stated as follows:

> *A syllogism is valid iff the diagram of the conclusion does not contain any more information than is already present in the diagram of the two premises. (It may, of course, contain the same information or less.)*

We first apply this rule to syllogistic forms with universal premises and conclusions. Recall that the information conveyed by universal sentence forms is entered in the diagrams by *shading out* appropriate regions. Thus in a three-circle system, the sentence form 'All *M* are *P*' (which says that there are no *M*s outside of the class *P*) is represented by shading out regions 4 and 7:

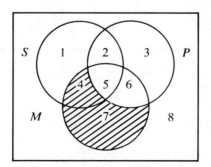

All *M* are *P*: regions 4 and 7 are empty, or, for short, #4 = 0 and #7 = 0

Here is a list of the universal sentence forms that may serve as premisses or conclusions of syllogistic forms, together with the information that each conveys:

All M are P: #4 = 0 and #7 = 0
All P are M: #2 = 0 and #3 = 0
No M are P: #5 = 0 and #6 = 0
No P are M: #5 = 0 and #6 = 0
All S are M: #1 = 0 and #2 = 0
All M are S: #6 = 0 and #7 = 0
No S are M: #4 = 0 and #5 = 0
No M are S: #4 = 0 and #5 = 0
All S are P: #1 = 0 and #4 = 0
No S are P: #2 = 0 and #5 = 0

As examples of syllogistic forms with universal premisses and conclusions, we take (11') and (12'). For each, we present two diagrams—one for the two premisses and one for the conclusion.

(11')   All M are P
         All S are M
         Hence all S are P
         (AAA-1)

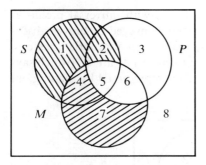 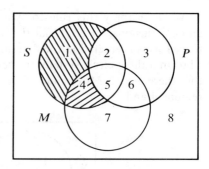

All M are P: #4 = 0 and #7 = 0   All S are P: #1 = 0 and #4 = 0
All S are M: #1 = 0 and #2 = 0

(12')   No M are P
         All S are M
         Hence no S are P
         (EAE-1)

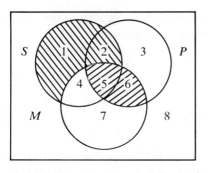

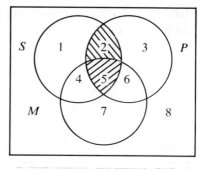

No *M* are *P*: #5 = 0 and #6 = 0   No *S* are *P*: #2 = 0 and #5 = 0

All *S* are *M*: #1 = 0 and #2 = 0

Thus (11′) and (12′) are valid forms, because the information contained in the diagrams of their conclusions does not go beyond the information contained in the diagrams of their premisses. Notice that the information in the conclusion is contained literally in the information given by the two premisses: each premiss declares empty one of the two regions declared empty by the conclusion.

Consider now the syllogistic form

(15′)   All *P* are *M*

All *S* are *M*

Hence all *S* are *P*

(AAA-2)

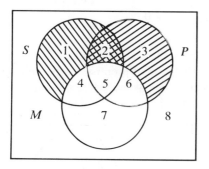

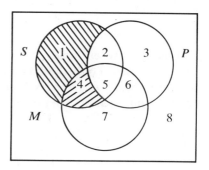

All *P* are *M*: #2 = 0 and #3 = 0   All *S* are *P*: #1 = 0 and #4 = 0

All *S* are *M*: #1 = 0 and #2 = 0

Here the diagram of the conclusion states that regions 1 and 4 are empty, but the premisses tell us nothing about region 4. Hence (15′) fails the

diagram test: its conclusion contains information not present in the premisses.   It is an *invalid* form, as the following example confirms:

(15)   All sophomores are students.

   All freshmen are students.

   Therefore all freshmen are sophomores.

Next we apply the diagram rule to syllogistic forms that involve particular sentence forms.   Recall that a particular affirmative (form) says
there are things that belong to both the subject class and the predicate class.
In a two-circle system, this information is entered by *inserting* an X in the
region common to the two circles.   But in a three-circle system, each circle
has two regions in common with each of the other circles.   Where, then,
does the X go?   The answer is that it goes on the boundary line of the two
regions.   Thus, for 'Some *M* are *P*', we have

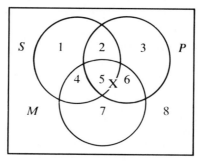

Some *M* are *P*: region 5 is not empty *or* region 6 is not empty, or, for
short, #5 ≠ 0 *or* #6 ≠ 0

Here are two examples of how to apply the diagram rule.   To save
time we construct only the diagrams for the pairs of premisses.   (*Caution*:
whenever there is one universal premiss and one particular premiss, always
enter the information from the universal first.)

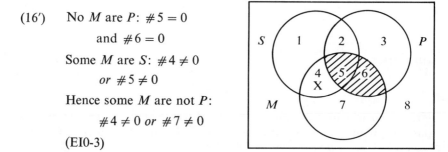

(16′)   No *M* are *P*: #5 = 0

   and #6 = 0

Some *M* are *S*: #4 ≠ 0

   or #5 ≠ 0

Hence some *M* are not *P*:

   #4 ≠ 0 *or* #7 ≠ 0

(EIO-3)

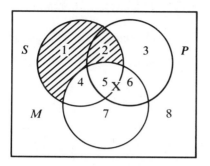

(17')   Some *M* are *P*: #5 ≠ 0 *or* #6 ≠ 0

All *S* are *M*: #1 = 0 and #2 = 0

Hence some *S* are *P*: #2 ≠ 0 *or* #5 ≠ 0

(IAI-1)

Notice that in the diagram for (16') the X is placed *within* region 4, because region 5 has already been declared empty by the universal premiss. Since the conclusion says that region 4 is not empty *or* region 7 is not empty, (16') is valid: the information contained in its conclusion does not go beyond that shown in the diagram of its premisses.   On the other hand, in (17') the combined effect of the two premisses is to leave the X on the boundary between regions 5 and 6.   But the conclusion would place the X on the boundary between regions 2 and 5 (and since the universal premiss declares region 2 empty, the conclusion would then place the X *within* region 5).   This information is not contained in the diagram of the premisses.   Hence (17') is *invalid*, as is confirmed by

(17)   Some Europeans are Belgians.

All Italians are Europeans.

Therefore some Italians are Belgians.

TWO INTERPRETATIONS OF THE LOGIC OF CATEGORICAL SENTENCES

As observed earlier, immediate inferences—with some exceptions—are valid by the Venn Diagram test iff they are valid by the TL test.   The same is true—again with exceptions—of syllogistic inferences.   In general, the choice between the two tests is a matter of convenience.   The exceptions, however, are quite important, for they point to a problem in interpreting

TL sentence forms.   We conclude this survey with comments on the exceptions and on the problem of interpretation.

In immediate inference, TL admits as a valid form of argument

D   U   U   U

(18′)   All *S* are *P*   Therefore *some P* are *S*

This form is called "conversion by limitation," as distinguished from simple conversion (which in the case of 'All *S* are *P*' is invalid), because the *P*-term is limited in the conclusion by putting 'some' for 'all'.   As a result, no term is distributed in the conclusion that was not distributed in the premiss; hence (18′), according to TL, is valid.

But if we apply the diagram rule to (18′), we obtain

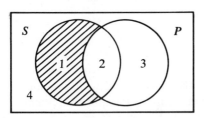   All *S* are *P*

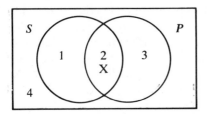   Some *P* are *S*

Clearly, (18′) violates the diagram rule.   And it does so not because the diagram of the conclusion omits the shading out of region 1—the diagram of a conclusion may contain less information than or the same information as the diagram of the premiss—but because it includes an X in region 2. It thus contains information not present in the diagram of the premiss.

Similarly, TL accepts AAI-1 and the other "weakened" syllogistic forms as valid.   But on the diagram rule these are all invalid, because the diagrams of the particular conclusions contain information—the presence of an X—not contained in the diagrams of the premisses.

These divergences are not incidental.   They have their source in two differing interpretations of categorical sentences: the *traditional* and the *modern*.   The traditional interpretation finds expression in the TL rules for validity, the modern in the Venn Diagram procedure.

According to the traditional, or *existential*, view, all categorical sentences are to be construed as asserting the existence of members of the class denoted by the subject term.   On this interpretation, all classes referred to by subject terms have members, and the empty class is not considered. According to the modern, or *hypothetical*, view, however, only particular sentences make existence claims; universal sentences do not.   On this interpretation, the empty class is admitted into consideration.   (An example of an expression denoting the empty class is 'all women ex-Presidents of the United States'.)

The two interpretations may be summarized as follows:

	Traditional	Modern
A	All *S* are *P*, and there are *S*s	If anything is *S*, then it is *P* (and there may or may not be any *S*s)
E	No *S* are *P*, and there are *S*s	If anything is *S*, then it is not *P* (and there may or may not be any *S*s)
I	There is at least one thing that belongs to *S* and belongs to *P*	Same as the traditional
O	There is at least one thing that belongs to *S* and does not belong to *P*	Same as the traditional

Notice that on the modern, or hypothetical, interpretation, universal sentence forms ('All *S* are *P*') are regarded as if-then sentence forms ('If anything is *S*, then it is *P*').

It is a simple matter to "traditionalize" the Venn Diagrams—that is, to adapt them to the existential interpretation.   We need only insert an X in the subject circles of diagrams of universal premises.   The divergences then disappear, and conversion by limitation and the weakened syllogistic forms pass the diagram test:

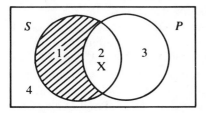
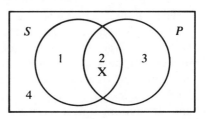

All *S* are *P*: #1 = 0, and #1 ≠ 0   Some *P* are *S*: #2 ≠ 0
        or #2 ≠ 0

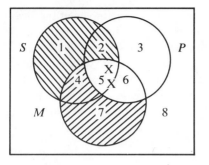

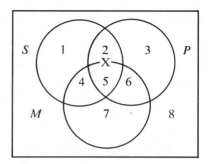

All *M* are *P*: #4 = 0 and #7 = 0,   Some *S* are *P*: #2 ≠ 0 or #5 ≠ 0
   and #   4 or 5 or 6 or 7 ≠ 0

All *S* are *M*: #1 = 0 and #2 = 0,
   and #   1 or 2 or 4 or 5 ≠ 0

But the notion of an empty class is not to be given up lightly.   It plays a major role not only in modern mathematics and logic, but even in daily life.   We often make negative existential statements, such as "There are no centaurs."   Still more often, we have occasion to refer to a possibly empty class, as when we say, "If anyone fails to complete the work of the course, he or she will not receive credit."

It therefore seems preferable to "modernize" TL—that is, to admit the empty class and to construe universal sentences as not necessarily asserting the existence of members of their subject classes.   Conversion by limitation is rejected, and the weakened syllogistic forms are banned as invalid.   The ban is made official by adding to the TL rules a Rule 5:

> No syllogism is valid if it has two universal premisses and a particular conclusion.

Notice that by adding Rule 5, we demote 4b from an original rule to a derived one.   For AAO-3, the only *invalid* form for which we need the services of 4b as an independent rule, is now blocked by Rule 5.

In conclusion, we note the drastic effect that the modernization of TL has on the Traditional Square of Opposition.   First, subalternation, the inference from A to I and from E to O, is barred.   Second, A and E may now both be true and hence are no longer contraries.   (According to modern logic, if there are no *S*s, then both 'If anything is *S*, then it is *P*' and 'If anything is *S*, it is not *P*' count as true.)   Third, I and O may both be false (again if there are no *S*s) and thus are no longer subcontraries. The sole survivors are the diagonals, the contradictories:

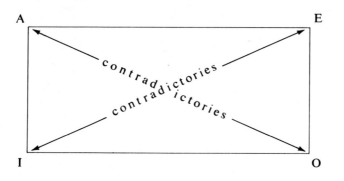

This may seem an exorbitant admission fee to pay for the empty class. But modern logic and mathematics find it worth the price.   And logic is entitled to some little ironies of its own.

Solutions

2.1. *a*, *c*, and *d* contain arguments.

2.2. *a* and *c* are narratives; *b*, *d*, *e*, and *f* contain arguments. Thus in *b*, the premisses may be stated as follows:

If we can go fusion for Lindsay, there's a contest.

If we can't go fusion for Lindsay, there's no contest.

If we go independent or take a Democrat, we can't go fusion for Lindsay.

The conclusion then is:

If we go independent or take a Democrat, there's no contest.

Notice that the third premiss listed above does not actually appear in the quoted passage. As we shall see, premisses and even conclusions often are implicit rather than explicit, and must therefore be supplied if the argument is to be set forth in full.

4.1. *a*, *d*, *g*, and *j* are valid deductive arguments.

4.2. *a*, *c*, *f*, *g*, and *h* are valid; *a*, *f*, and, some would say, *h* are sound.

4.3. *a*, *b*, and *e* are true; *c* and *d* are false.

4.5. Argument *b* in 2.2 is deductive and valid.

4.6. *Proofs*:

    a. By the commonsense criterion of validity, a valid deductive argument cannot, if its premisses are all true, have a false conclusion. But a sound deductive argument, by definition, is simply a valid deductive argument with all true premisses. Therefore a sound deductive argument cannot have a false conclusion.

b. By the commonsense criterion of validity, a valid deductive argument cannot, if its premisses are all true, have a false conclusion. Hence if a valid deductive argument does have a false conclusion, then its premisses cannot all be true—that is, at least one of them must be false.

5.1. *a*, *b*, *c*, and *e* are incorrect. When corrected, they should read:

a. The argument is *unsound* because its first premiss is *false*.

b. Since the first premiss is *false*, the argument, though valid, is *unsound*.

c. The argument is *valid* because if the premisses were all true, the conclusion would have to be true.

e. The conclusion is *true*; but since the first premiss is false, the argument is unsound.

6.1. Answers are suggested here for *a*, *c*, and *d*.

a. *First premiss:* If Thieu implements the Paris agreements, he loses.
Second premiss: If Thieu does not implement the agreements, he loses.
Third premiss (supplied): Either Thieu implements the agreements or he does not.
Conclusion (supplied): Therefore Thieu loses.

c. This passage may be viewed as containing two linked arguments:
First premiss: If the truth '*God is to be worshipped*' is innate, then the ideas of *God* and *worship* are innate.
Second premiss (supplied): If an idea is innate, then it must be in the understanding of children and be a character stamped on the mind in its first original.
Third premiss: The idea of *worship* is not in the understanding of children, and so forth (as shown by the fact that few grown persons, even, have a clear and distinct notion of it).
First conclusion (supplied): Therefore the idea of *worship* is not innate. (This conclusion follows from premisses two and three.)
Second conclusion: Therefore the truth '*God is to be worshipped*' is not innate. (This follows from premiss one and conclusion one.)

d. This passage amounts to the following:
Premiss: I am the first American President ever to pay a state visit to Indonesia.
Conclusion: Therefore the next American President to pay a state visit to Indonesia will not be the first one.

6.2. While the argument in passage *b* is clearly intended as nondeductive, the arguments contained in *a*, *c*, and *d* may be regarded as deductive. These deductive arguments are all valid, and *d* is obviously sound. The question of the soundness of *a* and *c* we leave to experts in the appropriate fields.

11.1. Examples *a* and *k* are valid. The others involve or commit the fallacies of

b. Equivocation (on the term 'friendly').

c. Division.

d. Argument *ad hominem*.

e. *Ignoratio elenchi.*

f. *Petitio principii* (circular).

g. Many questions.

h. Composition.

i. Inconsistent premisses.

j. Arguments *ad verecundiam* and *ad ignorantiam*.

      l.   Equivocation (on the term 'money': J. S. Mill distinguishes money as the amount of capital seeking investment and money as the amount of the circulating medium).

      m.   An answer for *m* is postponed; see the solution to Exercise 27.3*f*.

11.2. Quotation *g* describes a fallacy in belief only. The others (except *f*, see below) involve fallacies in argument only, as follows:

      a.   Equivocation (on the term 'know ').

      b.   *Petitio principii.*

      c.   Argument *ad baculum.*

      d.   Equivocation (on the term 'criminal actions').

      e.   Division.

      f.   Accident.   But doesn't the author, in illustrating the fallacy (in argument) of accident, himself commit a *fallacy in belief* when he writes of "races" and the extent to which they are "fit" for freedom?

      h.   Here Whately, like Homer, nodded.   Can you identify the fallacy?

15.1. They may all be taken as definitions except *c*, *f*, *j*, and *k*. For example:

      a.   *Definiendum:* 'sound deductive argument'.
           Definiens: 'valid argument with all true premisses'.

      b.   *Definiendum:* 'definition'.
           Definiens: 'any explanation of the meaning or use of a word or phrase'.

      g.   *Definiendum:* 'ontology'.
           Definiens: 'the study of what there is'.

15.2.   a.   Explicative.

      b.   Borderline lexical-explicative.

      d.   Stipulative.

      e.   Stipulative.

      g.   Lexical (and perhaps persuasive).

      h.   Theoretical-explicative.

      i.   Stipulative.

15.3.   a.   Lexical.

      b.   Stipulative.

      c.   Stipulative (notice the change in stipulation from *b* to *c*).

      d.   Theoretical and explicative.

      e.   Stipulative.

      f.   Explicative.

      g.   Persuasive (perhaps intended as explicative).

      h.   Persuasive.

      i.   Stipulative.

      j.   Explicative.

      k.   Theoretical.

      l.   Lexical.

      m.   Explicative.

      n.   Lexical.

      o.   Explicative-theoretical.

      p.   Stipulative.

      q.   Persuasive (?).

15.6.   a.   Contextual.

      b.   Definition 1 is circular, hence bad in this instance.
           Definition 2 is a standard theoretical definition.

      c.   An open question.

      d.   Definition 1 is: 'an extended fictional narrative in prose'.
           Definition 2 is Northrop Frye's.
           Definition 3 is Professor Levine's—a modification of the Frye definition with emphasis on character portrayal and "the related conventions of realism." Professor Levine's definition seems intended as an

explicative one (and thus like all such definitions has in it a stipulative element).   On the other hand, his comment that the qualities he has in mind are "perhaps never uniformly present in any single novel" strongly suggests not so much a definition as a Wittgenstein-style description in terms of "family resemblances."

17.1.   *b, c, d,* and *f* are valid; *a* and *e* are invalid.

18.1.   The argument forms are:

    a.   If *P,* then *Q*
        Not-*Q*
        Therefore not-*P*

    b.   *P* or not-*Q*
        Q
        Therefore *P*

    c.   If *P,* then *Q*
        Therefore if not-*Q,* then not-*P*

    d.   If *P,* then *Q*
        If not-*P,* then not-*R*
        P or not-*P*
        Therefore *Q* or not-*R*

    e.   If *P,* then *Q*
        If *Q,* then *R*
        Therefore if *P,* then *R*

For *a* the corresponding conditional is

If [(if *P,* then *Q*) and not-*Q*], then not-*P,*

and another argument of the same form as *a* is

    If you understand Hume, you understand Kant.
    You do not understand Kant.
    Hence you do not understand Hume.

18.2.   The logical truths are *a, b, d, f,* and *g.*   An argument whose corresponding conditional is of the same form as *d* is

    The Democrats will name Johnson or they will name Walton.
    If they name Johnson, they will lose the election.
    If they name Walton, they will lose the election.
    Hence the Democrats will lose the election.

20.1.   *a, c, d, e,* and *f* are sentences normally used to make statements.

20.2.   The compounds are *a, d, e,* and possibly *f.*   The truth-functional compounds are *a* and *e.*

21.2.   a.

P	*Q*	*P* ∨ *Q*	~(*P* ∨ *Q*)
T	T	T	F
T	F	T	F
F	T	T	F
F	F	F	T

21.3.   a.   Three different readings are

    P ∨ (~*Q* → *R*)
    P ∨ ~(*Q* → *R*)
    (*P* ∨ ~*Q*) → *R*

21.4.   a. *P* ∨ (~*Q* → *R*)
     b. *P* ∨ ~(*Q* → *R*)
     c. (*P* ∨ ~*Q*) → *R*

21.5.   The tables for '*Q* ∨ *P*' and '*P* ∨ *Q*' are the same, and so are the tables for '*Q* & *P*' and '*P* & *Q*' (that is, the operations of disjunction and conjunction are commutative). But the tables for '$Q \rightarrow P$' and '$P \rightarrow Q$' are different:

P	Q		$P \rightarrow Q$		$Q \rightarrow P$
T	T		T		T
T	F		F		T
F	T		T		F
F	F		T		T

21.6. The tables are the same.

22.1. The occurrences in *a*, *c*, and *e* are truth-functional. The corresponding symbolic expressions are:

    a. *P* & *Q*

    c. $\sim(P \lor Q)$

    e. *P* alt *Q*   (the strong 'or', obviously)

22.2.   a. $\sim P \rightarrow \sim W$

    b. $(P \,\&\, C) \rightarrow W$

    c. $R \rightarrow (J \rightarrow \sim W)$

    d. $(F \,\&\, J) \rightarrow I$

22.3.   a. False.

    b. True.

    c. False.

    d. True.

22.4.   a. $E \rightarrow G$

    b. $G \rightarrow C$ (or, $\sim C \rightarrow \sim G$)

    c. $E \leftrightarrow G$

    d. $(C \,\&\, E) \leftrightarrow G$

    e. $G \rightarrow E$ (or, $\sim E \rightarrow \sim G$)

    f. $\sim E \rightarrow \sim G$ (or, $G \rightarrow E$)

    g. $\sim E \rightarrow \sim G$ (or, $G \rightarrow E$)

Notice that, taken truth-functionally, *e*, *f*, and *g* all say the same thing: that for Rogers to graduate it is necessary that he have 120 credits, that if he doesn't earn 120 credits he won't graduate, that he won't graduate without 120 credits—in short, that earning 120 credits is a necessary condition for Rogers to graduate.

23.1. The SL expressions are *a*, *c*, *e*, and *f*.

23.2. The SL sentence forms are *b*, *c*, *e*, *g*, and *h*.

23.3. An answer for *b* would be, "If the Democrats adopt a good program, then, if they name Canavan, they will win."

23.4.   a. $(P \,\&\, Q) \lor \sim R$

    b. $\sim P \rightarrow (Q \lor R)$

    c. $(P \lor Q) \leftrightarrow (R \,\&\, S)$

    d. $P \rightarrow [(Q \,\&\, R) \rightarrow S]$

    e. $[(P \,\&\, \sim Q) \rightarrow R] \lor (\sim R \rightarrow S)$

    f. $(\sim P \rightarrow \sim Q) \,\&\, [\sim Q \rightarrow (R \rightarrow S)]$

    g. $P \rightarrow Q$; alternatively, '$\sim Q \rightarrow \sim P$'—where '*P*' is put for 'Perkins will get his Ph.D' and '*Q*' for 'His dissertation is approved'.

    h. $P \rightarrow [Q \lor (R \,\&\, S)]$; alternatively, '$\sim [Q \lor (R \,\&\, S)] \rightarrow \sim P$'

24.1.   a.

P	Q		$Q \rightarrow (Q \rightarrow P)$					
T	T		T	T	T	T	T	The major connective is the first
T	F		F	T	F	T	T	occurrence of '$\rightarrow$'.
F	T		T	F	T	F	F	
F	F		F	T	F	T	F	

d.

P	Q	R	$[P \to (Q \to R)] \to (P \to R)$	
T	T	T	T T T T T T T T	The major connective
T	T	F	T F T F F T T F F	is the third occurrence
T	F	T	T T F T T T T T T	of ' → '.
T	F	F	T T F T F F T F F	
F	T	T	F T T T T T F T T	
F	T	F	F T T F F T F T F	
F	F	T	F T F T T T F T T	
F	F	F	F T F T F T F T F	

e. $(P \leftrightarrow Q) \& (P \& \sim Q)$

T T T	F	T	F	FT	The major connective is the
T F F	F	T T	TF		first occurrence of ' & '.
F F T	F	F F	FT		
F T F	F	F F	TF		

f. $[P \& (P \to Q)] \to Q$

T T T T T	T T	The major connective is the
T F T F F	T F	second occurrence of ' → '.
F F F T T	T T	
F F F T F	T F	

24.2. The compounds *b, d, e, f, g, i, l* are true.

24.3. a.

P	Q	R
T	T	T
T	T	F
T	F	T

b.

P	Q	R
T	T	T
T	F	T
T	F	F

c.

P	Q
T	F
F	T
F	F

d.

P	Q	R
T	F	T
T	F	F
F	T	F
F	F	T
F	F	F

e.

P	Q	R
T	T	T
T	T	F
T	F	T
T	F	F
F	T	T
F	T	F
F	F	T
F	F	F

f.

P	Q	R
T	T	T
T	T	F
T	F	F
F	T	T
F	T	F
F	F	T
F	F	F

g.

P	Q	R
T	T	T
T	T	F
T	F	T
T	F	F
F	T	T
F	T	F
F	F	T
F	F	F

h.

P	Q	R	S
T	F	T	T
T	F	F	T
T	T	T	F
T	F	T	F
T	F	F	F
F	T	T	F
F	F	T	F

24.4. The desired SL sentence forms are

   a. $\sim(\sim P \vee \sim Q)$
   b. $\sim P \vee Q$
   c. $\sim(\sim P \vee \sim Q) \vee \sim(P \vee Q)$

25.1. The expressions *a*, *d*, and *f* are SL argument forms; *b*, *e*, and *g* are *not* sequences of SL sentence forms, and *c* does *not* yield an argument when appropriate substitutions are made.

25.2. For *a*, a substitution instance would be the following argument:

   If Quincy graduates, she has at least 120 credits.
   She has at least 120 credits.
   Therefore she graduates.

26.1. *a*, *e*, and *g* are tautologies; *b* and *f* are contradictions; *c*, *d*, and *h* are contingent sentence forms.

26.2.   a. If *A* and *A* ↔ *B* are tautologies, so is *B*.

     Proof. Suppose *B* is not a tautology. Then there is some truth-table line on which *A*, a tautology, takes T and *B* takes F. But if *A* takes T and *B* takes F, then *A* ↔ *B* must take F. This contradicts the assumption that *A* ↔ *B* is a tautology. Hence *B* must be a tautology.

    b. If *A* & *B* is a tautology, so are *A* and *B*.

     Proof. A conjunction takes the truth-value T iff both conjuncts take T. But *A* & *B*, as a tautology, takes T on all lines of the truth table. Hence its conjuncts, *A* and *B*, take T on all lines—that is, *A* and *B* are tautologies.

27.1. *a*, *g*, and *i* are invalid; the others are valid.

27.2. The desired SL argument forms are

    a. $P \rightarrow Q$
        Q
        Therefore P *Invalid*
    b. $P \rightarrow Q$
        Therefore $\sim Q \rightarrow \sim P$ *Valid*
    c. $P \rightarrow Q$
        $Q \rightarrow R$
        Therefore $P \rightarrow R$ *Valid*
    d. $(P \mathbin{\&} Q) \rightarrow R$
        Therefore $P \rightarrow (Q \rightarrow R)$ *Valid*
    e. $\sim(P \mathbin{\&} Q) \rightarrow \sim R$
        $P \rightarrow Q$
        Therefore $P \rightarrow R$ *Invalid*
    f. $(P \leftrightarrow Q) \rightarrow (P \leftrightarrow R)$
        $Q \rightarrow P$
        Therefore $P \rightarrow R$ *Invalid*

27.3. Answers are suggested for *c* and *f*.

    c. There are two arguments here. The first is one that Mr. Palme wishes to rebut; the second is the argument he uses to rebut the first. The first one may be put as follows:

    Premiss: The United States sends an ambassador to Sweden iff it approves of the Swedish Government.
    Premiss: The United States is not sending an ambassador to Sweden.
    Conclusion: Therefore the United States does not approve of the Swedish Government.

The SL argument form is

    $P \leftrightarrow Q$
    $\sim P$
    Therefore $\sim Q$,

and it is valid. The second argument attacks the first premiss of the first argument, and may be stated as follows:

    Premiss: If the United States sends an ambassador iff it approves of the government of the country, then if it sends an ambassador it approves of the government of the country.
    Premiss: But the United States sends ambassadors to countries of whose governments it does not approve.
    Conclusion: Therefore it is not the case that the United States sends an ambassador iff it approves of the government of the country.

Here the SL argument form is

    $(P \leftrightarrow Q) \rightarrow (P \rightarrow Q)$
    $P \mathbin{\&} \sim Q$
    Therefore $\sim(P \leftrightarrow Q)$,

and it too is valid.

    f. Yossarian's situation, it seems, is described by this argument:

    Premiss: Yossarian is grounded iff both he is crazy and he asks to be grounded.
    Premiss: If he keeps flying (i.e., if he doesn't ask to be grounded), he is crazy.
    Premiss: If he asks to be grounded, he is not crazy.
    Conclusion: Therefore, if Yossarian asks to be grounded, he won't be (because then he isn't crazy); and if he doesn't ask to be grounded, he won't be (because then he hasn't asked).

If we take this conclusion as a premiss and add the obvious premiss

Either Yossarian asks to be grounded or he doesn't

we then obtain the conclusion

Yossarian won't be grounded.

The SL argument forms that figure here are

$$P \leftrightarrow (Q \,\&\, R)$$
$$\left. \begin{array}{l} \sim R \to Q \\ R \to \sim Q \end{array} \right\} \quad \text{or} \quad R \leftrightarrow \sim Q$$

Therefore $(R \to \sim P) \,\&\, (\sim R \to \sim P)$

But $R \lor \sim R$

Therefore $\sim P$

Both SL argument forms are valid. So what is involved in *Catch 22* is not a fallacy, but without doubt, a predicament.

27.4. a. Equivalent.
 b. Equivalent.
 c. Not equivalent.
 d. Equivalent.
 e. Not equivalent.

28.1. *a, g, i,* and *m* are invalid; the others are all valid. Here are the trees for *a, j,* and *n,* and a note on *o.*

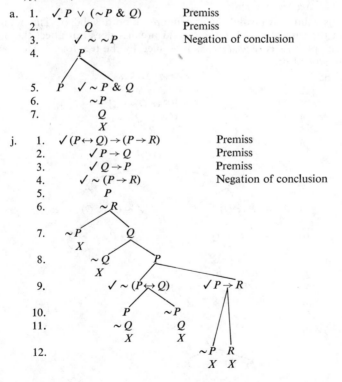

a. 1. $\checkmark P \lor (\sim P \,\&\, Q)$ Premiss
 2. Q Premiss
 3. $\checkmark \sim \sim P$ Negation of conclusion
 4. P

 5. $P \quad \checkmark \sim P \,\&\, Q$
 6. $\sim P$
 7. Q
      X

j. 1. $\checkmark (P \leftrightarrow Q) \to (P \to R)$ Premiss
 2. $\checkmark P \to Q$ Premiss
 3. $\checkmark Q \to P$ Premiss
 4. $\checkmark \sim (P \to R)$ Negation of conclusion
 5. P
 6. $\sim R$

 7. $\sim P \quad\quad Q$
      X
 8. $\sim Q \quad\quad P$
      X
 9. $\checkmark \sim (P \leftrightarrow Q) \quad\quad \checkmark P \to R$
 10. $P \quad\quad \sim P$
 11. $\sim Q \quad\quad Q$
      X $\quad\quad$ X
 12. $\sim P \quad R$
      X $\quad$ X

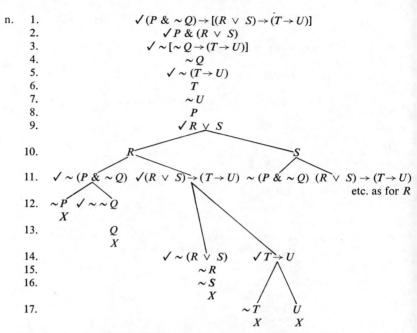

n. 1. $\checkmark(P\ \&\ \sim Q)\to[(R\ \vee\ S)\to(T\to U)]$
    2. $\checkmark P\ \&\ (R\ \vee\ S)$
    3. $\checkmark\sim[\sim Q\to(T\to U)]$
    4. $\sim Q$
    5. $\checkmark\sim(T\to U)$
    6. T
    7. $\sim U$
    8. P
    9. $\checkmark R\ \vee\ S$

    10. R S

    11. $\checkmark\sim(P\ \&\ \sim Q)$ $\checkmark(R\ \vee\ S)\to(T\to U)$ $\sim(P\ \&\ \sim Q)$ $(R\ \vee\ S)\to(T\to U)$
                                                                            etc. as for R

    12. $\sim P$ $\checkmark\sim\sim Q$
         X

    13. Q
                     X

    14. $\checkmark\sim(R\ \vee\ S)$ $\checkmark T\to U$
    15. $\sim R$
    16. $\sim S$
                     X

    17. $\sim T$ U
                                     X X

o. Notice that o, though valid, has no substitution instance that is a *sound*
    argument. The conjunction of its premises is a contradiction, as the
    reader may verify.

28.2. *a* is valid, *b* is invalid.   Yet *c* and *d* are both valid.   The point is that
    in the case of *c* and *d*, the second premiss does not affect the outcome.
    The premiss is *redundant*, as is verified by the tree for *e*. Here are trees
    for *b* and *d*:

b. 1. $\checkmark(P\ \&\ Q)\to R$
    2. $\checkmark P\to S$
    3. $\checkmark\sim[(S\ \&\ Q)\to R]$
    4. $\checkmark S\ \&\ Q$
    5. $\sim R$
    6. S
    7. Q

    8. $\sim P$ S

    9. $\checkmark\sim(P\ \&\ Q)$ R $\checkmark\sim(P\ \&\ Q)$ R
                              X X
    10. $\sim P$ $\sim Q$ $\sim P$ $\sim Q$
                    X X

d. 1. $\checkmark(P\to Q)\to R$
    2. $P\to S$
    3. $\checkmark\sim[(S\ \&\ Q)\to R]$
    4. $\checkmark S\ \&\ Q$
    5. $\sim R$
    6. S
    7. Q

    8. $\checkmark\sim(P\to Q)$ R
                                     X

9. P
        $\sim Q$
         X

Notice that in *d* all paths close *before* the information contained in premiss '$P \to S$' is entered.

28.3. All are tautologies except *c*, *e*, *h*, and *i*. Trees are given for *c* and *h*. For *j*, define '*A & B*' as '$\sim(A \to \sim B)$', and then proceed with the tree.

c.   1. ✓ $\sim[(P \to \sim P) \to P]$
    2.   ✓ $P \to \sim P$
    3. $\sim P$

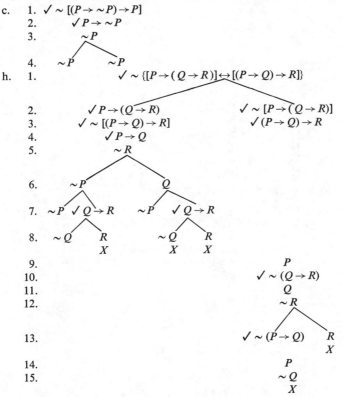

12. $\sim I$ $\sim I$
13. $\sim D$ $\sim D$
       X X Premiss '$P \to Q$' is not needed

g. 1. $\checkmark [(P \vee Q) \mathbin{\&} (R \vee S)] \to T$
    2. $\sim Q$
    3. $\sim S$
    4. $\checkmark \sim [(P \mathbin{\&} R) \to T]$ Negation of conclusion
    5. $\checkmark P \mathbin{\&} R$
    6. $\sim T$
    7. P
    8. R

    9. $\checkmark \sim [(P \vee Q) \mathbin{\&} (R \vee S)]$ T
                                                                        X
    10. $\checkmark \sim (P \vee Q)$
    11. $\sim P$
    12. $\sim Q$
    13. X $\checkmark \sim (R \vee S)$
    14. $\sim R$
    15. $\sim S$
                                           X

29.1. Answers are given for a, c, and d.

a. 1. $P \to Q$
    2. $R \vee \sim Q$
    3. $\sim R$
    4. $\sim Q$ From steps 2 and 3, by Rule (c)
    5. $\sim P$ From steps 1 and 4, by Rule (b)

c. 1. $P \vee (Q \to R)$
    2. $Q \vee \sim P$
    3. $\sim Q$
    4. $\sim P$ 2, 3 (c)
    5. $Q \to R$ 1, 4 (c)

d. 1. $R \to Q$
    2. $Q \to P$
    3. $P \to S$
    4. $\sim S$
    5. $\sim P$ 3, 4 (b)
    6. $R \to P$ 1, 2 (a)
    7. $\sim R$ 6, 5 (b)

31.1.   a.   {1}   1. $(Q \vee R) \to P$ Premiss
                  {2}   2. $\sim R \to S$ Premiss
                  {3}   3. $\sim S$ Premiss
               {2, 3}   4. $\sim \sim R$ 2, 3 MT
               {2, 3}   5. R 4 DN
               {2, 3}   6. $R \vee Q$ 5 Add.
               {2, 3}   7. $Q \vee R$ 6 Com.
            {1, 2, 3}   8. P 1, 7 MP

            b.   {1}   1. $(P \mathbin{\&} Q) \to R$ Premiss
                  {2}   2. $S \to Q$ Premiss
                  {3}   3. $P \vee \sim S$ Premiss
                  {4}   4. S Premiss
               {2, 4}   5. Q 2, 4 MP
                  {3}   6. $\sim S \vee P$ 3 Com.
                  {4}   7. $\sim \sim S$ 4 DN

{3, 4}	8.	P	6, 7 DS
{2, 3, 4}	9.	$P \& Q$	8, 5 Adj.
{1, 2, 3, 4}	10.	R	1, 9 MP

c.
{1}	1.	$P \leftrightarrow Q$	Premiss
{2}	2.	$\sim P$	Premiss
{3}	3.	$Q \vee R$	Premiss
{4}	4.	$R \to S$	Premiss
{1}	5.	$(P \to Q) \& (Q \to P)$	1 Bicon.
{1}	6.	$Q \to P$	5 Com., Simp.
{1, 2}	7.	$\sim Q$	6, 2 MT
{1, 2, 3}	8.	R	7, 3 DS
{1, 2, 3, 4}	9.	S	4, 8 MP

d.
{1}	1.	$(P \vee Q) \to R$	Premiss
{2}	2.	$(Q \vee \sim R) \to S$	Premiss
{3}	3.	$\sim R \vee \sim S$	Premiss
{1}	4.	$\sim R \to \sim (P \vee Q)$	1 Trans.
{2}	5.	$\sim S \to \sim (Q \vee \sim R)$	2 Trans.
{1, 2}	6.	$[\sim R \to \sim (P \vee Q)] \&$ $[\sim S \to \sim (Q \vee \sim R)]$	4, 5 Adj.
{1, 2, 3}	7.	$\sim (P \vee Q) \vee \sim (Q \vee \sim R)$	3, 6 CD
{1, 2, 3}	8.	$(\sim P \& \sim Q) \vee (\sim Q \& \sim \sim R)$	7 DeM
{1, 2, 3}	9.	$(\sim P \& \sim Q) \vee (\sim Q \& R)$	8 DN
{1, 2, 3}	10.	$(\sim Q \& \sim P) \vee (\sim Q \& R)$	9 Com.
{1, 2, 3}	11.	$\sim Q \& (\sim P \vee R)$	10 Dist.
{1, 2, 3}	12.	$\sim Q \& (P \to R)$	11 Con.

31.2. a.
{1}	1.	$(P \& Q) \to R$	Premiss
{2}	2.	$\sim P \vee Q$	Premiss
{3}	3.	P	Premiss
{3}	4.	$\sim \sim P$	3 DN
{2, 3}	5.	Q	2, 4 DS
{2, 3}	6.	$P \& Q$	3, 5 Adj.
{1, 2, 3}	7.	R	1, 6 MP

b.
{1}	1.	$(P \vee Q) \to R$	Premiss
{2}	2.	$P \vee S$	Premiss
{3}	3.	$\sim S$	Premiss
{2}	4.	$S \vee P$	2 Com.
{2, 3}	5.	P	4, 3 DS
{2, 3}	6.	$P \vee Q$	5 Add.
{1, 2, 3}	7.	R	1, 6 MP

c.
{1}	1.	$P \to Q$	Premiss
{2}	2.	$R \to S$	Premiss
{3}	3.	$(Q \vee S) \to T$	Premiss
{4}	4.	$P \vee R$	Premiss
{1, 2}	5.	$(P \to Q) \& (R \to S)$	1, 2 Adj.
{1, 2, 4}	6.	$Q \vee S$	5, 4 CD
{1, 2, 3, 4}	7.	T	3, 6 MP

d.
{1}	1.	$P \to R$	Premiss
{2}	2.	$Q \to \sim R$	Premiss
{3}	3.	$Q \vee S$	Premiss
{4}	4.	$S \to \sim P$	Premiss
{1}	5.	$\sim R \to \sim P$	1 Trans.
{1, 2}	6.	$Q \to \sim P$	2, 5 HS
{1, 2, 4}	7.	$(Q \to \sim P) \& (S \to \sim P)$	6, 4 Adj.
{1, 2, 3, 4}	8.	$\sim P \vee \sim P$	7, 3 CD
{1, 2, 3, 4}	9.	$\sim P$	8 Taut.

e. {1}   1. $P \to (Q \ \& \ R)$ Premiss
    {2}   2. $Q \to S$ Premiss
    {3}   3. $\sim S$ Premiss
    {2, 3}   4. $\sim Q$ 2, 3 MT
    {2, 3}   5. $\sim Q \ \lor \ \sim R$ 4 Add.
    {2, 3}   6. $\sim (Q \ \& \ R)$ 5 DeM
    {1, 2, 3} 7. $\sim P$ 1, 6 MT
f. {1}   1. $P \to Q$ Premiss
    {2}   2. $R \to S$ Premiss
    {3}   3. $\sim P \to T$ Premiss
    {4}   4. $\sim T$ Premiss
    {3, 4}   5. $\sim \sim P$ 3, 4 MT
    {3, 4}   6. P 5 DN
    {1, 3, 4} 7. Q 1, 6 MP
    {1, 3, 4} 8. $Q \ \lor \ S$ 7 Add.

(Note that premiss 2 is not required for the derivation.)

g. {1}   1. $P \to (Q \ \lor \ R)$ Premiss
    {2}   2. $\sim P \to S$ Premiss
    {3}   3. $\sim T \to \sim S$ Premiss
    {4}   4. $\sim T \ \lor \ U$ Premiss
    {5}   5. $\sim U$ Premiss
    {4, 5}   6. $\sim T$ 4, 5 DS
    {3, 4, 5} 7. $\sim S$ 3, 6 MP
    {2, 3, 4, 5} 8. $\sim \sim P$ 2, 7 MT
    {2, 3, 4, 5} 9. P 8 DN
    {1, 2, 3, 4, 5} 10. $Q \ \lor \ R$ 1, 9 MP
h. {1}   1. $P \to (Q \to R)$ Premiss
    {2}   2. $\sim Q \to \sim S$ Premiss
    {3}   3. $S \ \lor \ T$ Premiss
    {4}   4. $\sim T \ \lor \ U$ Premiss
    {5}   5. $\sim U$ Premiss
    {4, 5}   6. $\sim T$ 4, 5 DS
    {3, 4, 5} 7. S 3, 6 DS
    {3, 4, 5} 8. $\sim \sim S$ 7 DN
    {2, 3, 4, 5} 9. $\sim \sim Q$ 2, 8 MT
    {2, 3, 4, 5} 10. Q 9 DN
    {1}   11. $(P \ \& \ Q) \to R$ 1 Exp.
    {1}   12. $(Q \ \& \ P) \to R$ 11 Com.
    {1}   13. $Q \to (P \to R)$ 12 Exp.
    {1, 2, 3, 4, 5} 14. $P \to R$ 13, 10 MP

31.3. Answers are given for *b*, *c*, and *e*.

b. {1}   1. $P \to (\sim Q \to R)$ Premiss
    {2}   2. P Premiss
    {3}   3. $\sim R$ Premiss / $\therefore \ Q$
    {1, 2}   4. $\sim Q \to R$ 1, 2 MP
    {1, 2, 3} 5. $\sim \sim Q$ 4, 3 MT
    {1, 2, 3} 6. Q 5 DN
c. {1}   1. $P \to (Q \ \& \ R)$ Premiss
    {2}   2. $R \to S$ Premiss
    {3}   3. $\sim S$ Premiss / $\therefore \ \sim P$
    {2, 3}   4. $\sim R$ 2, 3 MT
    {2, 3}   5. $\sim R \ \lor \ \sim Q$ 4 Add.
    {2, 3}   6. $\sim Q \ \lor \ \sim R$ 5 Com.
    {2, 3}   7. $\sim (Q \ \& \ R)$ 6 DeM
    {1}   8. $\sim (Q \ \& \ R) \to \sim P$ 1 Trans.
    {1, 2, 3} 9. $\sim P$ 8, 7 MP

e.

{1}	1.	$(P \& Q) \to R$	Premiss
{2}	2.	$R \to (S \lor T)$	Premiss
{3}	3.	$P \to \sim S$	Premiss
{4}	4.	$\sim T$	Premiss / $\therefore P \to \sim Q$
{2}	5.	$\sim R \lor (S \lor T)$	2 Con.
{2}	6.	$(\sim R \lor S) \lor T$	5 Assoc.
{2}	7.	$T \lor (\sim R \lor S)$	6 Com.
{2, 4}	8.	$\sim R \lor S$	7, 4 DS
{1}	9.	$\sim R \to \sim (P \& Q)$	1 Trans.
{3}	10.	$\sim \sim S \to \sim P$	3 Trans.
{3}	11.	$S \to \sim P$	10 DN
{3}	12.	$\sim S \lor \sim P$	11 Con.
{3}	13.	$(\sim S \lor \sim P) \lor \sim Q$	12 Add.
{3}	14.	$\sim S \lor (\sim P \lor \sim Q)$	13 Assoc.
{3}	15.	$S \to (\sim P \lor \sim Q)$	14 Con.
{3}	16.	$S \to \sim (P \& Q)$	15 DeM
{1, 3}	17.	$[\sim R \to \sim (P \& Q)]$ & $[S \to \sim (P \& Q)]$	9, 16 Adj.
{1, 2, 3, 4}	18.	$\sim (P \& Q) \lor \sim (P \& Q)$	17, 8 CD
{1, 2, 3, 4}	19.	$\sim (P \& Q)$	18 Taut.
{1, 2, 3, 4}	20.	$\sim P \lor \sim Q$	19 DeM
{1, 2, 3, 4}	21.	$P \to \sim Q$	20 Con.

31.4. The arguments *a*, *b*, *c*, and *e* are valid; *d* is invalid. Derivations are given for the argument forms of *a*, *b*, *c*, and *e*, and a counterexample for the argument form of *d*.

a.

{1}	1.	$\sim P \to Q$	Premiss
{2}	2.	$Q \to R$	Premiss
{3}	3.	$P \to R$	Premiss
{4}	4.	$P \lor \sim P$	Supplied Premiss / $\therefore R$
{1, 2}	5.	$\sim P \to R$	1, 2 HS
{1, 2, 3}	6.	$(P \to R) \& (\sim P \to R)$	3, 5 Adj.
{1, 2, 3, 4}	7.	$R \lor R$	6, 4 CD
{1, 2, 3, 4}	8.	R	7 Taut.

b.

{1}	1.	$P \to (Q \& R)$	Premiss
{2}	2.	$(Q \& R) \to S$	Premiss
{3}	3.	$S \to T$	Premiss
{4}	4.	$T \to \sim P$	Premiss / $.. \sim P$
{1, 2}	5.	$P \to S$	1, 2 HS
{1, 2, 3}	6.	$P \to T$	5, 3 HS
{1, 2, 3, 4}	7.	$P \to \sim P$	6, 4 HS
{1, 2, 3, 4}	8.	$\sim P \lor \sim P$	7 Con.
{1, 2, 3, 4}	9.	$\sim P$	8 Taut.

c.

{1}	1.	$P \to (Q \to R)$	Premiss
{2}	2.	$Q \& S$	Premiss
{3}	3.	$\sim R$	Premiss / $\therefore \sim P$
{2}	4.	Q	4 Simp.
{2}	5.	$\sim \sim Q$	4 DN
{2, 3}	6.	$\sim \sim Q \& \sim R$	5, 3 Adj.
{2, 3}	7.	$\sim (\sim Q \lor R)$	6 DeM
{2, 3}	8.	$\sim (Q \to R)$	7 Con.
{1, 2, 3}	9.	$\sim P$	1, 8 MT

e.

{1}	1.	$P \to (Q \to R)$	Premiss
{2}	2.	$R \to (S \to T)$	Premiss
{3}	3.	$Q \lor U$	Premiss
{4}	4.	$U \to V$	Premiss
{5}	5.	$\sim V$	Premiss / $\therefore (P \& S) \to T$

$$\{4, 5\} \quad 6. \quad \sim U \qquad\qquad 4, 5 \text{ MT}$$
$$\{3, 4, 5\} \quad 7. \quad Q \qquad\qquad 3, 6 \text{ DS}$$
$$\{1\} \quad 8. \quad (P \& Q) \to R \qquad 1 \text{ Exp.}$$
$$\{1\} \quad 9. \quad (Q \& P) \to R \qquad 8 \text{ Com.}$$
$$\{1\} \quad 10. \quad Q \to (P \to R) \qquad 9 \text{ Exp.}$$
$$\{1, 3, 4, 5\} \quad 11. \quad P \to R \qquad\qquad 10, 7 \text{ MP}$$
$$\{1, 2, 3, 4, 5\} \quad 12. \quad P \to (S \to T) \qquad 11, 2 \text{ HS}$$
$$\{1, 2, 3, 4, 5\} \quad 13. \quad (P \& S) \to T \qquad 12 \text{ Exp.}$$

As to Exercise *d* in §31.4: the SL argument form is

$$P \to Q$$
$$P \to (R \& S)$$
$$S \to T$$
$$T \to Q$$

Therefore $Q \leftrightarrow S$

A counterexample would be

You are a philosophy major only if you are exposed to arguments.
If you are a philosophy major, you take history of philosophy and logic.
If you take logic, you engage in reasoning.
If you engage in reasoning, you are exposed to arguments.
Therefore you are exposed to arguments iff you take logic.

Now these premisses (on a reasonable view of things) are acknowledgedly true and the conclusion is obviously false. Thus we have a counterexample to the claim that the SL argument form for *d* is valid. Hence this argument form is *invalid*, and since for us all substitution instances of invalid SL argument forms are invalid, argument *d* is invalid.

Notice that if we *err* in interpreting the 'only if' in the first premiss of *d* and write it as

If inflation is arrested, confidence will be restored

we obtain a different argument from *d*, and one that happens to be valid. Its SL argument form is

$$Q \to P$$
$$P \to (R \& S)$$
$$S \to T$$
$$T \to Q$$

Therefore $Q \leftrightarrow S$

As the reader may verify, this is a valid form.

33.1.   a.

$\{1\}$	1.	$(S \& T) \to (R \lor \sim P)$	Premiss
$\{2\}$	2.	$P \to S$	Premiss
$\{3\}$	3.	$Q \to T$	Premiss
$\{4\}$	4.	$P \& Q$	Premiss*
$\{4\}$	5.	P	4 Simp.
$\{4\}$	6.	Q	4 Com., Simp.
$\{2, 4\}$	7.	S	2, 5 MP
$\{3, 4\}$	8.	T	3, 6 MP
$\{2, 3, 4\}$	9.	$S \& T$	7, 8 Adj.
$\{1, 2, 3, 4\}$	10.	$R \lor \sim P$	1, 9 MP
$\{1, 2, 3, 4\}$	11.	$\sim P \lor R$	10 Com.
$\{4\}$	12.	$\sim \sim P$	5 DN
$\{1, 2, 3, 4\}$	13.	R	11, 12 DS
$\{1, 2, 3\}$	14.	$(P \& Q) \to R$	4-13 CP

b.

$\{1\}$	1.	$P \to S$	Premiss
$\{2\}$	2.	$Q \to \sim P$	Premiss
$\{3\}$	3.	$Q \lor (R \lor T)$	Premiss

{4}	4.	$\sim T \, \& \, P$	Premiss*
{3}	5.	$(Q \lor R) \lor T$	3 Assoc.
{4}	6.	$\sim T$	4 Simp.
{3, 4}	7.	$Q \lor R$	5, 6 Com., DS
{4}	8.	P	4 Com., Simp.
{2, 4}	9.	$\sim Q$	2, 8 DN, MT
{2, 3, 4}	10.	R	9, 7 DS
{1, 4}	11.	S	1, 8 MP
{1, 2, 3, 4}	12.	$S \, \& \, R$	11, 10 Adj.
{1, 2, 3}	13.	$(\sim T \, \& \, P) \rightarrow (S \, \& \, R)$	4-12 CP

c.

{1}	1.	$P \rightarrow (Q \, \& \, S)$	Premiss
{2}	2.	$(Q \lor R) \rightarrow T$	Premiss
{3}	3.	$T \rightarrow \sim S$	Premiss
{4}	4.	$\sim \sim (P \, \& \, R)$	Premiss*
{4}	5.	$P \, \& \, R$	4 DN
{4}	6.	P	5 Simp.
{1, 4}	7.	$Q \, \& \, S$	1, 6 MP
{1, 4}	8.	S	7 Com., Simp.
{1, 3, 4}	9.	$\sim T$	3, 8 DN, MT
{1, 2, 3, 4}	10.	$\sim (Q \lor R)$	2, 9 MT
{1, 2, 3, 4}	11.	$\sim Q \, \& \, \sim R$	10 DeM
{1, 4}	12.	Q	7 Simp.
{1, 2, 3, 4}	13.	$\sim Q$	11 Simp.
{1, 2, 3, 4}	14.	$Q \, \& \, \sim Q$	12, 13 Adj.
{1, 2, 3}	15.	$\sim (P \, \& \, R)$	4-14 IP

d.

{1}	1.	$\sim P \rightarrow R$	Premiss
{2}	2.	$\sim Q \rightarrow T$	Premiss
{3}	3.	$T \rightarrow \sim R$	Premiss
{4}	4.	$\sim (P \lor Q)$	Premiss*
{4}	5.	$\sim P \, \& \, \sim Q$	4 DeM
{4}	6.	$\sim P$	5 Simp.
{4}	7.	$\sim Q$	5 Com., Simp.
{1, 4}	8.	R	1, 6 MP
{2, 4}	9.	T	2, 7 MP
{2, 3, 4}	10.	$\sim R$	3, 9 MP
{1, 2, 3, 4}	11.	$R \, \& \, \sim R$	8, 10 Adj.
{1, 2, 3}	12.	$P \lor Q$	4-11 IP

e.

{1}	1.	$P \rightarrow (R \rightarrow T)$	Premiss
{2}	2.	$Q \rightarrow (S \, \& \, \sim T)$	Premiss
{3}	3.	$P \, \& \, (Q \lor R)$	Premiss*
{4}	4.	$\sim T$	Premiss*
{3}	5.	P	3 Simp.
{1, 3}	6.	$R \rightarrow T$	1, 5 MP
{3}	7.	$Q \lor R$	3 Com., Simp.
{1, 3, 4}	8.	$\sim R$	6, 4 MT
{1, 3, 4}	9.	Q	7, 8 DS
{1, 2, 3, 4}	10.	$S \, \& \, \sim T$	2, 9 MP
{1, 2, 3, 4}	11.	S	10 Simp.
{1, 2, 3}	12.	$\sim T \rightarrow S$	4-11 CP
{1, 2}	13.	$[P \, \& \, (Q \lor R)] \rightarrow (\sim T \rightarrow S)$	3-12 CP

33.2. a. (i.e., §31.2*d*)

{1}	1.	$P \rightarrow R$	Premiss
{2}	2.	$Q \rightarrow \sim R$	Premiss
{3}	3.	$Q \lor S$	Premiss
{4}	4.	$S \rightarrow \sim P$	Premiss

{5}	5.	P	Premiss*
{4, 5}	6.	$\sim S$	4, 5 DN, MT
{3, 4, 5}	7.	Q	3, 6 Com., DS
{2, 3, 4, 5}	8.	$\sim R$	2, 7 MP
{1, 2, 3, 4, 5}	9.	$\sim P$	1, 8 MT
{1, 2, 3, 4, 5}	10.	$P \ \& \sim P$	5, 9 Adj.
{1, 2, 3, 4}	11.	$\sim P$	5-10 IP

b. (i.e., §31.2e)

{1}	1.	$P \rightarrow (Q \ \& \ R)$	Premiss
{2}	2.	$Q \rightarrow S$	Premiss
{3}	3.	$\sim S$	Premiss
{4}	4.	P	Premiss*
{1, 4}	5.	$Q \ \& \ R$	1, 4 MP
{1, 4}	6.	Q	5 Simp.
{1, 2, 4}	7.	S	2, 6 MP
{1, 2, 3, 4}	8.	$S \ \& \sim S$	7, 3 Adj.
{1, 2, 3}	9.	$\sim P$	4-8 IP

c. (i.e., 31.3e)

{1}	1.	$(P \ \& \ Q) \rightarrow R$	Premiss
{2}	2.	$R \rightarrow (S \ \lor \ T)$	Premiss
{3}	3.	$P \rightarrow \sim S$	Premiss
{4}	4.	$\sim T$	Premiss
{5}	5.	P	Premiss*
{3, 5}	6.	$\sim S$	3, 5 MP
{3, 4, 5}	7.	$\sim S \ \& \sim T$	6, 4 Adj.
{3, 4, 5}	8.	$\sim (S \ \lor \ T)$	7 DeM
{2, 3, 4, 5}	9.	$\sim R$	2, 8 MT
{1, 2, 3, 4, 5}	10.	$\sim (P \ \& \ Q)$	1, 9 MT
{1, 2, 3, 4, 5}	11.	$\sim P \ \lor \ \sim Q$	10 DeM
{1, 2, 3, 4, 5}	12.	$\sim Q$	11, 5 DN, DS
{1, 2, 3, 4}	13.	$P \rightarrow \sim Q$	5-12 CP

33.3.

a.

{1}	1.	$(P \ \lor \ Q) \ \& \ (\sim R \ \lor \ \sim Q)$	Premiss*
{2}	2.	$\sim P$	Premiss*
{1}	3.	$P \ \lor \ Q$	1 Simp.
{1}	4.	$\sim R \ \lor \ \sim Q$	1 Com., Simp.
{1, 2}	5.	Q	2, 3 DS
{1, 2}	6.	$\sim R$	4, 5 Com., DN, DS
{1}	7.	$\sim P \rightarrow \sim R$	2-6 CP
$\land$	8.	$[(P \ \lor \ Q) \ \& \ (\sim R \ \lor \ \sim Q)] \rightarrow (\sim P \rightarrow \sim R)$	1-7 CP

b.

{1}	1.	$(P \ \& \ Q) \ \lor \ (Q \ \& \ R)$	Premiss*
{1}	2.	$(Q \ \& \ P) \ \lor \ (Q \ \& \ R)$	1 Com.
{1}	3.	$Q \ \& \ (P \ \lor \ R)$	2 Dist.
{1}	4.	Q	3 Simp.
{1}	5.	$Q \ \lor \ R$	4 Add.
$\land$	6.	$[(P \ \& \ Q) \ \lor \ (Q \ \& \ R)] \rightarrow (Q \ \lor \ R)$	1-5 CP

c.

{1}	1.	P	Premiss*
{2}	2.	$Q \ \lor \ R$	Premiss*
{2}	3.	$(Q \ \lor \ R) \ \lor \ \sim P$	2 Add.
{2}	4.	$\sim P \ \lor \ (Q \ \lor \ R)$	3 Com.
{2}	5.	$P \rightarrow (Q \ \lor \ R)$	4 Con.
$\land$	6.	$(Q \ \lor \ R) \rightarrow [P \rightarrow (Q \ \lor \ R)]$	2-5 CP
$\land$	7.	$P \rightarrow \{(Q \ \lor \ R) \rightarrow [P \rightarrow (Q \ \lor \ R)]\}$	1-7 CP

d.

{1}	1.	$\sim \{[P \ \lor \ (\sim P \ \& \ Q)] \ \lor \ (\sim P \ \& \sim Q)\}$	Premiss*
{1}	2.	$\sim [P \ \lor \ (\sim P \ \& \ Q)] \ \& \sim (\sim P \ \& \sim Q)$	1 DeM

{1}	3.	$[\sim P \ \& \ (P \ \vee \ \sim Q)] \ \& \ (P \ \vee \ Q)$	2 DeM, DN
{1}	4.	$\sim P$	3 Simp.
{1}	5.	$P \ \vee \ \sim Q$	3 Assoc., Com., Simp.
{1}	6.	$P \ \vee \ Q$	3 Com., Simp.
{1}	7.	$\sim Q$	5, 4 DS
{1}	8.	P	6, 7 Com., DS
{1}	9.	$P \ \& \ \sim P$	8, 4 Adj.
$\wedge$	10.	$[P \ \vee \ (\sim P \ \& \ Q)] \ \vee \ (\sim P \ \& \ \sim Q)$	1-9 IP, DN

e.

{1}	1.	$P \ \& \ Q$	Premiss*
{2}	2.	$\sim R$	Premiss*
{3}	3.	$P \rightarrow (Q \ \& \ R)$	Premiss*
{1}	4.	P	1 Simp.
{1, 3}	5.	$Q \ \& \ R$	3, 4 MP
{1, 3}	6.	R	5 Com., Simp.
{1, 2, 3}	7.	$R \ \& \ \sim R$	6, 2 Adj.
{1, 2}	8.	$\sim (P \rightarrow (Q \ \& \ R)$	3-7 IP
{1}	9.	$\sim R \rightarrow \sim (P \rightarrow (Q \ \& \ R)$	2-8 CP
$\wedge$	10.	$(P \ \& \ Q) \rightarrow \{\sim R \rightarrow \sim [P \rightarrow (Q \ \& \ R)]\}$	1-9 CP

f.

{1}	1.	$\sim (P \rightarrow Q)$	Premiss*
{1}	2.	$\sim (\sim P \ \vee \ Q)$	1 Con.
{1}	3.	$P \ \& \ \sim Q$	2 DeM, DN
$\wedge$	4.	$\sim (P \rightarrow Q) \rightarrow (P \ \& \ \sim Q)$	1-3 CP
$\wedge$	5.	$(P \rightarrow Q) \ \vee \ (P \ \& \ \sim Q)$	4 Con. , DN

34.1. All the sentences exhibit *inessential* departures, except *c*, *e*, *h*, and probably *k* and *l*. For the others, the desired truth-functional compounds, and their forms, are

a. The Democrats named Canavan for President *and* chose Walton to run with her for Vice-President.   Form: $P \ \& \ Q$

b. It is *not* the case that Perkins seeks fame *or* Perkins seeks fortune.
Form: $\sim (P \ \vee \ Q)$

d. *If* certain measures are *not* taken, *then* inflation will *not* be checked.
Form: $\sim P \rightarrow \sim Q$

f. Rogers will *not* graduate *and* he has 120 credits.   Form: $\sim P \ \& \ Q$

g. *If* you are a mathematician, *then* algebra is useful; *and if* you are *not* a mathematician, *then* algebra is useful.   Form: $(P \rightarrow Q) \ \& \ (\sim P \rightarrow Q)$

i. Perkins will vacation in the Poconos *or* ("strong") he will stay home all summer.   Form: $\sim (P \leftrightarrow Q)$, i.e., P alt Q

j. Quincy's argument is valid *and* it is *not* sound.   Form: $P \ \& \ \sim Q$

As to *k* and *l*, we could perhaps try to represent them truth-functionally as

k. The Supreme Court handed down a decision *and* this action pleased no one.

l. The Supreme Court handed down a decision *and* this decision pleased no one.

But the question of relative clauses still awaits definitive treatment.

35.1. Examples *a*, *e*, and *g* do *not* involve essential departures. But the other examples do, since they contain occurrences of the following kinds of conditionals:

b. Counterfactual.

c. Generalized.

d. Definitional.

f.   Implicational (and generalized).
h.   Implicational (and generalized).

37.1. a.   ~Fa
b.   Fa & Fb
c.   Fab
d.   Fa & Ga & Ha
e.   Fa & Gab
f.   ~Fab & Fac
g.   Fabc
h.   Fabcd

37.2. a. $(x)(Fx \rightarrow Gx)$
b. $(\exists x)(Fx \& \sim Gx)$
c. $(\exists x)Fx \& (\exists x)Gx \& (\exists x)(Fx \& Gx)$
d. $\sim(\exists x)Fxa$
e. $(\exists x)(\exists y)Fxy$
f. $(x)(\exists y)Fxy$
g. $\sim Fab \rightarrow (x) \sim Fxb$
h. $(x)(Fx \rightarrow Gx)$; possibly '$(x)(y)[(Fx \& Gy \& Hxy) \rightarrow Ixy]$'

37.3. a. $(\exists x)Fxa \& \sim(\exists x)Gxa$
b.   Fab & Fca
c. $(Fxy \& Fyz) \rightarrow Fxz$
d.   Fabc
e. $(x)(Fx \rightarrow \sim Gx)$
f. $\sim(\exists x)(y)Fxy$
g. $(y)(Fxy \rightarrow Gxy)$
h. $(x)(y)(z)[(Fxz \& Fyz) \rightarrow Fxy]$

b is compound singular, d is simple singular.
c and g are compound open sentences.
a is a compound with a general part; f is simple general; e and h are simple general sentences formed from compound open sentences.

37.4. Answers are suggested for g through n.

g.   Someone did not brief Chamberlain about Hitler.
h.   Every number is equal to itself.
i.   If someone helps everyone, then for everyone there is someone who helps him or her.
j.   If one person is a descendant of another, then the latter is not a descendant of the former.
k.   All are saved or x is not saved.
l.   All are saved or it is not the case that all are saved.
m.   All are saved or none is saved.
n.   Everyone is either saved or not saved.

37.5. Answers are given for f through k.

f.   The first two occurrences of 'x' are bound, the third is free.
g.   Both are bound.
h.   All three are bound.
i and j.
All occurrences of 'x' and 'y' are bound.
k.   The first two occurrences of 'x' are bound, the third is free.

37.6. Answers are given for a and c.

a.   '$(x)Fx \rightarrow Ga$' says that *if* everything is 'F' then 'a' is 'G'. But '$(x)(Fx \rightarrow Ga)$' says that each thing is such that if it is 'F' then 'a' is 'G'. The first is the form of a compound sentence (a conditional) with a general sentence as antecedent. The second is the form of a simple general sentence formed from the compound open sentence '$Fx \rightarrow Ga$'.

c. '$(x)Fx \lor (x) \sim Fx$' says that *either everything* is 'F' or nothing is 'F'. But '$(x)(Fx \lor \sim Fx)$' says that *everything* (each thing) *either* is 'F' or is not 'F'. The first is the form of a compound sentence (a disjunction) with general sentences as disjuncts. The second is the form of a simple general sentence formed from the compound open sentence '$Fx \lor \sim Fx$'.

38.1
a. $(x)(Fxx \rightarrow Fax)$
b. $(\exists x)(Fx \& Gx) \& \sim(x)(Fx \rightarrow Gx)$
c. $(x)[(Fx \& \sim Gx) \rightarrow Hx]$
d. $(x)(\sim Fx \rightarrow \sim Gx)$
e. $\sim(\exists x)(Fx \& Gx)$
f. $(x)[Fx \rightarrow (Gx \lor Hx)]$
g. $(\exists x)(y)Fyx$
h. $[(x)Fx \& (x) \sim Gx] \rightarrow (x)(y) \sim Hxy$
i. $(x)(Fx \rightarrow Gx)$; possibly '$(x)[Fx \rightarrow (\exists y)(Fy \& Gy)]$'
j. $(x)(Fx \rightarrow Gx)$

38.2.

	Original Sentence Symbolized	Negation	Negation Symbolized
a.	$(x)(Fx \rightarrow Gx)$	Some faculty are not effective teachers.	$(\exists x)(Fx \& \sim Gx)$
b.	$(x)(Fx \rightarrow \sim Gx)$	Some faculty are effective teachers.	$(\exists x)(Fx \& Gx)$
c.	$(\exists x)(Fx \& Gx)$	No faculty are effective teachers.	$(x)(Fx \rightarrow \sim Gx)$
d.	$(\exists x)(Fx \& \sim Gx)$	All faculty are effective teachers.	$(x)(Fx \rightarrow Gx)$
e.	$\sim(x)(Fx \rightarrow Gx)$	All faculty are effective teachers.	$(x)(Fx \rightarrow Gx)$
f.	$(x)(Gx \rightarrow Fx)$	Some effective teachers are not faculty.	$(\exists x)(Gx \& \sim Fx)$

39.1. Only *b*, *e*, and *f* are *not* PL-1 expressions.

39.2. *a*, *c*, and *f* are *not* PL-1 sentence forms; the others are.

40.1.
a. $(Fa_1 \lor \sim Fa_1) \& (Fa_2 \lor \sim Fa_2) \& \ldots \& (Fa_n \lor \sim Fa_n)$
b. $(Fa_1 \& \sim Ga_1) \lor (Fa_2 \& \sim Ga_1) \lor \ldots \lor (Fa_n \& \sim Ga_1)$

40.2. *c*, *d*, *f*, and *g* are pairs of equivalent PL-1 sentence forms.

40.3.
a. $(x)[Fx \rightarrow (\exists y)(Gy \& Hxy)]$
b. $\sim(\exists x)[Fx \& (y)(Gy \rightarrow \sim Hxy)]$
c. $(\exists x)[Fx \& (y)(Gy \rightarrow \sim Hyx)]$
d. $(\exists x)(\exists y)[Fx \& Gy \& Hxy \& (z)(Fz \rightarrow \sim Izy)]$
e. $(x)(y)(z)[(Fx \& Gy \& Hz) \rightarrow Ixyz]$
f. $(x)\{Fx \rightarrow (y)(\exists z)[(Gy \& Hz) \rightarrow Ixzy]\}$
g. $(\exists x)\{Fx \& (y)(z)[(Gy \& Hz) \rightarrow Iyxz]\}$
h. $(x) \{Fx \rightarrow [\sim(\exists y)(Gy \& Hxy) \rightarrow (z)(Iz \rightarrow \sim Jxz)]\}$
i. $(x)(y)[(Fx \& Gy) \rightarrow (\exists z)(Hz \& Ixzy)]$
j. $(x)\{(Fx \& Gx) \rightarrow (y)[Hy \rightarrow \sim(Iyx \lor Jyx \lor Kyx)]\}$

40.4. Here is one way of symbolizing the sentence:

$(\exists x_1)(Ix_1 \& (x_2)(Sx_2 \rightarrow Cx_2 x_1) \& (x_3)\{[(Ex_3 \lor Mx_3) \& Gx_1x_3] \rightarrow Fx_3\} \& (x_4)$
$\{Sx_4 \rightarrow [\sim(Px_1x_4 \lor Hx_1x_4) \& (Rx_1x_4 \& Ax_1x_4)]\})$

42.1. Counterexamples are suggested and domains specified for *a* through *f*.

a. Everyone is happy or no one is happy.   *D = people*

b. If some students understand, all do.   *D = students*

c. Aristotle is French or (Aristotle is not French and is a poet).   *D = people* (i.e., the domain for which '*F*' and '*G*' are defined and a member of which is named by the word 'Aristotle')

d. If all members of the French Academy are men, then all men are members of the French Academy.   *D = people*

e. If some students are not sophomores, then some sophomores are not students.   *D = people*

f. If *x* is equal to *y*, then *y* is not equal to *x*.   *D = integers*

42.2. Sentence forms *b*, *d*, and *g* are valid; *a*, *e*, and *h* are not true under any interpretation.

42.3.   a. If *B* is valid, so is $A \rightarrow B$.

Proof: By the definition of the conditional, $A \rightarrow B$ is true under any interpretation for which *A* is false or *B* is true. But since *B* is valid, *B* is true under all interpretations. Hence $A \rightarrow B$ will also be true under all interpretations. Thus if *B* is valid, so is $A \rightarrow B$.

b. If $A \rightarrow B$ and *A* are valid, so is *B*.

Proof: By definition, a conditional cannot be true if its antecedent is true and its consequent is false. Now $A \rightarrow B$ is valid, thus true under all interpretations. Hence there is no interpretation under which the antecedent *A* is true and the consequent *B* is false. But *A* is valid and therefore true under all interpretations. Consequently, there is no interpretation under which *B* is false; in other words, *B* is valid. Thus if $A \rightarrow B$ and *A* are valid, so is *B*.

43.1.   a. *Counterexample:* Replace '*F*' by 'is a Belgian'; '*G*' by 'is a German'; '*H*' by 'is a European'. The domain is *people*.

b. *Counterexample:* Replace '*F*' by 'is a man'; '*G*' by 'is a god'; '*H*' by 'is an animal'. The domain is the *universe*.

c. *Counterexample:* Replace '*F*' by 'is a Vietnamese'; '*G*' by 'is a Nigerian'; '*H*' by 'is an Asian'. The domain is *people*.

d. *Counterexample:* Replace '*F*' by 'is an empiricist'; '*G*' by 'is a Hegelian'; '*H*' by 'is a logical positivist'. The domain is *philosophers*.

e. *Counterexample:* Replace '*F*' by 'leaked the story'; '*G*' by 'is a clairvoyant'; '*a*' by 'Kissinger'. The domain is *people*.

f. *Counterexample:* Replace '*F*' by 'believes in astrology'; '*G*' by 'believes in science'; '*H*' by 'believes in astronomy'. The domain is *people*.

g. *Counterexample:* Replace '*F*' by 'is immediately succeeded by'; '*a*' by '0'; '*b*' by '1'. The domain is *natural numbers*. The argument then is

0 is immediately succeeded by 1.
For every number there is a number that immediately succeeds it.
Therefore there is a number that is immediately succeeded by 0.

43.2.   a. *Argument form:*

$(\exists x)(Gx \ \& \ Hx)$
$(\exists x)(Fx \ \& \ Gx)$
Therefore $(\exists x)(Fx \ \& \ Hx)$

Counterexample: Replace '*F*' by 'is a conservative'; '*G*' by 'is a Republican'; '*H*' by 'is a liberal'. The domain is *people*.

b. *Argument form:*

    $(\exists x)(Fx \ \& \ Gx)$

    Fa

Therefore Ga

Counterexample: Replace 'F' by 'is an officeholder'; 'G' by 'is a Democrat'; 'a' by 'Gerald Ford'. The domain is *people*.

c. *Argument form:*

    $(x)(Fx \rightarrow \sim Gx)$

    $(\exists x)(Gx \ \& \ Hx)$

    Therefore $(\exists x)(Fx \ \& \ \sim Hx)$

Counterexample: Replace 'F' by 'is an economist'; 'G' by 'is a soothsayer'; 'H' by 'is mortal'. The domain is *people*.

d. *Argument form:*

    $(x)(y)(z)[(Fxy \ \& \ Fyz) \rightarrow Fxz]$

    $(x)(y)(Fxy \rightarrow Fyx)$

    Therefore $(x)Fxx$

Counterexample: Replace 'F' by 'is a sibling of'. The domain is *people*.

44.1. c, f, h, and j are not valid; the others are all valid. Truth trees are given here for a, c, f, g, h, and i.

a.

1.	✓ $(\exists x)Fx$	Premiss
2.	$(x)(Fx \rightarrow Gx)$	Premiss
3.	✓ $\sim(\exists x)Gx$	Negation of conclusion
4.	$(x) \sim Gx$	3 NQ
5.	Fa	1 EQ
6.	$\sim Ga$	4 UQ
7.	✓ $Fa \rightarrow Ga$	2 UQ

8. $\sim Fa$ Ga $7 \rightarrow$

        X   X

c.

1.	✓ $(\exists x)(Fx \lor Gx)$	Premiss
2.	$(x)(Gx \rightarrow Hx)$	Premiss
3.	✓ $\sim(\exists x)Hx$	Negation of conclusion
4.	$(x) \sim Hx$	3 NQ
5.	✓ $Fa \lor Ga$	1 EQ

6. Fa Ga $5 \lor$

7. $\sim Ha$ $\sim Ha$ 4 UQ

8.   ✓ $Ga \rightarrow Ha$ ✓ $Ga \rightarrow Ha$ 2 UQ

9. $\sim Ga$ Ha $\sim Ga$ Ha $8 \rightarrow$

         X   X   X

f.

1.	$(x)(Gx \rightarrow \sim Hx)$	Premiss
2.	$(x)(Gx \rightarrow Fx)$	Premiss
3.	✓ $\sim(x)(Fx \rightarrow \sim Hx)$	Negation of conclusion
4.	✓ $(\exists x) \sim (Fx \rightarrow \sim Hx)$	3 NQ
5.	✓ $\sim(Fa \rightarrow \sim Ha)$	4 EQ
6.	Fa	$5 \sim (\rightarrow)$
7.	✓ $\sim \sim Ha$	$5 \sim (\rightarrow)$
8.	Ha	7 Cancellation law
9.	✓ $Ga \rightarrow \sim Ha$	1 UQ

10. $\sim Ga$ $\sim Ha$ $9 \rightarrow$

               X

11.   ✓ $Ga \rightarrow Fa$ 2 UQ

12. $\sim Ga$ Fa $11 \rightarrow$

g.　1.　　$(x)(Gx \to \sim Hx)$　　　　　Premiss
　　2.　　$(x)(Fx \to Gx)$　　　　　Premiss
　　3.　✓$\sim(x)(Fx \to \sim Hx)$　　Negation of conclusion
　　4.　✓$(\exists x)\sim(Fx \to \sim Hx)$　3 NQ
　　5.　✓$\sim(Fa \to \sim Ha)$　　　4 EQ
　　6.　　　Fa　　　　　　　　$5 \sim (\to)$
　　7.　✓$\sim \sim Ha$　　　　　$5 \sim (\to)$
　　8.　　　Ha　　　　　　　　7 Cancellation law
　　9.　✓$Ga \to \sim Ha$　　　　1 UQ

　　10.　　$\sim Ga$　　　$\sim Ha$　　　$9 \to$
　　　　　　　　　　　　X

　　11.　✓$Fa \to Ga$　　　　　2 UQ

　　12.　　$\sim Fa$　　　Ga　　　$11 \to$
　　　　　　　X　　　X

h.　1.　$(x)(\exists y)(Fx \lor \sim Fy)$　　Premiss
　　2.　　　$\sim Fa$　　　　　　　Premiss
　　3.　✓$\sim(\exists x)Fx$　　　　Negation of conclusion
　　4.　　$(x)\sim Fx$　　　　　　3 NQ
　　5.　✓$(\exists y)(Fa \lor \sim Fy)$　1 UQ
　　6.　✓$Fa \lor \sim Fb$　　　　5 EQ

　　7.　　Fa　　　$\sim Fb$　　　$6 \lor$
　　　　　X

　　8.　✓$(\exists y)(Fb \lor \sim Fy)$　1 UQ
　　9.　✓$Fb \lor \sim Fc$　　　　8 EQ

　　10.　　　Fb　　　$\sim Fc$　　　$9 \lor$
　　　　　　　　X

Etc.

i.　1.　✓$\sim(\{[(x)Fx \lor Ga] \& \sim Ga\} \to Fa)$　Negation of sentence form
　　2.　✓$[(x)Fx \lor Ga] \& \sim Ga$　$1 \sim (\to)$
　　3.　　　$\sim Fa$　　　　　　$1 \sim (\to)$
　　4.　✓$(x)Fx \lor Ga$　　　　2 &
　　5.　　$\sim Ga$　　　　　　　2 &

　　6.　　$(x)Fx$　　　Ga　　　$4 \lor$
　　　　　　　　　　　X
　　7.　　　Fa　　　　　　　　6 UQ
　　　　　　X

44.2.　a.　*Error:*　The application of EQ to step 3 uses 'a', which has appeared earlier in the path at step 1.

　　　Counterexample:　Replace 'F' by 'is famous' and 'a' by the word 'Aristotle'.　The domain is *people*.

　　b.　*Error:*　Step 4 is obtained by applying UQ to step 1; but '$(x)Fx \to Ga$' is a *conditional*, to which only Rule $\to$ is applicable.

　　　Counterexample:　Replace 'F' by 'votes Republican', 'G' by 'wins', and 'a' by 'Goldwater'.　The domain is *people*.

　　c.　*Error:*　The application of EQ to step 7 uses 'a', which has appeared earlier in the path at step 5.

　　　Counterexample:　Replace 'F' by 'votes Republican'.　The domain is *eligible voters*.

d. *Error:* Rule → has been incorrectly applied at step 11. Step 12 should read

~ *Fa*   *Ga*   and not   *Fa*   ~ *Ga*

Counterexample: Replace '*F*' by 'is sound'; '*G*' by 'is valid'; '*H*' by 'has true premisses'. The domain is *deductive arguments*.

e. *Error:* The application of EQ to step 6 uses '*a*', which has already appeared in the path at step 5.

Counterexample: Replace '*F*' by '(logically) implies'. The domain is *PL-1 sentence forms*.

44.3. *a* and *d* are invalid; the others are valid.

a. *Argument form:*

$(x)(Gx \rightarrow Hx)$
$(\exists x)(Fx \ \& \sim Gx)$
Therefore $(\exists x)(Fx \ \& \sim Hx)$

Counterexample: Replace '*F*' by 'is an animal'; '*G*' by 'is a man'; '*H*' by 'is mortal'. The domain is the *universe*.

b. *Argument form:*

Ia & *Ga*
$(x)[Gx \rightarrow (Hx \lor Fxb)]$
$\sim Fab$
Therefore *Ha*

Truth tree:

1.	✓*Ia* & *Ga*	Premiss
2.	$(x)[Gx \rightarrow (Hx \lor Fxb)]$	Premiss
3.	~ *Fab*	Premiss
4.	~ *Ha*	Negation of conclusion
5.	*Ia*	1 &
6.	*Ga*	1 &
7.	✓ *Ga* → (*Ha* ∨ *Fab*)	2 UQ

8.   ~ *Ga*   ✓ *Ha* ∨ *Fab*   7 →
      X
9.   *Ha*   *Fab*   8 ∨
                   X   X

c. *Argument form:*

$(x)[(\exists x)Fxy \rightarrow (z)Fzx]$
$\sim Fab$
Therefore $\sim Fbb$

Truth tree:

1.	$(x)[(\exists y)Fxy \rightarrow (z)Fzx]$	Premiss
2.	~ *Fab*	Premiss
3.	~ ~ *Fbb*	Negation of conclusion
4.	*Fbb*	3 Cancellation law
5.	✓ $(\exists y)Fby \rightarrow (z)Fzb$	1 UQ

6.   ✓ ~(∃*y*)*Fby*   (*z*)*Fzb*   5 →
7.   (*y*)~ *Fby*   6 NQ
8.   ~ *Fbb*   7 UQ
            X
9.   *Fab*   6 UQ
                             X

d. *Argument form:*

> ~ *Fab*
> *Gb*
> (*x*)(*Gx* → ~ *Fxb*)
> Therefore *Ga*

Counterexample: Replace '*F*' by 'has forgotten'; '*G*' by 'is a Progressive'; '*b*' by 'Theodore Roosevelt'; '*a*' by 'Richard Nixon'.

e. *Argument form:*

> (*x*)[*Fx* → (*Gax* → *Hx*)]
> (*x*)(*Fx* → ~ *Hx*)
> Therefore (*x*)(*Fx* → ~ *Gax*)

Truth tree:

1.	(*x*)[*Fx* → (*Gax* → *Hx*)]	Premiss
2.	(*x*)(*Fx* → ~ *Hx*)	Premiss
3.	✓ ~(*x*)(*Fx* → ~ *Gax*)	Negation of conclusion
4.	✓ (∃*x*) ~ (*Fx* → ~ *Gax*)	3 NQ
5.	✓ ~(*Fb* → ~ *Gab*)	4 EQ
6.	*Fb*	5 ~ (→)
7.	~ ~ *Gab*	5 ~ (→)
8.	*Gab*	7 Cancellation law
9.	✓ *Fb* → (*Gab* → *Hb*)	1 UQ

```
10.     ~ Fb          ✓ Gab → Hb        9 →
         X

11.                ~ Gab      Hb         10 →
                    X

12.                    ✓ Fb → ~ Hb       2 UQ


13.                  ~ Fb    ~ Hb        12 →
                      X       X
```

44.4. *a, b, e,* and *f* are valid. The others are not valid. Answers are given for *b, f,* and *h*.

b. *Truth tree:*

1.	✓ *Ga* & *Fab*	Premiss
2.	(*x*)(~ *Gx* ∨ ~ *Hbx*)	Premiss
3.	✓ ~ (∃*x*)(*Fxb* & ~ *Hbx*)	Negation of conclusion
4.	(*x*) ~ (*Fxb* & ~ *Hbx*)	3 NQ
5.	*Ga*	1 &
6.	*Fab*	1 &
7.	✓ ~(*Fab* & ~ *Hba*)	4 UQ

```
8.    ~ Fab        ✓ ~ ~ Hba          7 ~ (&)
       X

9.                     Hba            8 Cancellation law
10.               ~ Ga ∨ ~ Hba        2 UQ


11.               ~ Ga      ~ Hba      10 ∨
                   X          X
```

f. *Truth tree:*

1.	$(x)[(Fx \rightarrow Gx) \rightarrow Hx]$	Premiss
2.	✓ $\sim(x)[Fx \rightarrow (Gx \rightarrow Hx)]$	Negation of conclusion
3.	✓ $(\exists x) \sim [Fx \rightarrow (Gx \rightarrow Hx)]$	2 NQ
4.	✓ $\sim[Fa \rightarrow (Ga \rightarrow Ha)]$	3 EQ
5.	Fa	$4 \sim (\rightarrow)$
6.	✓ $\sim(Ga \rightarrow Ha)$	$4 \sim (\rightarrow)$
7.	Ga	$6 \sim (\rightarrow)$
8.	$\sim Ha$	$6 \sim (\rightarrow)$
9.	✓ $(Fa \rightarrow Ga) \rightarrow Ha$	1 UQ

10.   ✓ $\sim (Fa \rightarrow Ga)$ Ha $9 \rightarrow$
                                  X

11.	Fa	$10 \sim (\rightarrow)$
12.	$\sim Ga$	$10 \sim (\rightarrow)$
	X	

h. *Counterexample:* Replace 'F' by 'loves' (as a two-place predicate); 'G' by 'is a misanthrope'. The domain is *people*.

44.5. *c, d, f,* and *g* are pairs of equivalent PL-1 sentence forms. We give the answer for *b*.

First argument form:

$(\exists x)[(y)(Fxy \ \& \ Gx)]$

Therefore $(\exists x)(y)Fxy \ \& \ (\exists x)Gx$

First truth tree:

1.	✓ $(\exists x)[(y)Fxy \ \& \ Gx]$	Premiss
2.	✓ $\sim [(\exists x)(y)Fxy \ \& \ (\exists x)Gx]$	Negation of conclusion

3.	✓ $\sim (\exists x)(y)Fxy$	✓ $\sim (\exists x)Gx$	$2 \sim (\&)$
4.	$(x) \sim (y)Fxy$		3 NQ
5.	$(y)(Fay \ \& \ Ga)$		1 EQ
6.	✓ $\sim(y)Fay$		4 UQ
7.	✓ $(\exists y) \sim Fay$		6 NQ
8.	$\sim Fab$		7 EQ
9.	✓ $Fab \ \& \ Gb$		5 UQ
10.	Fab		9 &
11.	Gb		9 &
	X		
12.		$(x) \sim Gx$	3 NQ
13.		$(y)(Fay \ \& \ Ga)$	1 EQ
14.		$\sim Ga$	12 UQ
15.		✓ $Fab \ \& \ Ga$	13 UQ
16.		Fab	15 &
17.		Ga	15 &
		X	

Second argument form:

$(\exists x)(y)Fxy \ \& \ (\exists x)Gx$
Therefore $(\exists x)[(y)Fxy \ \& \ Gx]$

Second truth tree:

1.	✓(∃x)(y)Fxy & (∃x)Gx	Premiss
2.	✓ ~{(∃x)[(y)Fxy & Gx]}	Negation of conclusion
3.	(x) ~ [(y)Fxy & Gx]	2 NQ
4.	✓(∃x)(y)Fxy	1 &
5.	✓(∃x)Gx	1 &
6.	(y)Fay	4 EQ
7.	Gb	5 EQ
8.	✓ ~[(y)Fay & Ga]	3 UQ

9.	~ (y)Fay ~ Ga	[8 ~ (&)
10.	(∃y) ~ Fay	9 NQ
11.	~ Fac	10 EQ
12.	Fac	6 UQ
	X	

Etc.

45.1. a.

{1}	1.	(x)Fx ∨ Ga	Rule P
{2}	2.	~Ga	Rule P
{1, 2}	3.	(x)Fx	1, 2 Rule T
{1, 2}	4.	Fa	3 Rule UI
{1, 2}	5.	(∃x)Fx	4 Rule EG

b.

{1}	1.	(x)[Fx → (Gx & Hx)]	P
{2}	2.	Fa	P
{1}	3.	Fa → (Ga & Ha)	1 UI
{1, 2}	4.	Ga & Ha	2, 3 T
{1, 2}	5.	Ga	4 T

c.

{1}	1.	(x)[Fx & (Gx ∨ ~Hx)]	P
{2}	2.	Ha	P
{1}	3.	Fa & (Ga ∨ ~Ha)	1 UI
{1}	4.	Ga ∨ ~Ha	3 T
{1, 2}	5.	Ga	2, 4 T
{1}	6.	Fa	3 T
{1, 2}	7.	Fa & Ga	5, 6 T

d.

{1}	1.	Ga & Ha	P
{2}	2.	(x)[Gx → (Fx ∨ ~Hx)]	P
{2}	3.	Ga → (Fa ∨ ~Ha)	2 UI
{1}	4.	Ga	1 T
{1, 2}	5.	Fa ∨ ~Ha	3, 4 T
{1}	6.	Ha	1 T
{1, 2}	7.	Fa	5, 6 T
{1, 2}	8.	(∃x)Fx	7 EG

e.

{1}	1.	Ga & Fab	P
{2}	2.	(x)(~Gx ∨ ~Hbx)	P
{2}	3.	~Ga ∨ ~Hba	2 UI
{1}	4.	Ga	1 T
{1, 2}	5.	~Hba	3, 4 T
{1}	6.	Fab	1 T
{1, 2}	7.	Fab & ~Hba	6, 5 T
{1, 2}	8.	(∃x)(Fxb & ~Hbx)	7 EG

f.

{1}	1.	Ia & Ga	P
{2}	2.	(x)[Gx → (Hx ∨ Fxb)]	P
{3}	3.	~Fab	P
{2}	4.	Ga → (Ha ∨ Fab)	2 UI
{1}	5.	Ga	1 T
{1, 2}	6.	Ha ∨ Fab	4, 5 T
{1, 2, 3}	7.	Ha	6, 3 T

g.

{1}	1.	*Ga & Fab*	P
{2}	2.	$(x)[Fxb \rightarrow (\sim Gx \lor Fbx)]$	P
{2}	3.	$Fab \rightarrow (\sim Ga \lor Fba)$	2 UI
{1}	4.	*Fab*	1 T
{1, 2}	5.	$\sim Ga \lor Fba$	3, 4 T
{1}	6.	*Ga*	1 T
{1, 2}	7.	*Fba*	5, 6 T
{1, 2}	8.	*Fab & Fba*	4, 8 T
{1, 2}	9.	$(\exists y)(Fay \& Fya)$	8 EG
{1, 2}	10.	$(\exists x)(\exists y)(Fxy \& Fyx)$	9 EG

45.2. a. *Error:* When UI is applied, occurrences of the constant thus introduced must replace *all* occurrences of the variable for which the constant is put. UI correctly applied here yields '*Faa*'.

Counterexample: Replace '*F*' with 'is equal to' and '*a*' with '2'. The domain is the set of *natural numbers*.

b. *Error:* UI is applied to a *part* of a sentence form.

Counterexample: Replace '*F*' with 'votes Republican'; '*G*' with 'wins'; and '*a*' with 'Goldwater'. The domain is *people*.

c. *Error:* EG is applied to a *part* of a sentence form. The argument form, however, is valid, and a correct derivation is

{1}	1.	$Fb \lor Ga$	P
{2}	2.	$\sim Fb$	P
{1, 2}	3.	*Ga*	1, 2 T
{1, 2}	4.	$(\exists x)Gx$	3 EG

d. *Error:* If EG is correctly applied to '$\sim Ga$', it yields '$(\exists x) \sim Gx$', not '$\sim (\exists x)Gx$'.

Counterexample: Replace '*F*' with 'is a woman'; '*G*' with 'is a member of the French Academy'; '*a*' with 'Simone de Beauvoir'. The domain is *people*.

45.3. a. *Argument form:*

$(x)(Ex \rightarrow Lx)$
$(x)(Lx \rightarrow \sim Ox)$
$Ef \& Eg$ (supplied premiss)
Therefore $\sim Of \& \sim Og$

Derivation: Simply apply UI to the first two premisses, then use Rule T to obtain the desired conclusion.

b. *Argument form:*

Ffe
Bej
$(x)(y)(z)[(Fxy \& Byz) \rightarrow Fxz]$ (supplied premiss)
Therefore *Ffj*

Derivation:

{1}	1.	*Ffe*	P
{2}	2.	*Bej*	P
{3}	3.	$(x)(y)(z)[(Fxy \& Byz) \rightarrow Fxz]$	P
{3}	4.	$(y)(z)[(Ffy \& Byz) \rightarrow Ffz]$	3 UI
{3}	5.	$(z)[(Ffe \& Bez) \rightarrow Ffz]$	4 UI
{3}	6.	$(Ffe \& Bej) \rightarrow Ffj$	5 UI
{1, 2}	7.	*Ffe & Bej*	1, 2 T
{1, 2, 3}	8.	*Ffj*	6, 7 T

c. *Argument form:*

$(x)(Gx \rightarrow Tx) \lor (\exists x)Cx$
$(\exists x)Cx \rightarrow Uh$

$\sim Uh$

Gq (supplied premiss)

Therefore Tq

Derivation:

{1}	1.	$(x)(Gx \to Tx) \lor (\exists x)Cx$	P
{2}	2.	$(\exists x)Cx \to Uh$	P
{3}	3.	$\sim Uh$	P
{4}	4.	Gq	P
{2, 3}	5.	$\sim(\exists x)Cx$	2, 3 T
{1, 2, 3}	6.	$(x)(Gx \to Tx)$	1, 5 T
{1, 2, 3}	7.	$Gq \to Tq$	6 UI
{1, 2, 3, 4}	8.	Tq	7, 4 T

d. *Argument form:*

Lpb

Lbn

$\sim Lpc$

$(x)(y)(z)[(Lxy \ \& \ Lyz) \to Lxz]$ (supplied premiss)

$(x)(y)(z)[(Lxy \ \& \ \sim Lxz) \to Lzy]$ (supplied premiss)

Therefore Lcn

Derivation:

{1}	1.	Lpb	P
{2}	2.	Lbn	P
{3}	3.	$\sim Lpc$	P
{4}	4.	$(x)(y)(z)[(Lxy \ \& \ Lyz) \to Lxz]$	P
{5}	5.	$(x)(y)(z)[(Lxy \ \& \ \sim Lxz) \to Lzy]$	P
{4}	6.	$(y)(z)[(Lpy \ \& \ Lyz) \to Lpz]$	4 UI
{4}	7.	$(z)[(Lpb \ \& \ Lbz) \to Lpz]$	6 UI
{4}	8.	$(Lpb \ \& \ Lbn) \to Lpn$	7 UI
{1, 2}	9.	$Lpb \ \& \ Lbn$	1, 2 T
{1, 2, 4}	10.	Lpn	8, 9 T
{5}	11.	$(y)(z)[(Lpy \ \& \ \sim Lpz) \to Lzy]$	5 UI
{5}	12.	$(z)[(Lpn \ \& \ \sim Lpz) \to Lzn]$	11 UI
{5}	13.	$(Lpn \ \& \ \sim Lpc) \to Lcn$	12 UI
{1, 2, 3, 4}	14.	$Lpn \ \& \ \sim Lpc$	10, 3 T
{1, 2, 3, 4, 5}	15.	Lcn	13; 14 T

46.1.   a.

{1}	1.	$(x)(Fx \to Gx)$	P
{2}	2.	$(x)(Gx \to \sim Hx)$	P
{1}	3.	$Fa \to Ga$	1 UI
{2}	4.	$Ga \to \sim Ha$	2 UI
{1, 2}	5.	$Fa \to \sim Ha$	3, 4 T
{1, 2}	6.	$(x)(Fx \to \sim Hx)$	5 UG

b.

{1}	1.	$(x)(Fx \to Gx)$	P
{2}	2.	$(\exists x) \sim Gx$	P
{2}	3.	$\sim Ga$	2 EI
{1}	4.	$Fa \to Ga$	1 UI
{1, 2}	5.	$\sim Fa$	3, 4 T
{1, 2}	6.	$(\exists x) \sim Fx$	5 EG

c.

{1}	1.	$(x)(Fx \to \sim Gx)$	P
{2}	2.	$(\exists x)(Gx \ \& \ Hx)$	P
{2}	3.	$Ga \ \& \ Ha$	2 EI
{1}	4.	$Fa \to \sim Ga$	1 UI
{2}	5.	Ga	3 T
{2}	6.	Ha	3 T
{1, 2}	7.	$\sim Fa$	4, 5 T

	{1, 2}	8.	Ha & $\sim Fa$	6, 7 T
	{1, 2}	9.	$(\exists x)(Hx$ & $\sim Fx)$	8 EG
d.	{1}	1.	$(x)(Fx \rightarrow Gx)$	P
	{2}	2.	$(x)(Gx \rightarrow Hx)$	P
	{3}	3.	$(x)(Hx \rightarrow \sim Ix)$	P
	{4}	4.	$(\exists x)Fx$	P
	{4}	5.	Fa	4 EI
	{1}	6.	$Fa \rightarrow Ga$	1 UI
	{2}	7.	$Ga \rightarrow Ha$	2 UI
	{3}	8.	$Ha \rightarrow \sim Ia$	3 UI
	{1, 2}	9.	$Fa \rightarrow Ha$	6, 7 T
	{1, 2, 3}	10.	$Fa \rightarrow \sim Ia$	9, 8 T
	{1, 2, 3, 4}	11.	$\sim Ia$	10, 5 T
	{1, 2, 3, 4}	12.	$(\exists x) \sim Ix$	11 EG
e.	{1}	1.	$(x)(Hx \rightarrow Gx)$	P
	{2}	2.	$(x)(\exists y)(Fxy \vee \sim Gx)$	P
	{2}	3.	$(\exists y)(Fay \vee \sim Ga)$	2 UI
	{2}	4.	$Fab \vee \sim Ga$	3 EI
	{1}	5.	$Ha \rightarrow Ga$	1 UI
	{2}	6.	$Ga \rightarrow Fab$	4 T
	{1, 2}	7.	$Ha \rightarrow Fab$	5, 6 T
	{1, 2}	8.	$Fab \vee \sim Ha$	7 T
	{1, 2}	9.	$(\exists y)(Fay \vee \sim Ha)$	8 EG
	{1, 2}	10.	$(x)(\exists y)(Fxy \vee \sim Hx)$	9 UG
f.	{1}	1.	$(x)[(Fx$ & $Gx) \rightarrow Hx]$	P
	{2}	2.	$(\exists x)Hx \rightarrow (x)(Iax$ & $Gx)$	P
	{3}	3.	$(\exists x)(Fx$ & $Gx)$	P* (borrowed premiss)
	{3}	4.	Fa & Ga	3 EI
	{1}	5.	$(Fa$ & $Ga) \rightarrow Ha$	1 UI
	{1, 3}	6.	Ha	4, 5 T
	{1, 3}	7.	$(\exists x)Hx$	6 EG
	{1, 2, 3}	8.	$(x)(Iax$ & $Gx)$	2, 7 T
	{1, 2, 3}	9.	Iaa & Ga	8 UI
	{1, 2}	10.	$(\exists x)(Fx$ & $Gx) \rightarrow (Iaa$ & $Ga)$	3-9 CP
g.	{1}	1.	$(\exists x)Fx \rightarrow (x)(\sim Gx \rightarrow Fx)$	P
	{2}	2.	$(\exists x)Hx \rightarrow (x)(Fx \rightarrow Hx)$	P
	{3}	3.	$(\exists x)(Fx$ & $Hx)$	P
	{3}	4.	Fb & Hb	3 EI
	{3}	5.	Fb	4 T
	{3}	6.	Hb	4 T
	{3}	7.	$(\exists x)Fx$	5 EG
	{3}	8.	$(\exists x)Hx$	6 EG
	{1, 3}	9.	$(x)(\sim Gx \rightarrow Fx)$	1, 7 T
	{2, 3}	10.	$(x)(Fx \rightarrow Hx)$	2, 8 T
	{1, 3}	11.	$\sim Ga \rightarrow Fa$	9 UI
	{2, 3}	12.	$Fa \rightarrow Ha$	10 UI
	{1, 2, 3}	13.	$\sim Ga \rightarrow Ha$	11, 12 T
	{1, 2, 3}	14.	$(x)(\sim Gx \rightarrow Hx)$	13 UG

46.2. The errors are as follows:

a. The application of UG to the sentence form '$Faa \rightarrow Ga$' fails to replace *all* occurrences of 'a' by occurrences of 'x', the variable of quantification.

b. The constant generalized on ('a') *appears in a premiss* of the sentence form to which UG is applied.

    c. The application of EI to obtain step 3 uses a constant that *appears earlier* in the derivation.

    d. UG is used on a constant ('*a*') *introduced* into the derivation *by an application of EI.*

    e. Rule T is misapplied to obtain '*Fa*' from '*Fa → Ga*' and '*Ga*'.

    f. UG is used on a constant ('*b*') *introduced* into the derivation *by an application of EI.*

    g. The *second* application of UG generalizes on a constant—'*a*'—introduced into the derivation by an application of EI.

46.3. EG is misused. Applied to '$\sim Aa$', it should yield '$(\exists x) \sim Ax$' and not '$\sim (\exists x)Ax$'. *Note:* We are also barred from applying UG to '$\sim Aa$' to obtain '$(x) \sim Ax$'—the equivalent of the conclusion '$\sim (\exists x)Ax$'. For this would involve generalizing on a constant introduced into the derivation by an application of EI.

46.4. *a* and *d* are valid; the others are not valid.

    a. *Derivation:*

{1}	1.	*Fa*	P
{2}	2.	$(\exists x)Gx$	P
{1}	3.	$(\exists x)Fx$	1 EG
{1, 2}	4.	$(\exists x)Fx$ & $(\exists x)Gx$	2, 3 T

    b. *Argument form:*

$(x)(Fx → Gx)$
$(\exists x)(Gx$ & $Hx)$
Therefore $(\exists x)(Fx$ & $Hx)$

Counterexample: Replace '*F*' with 'is Chinese'; '*G*' with 'is an Asian'; '*H*' with 'is Japanese'. The domain is *people.*

    c. *Argument form:*

$(\exists x)(Fx$ & $\sim Gx)$
$(x)(Gx → \sim Hx)$
Therefore $(\exists x)(Fx$ & $\sim Hx)$

Counterexample: Replace '*F*' with 'is a man'; '*G*' with 'is infallible'; '*H*' with 'is mortal'. The domain is "*beings.*"

    d. *Derivation:*

{1}	1.	$(x)(Fx \lor Gx)$	P
{2}	2.	$(x)(Gx → Hx)$	P
{3}	3.	$(\exists x) \sim Hx$	P
{3}	4.	$\sim Ha$	3 EI
{1}	5.	$Fa \lor Ga$	1 UI
{2}	6.	$Ga → Ha$	2 UI
{2, 3}	7.	$\sim Ga$	6, 4 T
{1, 2, 3}	8.	*Fa*	5, 7 T
{1, 2, 3}	9.	$(\exists x)Fx$	8 EG

    e. *Argument form:*

$(x)(y)(z)[(Fxy$ & $Fyz) → Fxz]$
$(x)(y)(Fxy → Fyx)$
$(x)Fxx$

Counterexample: Replace '*F*' by the two-place predicate 'is parallel to'. The domain is *straight lines.*

47.1. Answers are given for *b, c, e, g, h, j.*

    b. $(x)(Fx \lor Gx) → [(\exists x)Fx \lor (\exists x)Gx]$

Proof:

{1}	1.	$(x)(Fx \lor Gx)$	P*
{2}	2.	$\sim (\exists x)Fx$	P*

{2}	3.	$(x) \sim Fx$	2 Definition
{2}	4.	$\sim Fa$	3 UI
{1}	5.	$Fa \lor Ga$	1 UI
{1, 2}	6.	Ga	5, 4 T
{1, 2}	7.	$(\exists x)Gx$	6 EG
{1}	8.	$\sim(\exists x)Fx \rightarrow (\exists x)Gx$	2-7 CP
{1}	9.	$(\exists x)Fx \lor (\exists x)Gx$	8 T
$\land$	10.	$(x)(Fx \lor Gx) \rightarrow [(\exists x)Fx \lor (\exists x)Gx]$	1-9 CP

c. $(\exists x)[(y)Fxy \,\&\, Gx] \rightarrow [(\exists x)(y)Fxy \,\&\, (\exists x)Gx]$

Proof:

{1}	1.	$(\exists x)[(y)Fxy \,\&\, Gx]$	P*
{1}	2.	$(y)Fay \,\&\, Ga$	1 EI
{1}	3.	$(y)Fay$	2 T
{1}	4.	Ga	2 T
{1}	5.	$(\exists x)(y)Fxy$	3 EG
{1}	6.	$(\exists x)Gx$	4 EG
{1}	7.	$(\exists x)(y)Fxy \,\&\, (\exists x)Gx$	5, 6 T
$\land$	8.	$(\exists x)[(y)Fxy \,\&\, Gx] \rightarrow [(\exists x)(y)Fxy \,\&\, (\exists x)Gx]$	1-7 CP

e. $(x) \sim Fx \lor (\exists x)Fx$

Proof:

{1}	1.	$\sim[(x) \sim Fx \lor (\exists x)Fx]$	P*
{1}	2.	$\sim(x) \sim Fx \,\&\, \sim(\exists x)Fx$	1 T
{1}	3.	$\sim(x) \sim Fx$	2 T
{1}	4.	$(\exists x)Fx$	3 Definition
{1}	5.	$\sim(\exists x)Fx$	2 T
{1}	6.	$(\exists x)Fx \,\&\, \sim(\exists x)Fx$	4, 5 T
$\land$	7.	$\sim[(x) \sim Fx \lor (\exists x)Fx] \rightarrow [(\exists x)Fx \,\&\, \sim(\exists x)Fx]$	1-6 CP
$\land$	8.	$\sim \sim[(x) \sim Fx \lor (\exists x)Fx]$	7 T
$\land$	9.	$(x) \sim Fx \lor (\exists x)Fx$	8 T

(right brace joining 7–9) IP

g. $(\exists x)(Fx \lor Gx) \leftrightarrow [(\exists x)Fx \lor (\exists x)Gx]$

Proof:

{1}	1.	$(\exists x)(Fx \lor Gx)$	P*
{2}	2.	$\sim(\exists x)Fx$	P*
{2}	3.	$(x) \sim Fx$	2 Definition
{1}	4.	$Fa \lor Ga$	1 EI
{2}	5.	$\sim Fa$	3 UI
{1, 2}	6.	Ga	4, 5 T
{1, 2}	7.	$(\exists x)Gx$	6 EG
{1}	8.	$\sim(\exists x)Fx \rightarrow (\exists x)Gx$	2-7 CP
{1}	9.	$(\exists x)Fx \lor (\exists x)Gx$	8 T
$\land$	10.	$(\exists x)(Fx \lor Gx) \rightarrow [(\exists x)Fx \lor (\exists x)Gx]$	1-9 CP
{11}	11.	$(\exists x)Fx \lor (\exists x)Gx$	P*
{12}	12.	$\sim(\exists x)(Fx \lor Gx)$	P*
{12}	13.	$(x) \sim (Fx \lor Gx)$	12 Definition
{12}	14.	$(x)(\sim Fx \,\&\, \sim Gx)$	13 T
{12}	15.	$\sim Fa \,\&\, \sim Ga$	14 UI
{12}	16.	$\sim Fa$	15 T
{12}	17.	$(x) \sim Fx$	16 UG
{12}	18.	$\sim(\exists x)Fx$	17 Definition
{11, 12}	19.	$(\exists x)Gx$	11, 18 T
{12}	20.	$\sim Ga$	15 T
{12}	21.	$(x) \sim Gx$	20 UG
{12}	22.	$\sim(\exists x)Gx$	21 Definition
{11, 12}	23.	$(\exists x)Gx \,\&\, \sim(\exists x)Gx$	19, 22 T

$\{11\}$ 　24.　$(\exists x)(Fx \lor Gx)$ 　　　　　　　　　　　12, 23 IP

$\wedge$ 　25.　$[(\exists x)Fx \lor (\exists x)Gx] \to (\exists x)(Fx \lor Gx)$ 　11-24 CP

$\wedge$ 　26.　$(\exists x)(Fx \lor Gx) \leftrightarrow [(\exists x)Fx \lor (\exists x)Gx]$ 　10, 25 T

h. $(x)\{[(Fx \,\&\, Gx) \to Hx] \to [Fx \to (Gx \to Hx)]\}$

Proof:

$\{1\}$ 　1.　$(Fa \,\&\, Ga) \to Ha$ 　　　　　　　　　　　P*

$\{1\}$ 　2.　$Fa \to (Ga \to Ha)$ 　　　　　　　　　　　1 T

$\wedge$ 　3.　$[(Fa \,\&\, Ga) \to Ha] \to [Fa \to (Ga \to Ha)]$ 　1-2 CP

$\wedge$ 　4.　$(x)\{[(Fx \,\&\, Gx) \to Hx] \to [Fx \to (Gx \to Hx)]\}$ 　3 UG

j. $(x)((Fx \,\&\, Gx) \to \{(y)[Hy \to (\sim Gy \lor \sim Fy)] \to \sim Hx\})$

Proof:

$\{1\}$ 　1.　$Fa \,\&\, Ga$ 　　　　　　　　　　　　　　P*

$\{2\}$ 　2.　$(y)[Hy \to (\sim Gy \lor \sim Fy)]$ 　　　　　P*

$\{2\}$ 　3.　$Ha \to (\sim Ga \lor \sim Fa)$ 　　　　　　2 UI

$\{1\}$ 　4.　$\sim(\sim Ga \lor \sim Fa)$ 　　　　　　　　1 T

$\{1, 2\}$ 　5.　$\sim Ha$ 　　　　　　　　　　　　　　3, 4 T

$\{1\}$ 　6.　$(y)[Hy \to (\sim Gy \lor \sim Fy)] \to \sim Ha$ 　2-5 CP

$\wedge$ 　7.　$(Fa \,\&\, Ga) \to \{(y)[Hy \to (\sim Gy \lor \sim Fy)] \to \sim Ha\}$ 　1-6 CP

$\wedge$ 　8.　$(x)((Fx \,\&\, Gx) \to \{(y)[Hy \to (\sim Gy \lor \sim Fy)] \to \sim Hx\})$

　　　　　　　　　　　　　　　　　　　　　　　7 UG

49.1. All are valid except *b* and *d*. Answers are given for *b*, *c*, *d*, *g*, *h*.

b. *Counterexample:* Replace '*F*' by 'is well read'; '*G*' by 'is omniscient'; '*H*' by 'is infallible'. The domain is *people*.

c. *Derivation:*

$\{1\}$ 　1.　$Fa \lor Gb$ 　　　　　　　　　　　　P

$\{2\}$ 　2.　$[(\exists x)Fx \lor (\exists x)Gx] \to (x)(Fx \lor Gx)$ 　P

$\{3\}$ 　3.　$(\exists x) \sim Gx$ 　　　　　　　　　　P

$\{4\}$ 　4.　$\sim(\exists x)Fx$ 　　　　　　　　　　P*

$\{4\}$ 　5.　$(x) \sim Fx$ 　　　　　　　　　　　4 Definition

$\{4\}$ 　6.　$\sim Fa$ 　　　　　　　　　　　　5 UI

$\{1, 4\}$ 　7.　Gb 　　　　　　　　　　　　　1, 6 T

$\{1, 4\}$ 　8.　$(\exists x)Gx$ 　　　　　　　　　　　7 EG

$\{1, 4\}$ 　9.　$(\exists x)Fx \lor (\exists x)Gx$ 　　　　　8 T

$\{1, 2, 4\}$ 　10.　$(x)(Fx \lor Gx)$ 　　　　　　　2, 9 T

$\{3\}$ 　11.　$\sim Gc$ 　　　　　　　　　　　3 EI

$\{1, 2, 3, 4\}$ 　12.　$Fc \lor Gc$ 　　　　　　　　10 UI

$\{1, 2, 3, 4\}$ 　13.　Fc 　　　　　　　　　　11, 12 T

$\{4\}$ 　14.　$\sim Fc$ 　　　　　　　　　　5 UI

$\{1, 2, 3, 4\}$ 　15.　$Fc \,\&\, \sim Fc$ 　　　　　　　13, 14 T

$\{1, 2, 3\}$ 　16.　$(\exists x)Fx$ 　　　　　　　　4-15 IP

d. *Counterexample:* Replace '*F*' by 'is very young'; '*G*' by 'is very old'; '*H*' by 'is mortal'. The domain again is *people*.

g. *Derivation:*

$\{1\}$ 　1.　$(x)(y)(z)[(Fxy \,\&\, Fyz) \to Fxz]$ 　P

$\{2\}$ 　2.　$(x)(y)(Fxy \,\&\, Fyx)$ 　　　　　　P

$\{1\}$ 　3.　$(Fab \,\&\, Fba) \to Faa$ 　　　　　1 UI (three times)

$\{2\}$ 　4.　$Fab \,\&\, Fba$ 　　　　　　　　2 UI (twice)

$\{1, 2\}$ 　5.　Faa 　　　　　　　　　　3, 4 T

$\{1, 2\}$ 　6.　$(x)Fxx$ 　　　　　　　　　5 UG

h. *Derivation:*

$\{1\}$ 　1.　$(x)(y)(\exists z)[Fxyz \,\&\, (Gx \lor Gy)]$ 　P

$\{2\}$ 　2.　$(x)(y)(z)(Fyzx \to \sim Gx)$ 　　　P

{3}	3.	(∃x)Fxxx	P*
{3}	4.	Faaa	3 EI
{2}	5.	Faaa → ~ Ga	2 UI
{1}	6.	(∃z)[Faaz & (Ga ∨ Ga)]	1 UI
{1}	7.	Faab & (Ga ∨ Ga)	6 EI
{1}	8.	Ga	7 T
{1, 2}	9.	~ Faaa	5,8 T
{1, 2, 3}	10.	Faaa & ~ Faaa	4, 9 T
{1, 2}	11.	~ (∃x)Fxxx	3-10 IP

Glossary of Terms
in Logic

absorption (Abs.), law of (§31) If A and B are sentence forms, then $A \rightarrow B$ is equivalent to $A \rightarrow (A \ \& \ B)$.

accident, fallacy of (§11) A fallacy of irrelevance committed when some general principle is applied to a particular case whose accidental features make it an exception.

ad baculum *argument (appeal to force)* (§11) An argument that commits a fallacy of irrelevance by using force or the threat of force in place of relevant premisses to obtain assent to a conclusion. More accurately, it is the substitution of force for argument.

ad hominem *argument ("to the person")* (§11) An argument that commits a fallacy of irrelevance by offering as premisses statements about a person's character or circumstances that have nothing to do with the conclusion of the argument. An *ad hominem* argument is abusive if these statements attack the character or motives of the person, circumstantial if they make the circumstances of the person the issue.

ad ignorantiam *argument ("from ignorance")* (§11) An argument that commits a fallacy of irrelevance by offering as a premiss either the fact that the conclusion has not yet been proved or the fact that the conclusion has not yet been disproved.

ad misericordiam *argument (appeal to pity)* (§11) An argument that commits a fallacy of irrelevance by presenting an appeal to pity as if it were a proper premiss from which to infer a conclusion.

ad populum *argument* ("*to the people*") (§11)   An argument that commits a fallacy of irrelevance by relying on an appeal to mass sentiment or prejudice, rather than on proper premises, to gain assent to its conclusion.

ad verecundiam *argument* (*appeal to authority*) (§11)   An argument that commits a fallacy of irrelevance by appealing to an authority in an area outside the competence of that authority.

addition (*Add.*) (§31)   A form of argument or rule of inference whereby, if A and B are sentence forms, from A we may validly infer $A \lor B$.

adjunction (*Adj.*) (§31)   A form of argument or rule of inference whereby, if A and B are sentence forms, from A and B we may validly infer $A \& B$.

affirmative sentence (**appendix***)   Any categorical sentence of the form 'All S are P' (the A form) or 'Some S are P' (the I form).

affirming the consequent (§27)   A formal fallacy in which the conclusion A is wrongly inferred from the premises $A \rightarrow B$ and B.

alternation (§21)   An 'or' sentence in which 'or' has the force of 'either but not both'.

ambiguity and vagueness (§11)   An expression is ambiguous in a particular context if the expression has more than one meaning, the meanings are easily confused, and it is not clear in that context which of the meanings is intended. An expression is vague if its use is imprecise.

ambiguity, fallacy of (§11)   A nonformal fallacy in which a deductive argument, though unsound, is wrongly taken to be sound due to multiple and shifting uses of expressions occurring in the argument.

amphiboly, fallacy of (§11)   A fallacy of ambiguity in which the ambiguity attaches not to a word or phrase but to an entire sentence.

analogy, argument by (§53)   A nondeductive argument whose premises state that two things have several properties in common and that one of the two has an additional property, and whose (probable) conclusion states that the other thing will also be found to have that additional property.

anecdotal evidence, fallacy of (§55)   A fallacy in nondeductive argument that consists in offering mere illustration, in lieu of substantial supporting evidence, as the basis for a generalization.

antecedent (§21)   In a conditional sentence, the 'if' part.

appeal to authority   *See ad verecundiam* argument.

appeal to force   *See ad baculum* argument.

appeal to ignorance   *See ad ignorantiam* argument.

appeal to pity   *See ad misericordiam* argument.

arguing beside the point   *See ignoratio elenchi.*

argument (§2)   A sequence of sentences together with a claim that one of these sentences, the conclusion, follows in some sense from the others, the premises. *See* sentence and statement.

argument, deductive (§3)   An argument is deductive if the claim is that the conclusion follows from the premises in the sense that it is impossible for the conclusion to be false if the premises are all true.

argument form, PL-1 (§41)   A sequence of closed first-order predicate-logic sentence forms such that when we uniformly replace n-place predicate letters with ordinary-language n-place predicates, individual constants with the

---

* Hereafter abbreviated as 'app'.

names of particular individuals belonging to a specified set, sentence letters with true-false sentences, and quantifiers and truth-functional connective symbols with their ordinary-language counterparts, the result is a deductive argument, either valid or invalid.

argument form, SL (§25)   A sequence of sentence logic sentence forms such that when distinct sentence letters are uniformly replaced by distinct true-false sentences, and SL connective symbols are uniformly replaced by their ordinary-language counterparts, the result is a deductive argument, either valid or invalid.

argument, nondeductive (§3)   An argument is nondeductive if the claim is that the conclusion follows from the premisses in the sense that it is improbable (not impossible) that the conclusion will be false, given that the premisses are all true.

association (*Assoc.*), *law of* (§31)   For disjunction, the law that if A, B, and C are sentence forms, then $A \vee (B \vee C)$ is equivalent to $(A \vee B) \vee C$. For conjunction, the law that if A, B, and C are sentence forms, then $A \,\&\, (B \,\&\, C)$ is equivalent to $(A \,\&\, B) \,\&\, C$.

begging the question   *See petitio principii.*

biconditional (§21)   An 'if-and-only-if' sentence—that is, a sentence of the form '$P \leftrightarrow Q$'. The sentence is true iff 'P' and 'Q' are both true or 'P' and 'Q' are both false.

biconditional (*Bicon.*), *law for the* (§31)   If A and B are sentence forms, then $A \leftrightarrow B$ is equivalent to $(A \to B) \,\&\, (B \to A)$.

bound variable   *See* free and bound variables.

cancellation law for negation (§28)   In the truth-tree method, the rule permitting us to rewrite $\sim \sim A$ as A, where A is any sentence form.

categorical sentence (**app.**)   Any sentence of the form A, E, I, or O. It consists of a subject term and a predicate term, joined by the copula 'are'.

chain syllogism   *See* hypothetical syllogism.

closed PL-1 sentence form (§37)   A PL-1 sentence form is closed if it contains no free occurrence of a variable.

commutation (*Com.*), *law of* (§31)   For disjunction, the law that if A and B are sentence forms, then $A \vee B$ is equivalent to $B \vee A$. For conjunction, the law that if A and B are sentence forms, then $A \,\&\, B$ is equivalent to $B \,\&\, A$.

completeness (§29)   A system of deduction is complete if it takes us from true premisses to all the conclusions they logically imply.

complex question, fallacy of the (§11)   A fallacy of irrelevance arising when a question is asked that carries a presupposition such that any responsive answer to the question appears to concede the truth of the presupposition.

composition and division, fallacies of   *See* division, fallacy of.

compound sentence (§20)   A sentence that has a proper part that is itself a sentence.

conditional (§21)   An 'if-then' sentence—that is, a sentence of the form '$P \to Q$'. The sentence is true if 'P' is false or if 'Q' is true; it is false only if 'P' is true and 'Q' is false.

conditional (*Con.*), *law for the* (§§27, 31)   If A and B are sentence forms, then $A \to B$ is equivalent to $\sim A \vee B$, and to $\sim (A \,\&\, \sim B)$.

conditional proof   *See* Rule CP.

conjunction (§§20, 21)   An 'and' sentence—that is, a sentence of the form '$P \,\&\, Q$'. The sentence is true iff both 'P' and 'Q' are true.

consequent (§21)   In a conditional sentence or sentence form, the 'then' part.

contextual definition (§15)   A definition that specifies how contexts in which the *definiendum* occurs may be rephrased as contexts in which the *definiendum* does not occur.

contingent sentence form (§26)   An SL sentence form whose truth table contains at least one T and at least one F under its major connective.

contradiction or self-contradiction (§14)   A sentence used to make a statement that is necessarily false, such as 'It is raining and it is not raining'.

contradictories (app.)   Two categorical sentences that differ both in quality and quantity.   If one is true, the other is false, and vice versa.

contradictory sentence form (§26)   An SL sentence form that takes the truth-value F for all assignments of truth-values to its sentence letters.

contraposition (app.)   A form of immediate inference that consists in interchanging the subject term and the predicate term, and negating each.   It is valid for the A and O forms, but not for E and I.

contraposition, law of   See transposition, law of.

contraries (app.)   Two universal categorical sentences that differ only in quality. Both may be false, but both cannot be true.

converse fallacy of accident (§§11, 55)   A fallacy in nondeductive argument committed when a case whose accidental features make it exceptional is taken as the basis for a generalization.

conversion (app.)   A form of immediate inference that consists in interchanging subject term and predicate term, leaving all else unchanged.   It is valid for the E and I forms, but not for A and O.

conversion by limitation (app.)   Conversion of the A form, not by simple conversion (which is invalid), but by replacing 'all' with 'some', thus limiting the *P*-term.   From 'All *S* are *P*', we infer 'Some *P* are *S*'.

copula (app.)   In a categorical sentence, the word 'are', which joins the subject term and the predicate term.

corresponding conditional (§18)   For an argument or argument form, the conditional sentence or sentence form constructed by taking the conjunction of the premises as the antecedent and the conclusion as the consequent.

deductive argument   See argument.

definiendum (§15)   In a definition, the word or phrase to be defined.

definiens (§15)   In a definition, the word or phrase in terms of which a word or phrase is being defined.

definition and verbal definition (§15)   A definition is any explanation of the meaning or use of a word or phrase.   A verbal definition is a sentence used to fix or explain the meaning or use of a word or phrase.

De Morgan's laws (*DeM*) (§27)   If A and B are sentence forms, then $\sim(A \vee B)$ is equivalent to $\sim A$ & $\sim B$, and $\sim(A$ & $B)$ is equivalent to $\sim A \vee \sim B$.   In words, the negation of a disjunction is equivalent to the conjunction of the negations of the disjuncts; the negation of a conjunction is equivalent to the disjunction of the negations of the conjuncts.

denying the antecedent (§27)   A formal fallacy in which a conclusion of the form $\sim B$ is wrongly inferred from the premises $A \rightarrow B$ and $\sim A$.

derivability-in-S (§30)   A sentence form B is derivable in a natural-deduction system S from a set of premises $\{A_1, \ldots, A_n\}$ iff there is a derivation in S of B from $\{A_1, \ldots, A_n\}$.

derivation (§30)   A derivation in a natural-deduction system S of a sentence form B from a set of sentence forms $\{A_1, \ldots, A_n\}$ as premises is a column of sentence forms such that 1) each entry either is a premiss or may be inferred from preceding entries in the column by virtue of one of the inference rules of S and 2) the last entry in the column is *B*.

dilemmas (§§**27, 31**)   Forms of argument or rules of inference that proceed from three premisses, two conditionals and a disjunction.   A dilemma is simple if it contains only three distinct terms: $A \to C$, $B \to C$, $A \vee B$, therefore *C*.   It is complex if it contains four distinct terms: $A \to C$, $B \to D$, $A \vee B$, therefore $C \vee D$.   A complex dilemma is constructive if, as in the preceding case, the disjuncts of the disjunctive premiss are the antecedents of the conditional premiss.   It is destructive if the disjuncts of the disjunctive premiss are the negations of the consequents of the conditional premisses: $A \to C$, $B \to D$, $\sim C \vee \sim D$, therefore $\sim A \vee \sim B$.

disjunction (§§**20, 21**)   An 'or' sentence, in which 'or' has the force of 'either or both'—that is, a sentence of the form '$P \vee Q$'.   It is true if '*P*' is true or '*Q*' is true or both are true.

disjunctive syllogism (**DS**) (§§**27, 31**)   A form of argument or rule of inference whereby, if *A* and *B* are sentence forms, from $A \vee B$ and $\sim A$ we may validly infer *B*.

distribution (**app**.)   A term is said to be distributed in a given sentence if that sentence, as ordinarily used, says something about (does not merely refer to) all of the class denoted by that term.

distribution (**Dist**.), **laws of** (§**31**)   If *A*, *B*, and *C* are sentence forms, then $A \& (B \vee C)$ is equivalent to $(A \& B) \vee (A \& C)$, and $A \vee (B \& C)$ is equivalent to $(A \vee B) \& (A \vee C)$.

distribution, rule of (**app**.)   The rule governing immediate inference in traditional logic: no term may be distributed in the conclusion unless it was distributed in the premiss.

division, fallacy of (§**11**)   A fallacy of ambiguity in which it is argued that what is true collectively of a whole or class must be true distributively of each part or member.   The fallacy of composition is the same kind of error in reverse.

domain   *See* interpretation relative to a domain.

double negation (**DN**), **law of** (§§**27, 31**)   If *A* is a sentence form, then *A* is equivalent to $\sim \sim A$.

eduction (§**53**)   A nondeductive argument whose premisses state that all observed things of a certain kind have a certain property and whose (probable) conclusion states that the next thing of that kind encountered will also have that property.

enumerative generalization (§**53**)   A nondeductive argument whose premisses state that *all observed* things of a certain kind have a certain property and whose (probable) conclusion states that *all* things of that kind have that property.

equivalence (**logical**) (§**27**)   If *A* and *B* are SL sentence forms, then *A* is equivalent to *B* iff $A \leftrightarrow B$ is a tautology; if *A* and *B* are PL-1 sentence forms, then *A* is equivalent to *B* iff $A \leftrightarrow B$ is valid.

equivocation (§**11**)   A fallacy of ambiguity committed when a word or phrase is used in shifting senses in the same argument, so that what has been established with respect to one sense of the term is then wrongly regarded as having been proved with respect to another sense.

existential generalization (§**37**)   A PL-1 sentence form, such as '$(\exists x)Fx$', that begins with an existential quantifier.

existential generalization of a sentence form containing an individual constant (§**45**)   A PL-1 sentence form obtained by replacing uniformly *some or all* occurrences of the individual constant with occurrences of a variable and pre-fixing to the result an existential quantifier binding all occurrences of that variable.   The Rule of Existential Generalization (Rule EG) allows us, given a sentence form containing an individual constant, to infer *any* existential generalization of that sentence form.

existential instantiation (§46)   A PL-1 sentence form obtained from an existential generalization by eliminating the quantifier at the head of the existential generalization and replacing uniformly all occurrences of the variable of quantification with occurrences of an individual constant.   The Existential Instantiation Procedure (EI-Procedure) specifies the conditions under which, given an existential generalization, we may use an instantiation of it in a derivation.

existential quantifier   See quantifiers.

explicative definition (§15)   A definition that is designed to clarify or make more precise the use or uses of a familiar but imprecisely used word or phrase.

explicit definition (§15)   A definition that specifies an expression for which the *definiendum* may always be directly substituted.

exportation (*Exp.*), *law of* (§§27, 31)   If *A*, *B*, and *C* are sentence forms, then $(A \And B) \rightarrow C$ is equivalent to $A \rightarrow (B \rightarrow C)$.

expression, PL-1 (§39)   An expression that consists exclusively of predicate letters, individual constants, individual variables, sentence letters, truth-functional connective symbols, quantifiers, and punctuation symbols.

expression, SL (§23)   An expression that consists exclusively of sentence letters, truth-functional connective symbols, and punctuation symbols.

fallacy (§11)   A typical error in belief or argument.

fallacy in deductive argument (§11)   A fallacy in argument in which an unsound (but seemingly sound) deductive argument is taken to be sound.

fallacy in nondeductive argument (§54)   A fallacy in argument in which a weak (but seemingly strong) nondeductive argument is taken to be strong.

figure (**app.**)   The position of the middle term in a syllogism or syllogistic form. There are four possible positions, hence four figures.

formal fallacy (§11)   A fallacy in deductive argument in which an invalid form of argument or inference is mistaken for a valid one.

free and bound variables (§37)   A variable is bound (free) in an expression if it has a bound (free) occurrence in that expression.   An occurrence of a variable is bound (free) in an expression if that occurrence does (does not) fall within the scope of a quantifier using that variable.   *See* scope of a quantifier.

general sentence (§37)   A sentence obtained from an open sentence by general-ization—that is, by prefixing to it a generalizing expression, such as 'For all *x*' or 'There is at least one *x* such that'.

generalization, statistical (§53)   A generalization to the effect that all things of a certain kind probably have a certain property.

hasty generalization, fallacy of (§55)   A fallacy in nondeductive argument that consists in proceeding to a generalization from too few or unrepresentative instances.

hypothetical syllogism (*HS*) *or chain syllogism* (§§27, 31)   A form of argument or rule of inference whereby, if *A*, *B*, and *C* are sentence forms, then from $A \rightarrow B$ and $B \rightarrow C$ we may validly infer $A \rightarrow C$.

ignoratio elenchi (*arguing beside the point*) (§11)   In a general sense, any fallacy of irrelevance; in a more specific sense, a fallacy of irrelevance that consists in offering premises directed to the wrong conclusion.

***immediate inference* (app.)** In traditional logic, forms of inference that proceed from a single premiss to a conclusion.

***implication* (*logical*) (§27)** If A and B are SL sentence forms, then A implies B iff $A \rightarrow B$ is a tautology; if A and B are PL-1 sentence forms, then A implies B iff $A \leftrightarrow B$ is valid.

***inconsistent premisses, fallacy of* (§11)** A fallacy that consists in offering as sound an argument whose premisses are inconsistent or mutually contradictory and thus cannot possibly all be true.

indirect proof *See* Rule for Indirect Proof.

***individual constant* (§36)** A symbol in PL-1, such as 'a' or 'b', that stands in place of the actual name of a particular individual or object.

***individual variable* (§36)** A variable whose values are members of a particular set or domain of individuals and whose substituends are the names of those individuals.

inductive argument *See* argument, nondeductive.

***inference* (§2)** The act of drawing a conclusion.

***informal* (*nonformal*) *fallacy* (§11)** Any fallacy in deductive argument that is not a formal fallacy.

instantiation *See* existential instantiation; universal instantiation.

***interpretation relative to a domain* (§42)** To interpret a closed PL-1 sentence form A relative to a domain D of individuals or objects is to obtain from A a true-false sentence S by 1) replacing the predicate letters of A (if any) with ordinary-language predicates defined for the individuals of D, 2) replacing the individual constants of A (if any) with the names of particular individuals belonging to D, 3) replacing the quantifier symbols and connective symbols of A (if any) with their ordinary-language counterparts, and 4) replacing the sentence letters of A (if any) with true-false sentences.

***irrelevance, fallacy of* (§11)** A nonformal fallacy in which the premisses of a deductive argument have no, or no appropriate, connection with the conclusion.

***laws of logic, valid argument forms, rules of inference* (§31)** If A and B are sentence forms, then $A \rightarrow B$ is a law or principle of logic

> iff A implies B
>
> iff $A \rightarrow B$ is a tautology or other valid sentence form
>
> iff the argument form 'A, therefore B' is valid
>
> iff 'from A, we may infer B' is an original or derived rule of inference in a sound and complete deduction system.

And $A \leftrightarrow B$ is a law or principle of logic

> iff A is equivalent to B
>
> iff $A \leftrightarrow B$ is a tautology or other valid sentence form
>
> iff the argument forms 'A therefore B' and 'B therefore A' are both valid
>
> iff 'from A, we may infer B' and 'from B, we may infer A' are both original or derived rules of inference in a sound and complete deduction system.

lexical definition (§15)   A definition that reports the accepted or standard usage(s) of a word or phrase.

logical form (§17)   The logical form of a sentence is, roughly, what remains of the sentence after place-holders are substituted for all nonlogical words or parts.   The logical form of an argument is constituted by the logical forms of the sentences that make up the argument.

logical impossibility and logical necessity (§§17, 18)   A sentence is logically impossible iff its negation is logically necessary.   A sentence is logically necessary iff it is logically true.

logical truth (§18)   Roughly, a sentence is logically true iff it is true and stays true under all reinterpretations of its nonlogical words (Quine).

major connective (§24)   In an SL sentence form, the connective that generates the compound that is the entire sentence form.

major premiss (**app.**)   In a syllogism, the premiss that contains the predicate term of the conclusion. It is generally written first.

many questions, fallacy of   *See* complex question, fallacy of the.

"material implication" (§35)   A term formerly used to designate the truth-functional conditional of SL.   The so-called paradoxes of material implication arise when the truth-functional conditional is confused with logical implication.

middle term (**app.**)   The term that appears in both premisses of a syllogism.

Mill's Methods (or Canons) of Induction (§57)   Five methods proposed by John Stuart Mill to aid in discovering the cause or causes of a phenomenon, where by 'cause' is meant invariable antecedent.   The methods are: agreement, difference, agreement and difference, concomitant variations, and residues.

minor premiss (**app.**)   In a syllogism, the premiss that contains the subject term of the conclusion.   It is generally written after the major premiss.

modus ponens (*MP*) (§§27, 31)   A form of argument or rule of inference whereby, if A and B are sentence forms, from $A \to B$ and A we may validly infer B.

modus tollens (*MT*) (§27, 31)   A form of argument or rule of inference whereby, if A and B are sentence forms, from $A \to B$ and $\sim B$ we may validly infer $\sim A$.

monadic quantification (§37)   The application of quantifiers to expressions with predicates of only one place.

mood (**app.**)   The mood of a syllogism or syllogistic form is determined by the quality and quantity of the sentences or sentence forms that make it up.   Thus 'All men are mortal, All mortals are fallible, Therefore all men are fallible' is a syllogism in the mood AAA.

names (§36)   Words, numerals, and the like ('Socrates', '7') that identify individual members of a set or domain of objects.

natural deduction systems (§29)   Systems of deduction made up entirely of rules of inference.

necessary condition   *See* necessary and sufficient conditions.

necessary and sufficient conditions (§22)   If a sentence of the form '$P \to Q$' is true, then the truth of 'P' is a sufficient condition for the truth of 'Q', and the truth of 'Q' is a necessary condition for the truth of 'P'.   If a sentence of the form '$Q \to P$' is true, then the truth of 'Q' is a sufficient condition for the truth of 'P' and the truth of 'P' is a necessary condition for the truth of 'Q'.   If a sentence of the form '$P \leftrightarrow Q$' is true, then the truth of 'P' is a necessary and sufficient condition for the truth of 'Q' and the truth of 'Q' is a necessary and sufficient condition for the truth of 'P'.

negation of a sentence or of a sentence form (§21)   For a sentence '*P*', the sentence 'not-*P*' or 'It is not the case that *P*'.   For a sentence form *A*, the sentence form $\sim A$, which takes the truth-value T iff *A* takes F.

negation of a term (app.)   The term non-T, denoting the class of everything outside of the class denoted by the term T.

negative sentence (app.)   Any categorical sentence of the forms 'No *S* are *P*' (the E form) or 'Some *S* are not *P*' (the O form).

nondeductive argument   *See* argument.

nonexclusive 'or'   *See* disjunction.

obversion (app.)   A form of immediate inference that consists in changing the quality of the sentence or sentence form and negating the predicate term.   It is valid for A, E, I, and O.

open sentence (§36)   An expression that 1) is like a sentence except that it contains at least one open place or variable instead of a name and 2) becomes a true-false sentence if appropriate names are inserted in the open places or for the variables.   An example is '——— defeated Napoleon', or if individual variables are used, '*x* defeated Napoleon'.

open sentence form (§37)   A PL-1 sentence form is open if it contains at least one free occurrence of a variable.

opposition (app.)   Two categorical sentences are opposed if they differ only in quantity or only in quality or in both.

particular sentence (app.)   Any categorical sentence of the form 'Some *S* are *P*' (the I form) or 'Some *S* are not *P*' (the O form).

petitio principii (*begging the question*) (§11)   A fallacy of irrelevance committed by an argument that has as its conclusion one of its premises, and thus begs the question by assuming what is to be proved.

polyadic or n-*adic quantification* (§37)   The application of quantifiers to expressions containing predicates of two or more places.

post hoc, ergo propter hoc (§57)   In nondeductive reasoning, the fallacy of inferring that because X follows X, therefore X must be a cause of Y.

predicate (§36)   An expression, such as '... is a person' or '... is larger than ...', used in attributing a property to an individual or a relation to two or more individuals.

predicate letter (§36)   A symbol, such as '*F*' or '*G*', used in PL-1 as a placeholder for ordinary-language predicates.

predicate term (app.)   In a categorical sentence, the term that follows the copula.

premiss number (§31)   In a derivation, the number of the line on which the premiss first appears in the derivation.

quality (app.)   In a categorical sentence or sentence form, the property of being affirmative or negative.

quantifiers (§37)   The symbolic counterparts to generalizing prefixes (*see* general sentence).   The counterpart to 'For all *x*' is '(*x*)' and is called the universal quantifier; the counterpart to 'There is at least one *x* such that' is '(∃*x*)' and is called the existential quantifier.

quantity (app.)   In a categorical sentence or sentence form, the property of being universal or particular.

reductio ad absurdum (§27)   Forms of argument by which, if *A* and *B* are sentence forms, we may validly infer $\sim A$ from $A \rightarrow \sim A$, and $\sim A$ from $A \rightarrow (B \,\&\, \sim B)$.   *See also* Rule for Indirect Proof.

Rule CP (*conditional proof*) (§33)   A rule of inference in the natural deduction system SNS ensuring that if there is a derivation in SNS of a sentence form B from a sentence form A together with a set of sentence forms $\{A_1, \ldots, A_n\}$ as premisses, then there is in SNS a derivation of $A \rightarrow B$ from the set $\{A_1, \ldots, A_n\}$ alone.

Rule for Indirect Proof, or proof by contradiction (§33)   A derived rule in the natural deduction system SNS to the effect that if a contradiction can be derived in SNS from a sentence form $\sim B$ together with a set of sentence forms $\{A_1, \ldots, A_n\}$ as premisses, then B is derivable-in-SNS from the set $\{A_1, \ldots, A_n\}$ alone.

rule of inference (§29)   A rule allowing us to infer a conclusion of a certain form from a premiss or premisses of a certain form.

Rule P (§32)   A rule of inference in the natural deduction system SNS according to which a premiss may be entered on any line of a derivation.

Rule T (§32)   A rule of inference in the natural deduction system SNS according to which any sentence form may be entered in a derivation if it is (tautologically) implied by a preceding entry or a conjunction of such entries.

scope of a quantifier (§37)   The quantifier itself and the open sentence to which it is prefixed.

sentence and statement (§§2, 10)   Sentences are expressions used to perform linguistic jobs of various sorts, such as to make a statement, to ask a question, to issue an instruction, and the like.   One of the uses of sentences is to make a statement—that is, to say something that is or is not the case.   Sentences so used are called 'true-false sentences' or 'statement-making sentences'.

sentence form, PL-1 (§39)   A PL-1 expression that becomes a true-false sentence or else an open sentence when we uniformly replace sentence letters by true-false sentences, n-place predicate letters by ordinary-language n-place predicates, individual constants by the names of particular individuals belonging to a specified set of individuals or objects, and quantifiers and connective symbols by their ordinary-language counterparts.

sentence form, SL (§23)   An SL expression that becomes a true-false sentence when distinct sentence letters are uniformly replaced by distinct true-false sentences and the connective symbols are uniformly replaced by their ordinary-language counterparts.

sentence letter (§20)   A symbol, such as 'P' or 'Q', used in SL as a place-holder for whole sentences.

simplification (Simp.) (§31)   A form of argument or rule of inference whereby, if A and B are sentence forms, from A & B we may validly infer A.

singular sentence (§36)   A sentence used to make a statement to the effect that a named individual object has a certain property or that two or more named individuals stand in a certain relation to one another.

soundness   A deductive argument is sound iff it is valid and has all true premisses (§4).   A system of deduction is sound if it never takes us from true premisses to false conclusions (§29).

statement   *See* sentence and statement.

stipulative definition (§15)   A definition that fixes the use of a newly introduced word or assigns a new use to an old word.

strength of a nondeductive argument (§54)   A nondeductive argument is strong if its premisses do in fact give its conclusion the degree of support claimed for the conclusion on the basis of the truth of the premisses.

subalterns and superalterns (app.)   Two categorical sentences that differ only in quantity. The universal sentence of the pair is the superaltern of the particular sentence; the particular sentence is the subaltern of the universal. In traditional logic, if the universal sentence is true, its subaltern must also be true.

subcontraries (**app.**) Two particular sentences that differ only in quantity. Both may be true, but they cannot both be false.

subject term (**app.**) In a categorical sentence, the term that precedes the copula.

substitution instance For a sentence form, a sentence obtained by making appropriate substitutions in that sentence form (§**23**). For an argument form, the argument obtained by making appropriate substitutions in that argument form (§**25**).

sufficient condition *See* necessary and sufficient conditions.

syllogism, categorical (**app.**) An argument consisting of three categorical sentences—two premises and a conclusion—and containing just three distinct terms, each of which appears in two of the sentences.

tautology or tautological SL sentence form (§**26**) An SL sentence form that receives the truth-value T for all possible assignments of truth-values to its sentence letters—that is, its truth table contains only Ts in the column under the major connective. Also, an SL sentence form all the substitution instances of which are true sentences.

tautology (*Taut.*), *law of* (§**31**) If A is a sentence form, then A is equivalent to $A \lor A$ and A is equivalent to $A \& A$.

theorem of a natural deduction system (§**33**) A sentence form that is derivable in the system from the empty set of premises.

transposition (*Trans.*), *law of* (§§**27, 31**) If A and B are sentence forms, then $A \to B$ is equivalent to $\sim B \to \sim A$.

truth-functional compound, truth-functional connective (§**20**) A sentence connective is a truth-functional connective if the compound sentence it forms is a truth-functional compound. A compound sentence is a truth-functional compound if its own truth-value is determined solely by the truth-values of its component sentences.

truth-functional expansion of generalized PL-1 sentence forms (§**40**) For a finite domain of n members, the truth-functional expansion of a universally generalized PL-1 sentence form, say '$(x)Fx$', is '$Fa_1 \& Fa_2 \& \ldots \& Fa_n$'; the expansion of an existentially generalized PL-1 sentence form, say '$(\exists x)Fx$', is '$Fa_1 \lor Fa_2 \lor \ldots \lor Fa_n$'.

truth table (§**21**) A device for listing all possible assignments of truth-values to a given number of sentences or sentence letters together with the particular truth-value that each such assignment determines for any truth-functional compound formed from these sentences or sentence letters.

truth trees (§**28**) A device for testing the validity of argument forms. We begin by assuming that the argument form is invalid—that is, we assign the truth-value T to the premises and to the negation of the conclusion. Then we develop the consequences of this assumption in accordance with rules for unpacking and entering in the tree the information contained in the premises and the negated conclusion. If the consequences prove contradictory, the assumption is false and the argument form is valid; if not, it is invalid.

truth-under-an-interpretation (§**42**) A closed PL-1 sentence form A is true under an interpretation I iff the sentence S obtained from A under that interpretation is true.

truth-values (§20)   In SL, there are two truth-values, truth and falsity. A statement-making sentence has the truth-value truth if it is true; it has the truth-value falsity if it is false.

undistributed middle, fallacy of (app.)   A formal fallacy committed by any syllogism or syllogistic form in which the middle term is not distributed at least once.

universal generalization (§37)   A PL-1 sentence form, such as '$(x)Fx$', that begins with a universal quantifier.

universal generalization of a sentence form containing an individual constant (§46)   The PL-1 sentence form obtained by replacing uniformly all occurrences of the constant with occurrences of a variable and prefixing to the result a universal quantifier binding all occurrences of that variable.   The Rule of Universal Generalization (Rule UG) specifies the conditions under which, given a sentence form that contains an individual constant, we may infer from that sentence form its universal generalization.

universal instantiation (§45)   A PL-1 sentence form obtained from a universal generalization by eliminating the quantifier at the head of the universal generalization and replacing uniformly all occurrences of the variable of quantification with occurrences of an individual constant.   The Rule of Universal Instantiation (Rule UI) allows us, given a universal generalization, to infer any instantiation of it.

universal quantifier   *See* quantifiers.

universal sentence (app.)   Any categorical sentence of the form 'All S are P' (the A form) or 'No S are P' (the E form).

vagueness   *See* ambiguity and vagueness.

valid deductive argument (§4)   A deductive argument is valid if its claim is justified—that is, if it is indeed impossible for the conclusion to be false if the premises are all true.

valid deductive argument, criteria for   An argument is valid according to the commonsense criterion iff it is "impossible" for the premises all to be true and the conclusion false (§17).   An argument is valid according to SL iff its corresponding conditional is a substitution instance of a tautology and thus is logically true (§§23, 27). An argument is valid according to PL-1 iff its corresponding conditional is a substitution instance of a valid PL-1 sentence form and thus is logically true (§42).

valid deductive argument form, criteria for   An argument form is valid according to SL iff its corresponding conditional is a tautology (§27).   An argument form is valid according to PL-1 iff its corresponding conditional is a valid PL-1 sentence form (§42).

valid PL-1 sentence form (§42)   A closed PL-1 sentence form A is valid iff it comes out true under every interpretation in any nonempty domain.

variable (§23)   A symbol, such as 'x' or 'y', that denotes any of a set of objects. The members of that set are said to be the values of the variable; the names of these members are called 'substituends' for the variable.

variable of quantification (§37)   A variable that appears in a quantifier. Its occurrences then are bound if they lie within the scope of that quantifier.

weakened form of a syllogism (app.)   One syllogistic form is a weakened form of another if the two are identical except that the conclusion of the former is the subaltern of the conclusion of the latter.   Thus AAI is a weakened form of AAA.

Bibliography

Except for a few items, this bibliography is limited to works in or on logic referred to in the text.

Alston, William P. *Philosophy of Language*. Englewood Cliffs, N.J.: Prentice-Hall, 1964.

———. "Language," in *The Encyclopedia of Philosophy*.

Bar-Hillel, Yehoshua. "Husserl's Conception of a Purely Logical Grammar," *Philosophy and Phenomenological Research*, Vol. 17 (1956–57), pp. 363–369.

Barker, Stephen F. *The Elements of Logic*. New York: McGraw-Hill, 1965, 2d ed. 1974.

———. "Must Every Inference Be Either Deductive or Inductive?" in Max Black (ed.), *Philosophy in America*. Ithaca, N.Y.: Cornell University Press, 1965.

Black, Max. "Induction," in *The Encyclopedia of Philosophy*.

———. *The Labyrinth of Language*. New York and Toronto: New American Library, 1968.

Carnap, Rudolf. *The Logical Foundations of Probability*. Chicago: University of Chicago Press, 1950.

Copi, Irving M. *Introduction to Logic*. New York: Macmillan, 1953, 1961, 1968, 4th ed. 1972.

Davidson, Donald. "Actions, Reasons, and Causes," *The Journal of Philosophy*, Vol. 60 (1963), pp. 685–700.

451

Dummett, Michael. "Truth," *Proceedings of the Aristotelian Society*, Vol. 59 (1958–59), pp. 141–162. Reprinted in P. F. Strawson (ed.), *Philosophical Logic*. London: Oxford University Press, 1967.

———. "Frege," in *The Encyclopedia of Philosophy*.

Edwards, Paul. "Why," in Paul Edwards (ed.), *The Encyclopedia of Philosophy*. New York: Macmillan, 1967.

Fischer, David Hackett. *Historians' Fallacies*. New York: Harper and Row, 1970.

Foot, Philippa (ed.). *Theories of Ethics*. London: Oxford University Press, 1967.

Frege, Gottlob. *Begriffsschrift*. Halle: Nebert, 1879. Translated by Stefan Bauer-Mengelberg, in van Heijenoort (ed.), *From Frege to Gödel*.

———. *Die Grundlagen der Arithmetik*. Breslau: Marcus, 1884. Translated by J. L. Austin as *Foundations of Arithmetic*. Oxford: Blackwell, 1950.

Hare, R. M *The Language of Morals*. London: Oxford University Press, 1952.

Heath, P. L. "Nothing," in *The Encyclopedia of Philosophy*.

Hempel, Carl. *Aspects of Scientific Explanation and Other Essays in the Philosophy of Science*. New York: Free Press, 1965.

———. *Philosophy of Science*. Englewood Cliffs, N.J.: Prentice-Hall, 1966.

Hockett, Charles F. "The Problem of Universals in Language," in Joseph H. Greenberg (ed.), *Universals of Language*. Cambridge, Mass.: The M.I.T. Press, 1963, 3rd ed. 1966.

Jeffrey, Richard C. *Formal Logic: Its Scope and Limits*. New York: McGraw-Hill, 1967.

Kim, Jaegwon. "Explanation in Science," in *The Encyclopedia of Philosophy*.

Kneale, William, and Martha Kneale. *The Development of Logic*. Oxford: Clarendon Press, 1962.

Kretzmann, Norman. "The Main Thesis of Locke's Semantic Theory," *Philosophical Review*, Vol. 77 (1966), pp. 175–196.

Lyons, John. *Introduction to Theoretical Linguistics*. Cambridge: Cambridge University Press, 1968.

Mackie, J. L. "Fallacies," in *The Encyclopedia of Philosophy*.

———. "Mill's Methods of Induction," in *The Encyclopedia of Philosophy*.

Mates, Benson. *Stoic Logic*. Berkeley: University of California Press, 1953, 2d ed. 1961.

———. *Elementary Logic*. New York: Oxford University Press, 1965, 2d ed. 1972.

Melden, A. I. *Free Action*. London: Routledge and Kegan Paul, 1961.

Mendelson, Elliott. *Introduction to Mathematical Logic*. Princeton, N.J.: Van Nostrand, 1964.

Mill, John Stuart. *A System of Logic*. London: Longmans, 8th ed., 1872.

Nagel, Ernest. *The Structure of Science*. New York: Harcourt, Brace and World, 1961.

Post, Emil L. "Introduction to a general theory of elementary propositions," *American Journal of Mathematics*, Vol. 43 (1921), pp. 163–185. Reprinted in van Heijenoort (ed.), *From Frege to Gödel*.

Quine, W. V. *Mathematical Logic*. Cambridge, Mass.: Harvard University Press, 1940, rev. ed. 1951.

———. *Methods of Logic*. New York: Holt, Rinehart and Winston, 1950, 1959, 3rd ed., 1972.

———. *From a Logical Point of View*. Cambridge, Mass.: Harvard University Press, 1953.

———. *The Ways of Paradox, and Other Essays*. New York: Random House, 1966.

———. *Philosophy of Logic*. Englewood Cliffs, N.J.: Prentice-Hall, 1970.

Robinson, Richard. *Definition*. Oxford: Clarendon Press, 1954.

Russell, Bertrand. *Introduction to Mathematical Philosophy*. London: George Allen and Unwin, 1919.

Ryle, Gilbert. *The Concept of Mind*. London: Hutchinson, 1949.

———. " 'If', 'So', and 'Because'," in Max Black (ed.), *Philosophical Analysis*. Englewood Cliffs, N.J.: Prentice-Hall, 1963.

Searle, John R. "How to Derive 'Ought' from 'Is'," in Foot (ed.), *Theories of Ethics*.

Skyrms, Brian. *Choice and Chance*. Belmont, Calif.: Dickenson, 1966.

Stevenson, Charles L. *Ethics and Language*. New Haven: Yale University Press, 1944.

———. "If-ficulties," *Philosophy of Science*, Vol. 37 (1970), pp. 27–49.

Suppes, Patrick. *Introduction to Logic*. Princeton, N.J.: Van Nostrand, 1957.

van Heijenoort, Jean (ed.). *From Frege to Gödel: A Source Book in Mathematical Logic*. Cambridge, Mass.: Harvard University Press, 1967.

———. "Subject and Predicate in Western Logic," *Philosophy East and West*, Vol. 24 (July 1974), pp. 253–268.

Vendler, Zeno. "Any and All," in *The Encyclopedia of Philosophy*.

Wang, Hao. *From Mathematics to Philosophy*. London: Routledge and Kegan Paul, 1974.

Wittgenstein, Ludwig. *Tractatus Logico-Philosophicus*. London: Kegan Paul, 1922. Reprint and translation of "Logisch-philosophische Abhandlung," *Annalen der Philosophie*, 1921.

———. *Philosophical Investigations*. Oxford: Basil Blackwell, 1953, 2d ed. 1958, translated by G. E. M. Anscombe.

Index

About the Author

Albert E. Blumberg was born in Baltimore, Maryland, and received his A.B. at the Johns Hopkins University. He did his graduate work in philosophy at Yale (M.A.), the Sorbonne, and the University of Vienna (Ph.D.). He has taught at Johns Hopkins, the New School for Social Research, and Rutgers College and is currently Professor of Philosophy at Livingston College-Rutgers University, where he was Chairman of the Philosophy Department from 1969 to 1975. He was a senior editor of the *Encyclopedia of Philosophy* (1967), for which he wrote the essay " Logic, Modern." Among his other publications are " Logical Positivism " (with Herbert Feigl), *Journal of Philosophy* (1931), and " The Nature of Philosophic Analysis," *Philosophy of Science* (1935), a journal of which he was one of the founding editors. His translations include Moritz Schlick's *Allgemeine Erkenntnislehre*, as *General Theory of Knowledge* (Springer-Verlag, 1974). He is married and lives in New York City.

The text of this book was set on the Monotype in a face called Times New Roman 327. This typeface cut by the Monotype Corporation was based on the original Times Roman, designed by Stanley Morison for The Times (London), and first introduced by that newspaper in 1932.

Among typographers and designers of the twentieth century, Stanley Morison has been a strong forming influence, as typographical advisor to the English Monotype Corporation, as a director of two distinguished English publishing houses, and as a writer of sensibility, erudition, and keen practical sense.

This book was printed and bound by the Kingsport Press, Kingsport, Tenn.

Designed by Susan Phillips